D1462405

LEARNING FROM THE FUTURE

LEARNING FROM THE FUTURE

COMPETITIVE FORESIGHT SCENARIOS

Editors

Liam Fahey
and
Robert M. Randall

John Wiley & Sons, Inc.

New York • Chichester • Weinheim • Brisbane • Singapore • Toronto

This text is printed on acid-free paper.

Copyright © 1998 by Liam Fahey and Robert M. Randall
Published by John Wiley & Sons, Inc.

This publication is designed to provide accurate and authoritative
information in regard to the subject matter covered. It is sold
with the understanding that the publisher is not engaged in
rendering legal, accounting, or other professional services. If
legal advice or other expert assistance is required, the services
of a competent professional person should be sought.

ISBN 0-471-30352-6

Printed in the United States of America

10   9   8   7   6   5   4   3   2   1

To my parents,
Michael C. Fahey and Veronica T. Fahey,
for teaching me that, "The future is what
you make it."

Liam Fahey

To my parents,
Randolph C. Randall and Ellen Moore Randall, who made
acknowledging "discerning judgment and consummate patience"
the family tradition for book dedications.

Robert M. Randall

Preface

Scenarios aim to stretch thinking about the future and widen the range of alternatives considered.

—Michael Porter, Competitive Advantage
(New York: The Free Press, 1985)

To create the future, a company must first be capable of imagining it.
—Gary Hamel and C. K. Prahalad,
Competing for the Future *(Boston:
Harvard Business School Press, 1994)*

The race to the future is the race to maximize the ratio of learning over investment. . . . Now you have to compete for industry foresight and reinvention opportunities.

—Gary Hamel interviewed by Robert M. Randall in
Planning Review, *January/February 1995*

We invite you on an exciting expedition to learn from the future. Unlike other books that offer a look beyond time's horizon, this one is not about a particular future that the authors foresee, nor does it contain forecasts by experts or predictions by seers. Instead, this book explains how to imagine and construct a set of alternative futures so you can explore the crucial decisions facing your organization. This is the analytical and imaginative process we refer to in our title, *Learning from the Future.*

Preparing an organization to anticipate that it could face a number of environments that are fundamentally different from the present is a radical departure from standard practice. Most corporations spend substantial effort forecasting and planning for one "likely" future. But if it doesn't occur, they are like a sports team that arrives in the wrong arena, with the wrong players, on the wrong day, with the wrong equipment.

This book offers a methodology for understanding the whole range of possibilities in store for all organizations—corporations, not-for-profits, and governments. By learning to develop and use competitive foresight scenarios, organizations can take actions to make a desirable future occur, quickly adapt to unfavorable environments, and efficiently implement strategies that will succeed in many different market conditions.

Learning from the Future shows you how to identify the forces that determine different possible future operating environments and how you can prepare an organization to be the first to understand and exploit the significant opportunities each future affords. In our rapidly changing world, your success, and the survival and growth of your organization, depend on mastering the ability to first project these futures and then to learn from them.

STRATEGY AND SCENARIOS

Understanding how to reinvent your business, nonprofit organization, or governmental agency to survive and prosper in the future is at the core of the exhilarating business of developing and executing strategy. Strategy is about placing bets: Risking your resources of time, energy, skills, attention, and capital to win 2, 5, 10, 15, and 20 years from now, while at the same time competing to win in today's marketplace. Strategy is always about competitive choices: Which products to offer, which customers to serve, and how to outmaneuver rivals. For those interested in learning more about strategic management we recommend our previous book in which 20 leading authorities address the topic of strategy, *The Portable MBA in Strategy* (New York: John Wiley & Sons, Inc., 1994).

This new book synthesizes some of what we have learned about managing strategy over the past several decades with the less widely known methodology of scenario development and learning. That's why we've subtitled it *Competitive Foresight Scenarios*. It offers readers the strategic scenario methodology for analyzing and understanding key competitive decisions.

A few leading organizations have already adopted the scenario-learning methodology described in this book, and their experiences are described in detail in several case studies. As you will see, scenario learning afforded these organizations a unique opportunity to unleash their creativity as they developed alternative futures, considered the strategy implications of each one, and devised new strategies that would thrive in a variety of future settings.

THE AUDIENCE FOR THIS BOOK

We believe this book will be especially useful to:

- Organization leaders who seek to understand the emerging future—and its implications for making immediate decisions—sooner and with more insight than their rivals.
- Managers of such functions as mergers and acquisitions, R&D, marketing, manufacturing, and sales who need to test the consequences of current and potential decisions in different competitive futures.
- Staff specialists who need to depict, assess, and communicate the implications of the alternative futures facing their organizations.
- Consultants who need to extend their knowledge of how scenarios can be used to their clients' advantage.
- Industry specialists who want to monitor emerging technologies and potential competitive conditions.
- Product and service marketers who track the rapid evolution of customers' needs.
- Government leaders, policy experts, and legislative advisors who need to sort through many social, political, and economic uncertainties to make public policy decisions for the long term.
- Directors of not-for-profit organizations who seek to ready their organizations for new missions.
- Securities analysts and professional investors who need to improve their understanding of the prospects of individual companies and whole industries.
- Academics and students who want to be able to project the future context of any business.

PURPOSES OF THE BOOK

This book explains how strategic scenarios can help any organization test how its own major strategy choices—its goals, posture and scope issues—would play out in various futures. Over the past three years, we have worked intensely with the world's leading authorities on scenarios to make each chapter contribute to four goals:

- To provide readers with a thorough conceptual and practical understanding of scenarios as a methodology to understand the future (and the present).
- To demonstrate how scenarios and strategic management can be interlinked.
- To enable readers to develop and use scenarios in their own strategy work.
- To institute scenario learning in their organization.

Taken as a whole, this book offers a new system to understand and prepare an organization for future opportunities and threats: scenario learning. This scenario-learning process is a truly new combination of strategic management and scenario technology combined with a collection of teamwork, creativity, and decision-making skills. But be advised that we're not offering a technology that can be patented or packaged. Each organization will have to adapt the scenario-learning techniques demonstrated by the contributors to this book to fit its own needs.

HEALTHY SKEPTICISM

We anticipate that a lot of experienced managers will greet the announcement of another foresight tool with more than a little skepticism. Enlisting managers in a new "futuring" crusade will be a tough sell because many learned to distrust forecasting and long-term planning. Neither work very well when the future can't be merely extrapolated from the past. When forecasting and planning don't work, industries experience unwanted surprises—unanticipated competitors, sudden technology obsolescence, unprecedented customer demands, and unforeseen regulatory pitfalls.

Over the past decades, a number of companies have attempted to use scenarios as a planning tool, with mixed results. A few pioneering attempts to use scenarios in the 1970s seemed to promise a new kind of foresight capability. However, the real reason these original scenarios were a success was not because they were predictive but because they shed new light on how an external environment could change in unexpected ways.

Unfortunately, a number of corporations rushed to embrace the technique, believing that it offered insights into which particular future would unfold; they were bitterly disappointed. Moreover, even the ardent supporters of scenario thinking became frustrated when it became clear that their efforts wouldn't have any effect on decision making unless their organization altered quite few of its systems and its mind-set, a tough sell. It's not surprising that some companies eventually abandoned their attempts to adopt scenario planning.

SOME CAVEATS

We believe that managers must be cognizant of the limitations of all management tools and the pitfalls that lie in wait for unwary implementers. So before you commit substantial resources to scenario learning, please heed these warnings and the many others prominently mentioned throughout this book:

- Scenario technology won't work if it's employed as a gimmick to help predict the likely long-term future environment.
- Be prepared to forget a lot you think you know about scenarios. For example, there aren't just three futures—the good, the bad, and the average—waiting in the wings.
- Scenario learning won't be effective unless it is integrated into the decision-making process. Keep asking yourself, "What actions need to be taken today and tomorrow?" This integration requires changing both the way people think about the future and the organizational systems that drive decisions. It's an ambitious goal, but this book is intended to show you how to do just that.

In sum, scenario learning is not a simplistic, one-shot predictive process; nor is it just a sophisticated form of industry analysis. Scenario learning is a search for an understanding of how the future could change, and how an organization could thrive by adapting to a number of particular changed circumstances. Scenario learning identifies what the indicators of change are, and what decisions and actions must be taken today to be ready to survive and win tomorrow and in the years to come.

STRUCTURE OF THE BOOK
This book has a four-part structure:

- Part I provides an introduction to the concept of scenarios and a preliminary understanding of how scenarios can be used to create winning strategies.
- Part II illustrates a number of different ways that scenarios can be constructed. A number of companies, consulting firms, military organizations, governmental institutions, and academics have developed and refined their own approach to constructing and using scenarios. The chapters in this part detail the scope, content, and rationale of the principal scenario methods used by business firms and other organizations. Each approach is carefully delineated using one or more detailed case examples.
- Part III then shows how scenarios can be applied to study alternative futures in a number of diverse contexts—how an industry might evolve; competitors' potential strategies; distinct technology futures; the evolution of customers' needs; different future states of the economy; and public decisions.
- Part IV is devoted to managing the organizational context for effective scenario learning. Scenarios that provide valuable foresight don't happen without preparation. Moreover, timely decisions don't flow from scenario learning without follow-up. These chapters address: how to introduce the notion of scenarios to an organization for the first time; how managers can use scenarios to communicate change imperatives; how to link scenarios to the organization's core business idea; how to use information technology to expedite scenario development and promote learning; and how to avoid some of the common pitfalls in the use of scenarios.

Liam Fahey
Robert M. Randall

Babson Park, Massachusetts
San Francisco, California

Acknowledgments

First and foremost we want to acknowledge the contributors—24 authors on three continents. Without their broad experience in developing scenarios and practicing scenario learning, this book would not have been possible. In addition, they deserve our gratitude for their forbearance when the process of putting this book together took much more time than anyone anticipated.

We all owe a debt to the early pioneers of scenario technology—talented people as disparate the late Herman Kahn, of the RAND Corporation and the Hudson Institute; and Pierre Wack, who was head planner of the Royal Dutch/Shell business environment division. Also among the pioneers are many of the contributors to this book who have implemented scenario planning in a wide range of organizations, refined their techniques, and taught others what they had learned about this new way of thinking about the future.

In addition to thanking the current John Wiley & Sons publishing team, we also wish to acknowledge the contribution of a former Wiley executive, John Mahaney, who originally encouraged us to pursue this project.

All during the editing process we were generously supported by a unique set of friends from the strategic management editorial community: Robert Allio, Sam Felton, Dan Simpson, and Mark Baroush are just a few who repeatedly provided wise advice and thoughtful criticism. Ian Wilson deserves individual mention for serving as contributor, reviewer, counselor, and editors' editor.

LF
RMR

CONTENTS

PART I

INTRODUCTION TO SCENARIO LEARNING

CHAPTER 1

WHAT IS SCENARIO LEARNING?

LIAM FAHEY and ROBERT M. RANDALL

This chapter introduces the concept of scenario learning: the development of scenarios and their integration into decision making. It highlights the twin purposes of scenario learning—augmenting decision makers' understanding of possible futures, and enhancing decision making—and the challenges and tasks that must be accomplished if scenarios are to truly inform decision makers and influence decision making. It defines what scenario learning is, corrects some common misconceptions about the use of scenarios, illustrates their key elements, and briefly reviews two distinctive approaches to constructing scenarios.

It's time that organizations reexamine how they anticipate and prepare for the future. Nowadays, most managers expect that sooner or later their own organization will experience some type of discontinuous change—new markets, new competitors, new customer needs, new combinations of technology, new distribution channels, new legislation. But too many managers still plan and invest based on forecasts of past trends or on a plan for a single "most likely" future, one that is addressed in the corporate plan. Over and over, organizations that await one "probable" future find themselves confused and disadvantaged when confronted with an unfavorable turn of events for which they are unprepared. Often this crisis is one of several futures that could easily have been anticipated; and if it had been, the organization could have readied itself to face the challenge.

SCENARIO LEARNING

We advocate that all organizations seeking to learn from the future use a methodology that combines scenario development with the decision-making processes of strategic management. This process that we call *scenario learning* can help an organization understand how to manage its future strategically—that is, how to lay the foundations for tomorrow's success while competing to win in today's marketplace.

An organization should adopt scenario learning if it has reason to believe that:

- Its future business context—products, customers, distribution channels, suppliers, competitors, technology, and governmental regulations—will be significantly different from that prevailing today.
- A set of "alternative futures," which are dramatically different from each other and from the current operating environment, should be considered as part of strategic decision making.
- Although the future will be strongly shaped by today's trends, many surprises may significantly affect the organization's operating environment.

Many organizations already have considerable experience using strategic management to identify, select, and execute choices for their business scope, competitive differentiation, and marketplace goals. As an important addition to the strategic management technology, scenario learning helps managers explore the true range of available choices involved in preparing for the future, test how well those choices would succeed in various possible futures, and prepare a rough timetable for future events. For those organizations committed to creating their own future, scenario learning is an invaluable tool. In short, this unique learning and preparation process helps school managers to cope with a variety of futures, even unexpected crises (see Box 1.1).

A central theme of this book is that scenario learning occurs when an organization:

- Uses scenarios to identify possible business opportunities.
- Tests its strategy in multiple scenarios.
- Refines its strategy based on its new understanding of what's required to succeed in a variety of possible futures.
- Monitors the results of strategy execution.
- Scans changes in the environment to determine whether further strategy change or adaptation is required.

Box 1.1
Scenario Learning

Scenario learning involves two elements: constructing or developing scenarios, and integrating the content of scenarios into decision making. Both elements are central to what we mean by scenario learning; neither one alone is sufficient for successful scenario use. We prefer scenario learning to the more common term scenario planning for a number of reasons.

First, learning, as now used in the management literature, is not just a means of generating or acquiring knowledge; management learning puts knowledge to use. Whether and how knowledge is acted upon is essential to learning. Scenario learning, thus, reinforces the need for scenarios and decision making to be intimately intertwined.

Second, scenarios, by definition, challenge the mind-set of managers by developing plausible alternatives. They take decision makers into new substantive terrain; they require them to be willing to suspend their beliefs, assumptions, and preconceptions; they compel them to grapple with questions that previously were not raised or were briefly considered and quickly shunted aside. Scenario learning therefore not only emphasizes the role of scenarios as a generator of thought and reflection, but also explicitly challenges conventional wisdom, historic ways of thinking and operating, and long-held assumptions about important issues.

Third, learning implies discussion and dialogue: Managers and others inside and outside the organization must engage each other in a free-ranging exchange of ideas, perceptions, concerns, alarms, and discoveries. Such exchanges will invariably provoke some degree of tension—between individuals, between functions holding opposing ideas, and between corporate and business unit perspectives. Such tension is the essence of collective learning—that is, individuals reflecting upon and challenging their own mind-sets.

Fourth, learning suggests that scenarios are a continual input to decision making and that actions and decisions in turn spawn further reflection and thinking—in short, further learning. Thus, scenarios provide views of the future against which managers can monitor and assess the world as it unfolds around them. Each distinct view of the future becomes a focus for learning.

A learning perspective suggests that the various tools and techniques involved in scenario development and use are a means to an end—aids to understanding how the world might unfold and how that understanding can be incorporated into decision making. If this objective is to be achieved, scenario methodologies must not and cannot take on a life of their own as they have in a few organizations. They are intended only to serve the purposes of augmenting understanding and informing decisions.

SCENARIOS: A PRELIMINARY DEFINITION

To learn about the future, most organizations either purchase forecasting or do their own. In contrast, relatively few organizations practice scenario learning. However, the success of forecasting is decidedly mixed, especially so in industries that are experiencing discontinuous change. Should your organization abandon forecasting and switch to scenario learning? We would suggest that organizations need to employ both technologies, because forecasting does shed light on how predictable trends may combine to produce significant changes in the business environment. Indeed, forecasting can help create well-researched scenarios.

Some senior managers are reluctant to engage in scenario learning because they equate scenarios with forecasting—which has a long history of unreliability when it was wrongly used to predict the unpredictable. Some of their reluctance stems from a misunderstanding of what scenarios are and what they can accomplish. For example, some critics argue that because the future is so uncertain, scenarios aren't of much use. The easiest way to overcome this prejudice is to define at the outset what scenario learning can and can't do.

What a Scenario Is

The dictionary definition of a scenario is "an outline of a natural or expected course of events." However, the scenario-learning methodology that has been developed and employed by many different types of business and nonbusiness organizations has a specialized definition. In this methodology, scenarios are descriptive narratives of plausible alternative projections of a specific part of the future. They are methodically researched and developed in sets of three, four, or more to study how an organization, or one of its decisions, would fare in each future in the set.

Based upon a combination of unfolding events that are quite predictable and those that aren't—what we know will happen and what we don't know—we can project a wide assortment of futures. Our pictures of the future are limited only by what information we have or can collect, by our understanding of this information, and by our imagination. That is, we are kept in the dark about the future because of what we don't know and what we can't imagine. Scenario learning trains managers to organize what they know and what they can imagine into logical, useful stories about the future and to discern and consider the implications of these "future histories" for their current and future strategy choices. A fringe benefit of scenario learning is that it prods the imagination, stimulating managers to think more audaciously about what is possible. It encourages managers to make informed, imaginative judgments about what they don't know.

As a tool for looking at the future, scenario learning is applicable to many topics, contexts, and organizations. In the three cases we are using as exemplars, the relevant futures include (see Box 1.2):

Case 1. The evolution of the multimedia business over the next three to five years.

Case 2. The evolution of the consumer goods industry in Europe.

Case 3. The evolution of macroenvironmental change that could affect the hospital industry in the United States.

Scenario sets provide vividly contrasting narrative descriptions of how several uncertain aspects of the future might evolve. These narratives might address, for example, the plausible future expansion or contraction of an industry, the advent of regulation or deregulation, or the emergence of a new technology. Thus, the consumer goods firm might develop scenarios that describe how distinctly different political and economic conditions in Europe could evolve by the year 2005 or 2010. These descriptions might include identification of key changes in Europe (such as the emergence of stable political institutions in Central and Eastern Europe) and the forces driving these changes (such as actions of different national governments or the European Union, and the conclusion of agreements among specific countries).

The scenarios are projections of a potential future. They are a combination of estimations of what might happen and assumptions about what could happen, but they are not forecasts of what will happen. Thus, projections should not be confused with predictions: A projection should be interpreted as one view of the future that is based upon specific information and a set of logical assumptions.

The multimedia firm in Case 1 might project a specific competitive environment three years ahead when intense rivalry erupted among three distinct technologies. The narrative for this scenario describes developments in specific technologies, interactions among these technologies, an increased sophistication upon the part of customers, and a relaxation of particular governmental regulations.

Box 1.2
Three Scenario Contexts

Case 1: Telecommunications. A leading telecommunications firm is trying to envision what the multimedia business will look like three to five years ahead. Multimedia products are produced by the coevolution of three media: voice, data, and video. They involve the integration of multiple product or technology domains including: telephones, television sets, computers, and software. Significant technological change is occurring in each of the component product domains.

Industry experts frequently revise their expectations about likely multimedia product configurations. A central challenge confronting the firm is to envisage how these various technologies might together create new product solutions.

Case 2: Consumer Goods. A consumer goods firm is trying to determine how aggressive its strategy should be in the new Europe, a region stretching from Ireland in the west to the Ural mountains in the east. It is concerned about the political and economic future of the new Europe in the last years of this millennium and the early years of the next. One view suggests a vibrant political and economic future: the European Union experiences an upsurge in economic growth and many of the Central and Eastern European countries experience a stabilization of their political processes and the first years of a sustained economic growth pattern. Another view suggests that the European Union's economic problems worsen and Central and Eastern European countries fail in their efforts to develop sustained economic growth.

Case 3: A Health Care Provider. A firm specializing in the purchase and management of hospitals is worried that emerging and potential changes in and around the U.S. health care system might spell disaster for many of its hospitals, but it also recognizes that these changes could open some new opportunities. The firm decides to examine how the political, regulatory, social, economic and technological forces affecting the health care system could lead to a hospital industry radically different from that prevailing today.

Scenarios need to be plausible—that is, possible, credible, and relevant. To be possible, and credible, they must pass the logic test. Thus, the consumer goods firm needs to articulate how and why various European government investment plans, economic policies, increases in discretionary income, political developments within specific countries, and agreements between specific nations might lead to an upsurge in industry demand across the continent of Europe. However, scenarios, are not intended to "prove" that what is projected will take place. They are based on a possible, credible, and relevant hypothesis. Plausible evidence should indicate that the projected narrative could take place (it is possible), demonstrate how it could take place (it is credible), and illustrate its implications for the organization (it is relevant).

In short, plausibility ultimately rests on judgments contained in the rationales or evidence that buttress any projection or narrative. All the key parts of a scenario should be stoutly questioned. And if one of the scenarios seems implausible—that is, if elements of its narrative are inconsistent or illogical—it should be reconceived. For example, a firm discovered that one of its technology scenarios was plainly flawed: It projected a date for a technology breakthrough by a competitor that independent analysis revealed was long before such an achievement could occur. The solution: rethink the logic of the scenario.

A SET OF SCENARIOS

For scenario learning, a set of these alternative stories or plots must be prepared. Three or four scenarios allow decision makers to compare and contrast how a particular future, such as the multimedia or consumer goods industry, or the political and economic state of Europe, might evolve. These comparisons allow decision makers to identify key indicators of the evolution of each future and to assess the importance of each scenario for specific strategies or decisions. Subsequently, the consumer goods manufacturer can assess the implications for each of its strategy alternatives in four scenarios depicting the European economic and political situation and the company's competitive environment.

In effect, the manufacturer can pretest three alternative strategies: build market share rapidly, penetrate at a modest pace into Central and Eastern Europe, or limit new investment in Europe to the minimum. Scenario learning allows the organization to explore how each of these strategies would play out in the four distinctly different plausible futures.

Exhibit 1.1
Key Scenario Elements

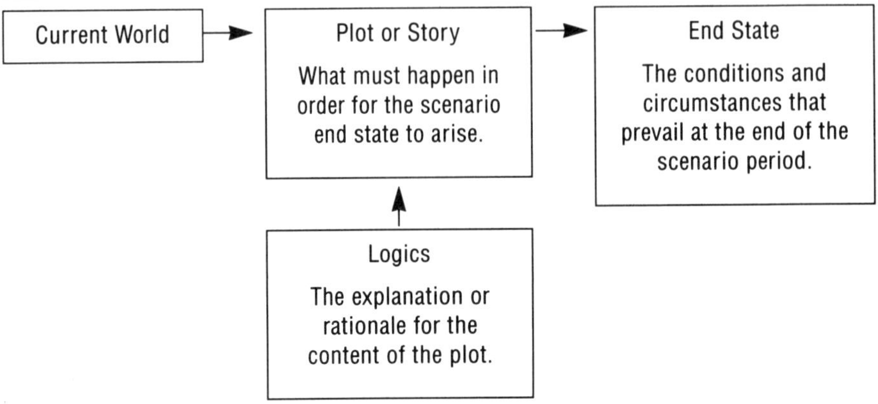

Current World	→	Plot or Story What must happen in order for the scenario end state to arise.	→	End State The conditions and circumstances that prevail at the end of the scenario period.

Logics

The explanation or rationale for the content of the plot.

The Elements of a Scenario

So far, this introduction to scenarios has identified a number of their key elements: driving forces, logics, plots, and end states. Although many business, governmental, and consulting organizations have developed their own particular approaches to crafting and using scenarios, generally speaking, the methodologies incorporate each of these elements (see Exhibit 1.1). These elements are briefly described here (and again in more detail in subsequent chapters).

Driving Forces.   Scenario plots are not merely exercises in creative writing. They are constructed out of driving forces, the forces that shape and propel the story described in a particular plot. While the individual forces that can affect any plot are in principle innumerable, at a very general level, they can be segmented into two categories: environmental forces and the actions of institutions. It is difficult to conceive of a scenario that does not incorporate driving forces such as economic, social, cultural, ecological, and technological events, trends, and developments. Similarly, the actions of institutions including many different types of business organizations, political parties, governmental agencies, and regional and international bodies are evident in every scenario.

Logics.   Scenario logics constitute the rationales that underlie a scenario's plot or story—the "why" underlying the "what" and "how" of a plot. Logics provide the explanation of why specific forces or players behave as they do. For example, why the American Medical Association would strongly support a particular legislative proposal, why a specific organization would be the force driving a plot in a particular direction, and why a set of driving forces would interact in a certain way. The logics underlying a plot built around increasing regulation of the health care market would not only identify which forces were likely to cause the health care market to evolve in a particular direction, but why they would do so. For example, it would identify why certain interest groups such as senior citizens, insurance companies, or governmental agencies would support specific types of legislation, and how they might come together to bring pressure to bear upon specific political parties and legislative committees.

In short, without an understanding of its logics, decision makers cannot assess the plausibility of a scenario: Could it happen? Are there inconsistencies? How could it happen? Why might it happen?

Plots. End states such as depictions of the multimedia industry at some future time are the outcome of one or more specific plots or stories. Each plot contains a story that connects the present to the end state; it illustrates what would have to happen for a specific future or world to come to be. Thus, in Case 3, the health care firm might end up considering plots around deregulation or increased regulation of the industry, or different forms of competition that might arise not only between current rivals but between them and new entrants. In Case 2, the consumer goods firm, as noted previously, might describe plots ranging from an economically buoyant to a depressed Europe.

End States. To make scenarios specific and unambiguous, they should describe a particular end state: What will happen in a particular future or world at some specific point in time. One way to generate end states is for decision makers to ask: What would happen if . . . ? For example, decision makers in Case 3 might ask what would be the configuration of the health care industry if the government rescinded particular major regulations and imposed some others? Depending upon the purpose of the scenarios, end states can be rich or sparse in details. For example, an end state intended to convey to managers the complexity and turbulence of competitive conditions in the multimedia industry five years from today might include:

- Specific descriptions of the solutions proffered by different groups of competitors.
- The rate of entry and exit of rivals.
- The types of customers who would use the solutions.
- How customers would purchase and use them.
- Why customers would purchase one solution rather than another.
- The dynamics of rivalry among competitors as they strive to attract and retain customers.

On the other hand, sometimes end states may be simple and straightforward. A sample end state: "In 2001, an inexpensive, pocket-sized computer terminal designed to play Internet games becomes the Model T of a new generation of computer products." Another: "In 2005, Internet outlets become common in retail and service establishments—gas stations, banks, grocery stores." A relatively small amount of detail may paint a picture that generates critical strategy or decision implications.

Two caveats, however, should be noted. One is that we should be careful not to fall into the trap of interpreting the description of end states as forecasts: They are merely speculative projections based on a specific set of assumptions. Two, it is more important to define clearly the dynamics of the future—how we reached the end state—than to aim for 100 percent accuracy about the end state itself. Scenarios are most valuable when they are understood to be movies of an evolving story, not a snapshot of a specific point in time.

THE PURPOSES OF SCENARIOS

Scenario learning is not just about constructing scenarios; it is ultimately about informing decision makers and influencing and enhancing decision making. Scenario learning emphasizes the importance of augmenting decision makers' understanding of possible futures as a prelude to decision making. As a bonus, managers learn even more from the results of actions they take to prepare for unorthodox futures.

To Augment Understanding. Scenarios help managers see what possible futures might look like (end states); how these futures might come about (plots or stories); and why they might occur (logics). As managers compare and contrast different futures and explore their decision implications, their shared mental models—how they view the future and the implicit assumptions they make about their industry, technologies and the economy—are inevitably raised and challenged.

Consider Case 1, the multimedia industry. New solutions are rapidly emerging; technology developments are in a constant state of flux; corporate and consumer needs vary greatly; and new competitors are constantly entering the marketplace. This rate of change is not likely to slow in the foreseeable future. Scenarios outlining distinct technology evolutions leading to a range of competitive end states are likely to cause decision makers in this firm to seriously consider how multiple technologies might interrelate and how different technology developments would lead to distinct solutions. If these solutions were not previously considered by the firm, its managers must now evaluate what would have to happen for these solutions to emerge. In doing so, they would identify beliefs and assumptions they previously held about future solutions and technologies and how they might have circumscribed questions they raised about technologies, the industry, and their own strategies.

In short, scenarios augment decision-makers' understanding of the world around them and how the future is unfolding. Scenarios provide one means by which decision makers can reflect upon, and if necessary, change their mind-set—their assumptions about how and why they do things. Scenario learning should aim to challenge organizational mindsets, otherwise they won't affect "what goes on between the ears" of top executives, middle managers, and workers.

Produce New Decisions. Scenarios may force new considerations to surface—decisions that were not previously on the organization's agenda. The multimedia scenarios may cause the firm in Case 1 to consider investing in technologies it had previously paid too little attention.

Reframe Existing Decisions. Scenarios can provide a new context for existing decisions. The scenarios generated by the consumer goods firm in Case 2 may cause reconsideration of some of the commitments in the firm's planned strategy in Central and Eastern European countries. A scenario with a high degree of plausibility suggesting a slower than anticipated rate of political evolution and economic development in many of these countries may cause the firm to reconsider many of the assumptions which underlay its planned aggressive penetration strategy. At a minimum, this new context might suggest the need to hedge the original strategy to make it effective across a variety of futures.

Identify Contingent Decisions.   Scenarios can help managers formulate important contingent decisions. That is, what the organization should or could do when certain circumstances arise. For example, in the multimedia case, the firm could determine what it would do were a new competitor's product to gain rapid market penetration. Scenario learning thus emphasizes knowing what the organization might or should do under sets of circumstances that might emerge at some future time.

SOME CORE CHALLENGES AND TASKS IN SCENARIO LEARNING

Every organization that seeks to adopt and execute scenario learning confronts three fundamental challenges. How can it learn about and from the future before the future happens? How can that learning be integrated into decision making? How can an organization learn about and prepare for the future better and faster than its competitors?

Consequently, organizations that hope to improve how they learn lessons from the future must master at least eight tasks:

1. *Understand the Present (and the Past).* Any attempt to project how a future might evolve necessitates identifying key current forces that are likely to shape that future. Typical key forces include demographic shifts, political and regulatory developments, technology changes, the emergence of new competitors, and changing customer tastes.

2. *Describe a Variety of Potential Futures.* Decision makers need to imagine, create and invent descriptions of what various futures might look like. Alternative futures such as different political and economic states of the new Europe or different states of the multimedia or health care industry five years from now provide distinct competitive environments in which to contemplate the consequences of a spectrum of strategies. In the consumer goods case, for example, what if the new Europe were to fragment into regional groups fighting protracted trade wars? If the firm's aggressive growth strategy were designed to capture market share in a united Europe, how would it play out in the new fractious environment?

3. *Delineate How Such Futures Might Evolve.* Specification of a particular future, such as the political and economic state of Europe in the year 2002, presumes some understanding of how that state might evolve—what would have to happen over the next five years to get from the Europe of today to the Europe of 2002? If a Europe dominated by national, racial, and ethnic tensions were to prevail in 2002, what sequence of actions taken by which social and political groups in which countries would lead to the disintegration?

4. *Identify Appropriate Indicators to Track.* The evolution of each projected future can be tracked by monitoring specific indicators. A Europe riven by religious and ethnic tensions or a Europe avidly accepting political and economic integration will not happen overnight; such political environments evolve. The recognizable precursors of transformation—pivotal events, measurable changes in attitude, enabling technology—forewarn observers that a particular future is headed their way before it arrives.

Integrating learning about and from the future into decision making also entails a number of specific tasks, each of which is central to ensuring that scenario learning is connected to decisions and action.

5. *Link to Specific Decisions.* Alternative views of a particular part of the future, such as how the multimedia industry in the United States might unfold, can be linked to specific decisions or issues of strategic importance to the organization in two ways. First, it is essential to derive their implications for decisions the organization is already making or contemplating. For example, projections of a slowly or rapidly evolving multimedia industry might have different implications for commitments to specific research and development projects. Second, many specific decisions that managers had previously either ignored or downplayed, or had simply not been aware of, may take on crucial significance if an alternative scenario becomes reality. For example, scenarios concerning the future of the multimedia industry might cause the firm in Case 1 to consider making alliances with partners owning particular technologies that are critical to specific product development.

6. *Link to Analysis Processes.* Understanding alternative futures and how they might unfold must be linked to the key analysis processes. As we shall see in Chapter 2, scenarios provide direct input to the identification, development, choice, and execution of strategy alternatives, to issues management and to capital allocation decisions.

7. *Link to Organizational Procedures.* A related means of ensuring that scenario learning is not an end in itself is to design organizational procedures that encourage widespread participation in scenario development and extensive sharing of the insights the developers gain. For example, it's a good practice to ask management teams performing business analysis to pool their insights, craft scenarios on specific business issues, write them up, and communicate their content to top management and to managers throughout the organization. It's even more crucial to incorporate such scenario learning into ongoing organizational procedures such as task forces, committees, and other groups that come together to understand the world around them. For instance, technology task forces charged with projecting technology developments and identifying potential strategy implications routinely use scenario methodology. But until representatives from different business units, different organizational levels, and various functions—such as finance, manufacturing, and marketing—assimilate the significance of the various scenarios, the organization will not integrate scenario learning into a new communal understanding of the future's possibilities.

8. *Involve Decision Makers.* Integration of alternative futures into decision making truly occurs only when managers both recognize and understand these futures. That is, can the executives imagine these strikingly different futures, envision how they happen, and "see" their particular implications for specific decisions? Such familiarity with and "feel for" alternative futures can occur only when decision makers are thoroughly involved in shaping them, in reflecting upon them, and in considering their implications for their own organization—especially their impact on investment decisions. This book explicates and demonstrates how these eight tasks are combined into a scenario-learning methodology to address the three survival challenges noted previously.

SCENARIO APPLICATIONS

As a tool for looking at the future, scenario learning is applicable to many topics, contexts, and organizations. (See Box 1.3 for a brief history of scenarios and the variety of circumstances in which they have been applied.) In this book, we show how scenarios can:

- Address the social changes resulting from demographic shifts, the political consequences of economic conditions, and the market dynamics of technological change.
- Explore the competitive conditions in an industry—the race among a number of corporations to develop and introduce a new product or service, the economic rivalry between geographic regions or nations, or the future political stance of a nation.

Box 1.3
A History of Scenarios

Scenarios have had a rich, though somewhat checkered, history in business, governmental, and military organizations over the last 30 years or so.

Most authors attribute the introduction of the notion of a scenario and the development of the first fully fledged scenarios to Herman Kahn during his tenure at RAND Corporation during the 1950s. His early scenarios were developed as part of military strategy studies conducted by RAND for the U.S. government. Kahn further developed the scope and use of scenarios when he founded the Hudson Institute in the mid-1960s. It seems fair to suggest that he single-handedly popularized the idea of developing scenarios in work he conducted on possible futures in the year 2000. "Thinking the unthinkable" is the phrase most frequently associated with his work and name.

Then in the 1970s, both Royal Dutch/Shell and the consulting firm SRI International, working separately, devised a formalized approach to scenario development that could be more readily linked to strategic planning. Shell is usually credited with having the first widespread use and application of scenarios in a corporate setting. Under the guidance of a succession of champions including Ted Newland, Pierre Wack, Arie de Geus, and Kees van der Heijden, Shell has continued to develop and evolve its scenario work. Most companies still put Shell at the top of their list when they consider firms to benchmark or investigate for best practice in the realm of scenarios. However, this does not mean that Shell maintains a large staff of scenario planners or commits great resources on scenario analysis.

Currently at Shell, scenarios play a significant role in the decision-making process, but they aren't allowed to steal the show. As one Shell planner put it, "Scenarios are like the scaffolding for a building. The building is what's important. Scenarios are used to frame a decision, but they must never divert attention away from the decision itself."

Over the last decade or so, as the chapters in this book will attest, the practice of scenarios has spread to many other corporations and governmental agencies as these organizations have endeavored to break out of the constraints and difficulties inherent in traditional forecasting methods.

A succession of consulting firms, notably Battelle, The Futures Group, Global Business Network, and Northeast Consulting, have played a major role in expanding the corporate use of scenarios in a wide variety of applications, many of them reflected in this book.

Energy companies create scenarios to understand potential interactions between public policies, oil reserves, and prices at the pump.
Consumer goods companies develop scenarios to understand how demographics, lifestyles, and economic conditions might interact to produce widely different market futures. High-tech companies devise
scenarios that paint a series of panoramas showing how multiple technologies could mingle and recombine to simultaneously destroy some
markets and create others. Financial services firms craft scenarios that
illustrate various ways the industry's historic boundaries among various
service products and services—insurance, banking, securities, and ad-
visory services—could collapse or integrate with other industries to
generate fundamentally new markets.

SOME MISCONCEPTIONS
ABOUT SCENARIOS

A number of misconceptions about scenarios inhibit (and in some cases
prohibit) the adoption and use of scenario learning in organizations.
These misconceptions contribute to the apprehension about using scenarios and the misuse of scenarios in many organizations.

First, unfortunately it is still common to find a scenario either depicted
or interpreted as a prediction. Therefore, it may help first-time users to
think of scenarios as something like the flight simulators used to train airline pilots. In fact, scenarios do allow executives to simulate the experience of operating an organization through a wide variety of potential
conditions. However, this analogy is only partially accurate. Scenarios
aren't just simulations of various combinations of present realities; they
are also experiments in rethinking how an organization will operate under
a variety of future possibilities. In effect, scenarios are flight simulators to
imaginative destinations to test real decisions. Imagine a simulated flight
to test the decision to buy a fleet of new fuel-efficient planes, which posed
such conditions as low fuel prices, a merger with a key rival, increased
ground delays resulting from counter-terrorist measures, and new government regulation. Such a scenario simulation would be a rich learning
experience, whether or not such a future ever came about. Clearly, the
criticism that a scenario "got the future wrong" reveals a misunderstanding of the purposes, uses, and limitations of scenario thinking.

Nor does a scenario have to capture and represent all the complexity
in the world to augment understanding and enhance decision making.

Sometimes very simple scenarios that are sufficiently different from current experience have the power to alert managers to new possibilities. What if your "cash cow" division could be rejuvenated? What if another industry began to use the Internet to deliver a customized product to your customers? What if a product ingredient or production method became the subject of a health scare?

SCENARIOS: MULTIPLE TYPES AND FORMS

There are many valid methods of constructing scenarios and performing scenario learning. The scenarios in this book illustrate a wide variety of techniques for developing and articulating plots, logics, and end states. Scenarios thus allow inventive minds myriad ways to depict and think about the future. But, at the risk of oversimplification, scenario construction can be segmented into two basic approaches:

- *Future Backward.* Select several significant futures and try to discover the paths that lead to them.
- *Future Forward.* Project sets of plausible futures based on analysis of present forces and their likely evolution.

The Future Backward Approach

This category includes methods some practitioners call the deductive and top-down approaches. In these processes, organizations first identify a number of end states that are integral to their future. Using this approach, sometimes only a small amount of data can suggest interesting and provocative scenarios. For example, a few years ago, a telecommunications firm noticed that a few of its customers had begun to use the Internet as an alternative means of communication with their customers. It then asked: What if many of our current and potential customers were to use the Internet as a means of interacting with their customers and other constituencies? Such an "event" could have devastating impact on the firm's sales and profitability.

Stories or plots are then developed to show what would have to happen for each end state to emerge from the present. Illustrations of this approach can be found in Mason (Chapter 6), Perrottet (Chapter 7), Fahey (Chapters 11 and 12), and Thomas (Chapter 13).

Future Forward Approach

This category includes the intuitive, or inductive methods. In these processes, organizations construct scenarios using knowledge about the present and the emerging future as the building blocks. A common starting point is the specific strategy alternatives or decisions confronting your firm. The construction materials include events and circumstances in and around your firm's competitive arena and its macroenvironment. Selecting which events and circumstances are most significant may require an analysis of your own organization's current and potential vision, resources, capabilities, opportunities, and threats. The competitive environment includes decisions and actions of other organizations—rivals, suppliers, market channels, and government—and changing needs and preferences of consumers.

As we shall see in many chapters throughout this book, determination of key forces driving an organization's environment and the major uncertainties facing the organization requires considerable analysis and reflection. The most critical driving forces must be matched with the uncertain conditions of greatest importance to the firm, for it is the various combinations of the two that produce different end states. For example, for a pharmaceutical company considering developing an antipregnancy vaccine, governmental regulation is one critical driving force of great uncertainty, and public acceptance/antagonism is another. Two critical forces of great uncertainty arrayed in a 2 × 2 matrix generate four scenario end states.

In this case, one axis of the two-axes matrix would be "onerous regulations" or "extensive deregulation." On the other axis are "public acceptance" and "public antagonism." The four qualitatively different scenario end states generated would be:

- Oncrous regulations and public support.
- Onerous regulations and public antagonism.
- Extensive deregulation and public support.
- Extensive deregulation and public antagonism.

Drawing upon the imagination, intuition, and assumptions of key managers and others, a story or plot is then constructed. Illustrations of this approach can be found in Schwartz and Ogilvy (Chapter 4) and Wilson (Chapter 5).

Models. Some consultants prepare analytic models or simulations to develop and study alternative futures. A frequent point of departure is to identify relationships in managers' mental conceptions of the world confronting them. These are then translated into models that can be analyzed or simulated using a computer. Illustrations of this approach can be found in Hinton and Paich (Chapter 9) and Behravesh (Chapter 16).

Influence Diagram. The influence diagram method is a new approach to scenario development that is closely related to the analytic or modeling technique. It involves building a series of cause–effect relationships in diagrammatic form among many data points or events so that an organization's managers can visualize the logic that connects what otherwise might appear to be unrelated events. This approach to developing alternative futures is illustrated by Ward and Schriefer (Chapter 8).

CONCLUSION

Scenarios offer decision makers an unrivaled methodology to learn from the future before it happens. Yet, as the contributors to this book clearly demonstrate, there is no single approach to developing and using scenarios. Organizations have many options for the types of scenarios they create, how they develop and explore them, and how they link them to decision making. The intent of this book is to explore these alternative scenario approaches and how they can be managed, and at the same time, show how scenario learning can support strategic management.

CHAPTER 2

INTEGRATING STRATEGY AND SCENARIOS

LIAM FAHEY and ROBERT M. RANDALL

A number of companies have had problems realizing the promise and potential of scenarios. The root cause seems to be that, in most organizations, scenario development initiatives and efforts to create and execute strategy have not been linked. In practice, scenario and strategy initiatives often address different issues, draw upon unrelated analysis processes, and are led by different sets of individuals. To make matters worse, few organizations have connected the execution of strategy with the scenario process. To help remedy this situation, this chapter illustrates how various types of companies have learned to use scenarios to improve the content of strategy, and to support and enrich the analysis processes and organizational procedures involved in strategy making and implementation.

When strategic analysis and scenario development are linked, the result can be a learning experience that will strongly influence the destiny of your organization. A requisite of this scenario learning is an understanding of the sophisticated process of integrating scenarios and strategy. In essence, how scenarios and strategy interrelate is, in one way or another, the focus of almost every chapter of this book.

Scenarios help managers discover and understand a variety of possible contexts for decisions about the future. In the renowned case of Royal Dutch/Shell's experiments with scenarios in the 1970s, for example, a scenario about a future world where an oil cartel controlled prices defined a profoundly different decision context for the firm. This scenario was so unlike the expected corporate future that it was initially considered almost subversive. Though it offered Shell an opportunity to consider alternative strategies in a new context, this scenario did not sway decision makers. To be effective, scenario learning must convincingly address strategic issues. Likewise, strategy makers would be well advised to test their plans in a number of possible futures.

The purpose of this chapter is to briefly introduce and illustrate three related ways in which scenarios can be used to greatly improve how organizations develop and execute strategy:

- Strategy content.
- Strategy analysis processes.
- Organizational procedures involved in strategy making.

These interconnections are of course also addressed in many later chapters.

STRATEGY CONTENT

Academicians, consultants, and practitioners alike struggle to define exactly what strategy means: how it can be defined; what its constituent elements are; and to what extent organizations are constrained in their strategy choices. Yet there is general agreement that any organization's strategy must confront and resolve three sets of elemental choices:

1. *Strategy Scope.* The segments of the marketplace in which the firm wishes to compete.
2. *Competitive Differentiation or Posture.* How the firm wishes to compete in its chosen segments; that is, how it differentiates its offering to attract, win, and retain customers.
3. *Goals.* What the firm wishes to achieve or accomplish.

Scenarios, as we shall see throughout this book, can be used to examine each of these elements of strategy content.

Strategy Scope.   Scope is the choice of products and services the firm offers and the customers it seeks to serve. Organizations with rapidly changing business environments must continually address scope questions: "Where in the marketplace does the firm want to compete?" or "What businesses does it want to be in?" Some fundamental issues affecting scope that must be confronted by every business include:

- *Product/Service Scope.* What products and services does the firm want to provide?
- *Customer Scope.* What customers does it want to reach or serve?
- *Geographic Scope.* What geographic regions does it want to be in?
- *Vertical Scope.* To what extent does the firm want operating control over activities from raw materials processing and supply logistics through manufacturing and distribution to marketing, sales, and service?
- *Stakeholder Scope.* What stakeholders can the firm leverage to aid in attaining its goals?

In most established firms, these scope issues are usually considered only from the perspective of the firm's historical approach to its competitive environment. However, a few organizations have used scenarios to reexamine the future in terms of these five scope questions. In some instances, scenarios have helped to identify new scope possibilities. Provocative scenario end states—specific future events or conditions that define a particular scenario—or scenario plots that managers have not previously considered or imagined often suggest opportunities to bring new products or solutions to the marketplace and to reach new customers. Four examples illustrate these possibilities:

- *New Product Ideas Tested in Scenarios.* One financial services firm recognized an entirely new way of combining parts of existing offerings to generate a new financial product for a particular segment of its corporate customers. By writing a set of scenarios about how the market would evolve, the managers of the financial services firm were able to consider the future needs of customers and to develop attractive new product combinations.
- *New Market Combinations Scenario.* By creating new views of interrelationships among existing products or industries, scenarios may suggest alliances or acquisitions that enable firms to enter new markets or businesses. For example, an electronics firm recognized that one scenario it had developed, the emergence of a new range of components, was actually going to occur. To seize the opportunity, it immediately launched a series of acquisitions so that it could introduce a range of new products for this marketplace.
- *New Customers Scenarios.* Scenarios can help decision makers identify ways to extend their present scope by widening the market for

existing products or solutions or by identifying new customers or new customer needs. One consumer firm began to consider how it could aggressively offer its services in a number of South American countries as a result of scenarios indicating that new opportunities would result from the greater political and economic stability in the region.

- *New Competitors Scenario.* Equally important, scenarios can help organizations avoid making detrimental scope decisions. For example, a surgical instrument firm recognized the potential folly of investing heavily in its current highly profitable product line after studying scenarios that showed how one or more competitors could easily introduce a substitute product that had clear cut advantages.

Competitive Differentiation or Posture. How an organization differentiates itself from current and future rivals in the eyes of its customers and other stakeholders determines its competitive posture. Posture analysis examines: How will the organization distinguish its offering to attract, win, and retain customers? Posture analysis also poses a crucial challenge to decision makers: How can they devise a way of competing that provides superior value to customers compared to current and potential rivals? Organizations that fail to develop a distinctive competitive posture—one that provides unique value to valuable customers—can't expect to succeed for long. In most likely scenarios, they won't gain market share from competitors, build customer loyalty, or even retain their existing customers.

Scenarios can play a pivotal role in the design and execution of competitive posture in at least two ways. First, scenarios can help identify a number of possible postures—new ways of competing. Scenarios addressing the future of industries, the interaction of technologies, the changing context of customers, and the likely actions of competitors can identify ways in which differentiation might be attained. For example, a major national retail chain is currently developing scenarios that compare and contrast a variety of competitive conditions over the next 10 years. It hopes to be able to identify the best way to compete for customers in each scenario to determine where stores should be located, the right range of products and services, the customer segments it should solicit, and the best pricing strategy.

Similarly, scenarios developed by a multimedia firm drew its managers' attention to customers' needs, product configurations, and ways of competing that were not previously on their radar screens. By focusing on strategies to achieve differentiation, managers considered:

- Product features that might be emphasized.
- Types of functionality that might be provided.
- Forms of service that might be appealing to various customers sets.
- Types of relationships that might be valued by different customer groups.
- Price structures that might be appropriate.

This enabled the firm to then conceptualize more distinctive offerings, ones that would be relatively difficult to quickly duplicate and that also would be attractive to particular customer segments. These potential offerings subsequently can be tested in a variety of scenarios to determine which choices are most likely to succeed in a variety of competitive environments.

Goals.   Scope and posture define the approach an organization will take to outmaneuver its competition and to win customers. Keep in mind that goals aren't static; they change as organizations get new information or work out new understandings about the future, therefore, scope and posture choices need to be continually reexamined to measure how well they help achieve key goals.

Scenarios can affect which goals an organization chooses to pursue in a number of ways. Scenarios may lead to fundamentally new goals, changes in existing goals, or changes in the timing of goal attainment, and each of these changes is closely aligned with the organization's scope and posture decisions. In one company, a set of scenarios compelled a much more rapid introduction of new products in order to preempt potential moves by rivals.

All organizations have an explicit or implicit "vision," "mission," or "strategic intent"; in other words, a unifying purpose the organization should strive to achieve over time. For example, Apple Computer's early vision was to build an innovative, easy to use computer. Scenarios can contribute greatly to the development of a new vision, mission, or strategic intent. By creating a new understanding of what the future could be, they alert decision makers to new views of what their organization might be able to attain or achieve at some future point in time. Apple's vision could have been explored in strategic scenarios that tested its vision against various combinations of scope, goals, and posture. For example, scenarios could have been constructed around driving forces such as technology developments, changes in home owner behaviors, changes in distribution channels, and new market entrants. Each scenario could then have been assessed to see if it would support strategies with the following goals:

- *A Macintosh in every home.* Scope: A line of trouble free, inexpensive small computers suitable for multiple purposes by different individuals in the home. Posture: Wide distribution, extensive service, and aggressive pricing.
- *A premium-priced Mac for affluent customers.* Scope: Selective product range aimed at "high-end demographics." Posture: Streamlined distribution, very extensive service, heavy emphasis upon product features, and mid- to premium price.
- *Apple dominance in key market segments.* Scope: Modest range of specialized products aimed at institutional customer segments such as schools, universities, and professionals such as graphic artists. Posture: Selective distribution channels, targeted service support, premium prices with quantity discounts.

STRATEGY ANALYSIS PROCESSES

The content of strategy—the choices of scope, posture, and goals and the allocation of enabling resources—is heavily influenced by the processes of analysis within the organization. Well-established strategy analysis frameworks such as the five forces industry model, value chain, and macroenvironmental analysis, are now widely used to generate description and understanding of an organization; the industry in which it competes; competitors, technology, and the political, social, and economic environment. To become truly useful to an organization, scenario learning should be directly integrated with its strategy analysis frameworks and processes. Many later chapters in this book will illustrate how scenarios can complement and extend specific types of strategy analysis. In this introductory chapter, it is sufficient to identify how scenarios can augment and contribute to a number of widely used approaches to strategy analysis.

Scenarios can contribute directly to the thinking and action that proceeds from the classic stages in strategic decision making:

- Understanding the (strategy) context.
- Identifying alternatives.
- Developing alternatives.
- Choosing among alternatives.
- Executing the chosen strategy.

Understanding Strategy Context.   Building a set of scenarios that is capable of stimulating managers to reconsider their present and future business strategy requires considerable investment of thought and energy. The actual payoff occurs when decision makers arrive at a better understanding of their present and future business choices. This understanding must lead to the development and assessment of significant business opportunities, a process that starts with identification of strategy alternatives and ends with implementation. To champion this process, it's wise to select managers with a predilection for strategy innovation and the skills to take effective action.

Identifying Alternatives.   In some organizations, scenarios are used to identify potential strategy alternatives, especially strategies that are different from those executives have traditionally considered. Unfortunately, however, in all too many organizations, the identification of strategy alternatives is an ad hoc process; initiatives to identify alternatives get little attention because senior executives erroneously believe they have fully weighed all the possibilities.

Before we consider the contribution of scenarios to alternative generation, it is appropriate to ask, "What is the meaning of strategic alternatives?" Furthermore, it is useful to distinguish between alternatives at the corporate and business unit levels. Strategic alternatives at the corporate level include: acquisition of other businesses; divestment of existing businesses; mergers with other organizations; and internal development of new products. Within each of these alternatives might be a number of subalternatives. For example, a corporation might be able to identify a number of possible acquisition candidates. At the business-unit level, strategic alternatives include: developing new products; amending existing products; adding to or deleting items from existing product lines; divesting product lines; and different ways of competing or achieving differentiation. Again, a firm may identify multiple distinct subalternatives within each type of alternative.

The challenge confronting any management team is to generate the broadest possible set of alternatives that either currently or at some point in the future might be available to the organization. It requires decision makers to extend their sights beyond the reach of the alternatives typically considered within the organization. In almost all instances, it requires decision makers to identify alternatives that extend well beyond extensions to their current strategy. Questions that might lead to identification of such alternatives include:

- What alternatives might be potentially available to the organization that historically have not been considered?
- What might happen in the future that would give rise to alternatives the organization has neglected?
- What alternatives might be associated with the organization's current strategy that might not have been considered?

These questions clearly indicate that scenarios can play an important role in identifying strategic alternatives at both the corporate and business unit levels. To the extent that the alternative futures depicted by diverse scenarios represent futures that are fundamentally distinct from the current world, decision makers are likely to discover and develop important strategy alternatives. Decision makers should address the following questions:

- What strategy alternatives are suggested by each scenario?
- How are these alternatives different from each other?
- How different are these alternatives to those currently being considered by the organization?

Developing Alternatives.   Before alternatives can be assessed and chosen, they must be developed and detailed so that decision makers can fully understand what the alternative entails. A strategic alternative such as introducing a new product may seem simple and straightforward until managers specify what the organization must do to execute it. The new product may consume substantial financial resources over a number of years and require the organization to hire many new people with specialized skills, to enter into one or more alliances, to develop a new manufacturing process, and to create new marketing and sales capabilities. In short, alternatives must be developed and defined before they can be fully understood and evaluated.

Unfortunately, in many organizations, few alternatives are fully developed, and those that are tend to be rather similar to each other, such as different types of acquisitions in a particular product area or a set of possible alliances in a particular geographic region. When the alternatives being

considered are largely similar, they all essentially presume only one future—thus the need for scenarios that challenge this presumption. Every
organization therefore needs to develop a set of distinct strategy alternatives. When they are compared and contrasted, distinct alternatives compel different points of view to be considered.

Fortunately, an organization need not develop and detail all the alternatives that are identified, only those that suggest significant opportunity
or that ward off serious threats. Scenarios can assist in determining which
alternatives should be examined in detail. Answering these questions can
aid in this task:

- Which alternatives suggest the greatest opportunity for the organization? Even a preliminary assessment of alternatives can identify
  those that constitute significant opportunities.
- Which alternatives most strongly challenge the assumptions underlying the current strategy? One or more of these alternatives may
  generate fundamental doubts and concerns about the viability of the
  current strategy under different scenario end states and plots.
- Which alternatives might be logical extensions of the current strategy? One or more of these alternatives may suggest ways in which the
  current strategy could be better leveraged if specific scenario plots
  were to unfold.
- Which alternatives seem to be suggested by a majority or all of the
  scenarios? It is usually essential to fully develop these specific alternatives since they may hold the key to success no matter which
  scenario actually transpires.

Choosing Among Alternatives.   Scenarios also directly influence the
choice of strategies: Different scenario end states and plots provide radically
distinct strategy evaluation criteria. For example, scenarios projecting intensely competitive or modestly competitive conditions suggest very different issues and questions that can easily lead to the rejection or acceptance of
a strategy alternative in one scenario that is accepted or rejected in another.

The role and importance of scenarios in strategy evaluation can be best
exemplified by considering the types of questions that are usually prescribed in choosing among a set of alternatives:

- How substantial is the opportunity presented by the alternative?
- What is the evidence to support the assumptions underlying each
  alternative?

- Is it feasible for the organization to execute the alternative?
- What risks and vulnerabilities are associated with each alternative and how can they be managed?
- What marketplace and financial returns might be associated with the alternative?

Developing a set of highly relevant but quite different scenarios is a critical step to answering these questions. The problem is that, in most organizations, the widely accepted mental model of the future of their industry and what it takes to succeed in it are the product of past experience. This model isn't based on anticipated or potential futures. Scenarios, by contrast, bring a future perspective to bear upon strategy choice. The future business environments delineated by the scenarios provide a unique testing ground for evaluating strategy alternatives.

Executing the Chosen Strategy.   Once strategies are chosen, the work of executing them can begin. Resources need to be allocated and plans prepared; for example, key action tasks need to be identified; personnel must be assigned to specific tasks; tasks must be sequenced; and action time lines need to be developed. In spite of the prevalence of the distinction between strategy formulation and strategy execution in both the strategic management literature and corporate parlance, it is wise to remember that any organization is always in the midst of executing strategy. Making strategy happen is an ongoing process. Regrettably, in many organizations, once major strategic changes have begun to be executed, decision makers ignore or forget about the scenarios that helped create them, when in fact, scenarios can benefit strategy execution in a number of ways.

First, as change occurs in the competitive and macroenvironment, decision makers must continually assess whether and to what extent they need to alter the strategy they are executing. Sometimes in the face of extensive change, decision makers may have little choice but to move to one of their contingent strategies. Consider the case of a consumer goods company that has begun to execute an aggressive marketing strategy by introducing a stream of new products and rapidly entering new channels in Central and Eastern Europe. It has taken this action based upon scenarios that projected modest or extensive economic growth in this broad region. As it implements its new strategy, it will begin to monitor economic and political indicators that signal whether or not this scenario is about to occur. So, if key indicators such as housing starts, wage levels, economic output, and employment growth begin to decline, indicating that the growth scenario is not on target, then the firm could rapidly scale back its aggressive marketing campaign. Second, decision makers need to continually review scenario plots. Indeed, changes in events and circumstances may suggest the need to craft a wholly new scenario.

Other Analysis Processes

Many hard-charging organizations like Microsoft Corporation use issues management as a major means of orchestrating the present and the future. Issues refer to those problems and opportunities that merit management's attention. They might include, for example, the potential emergence of a new substitute product, a change in strategy of a major competitor, technology developments that might give rise to new products, changes in governmental policies, or geographic mobility of key elements of the workforce. Managers can use each scenario to identify key issues and their implications. Issues that surface across a number of scenarios are what one organization refers to as "paramount issues." For example, a health care firm might discover that building better relationships with its key stakeholders is a paramount issue. In each one of a set of quite different scenarios, the firm's market and financial performance can be improved by working more closely with such stakeholders as regulatory agencies, professional health care institutions, community interest groups, and various groupings of its own employees.

Strategies, by definition, are always based upon implicit or explicit assumptions. Since scenarios represent alternative views of how an industry, the political and regulatory milieu, a set of related technologies, or a region's politics might unfold, they are used by many organizations to identify and challenge managers' assumptions about the future. For example, scenarios addressing a Balkanized Europe, a status quo Europe, and a politically integrated and economically buoyant Europe would be based on distinct assumptions such as political stability and economic growth. These assumptions could then be compared and contrasted to the assumptions underlying the firm's current strategy and the likelihood of new market entrants. In this way, many firms have discovered that their current assumptions about, for example, total industry sales, the lack of entrepreneurial spirit among competitors, or the slowness of change in key technology developments are far too optimistic. Some firms have also discovered that their explicit assumptions have overemphasized some issues and omitted others. For instance, one firm discovered by studying various scenarios that its future strategies were likely to be less sensitive to the future of the economy than to technology developments. Most of its efforts had been expended detailing the possible future course of the economy, and much less of its management's effort had gone into tracking technological possibilities.

A purpose of every strategy analysis framework is to identify and frame questions managers should ask. Scenarios always affect the perspective from which managers generate and pose these questions. One shift in perspective is from the present to the future: Each scenario raises its own unique issues and questions pertaining to a particular end state and how the future will evolve to reach that end state. Given a set of scenarios, managers can ask: How will our present decisions and commitments play out in each future? By developing a set of four or five pertinent but distinctly different scenarios, such questions can be asked in the context of all these plausible futures.

ORGANIZATIONAL PROCEDURES INVOLVED IN STRATEGY MAKING

Building scenario narratives, articulating diverse scenario end states, and integrating scenarios into decision making require the participation and contribution of many talented people inside and outside the organization. How these individuals come together to develop and make use of scenarios can be broadly referred to as organizational procedures. Because they determine who is involved (and to what extent) in scenario work, organizational procedures strongly affect how much learning scenarios generate, who does the learning, how widely the learning is diffused throughout the organization, and whether the learning informs decision makers and influences decision making—the ultimate rationale for scenario work in any organization. In short, how these procedures are designed and managed goes a long way to determining how well scenarios and strategy are interrelated.

Scenario Teams.   Ad hoc teams are frequently established to oversee, craft, and put scenarios to use. Team members should be drawn from a number of functional units, groups, or levels in the organization. The team conducts the research necessary to shape a plot, to articulate end states and to derive business implications.

Involvement of Line Management.   If line managers don't fully understand the need for developing scenarios, weren't involved in crafting them, or don't subscribe to the logics supporting particular plots, they cannot be expected to appreciate the critical implications of various scenarios, or even to know what questions they ought to ask that would link scenario content to current or future decisions. The rule of relevance is: Involve line managers in multiple ways. Some examples:

- Scenario thinking, content, and implications can be integrated into existing organizational procedures such as those involved in strategic planning or capital allocation. The intent here is to integrate scenarios into analysis that is part and parcel of the organization's business unit decision making.
- Several senior line managers can be asked to be associate or full members of the scenario team. The team's goal should be to include at least one influential line executive who is fully cognizant of both the content and nuances of scenario work.
- A number of line managers can be involved in early scenario team meetings to discuss the purpose of particular scenarios; how they will be developed, by whom; what the objectives might be and how scenarios might be used. The goal: Have senior line managers familiar with every phase of scenario work.
- Line managers can be given preliminary reports of progress in scenario development, including tentative end states, plots, and business implications. The goal: Give line managers an opportunity not just to influence scenario work but to become intimately involved in it.
- Senior line managers can be asked to appraise end states, plots, and their supporting logics. The goal: Monitor managerial understanding, obtain managers' input, and assess scenario implications.

Involvement of Outsiders.   Scenarios frequently require input from outsiders: management consultants; experts on topics such as demographics, political processes, and industry evolution; and representatives of distribution channels, end customers, technology sources, and suppliers. Some organizations have made outsiders active members of their scenario team. More often, however, outsiders are actively involved only in specific phases of scenario development; for example, experts can be used to help develop the outlines of plots or to challenge the logics supporting specific plots.

CONFLICTS THAT ARISE FROM INTEGRATING SCENARIOS AND STRATEGY

Scenarios provide a means to think about and analyze uncertain and important possible futures. After becoming familiar with these alternative futures, decision makers frequently challenge their organization's current strategy, its underlying assumptions, and both short- and long-term business prospects. A corporation's plan and its strategies are usually based on one "likely" scenario. Looking at a set of plausible, but very different alternatives may provoke decision makers to consider and sometimes adopt new strategies that are radically different from long-established strategies. In effect, well-crafted scenarios lure decision makers outside the comfort and familiarity of their historic mind-set and mode of operating. Doing so contributes to a number of conflicts that tend to characterize scenario learning. Unless the resulting polarizing tensions are carefully managed, scenarios will not realize their potential to inform decision makers at all levels of the organization and influence strategic and tactical decision making. Some of the principal conflicts are introduced briefly here. Each is discussed in further detail in later chapters.

Present versus Future. Scenarios and strategies require decision makers to simultaneously respect present realities and the logic of plausible futures. Developing and exploring alternative futures informs our understanding of the present and illuminates the risk of committing to a strategy (scope, posture, and goals) that is viable only for a particular future. Scenarios teach us that current commitments must always be made with an eye to the future. In developing scenarios and choosing among strategy alternatives, individuals cannot allow the present—or more precisely, their understanding of it—to blind them to imagining the future as it could be. It is necessary to thoroughly analyze the current environment in order to identify and understand the driving forces that may shape different futures and to understand why the current strategy is succeeding or failing.

Closed versus Open-Ended. Scenarios can be developed with specific strategy decisions in mind, or they may be constructed to ascertain to which strategy decisions managers should start analyzing. For example, a multimedia firm might construct a range of scenarios around different technology futures as an input to its technology investment decisions. On the other hand, in order to explore the future with as few preconceptions as possible, it would be appropriate to first construct a range of scenarios and only then consider their strategy implications. Such open-ended scenarios are especially appropriate when an organization is concerned that it may not know which strategies and decisions it should be considering or may have to consider at some future point. Thus, decision makers can use scenarios to explore some future in an open-ended manner—such as the likely configuration of an industry or possible sociopolitical futures that might be experienced by a specific geographic region—without regard to the organization's current issues, decisions, and concerns.

Grounded versus Imaginative.   Good scenarios are both thoroughly researched and thoroughly imagined; bad scenarios rely too much on uninformed speculation and are poorly researched. Don't go to the other extreme and get so caught up in detailed economic research for your scenarios that you lose sight of the need to take certain hints about the future and let your imagination soar.

Scenarios place heavy demands upon individuals' creative and imaginative faculties. Crafting scenario plots almost always challenges decision makers to envision a variety of futures that at best may be only dimly visible, if at all. Individuals with the capacity to generate rich and imaginative scenarios out of clues about environmental change can conjure up worlds or futures that startle or surprise others. Their intuition, and the explosive imaginative experiments it provokes, can blow open doors, clearing the way for more logical reasoned analysis. Other provocative scenarios are the product of reasoned analysis that make them plausible, credible, and pertinent. Whatever their origin, scenarios must compel managers to address strategic issues and strategy implementation.

Intellectual versus Emotional.   Scenarios are necessarily an intellectual or analytical activity: They involve thinking about what could be. They require managers to develop and analyze alternative end states and plots, to assess how different they might be from the present, and to identify their scope, posture, and goals implications. Furthermore, they must also appeal to and capture the emotions of both those who develop them and those who will be affected by them. Decision makers who are excited about and by a future they are envisioning and crafting, and the potential strategy choices that flow from it, are more likely to care about that future, to understand its driving forces, and to pursue its strategy implications for their own organization whether they are good, bad, or indifferent.

Advocacy versus Dialogue. Good scenarios are more likely to be forged when individuals advocate their point of view, argue how a plot might evolve, demonstrate the logics that might underpin it, and illustrate its implications for the organization's current and future strategies. True insight is likely to thrive when minds are engaged and energized by the clash or intersection of advocated perspectives and positions. Keep in mind that staunch advocacy helps a team, but unrelenting dissent hurts it.

The simultaneous consideration of two or three distinct scenario end states or plots—what they might look like, how they might come to be, and the strategies that might be suggested by them—should foster exciting dialogue. This happens when members of a team suspend old assumptions and rethink their possible futures together. This dialogue between top and middle management and among individuals within and outside the organization contributes to the synthesis of new perspectives and informed opinions about strategies that scenarios can help to generate.

Skepticism versus Expertise. Expertise is always required in the analytical processes of scenario development and in ways to integrate scenarios into organizational procedures. Scenarios of course cannot be developed without knowledge of the relevant substantive areas such as the peculiarities of a particular industry, the dynamics of technology development, or demographic shifts. Yet because the future can be so different from the past, and so many previous projections have proven false, a healthy skepticism must be maintained about the pronouncements, judgments, and assessments of experts and other individuals both within and outside the organization. Skepticism compels decision makers to critically reflect upon each scenario's logics, to compare and contrast alternative logics, and to challenge the strategy implications for their own organization of each scenario.

Quantitative versus Qualitative. Scenarios are essentially constructs of the imagination, and so are fundamentally qualitative in nature. Nevertheless, it is important to give some estimate of the extent of quantitative differences between scenarios if strategy is to be correctly calibrated. It is not enough to say, for instance, that "the market will grow faster in Scenario A than in Scenario B." Estimates of a doubling in size versus 20 percent growth not only give added dimension and "feel" to the story lines, but suggest different strategies. In sum, therefore, the primary effort should be given to fine-tuning the qualitative descriptions of the scenarios; selective quantitative details can add important dimensions to the story lines.

Probability versus Plausibility.   Perhaps the most divisive debate concerning the development and use of scenarios concerns the assignment of probability to the final scenarios. One school of thought (Battelle Management Consulting, for example) argues that assigning probabilities gives decision makers important information on which to base their strategies. According to this view, not assigning probabilities is an intellectual cop-out and constitutes a failure to complete the task. Another school (Global Business Network and SRI International, for example) believes that assigning probabilities is a hand-me-down from the days when forecasters tried to predict the future. Proponents argue that probabilities detract attention from scenarios' basic purpose of open-minded consideration of dramatically different futures. Assigning probabilities is, in this view, misleading, a distortion of the process, and probably no more likely to be right than are current attempts at forecasting. One solution to this conflict is to acknowledge that differing opinions about probabilities exist, and that discussion of these differences should be encouraged. In the team's initial analysis, *all* plausible scenarios—regardless of probability—should be considered.

CONCLUSION

The underlying premise in this book is that scenarios should be an invaluable component of the business strategist's toolkit. They generate a distinctive form of knowledge; they provide a productive laboratory by which decision makers can learn about the current and future world; they can be integrated into the making of strategic decisions in multiple ways. In short, they provide a process for enhancing management's understanding of how to prepare for and manage change and how to thrive in future environments that may be strikingly different from the present. Scenarios, thus, are and should be an integral part of strategic thinking. They give insight into the futures that tomorrow may bring, what will be needed to succeed in various futures, and how to set the stage for that success.

CHAPTER 3

USING SCENARIOS TO IDENTIFY, ANALYZE, AND MANAGE UNCERTAINTY

BRIAN MARSH

The goals of this chapter are threefold:
- *To explore and illuminate the concept of uncertainty.*
- *To show how scenarios can be used to identify and manage uncertainty.*
- *To provide some practical advice to managers about how to manage uncertainty.*

In the first act of Shakespeare's *Macbeth,* Lords Macbeth and Banquo are passing through a forest on their way home from a successful battle when they come across three witches. The crones amaze Macbeth by greeting him as king-to-be. After hearing the witches predict that Macbeth will reign one day, Banquo naturally also wants to know what's in store for him. He asks the three foreseers of future events what every manager of a large organization would like to know: "If you can look into the seeds of time and say which grain will grow and which will not, speak then to me. . . . "

In the theater, a little knowledge about the future can set protagonists on a dangerous path, as Macbeth and Banquo find out. But modern organizations must routinely search for insights about future possibilities as part of their business planning.

UNCERTAINTY: WHY IT DESERVES OUR ATTENTION

In our investigation of scenarios as a means to explain and manage uncertainty, let us start by examining some of the problems and difficulties commonly encountered in making forecasts. For purposes of illustration, we shall look at two quite different forecasts, from which a number of lessons can be gleaned.

Case 1: Commodity Supply Forecasts

In 1985, the Massachusetts Institute of Technology sponsored a project that reported on "Global Energy Futures."[1] The major conclusion was, in part, that: The supply of oil will fail to meet increasing demand before the year 2000, most probably between 1985 and 1995, even if energy prices rise 50 percent above current levels in real terms.

A company that invested heavily on the expectation of profiting from such a forecast would have been crippled. Oil and gas are in such abundant supply that the Gulf War caused only the briefest of upswings in price. Saudi Arabia has lost its power to manipulate prices by opening and closing the valves in its oil fields, and vast resources of oil and natural gas lie ready to satisfy the demand for energy. This excess supply of hydrocarbon fuels has kept energy prices remarkably low and prevented renewable energy sources—such as wind, solar, and tidal power—from becoming economically competitive. As a result, these alternative energy sources—and nuclear power—have never fulfilled the promise they seemed to offer in the early 1980s.

When we stop to think about it, we know that long-range estimates of the supply of raw materials have often been wrong, but we seldom allow singular lack of success to stand in the way of continuing the forecasting game. Consider Exhibit 3.1, Contrast between Forecast and Reality—the U.S. Oil Supply.[2] These forecasts were made by sensible people over many years. In hindsight, it's astonishing that despite their remarkable record of inaccuracy, the business world accepted their forecasts as gospel.

Gross miscalculations of this kind don't just occur in the oil business; future stocks of other commodities have also been greatly misforecast. In 1950, the known reserves of iron ore were 20 billion tons, but they increased to 250 billion tons by 1970. In the same period, known reserves of potash jumped from 5 to 120 billion tons and of copper from 100 to 280 million tons.

Over the past decades we've learned that forecasts of anything truly uncertain—that is, an important data point (such as the price of a barrel of oil 10 years from now) or a commodity availability estimate that

Exhibit 3.1
Contrast between Forecasts and Reality—The Oil Supply

Date on Which Forecast Was Made	The Forecast	The Reality
1885	Little or no chance of oil in California (U.S. Geological Survey)	8 billion barrels produced there since then
1891	Little or no chance of oil in Kansas or in Texas (U.S. Geological Survey)	14 billion barrels produced there since then
1908	Maximum future supply: 22.5 billion barrels (Geological Survey officials)	35 billion barrels produced since then
1920	Peak domestic production (then 0.45 billion barrels per year) almost reached (Director, U.S. Geological Survey)	1948 production was more than four times 1920 level
1947	Sufficient oil cannot be found in United States to satisfy domestic demand (Chief of Petroleum Division, State Department)	3 billion barrels found the next year, largest volume in history, and twice annual consumption
1949	End of U.S. oil supply almost in sight (Secretary of the Interior)	It wasn't and still isn't!

is not easily quantified (how much oil is a mile below the earth under the Amazon?)—almost always fail. In fact, such predictions fail so frequently that to rely on any numerical forecast dependent on many political, technological, and economic variables that can have a wide range of potential outcomes is to bet on very long odds!

Case 2: The Treasury Model and United Kingdom Economic Forecasts

Before we can develop a useful understanding of the notion of uncertainty, and of a way to manage it, we need to look at another important example of an ongoing failure to forecast how the future will unfold. Case in point is the continuing attempt to model the economy of the United Kingdom and the tribe of forecasting tinkerers this speculative process attracts.

For more than three decades, this attempt to predict the upturns and downturns in the economy of a relatively small nation, noted for its highly literate civil service and mature industrial base, has resulted in one missed forecast after another. Proponents of forecasting say that errors are the result of an incomplete or unperfected model. In sum, their argument is that only the "formula" they use to predict the future is somehow wrong. So their answer to better forecasting is to create better models of how the bit of the world we are interested in actually works. This is very well illustrated by the British Treasury's model of the United Kingdom economy.[3]

This model was developed in the 1960s—but kept secret until an act of Parliament in the late 1970s forced its guardians to make it public. By the 1980s, the forecasters had 25 years of experience tinkering with their model of the U.K. economy. After repeatedly having to amend, adjust, and enlarge the model to take account of new trends and evidence, and repeatedly having to admit to errors in forecasts, the forecasters decided to scrap it—and build another one! In this revision, the old model's 500 equations were reduced to 300; its variables were reduced from 1,275 to 530. Certainly, the new model ran faster and was less difficult to feed with data, but it was no more accurate than its predecessor.

Surprisingly, this failure didn't cast doubt on the value of computer models. Instead, it inspired a drive for "better" predictive systems. Other specialists emerged with their own particular brand of forecasting tool, such as neural networks. One such network, fed 30 years of back data of 16 key economic indicators, such as new car sales, "deduced" a model that announced that the United Kingdom recession was over. Chancellor Normal Lamont, began cheerfully reported sightings of the green shoots of recovery, annually, for several years! For example, in 1991, the governor of the Bank of England was "confident" in September that the United Kingdom was coming out of its recession.

Eleven months later the bank reported that "recovery remains elusive." Clearly, they should have suggested that economic recovery was unforecastable. That would at least have shown that some learning was taking place.

Instead, the bank decided to take a new tack. It reduced the number of people employed in its Econometrics Department and relied more on the models of the economy that economists carry around in their heads. To do this, the chancellor rounded up a posse of "wise men" in 1992 and reverentially consulted them on what was in store for Britain. Did that produce better results? It didn't, of course!

John Kay of the London Business School reported on a study of the attempt of economists to forecast economic performance in the short term.[4] The government's assembly of so-called wise men were "no better" than those economists not part of the inner circle. The more than 30 economists in Kay's sample were uniformly bad forecasters, and even when one of them got one of the predictions nearly right for a couple of years, he was just as wrong as his colleagues in later years. Kay concluded: "It is clear from the analysis that there is a consensus forecast which most forecasters cluster around—to such a degree that it is barely worth distinguishing between one estimate and another. Yet the consensus forecast failed to predict any of the most important developments in the economy over the past seven years."

Perhaps it is the irresistible desire to be believed that makes forecasters more likely to initially predict what business leaders and politicians wish for, and then to qualify their predictions with "ifs" and "buts." So it's wise to treat all forecasts with great circumspection, even when they're made by wise and respected people. However, forecasting can play a role in managing strategy, and we need to consider this authentic use of forecasting as we home in on the concept of uncertainty and how to confront it.

Predetermined Elements

Experience teaches us that some future events do seem to be predictable; or at least our expectations have some chance of occurring. A famous example Pierre Wack, the leader of Royal Dutch/Shell's original experiment with scenarios, used to illustrate predictability was that if heavy rains fall in the foothills of the Himalayas, the water of the Ganges River will rise and overflow its banks.[5] Many events that occur today will have predictable results tomorrow. Scenario writers call these events *predetermined elements,* and they are useful in making plans for the near future. If predictions are being made only for the immediate future, then the influence of predetermined elements is likely to be great. For example, though it may not be possible to forecast with absolute certainty whether it will rain on a given day next week, we can assume that the TV weather forecasters are frequently right on Friday about the need to take a raincoat to Saturday's football game. For another example, historic relationships between temperature and heating oil demand are helpful in forewarning fuel distributors of movements in short-term demand.

Too often, we wrongly assume that an event is predetermined. Only rigorous research, meticulous attention to detail, and testing ideas with fellow skeptics can help us avoid such mistakes. As the mistakes made by the forecasters in the Bank of England showed, much depends upon satisfactorily interpreting the facts as they are perceived, thus, considerable effort must be expended in understanding the present.

The Nature of Uncertainty

First, we need to clarify the nature of uncertainty. Obviously, we don't possess the tools to fully explain how today will become tomorrow. But uncertainty isn't *not* knowing what tomorrow will be like. Uncertainty is not knowing which issues, trends, decisions, and events will make up tomorrow.

Uncertainty, in the sense it is used in this chapter, should not be confused with probability, which is a quantified measure of likelihood. Dealing with uncertainty is not a problem of finding the degree of probability, nor is it a means of quantifying how much you do not really know. Probability quantifies the likelihood of a future event based upon the statistics of past similar events. So, for instance, given a good set of seismic surveys, the probability of finding oil can be estimated because we know from past records how often each sort of geologic formation has yielded oil.

If, however, a future outcome will be determined by a set of circumstances that we cannot now estimate or anticipate, then that outcome is uncertain and no probability can be ascribed to the various outcomes that can be envisaged.

One technique for tackling uncertainty—defined as not knowing which forces and trends really matter—is to surface an agenda of issues. The process uses an open-ended interviewing technique in which managers meet with an outside facilitator in a confidential one-to-one 90-minute meeting to respond to simple questions. In this process, interviewees are asked to talk about favorable and unfavorable outcomes for their organization and review significant events in the organization's past. They are urged to identify the issues that urgently require attention. They are asked what they might ask an oracle should one miraculously appear. They are offered an opportunity to muse about what contribution they would like to be recognized for when they leave the organization. Later, a trained facilitator analyzes the wealth of data from such interviews and prepares an agenda of issues that address the uncertainties the managers believe are shaping their organization's future.

This process of conducting structured interviews helps facilitators learn which issues are truly uncertain and which, after investigation, turn out to be predictable. The interviews also promote an objective confrontation of uncertainty, a necessary step before an organization can prioritize issues that need to be addressed.

Interpretations of the Present

The interviews help individual managers articulate their uncertainty and clarify their perceptions about what is causing the uncertainty. In times of rapid change, each manager's perception of the present is unique and valuable, and deserves attention. Organizations stressed by change have been compared to boats going through the rapids of a river. In fact, a company navigating discontinuous changes in technology, markets, legislation, and macroeconomics is operating in a much more complex environment than some Outward Bound river raft experience, even if it's running through white water.

Do the economic statistics tell you the same things about your company's prospects that they tell your colleagues? Isn't it likely that there is more than one interpretation of the market trends? Or of the forces at play in Europe? Or of why your customers buy your products? So, in fact, the present itself is uncertain!

If everyone in an organization is experiencing a different present, then tomorrow there will be more than one memory of today. Like witnesses to a motor accident, managers will describe a crisis they saw and experienced differently in the days to come. Thus, today there is more than one memory of the past; thus history, too, becomes uncertain!

Furthermore, one person's memory of the past dims and becomes selective. In the afterglow of the U.S. victory in Kuwait, who remembers, for example, that our adversary, Saddam Hussein, was formerly supported heavily by the West in his war against fundamentalist Iran? On the other hand, as memories dim, the desire to conform makes people susceptible to particular interpretations of the past. We are surrounded by a mixture of certainty and uncertainty. The uncertainty is so much a part of our everyday existence that we seldom recognize it. Though our organizations aren't good at methodically sorting the uncertain from the probable, as individuals and as managers we have developed techniques, conscious and unconscious, for coping with uncertainty.

When managers pause to think about it, they know all this to be true, and for the most part a certain level of uncertainty doesn't interfere with their everyday lives. The difficulty arises because it is singularly unhelpful to know that there are many pasts and a number of presents when what they really want is a straightforward answer to the question of what is going on in the world around them and what is going to happen in the future. People want a single interpretation of the present and a single forecast of the future. Managers believe they need to eliminate (or at least to quantify) uncertainty about the future in order to make decisions, even when they know that this is impossible.

The Benefits of Variety

This variety of experience and perception of experience, past as well as present, is a major cause of conflict in management teams. Managers invest time in eliminating that variety; they seek conformity. They build systems and structures to reinforce certainties that flow from unchallenged conformity. Organizations become more efficient and predictable: Rules, systems, procedures, and protocols are designed and applied and can be seen to work.

But variety is essential because the world outside of organizations is continuously in flux. If organizations are to survive, they must be able to adapt, to change modes of behavior, to break with practices that were essential to survival in the past. As a case in point, Peruvian peasants growing potatoes in the high Andes learned that if they grew only one variety that maximized yields they could be wiped out by a species-specific disease, or an adverse shift in climate. So they learned to cultivate many species, sacrificing yield each year in favor of propagating strains that would survive a variety of conditions that could one day occur. These peasants, not an MBA nor a Mendel among them, knew that variety was to be valued. They recognized that they faced unknown futures, quite unlike their presents and their pasts, for which they needed to be prepared.

The Management Paradox

This is not to suggest that peasants are more skilled at strategy than managers at successful companies in more developed countries. Rather, the reverse is generally true. However, all managers (and peasants farming Peru's harsh highlands) must address the same dilemma: Those who invest labor and resources today in hope of a reward tomorrow must acknowledge there is a real need to promote predictability, stability, and consistency, as well as to encourage change, variety, and flexibility.

The pressure to conform to the rules of management teams is so great that it becomes difficult and conspicuous to march out of step. In management teams, therefore, the pressures are toward conformity and consensus. The team often adopts the official axioms about the past and the present. There is also great pressure to reach a consensus view on what the future will be. People with divergent points of view are often judged "unsuitable" for membership on the team. In comparison, uncertainty is not easy to embrace. It doesn't inspire a rousing team fight song. For example, it would be surprising if none of the U.K.'s economists in the example referred to earlier did not know that his or her estimates would be wrong. But no one spoke up. All ended up conforming.

Managers, despite all of the doubts about and failure of previous forecasts, keep saying that they need to have forecasts. They maintain that they need to know the future so they can make good decisions today. So managers need to share a forecast of the future, whether or not it will be right. The rationale for this forecasting is clear: Managers need to make decisions for investment of resources and take responsibility for net profits. People affected by these decisions—shareholders, employees, and assorted stakeholders—need to believe that they're wise decisions. How then can the scenario approach help managers deal with uncertainty? We shall explore this in the remainder of this chapter.

The Scenario Approach

The scenario approach requires that managers first stop trying to make strategic decisions before they have done their best strategic thinking. To perform high-quality strategic thinking, they must start by learning how to have strategic conversations, or dialogues. These are nonadvocative communications among knowledgeable stakeholders that are quite distinct from debate, negotiation, and discussion.

Strategic decisions take time to play out and to have a significant impact on disposition of resources or alter the business portfolio. Often decisions emerge from the confusion of day-to-day operations and tactical maneuvering in the marketplace. When managers attempt to take strategic decisions, they are invariably confronting uncertainties that lie ahead.

The usual discussions and debates over strategy and tactics are combative arguments in which positions are defended and converts won. They are advocative procedures, whereas strategic dialogue involves talking through the issues and seeking collaborative understanding of implications and personal perceptions. Such conversations put a premium on listening, rather than talking, and on understanding rather than persuasion. Strategic dialogue allows managers to explore alternative opinions about what the future might be like without having to choose one possible path against which strategic decisions are to evaluate.

When performed properly, the scenario approach offers a way of formalizing such conversations, of focusing the dialogue on the really interesting aspects of the unknown and unknowable future. The scenario approach permits managers to explore lines of thought that are novel and that are "outside the box"; that is, beyond the normal limits of an organization's operations. By experimenting in the context of scenarios, managers don't need to risk either their corporations or their careers by exceeding these limits. Scenarios enable them to learn through "play" what it would be like to run their business in different circumstances and in different futures. Using the scenario approach, managers make hypotheses about the future in a structured and creative way, and in so doing place their uncertainties in some ordered perspective. By testing their decisions in several logical futures, they can assess the possible consequences of their actions without actually suffering the slings and arrows of outrageous fortune.

David Ingvar, a Swedish neurobiologist, has an insightful theory about how human beings model the future.[6] Ingvar believes that people continuously create sequences of events in their minds as to how the future could evolve. For example, an assembly line supervisor working on a repair of an old machine may start fantasizing about what could be done if the company bought a new one. This in turn could stimulate thinking about new layouts for the plant or for simplified product design to streamline product production. Suppose that one day, out of the blue, there is a need to reengineer the operation. At that point, the supervisor, because he or she has done some prior thinking, will be better prepared to respond. These strings of past suppositions are referred to, often unconsciously or informally, when assessing new choices that have to made about the direction in which the organization will go. Ingvar calls these "memories of the future." Scenarios allow managers to create a logic for their mental inventory of fragments of thought about possible futures.

Scenarios also focus attention on unknowns that are important and about which there is great uncertainty. They are stories about alternative ways in which these uncertainties about the future could be resolved. By practicing with the resulting scenarios, managers explore possible responses and reactions to future environments. As a result, they develop a resilience that better equips them to deal with surprises, because they have a wider, deeper, and more familiar inventory of Ingvar's "memories of the future." They become better prepared to face the future as it unfolds around them because they possess a greater inventory of memories of the future.

In essence, scenarios provide a vicarious experience from which something about the future has already been learned and about which various responses to different futures—even undesirable ones—can be tested. The actual future that emerges will then contain fewer surprises that could paralyze an organization. Many organizations are so unnerved by a particular turn of events, or fear of such events, that instead of counterpunching, they deny that the unwanted future is actually happening. Using scenarios makes it less likely that managers will attempt to defend the indefensible and more likely that they will react quickly and with confidence to unexpected challenges.

Strategic decisions often emerge quickly from a scenario exercise. If the scenarios have been well constructed to address the important issues faced by the business, and if they have been internalized and owned by the decision makers, then strategic choices will be more easily identified and exercised.

Good scenarios always challenge and surprise. Bad scenarios that merely confirm the prejudices of the management won't permit the organization to add to the inventory of memories of the future. It is tempting to delegate the task of creating scenarios to "experts" in the field, and to expect well-argued, finished products to stimulate decision making by the management team. Certainly, experts produce good scenarios. But unless the managers can truly "see" themselves in the worlds that have been created and can "feel" what it like to "live" in that world, they are unlikely to be convinced that they are authentic visions of the future. It is not enough that scenarios are logically sound and internally consistent—and therefore persuasive intellectually. They need also to be believable, visceral, and to excite emotions. To achieve this result, a management team should be actively involved, together with experienced scenario writers, in the creation of scenarios that they will own.

Time Parameters of Scenarios

How does a management team set the time frame for scenarios? A frequent initial question is, what is the right time period for a scenario? My suggestion is, write scenarios specifically for the time period affected by the decisions being made. If a major oil deposit is found in the North Sea, for instance, the time horizon for relevant oil price scenarios might be 20 years. In fact, the Troll gas field off Norway was discovered in 1979, and it was 15 years before the first gas deliveries began.

In contrast, scenarios for the textile industry should select a time horizon relevant to the likely changes in technology, foreign trade practices, and environmental priorities that greatly influence competition. Investing in research to create new colors and fabrics, and building more sophisticated manufacturing facilities to make the fabrics may take a dozen years. The client, the user of the scenarios, and the team of managers whose decision making is to be influenced by the scenarios should first define what it is that the scenarios are going to be used for, and then determine a sensible horizon year.

Keep in mind that it is important to avoid short-term thinking. Scenarios often are set in some purportedly stable end state; but in the real world, the train track never ends in Utopia Station and history does not reach a destination. When the horizon year eventually dawns, there will still be uncertainty and volatility: New businesses may arise from the ashes of failures; prices and demand and economic cycles will still be worrying managers. So having targeted a horizon year, consider whether it would be useful to extend the period just a little in order to stretch managers' minds a little further.

The scenario time frame should also stretch backward in time. It seems much easier to face up to the uncertainties of the future if the scenarios are placed in the context of a continuum. How far back in recent history should your scenarios explore? A rule of thumb might be: twice as far back as forward. The pace of change is accelerating so rapidly that transformations that might occur during the time period designated for the scenarios might be appreciated more fully in the context of changes that have already occurred over twice as many years in the past. But be forewarned that most organizations have selective memories, and they suppress their recollections of the true past. However, if the memories of the past are discussed objectively and if the path that the organization has followed in reaching its present situation is explored thoughtfully, then this revisiting of history will provide a sound foundation for the scenarios that consider the future.

In my experience it is not particularly useful to choose an historic event in the organization's own past as a starting point. For example: Don't choose the year in which the organization was listed on the stock market, the year the present CEO took office, or the launch of the mainstay product line. Likewise, avoid major breakpoints in the environment. Scenarios for Russia should not start will the fall of the Berlin Wall; likewise, those for the Balkans shouldn't really start with the death of Tito or even the death of Archduke Ferdinand.

History echoes around us; the present is the inheritance of past decisions. Gaining some insight into the dynamics of an organization's history is important, not because we should assume that the "model" that explains the past will predict the future. Instead, we should look for realizations about the past that challenge current assumptions about how the world works. Try to open minds to new possibilities, new outcomes, and new ways of addressing uncertainty. The hope is always that in analyzing the past, the scenario team will stumble across a truly surprising insight that will illuminate present uncertainty about the future.

Using Scenarios to Face Uncertainty:
Good and Bad News

Scenario planning was first practiced by Royal Dutch/Shell some 25 years ago. Shell continues to develop its techniques and to disseminate its "global scenarios" widely—to customers, the World Bank, many national governments, investment analysts, and special-interest lobbies. Most managers in Shell today cannot remember a time when scenarios were not part of the planning process. Mention of a particular scenario's name alone will still produce recognition from those who used it a decade or more ago. All senior managers get to debate the logics of each scenario with the head office specialists. Frequently, there is true dialogue on the local implications for the business of these scenarios. Scenario planning enabled Shell to become a "learning organization" decades before the term had gained currency.

Scenario Learning

Learning is an iterative process:[7]

- Experience leads to contemplation and appraisal,
- Which leads to theorizing and postulating,
- Which leads to plans and decisions,
- Which leads back to experience.

If learning is to lead to renewal, the organization must constantly appraise its performance. It must seek to understand why it performs the way it does; and that understanding must lead to new plans and new decisions. Richard Pascal warned in an article called "Nothing Fails Like Success": "Market leadership is difficult to sustain. . . . What is often missing is relentless questioning and obsessive concern that they aren't as good as they could be. . . . It is running scared that keeps a company on the edge of performance. . . . Successful companies feel they have answered the most relevant questions."[8]

Thus, a characteristic of the learning organization is its restlessness, its flexibility, its obsession with change. If it is successful, it advances over time: Each successive journey round the learning loop leads to new insights, new decisions, new experience. The organization can steadily improve performance for as long as it is able to learn. And if it is able to learn faster, it can catch those competitors ahead of it and open a gap between itself and those behind it.

CONCLUSION

Scenarios offer an organization a way to learn better and faster. They allow managers continually to test their perceptions of an uncertain future, for which there are two big payoffs:

- Enhanced learning by the organization.
- The successful continuance of the organization toward its desired future.

The real test is whether an organization has the insights and the stamina to undertake the learning journey and make the investment required to develop the skills necessary to create and use scenarios to identify, analyze, and manage uncertainty. This book can tempt the reader to give it a try, to run an experiment and learn first-hand about the benefits of learning from the future.

PART II

BASIC APPROACHES TO CONSTRUCTING SCENARIOS

CHAPTER 4

PLOTTING YOUR SCENARIOS

PETER SCHWARTZ and JAMES A. OGILVY

This chapter provides a step-by-step explanation of how to write a set of scenarios that portray a range of the most relevant alternative futures facing an organization. The scenarios are based on a logical hypothesis about how a few critical uncertain forces could interact to greatly alter the operating environment. Each scenario takes the form of a carefully plotted narrative that examines a unique combination of conditions. By imagining how well their current and prospective strategies would succeed in each scenario an organization's leaders can anticipate how to prepare for such momentous changes.

To be an effective planning tool, scenarios should be written in sets of four or five absorbing, convincing stories that describe the range of alternative futures most relevant to an organization's success. Each scenario story should have a unique plot and each plot should be flawlessly rational. Thoughtfully constructed, believable plots help managers to become deeply involved in the scenarios and perhaps gain new understanding of how their organizations can manage change as a result of this experience. The more involved managers are with scenarios, the more likely they will recognize the important but less obvious implications of these alternative worlds. Moreover, scenarios with engrossing plots can be swiftly communicated throughout the organization and will be more easily remembered by decision makers at all levels of management.

THE TWO-PART SCENARIO SET PROCESS: SELECTING THE PLOTS AND CREATING THE STORIES

Many organizations have learned to develop sets of alternative scenarios as powerful learning tools by using the simple process described in this chapter. The process presents a fundamental challenge: How to whittle the virtually infinite number of possible futures that could be described down to a manageable three or four plots that will shed the most light on a specific organization's future. The first part of this chapter lays out a methodology for creating a set of scenarios that deal with the issues that are most critical to an organization.

Once you have determined the logical rationale for three or four scenario plots, the next task is to create compelling stories. The second part of this chapter shows how organizations can prepare scenarios that are so thoroughly imagined that managers can "live" in them and gain valuable insight from this experience.

HOW TO SELECT THE PLOTS

Scenario plots—or scenario logics—can be effectively developed during a two-day workshop, which preferably takes place at an off-site location. When all goes well, a highly interactive, imaginative team process can occur at these sessions.

Composition of the Team.   Participants should be carefully recruited to include people with a thorough knowledge of the company, its competitive environment, and the critical issue or issues to be addressed. The team should include representatives of many levels of management, people with a variety of experience and roles. Management consultant Gary Hamel suggests that companies pay special attention to managers who operate on its frontiers—such as new ventures in Asia or Eastern Europe and technology start-ups—for new perspectives. A full spectrum of organizational functions should also be present—finance, R&D, manufacturing, marketing, and public affairs. Diversity of experience is critical to the success of the project.

If, on the other hand, people from inside and outside the organization who are unorthodox, original thinkers are excluded, the project is likely to fail. For example, at a workshop attended only by the intimidating head of a business unit and his malleable direct reports, little original thinking occurred. In contrast, at an AT&T scenario workshop for executives, it was an outsider whose ideas jump-started a provocative discussion about the future of telecommunications.

Decision Focus.   On the first morning, the team begins the first hour by identifying the key decision facing the organization, discussing it, and developing a clear understanding of insightful questions to ask about the decision. For scenarios to be truly useful learning and planning tools, they must teach lessons that are highly relevant to the company's decision makers. In other words, they must speak to decisions or direct concerns. When the team is developing such decision-focused scenarios, it is critically important to ask the right focal question: Should we build a new coal-fired power plant? Should we acquire, (or divest or expand) certain businesses (or product lines)? Should we build a manufacturing facility in China? Should we invest a substantial fraction of the firm's resources in a new interactive media venture?

When determining the focal issue, it is important to consider the appropriate time frame of the scenario, because it will affect the range of issues the scenario addresses. In medical scenarios, for example, biotechnology, genetic medicine, and noninvasive surgical procedures should be mature technologies by 2010, but they may not be relevant to a scenario with only a five-year time horizon.

Sometimes the focal question evolves after the initial discussion. For example, in a project to examine the future of white-collar work, the team started out thinking that the principal question was, How should white-collar work be physically and organizationally designed? But the pressing issue facing the company that emerged from a discussion with senior management was: Employees no longer see white-collar work as prestigious, so white-collar skills are not highly valued. Many of the employment pressures and discontents previously experienced in the blue-collar workforce were now souring the white-collar workforce. The project shifted from an effort to look simply at the future of the design and organization of white-collar work to one that asked, Will it be possible to reestablish white-collar prestige and its work ethic?

Not all scenarios must address a specific decision. Scenarios are also a learning tool for investigating general areas of risk and opportunity, such as, What will the office of the future be like? Or, What are the possible futures of China or Brazil? Such exploratory thinking can lead to the development of more focused scenarios and can also start a strategic dialogue with managers throughout the organization. But even exploratory scenarios must be built around a relevant question or the scenarios will lack focus and internal consistency.

Brainstorming a List of Key Factors

After selecting the decision focus of the session, the brainstorming begins. It pays to have this part of the workshop led by a person experienced at facilitating brainstorming sessions—usually someone from outside the business. One of the "rules" of successful creativity sessions is that no idea is immediately disparaged or discarded, a difficult rule to enforce when brainstorming sessions are headed by the CEO or led by the chief of a business unit for his or her direct reports.

Driving Forces

During the first day, much of the brainstorming revolves around identifying the driving forces and key trends. These are the most significant elements in the external environment. They drive the plots and determine their outcome. Be sure to consider five general categories: social, technological, economic, environmental, and political forces. The interaction of these forces creates complex and interesting plots.

Suppose Wal-Mart was looking at the future of shopping malls. A social force for consideration would be crime: A rising crime rate would keep shoppers off the streets. Would malls that invested heavily in security be perceived as a safer place to shop, and thus gain market share? A technological force that will affect malls is electronic shopping. An economic force that drives mall revenues is rising or falling disposable income. An environmental force—pressure for antipollution legislation—could lead to higher gas taxes and reduced personal automobile travel, and the result could be fewer mall trips for recreational shopping. A political force—the desire to revive local real estate assets—could lead to an effort to find creative new uses for shopping mall property.

Examples of other driving forces include: the impact of more women in the workplace; ever cheaper, yet more powerful computers; the emergence of China as an economic power; and the changing values of teenagers. Each organization must compile its own set of driving forces and key trends. However, the list for firms in the same industry will probably be quite similar.

While identifying driving forces, it is essential to distinguish the predetermined elements from uncertainties. Once the team has openly brainstormed a number of issues, it's time to look at the various forces and related environmental factors more closely:

- *Which key forces seem inevitable or predetermined?* These are trends that already evident and are unlikely to vary significantly in any of the scenarios. These might be slow-changing phenomena (the development of new oil resources), constrained situations (the U.S. social security crisis), trends already in the pipeline (the aging of baby boomers), or seemingly inevitable collisions (branch banking versus banking through personal computers). These forces should be reflected, implicitly or explicitly, in each of the scenario plots. For example, any set of scenarios about banking would include the globalization and integration of financial services, although these might assume a different shape or priority depending on political, regulatory, and technological factors.
- *Which forces are most likely to define or significantly change the nature or direction of the scenarios?* This assessment should be measured by two criteria: How uncertain are you about the net affect of a trend, and how important is the outcome to your organization? Organizations should develop the plots of their different scenarios by assuming they have to contend with the logical consequences of forces that may suddenly become both very important and very uncertain. One large professional services company, for example, identified an unusual key trend; the degree to which young college graduates would be motivated by individual values versus collective values. The outcome of this trend was considered a major uncertainty that would significantly affect its ability to attract top-notch recruits, a key driver of the firm's growth rate.

IDENTIFY THE SCENARIO LOGICS: THE INDUCTIVE AND DEDUCTIVE APPROACHES

Consensus about which of these forces are the most critical uncertainties only emerges after extensive discussion. There are two fundamentally different approaches to determining the basic premises of a small number of scenarios. One method is inductive, the other deductive. The inductive method is less structured and relies largely on the patience of a group to continue its discussions until consensus is reached. The group derives general logical principles from particular facts or instances. In contrast, the deductive approach uses simple techniques of prioritization to construct a 2 × 2 scenario matrix based on the two most critical uncertainties.

The Inductive Approach

The inductive approach has two variants. In one, the group brainstorms different events that are typical of different scenarios. In the other, the group agrees on what an "official future" will look like and then searches for influences that could cause the actual future to deviate substantially from that path.

Significant Events.   The first variant of the inductive approach starts by identifying significant future events or plot elements, and then spins larger stories around them. For a hospital that specializes in cardiology, for example, it might be worth asking: What if researchers at Johns Hopkins announce the successful testing of a pill that effectively treats arterial plaque deposits? Since 45 percent of the hospital's revenues come from performing bypass surgery on arteries clogged with arterial plaque, a pharmaceutical alternative would eventually have a serious impact. What might lead up to such an event? What would be a plausible chain of consequences resulting from such an event? By discussing the ramifications of such highly consequential events, a group can build a scenario that can be used to examine current decisions. Building scenarios around momentous events can yield powerful results, but the process is unsystematic and calls for a degree of creativity and imagination that not all organizations have.

The Official Future.   A slightly more systematic variant of the inductive approach begins by drafting the "official future." This may be the future that the decision makers really believe will occur. The official future is usually an unsurprising and relatively nonthreatening scenario, featuring no discontinuous changes to current trends, no crises, and continued stable growth.

But sometimes the official future can be excessively pessimistic, reflecting fears that the company is in serious trouble. In a scenario exercise for a utility, the official story was a projection of trends in the chief economist's annual forecast. The chief economist anticipated a serious and deep economic recession with very negative implications for the company's revenues. Clearly, this scenario had a number of serious implications rang-ing from layoffs and downsizing to the reduction or elimination of inno-vative service and R&D programs. To study other possibilities, the scenario team considered radically different and more optimistic futures. The next step was to chart the forces and factors that could produce such futures. Research indicated that major drivers of these scenarios could be the evolution of new industries, higher levels of investment and venture capital, and increasing entrepreneurial activity within the firm. In fact, these more optimistic scenarios gradually unfolded.

Identifying the important components of the official future—its key drivers—is best done through interviews with the scenario team and other key decision makers prior to any scenario exercise. This process usually re-quires 10 to 15 interviews with key decision makers—the CEO, top man-agers in different parts of the company who are likely to have different perspectives and concerns, as well as individuals who are known to be provocative or unorthodox thinkers. Sample questions are: "What will the future look like in 10 years," and "Where will you be sitting 10 years from now (and how did you get there)?" Use the interviews to elicit se-nior managers' concerns and fears ("What keeps you up at night?"). An-nual reports, forecasts, and the analysis done on individual business units are also valuable information sources.

The recent experience of the health care industry is a prime example of the dangers of planning for the official future without seriously ex-amining other scenarios. Insurance industry and consumer pressure, gov-ernment budget crises, the spread of managed care, technological change, and myriad other factors all pointed to a restructuring of the industry. Yet many health care organizations simply assumed that this restructuring would be defined by the Clinton administration's reform proposals, and scrambled to position themselves accordingly. When these reforms were derailed, many industry players were surprised, disadvantaged, and un-prepared to act—or to seize new and unexpected opportunities.

After identifying the key driving forces and uncertainties, it is usually easy to discover which ones are most important and influential in the official future. Next, have your team brainstorm variations to the offi-cial future that are based on possible but quite surprising changes in its key driving forces. Explore how different interactions between key forces might produce unexpected outcomes and build several new scenario log-ics. In the health care industry, for example, different scenarios might suggest an increasingly fragmented health care system differentiated entirely by the patient's ability to pay: one system for the poor, one for most of the middle class, and another for the upper middle class and the rich. Another possible scenario might be a privatized system with minimal government regulation or influence.

Using either of the two inductive approaches—starting with the official future or significant events—in order to reach consensus on which driving forces are truly of paramount importance can be a difficult group exercise. In cultures that lack the patience for the open-ended debate that these two inductive approaches require, beginning with the deductive approach can sometimes be more effective.

The Deductive Approach: Building a Scenario Matrix

Here the idea is to prioritize the long list of key factors and driving trends in order to find the two most critical uncertainties. One method—quick and dirty, but effective nonetheless—is to give 25 poker chips to every participant and to ask them to "bet" on which important forces are most uncertain. They should allot more chips for forces of greater importance and high uncertainty and fewer or no chips for forces of lesser importance and substantial certainty. This ranking exercise accelerates the discussion by narrowing the group's focus to the most crucial forces.

The Scenario Matrix

If you prioritize driving forces using the poker chips or another ranking exercise, your team can pick two forces that are voted the most unpredictable as well as most relevant to the focal issue. These become the axes of a 2 × 2 scenario matrix.

For example, in a Detroit study of the design criteria for an automobile intended for the first-time car buyer, the price of fuel (high or low) was an important and uncertain key factor, as were the values of consumers. So the matrix axes were "fuel price" and "values" (see Exhibit 4.1). Would the consumers of the '90s prefer more conventional family sedans or would they want a less conventional assortment of light trucks, hybrid car/van vehicles, and small cars of the sort that Japan and Germany were manufacturing? When the study was conducted in the early 1980s, very few marketers could imagine that Americans might want smaller, more versatile, and individualized cars. What most

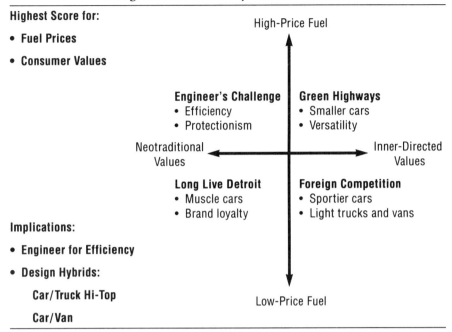

Exhibit 4.1
Design Criteria for Entry-Level Automobile

Highest Score for:

• **Fuel Prices**

• **Consumer Values**

High-Price Fuel

Engineer's Challenge
• Efficiency
• Protectionism

Green Highways
• Smaller cars
• Versatility

Neotraditional Values ←————→ Inner-Directed Values

Long Live Detroit
• Muscle cars
• Brand loyalty

Foreign Competition
• Sportier cars
• Light trucks and vans

Implications:

• **Engineer for Efficiency**

• **Design Hybrids:**

    Car/Truck Hi-Top

    Car/Van

Low-Price Fuel

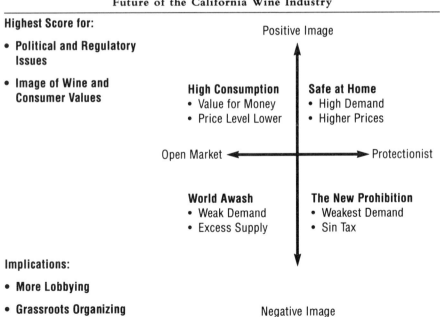

Exhibit 4.2
Future of the California Wine Industry

Highest Score for:

• **Political and Regulatory Issues**

• **Image of Wine and Consumer Values**

Positive Image

High Consumption
• Value for Money
• Price Level Lower

Safe at Home
• High Demand
• Higher Prices

Open Market ←————→ Protectionist

World Awash
• Weak Demand
• Excess Supply

The New Prohibition
• Weakest Demand
• Sin Tax

Implications:

• **More Lobbying**

• **Grassroots Organizing**

• **Monitor Leading Indicators**

Negative Image

industry observers imagined was a continuation of the status quo: Detroit's big auto companies continuing to produce cars with only stylistic differences, for similar markets, using similar production techniques. By using the matrix tool, the participants could see that this was only one of the possible scenarios.

The defining factors for a scenario matrix for the California wine industry were: the regulatory environment around the wine industry (open market versus protectionist) and the image of wine to consumers (positive or negative). So what happens when these most important and uncertain factors in the future of the market converge? (See Exhibit 4.2.) For example, what business environment can be expected when the industry experiences both an open market and a positive image? Suppose studies showed that a glass of wine every day was good for your health, and California wine sellers had no competition from imports. The result would be the "safe-at-home" scenario where there would be a high demand for wine and higher prices for California wine. In contrast, if a news story broke that California wine was tainted by a pesticide, and there were no restrictions or taxes on imported wine, the "world-awash" scenario—characterized by weak demand for California wine, excess supply, and falling prices—would likely result.

There are a number of advantages to building scenarios on a matrix. First, using a matrix assures that scenarios are qualitatively different in a logical, nonrandom way. Second, it assures that the top scoring key factors will be drivers in all scenarios. Deciding upon the axes is an interactive group process, driven as much by challenge as consensus.

In most cases, it is best to keep the number of dimensions in the matrix down to two for the sake of simplicity and ease of representation. Sometimes, the scenario logics can be represented by a spectrum (along one axis), or you may need a model with three axes. But as a rule, don't build a matrix with three dimensions; when it comes to communicating the scenario logics to decision makers who were not part of the scenario development process, three-dimensional, eight-celled frameworks sometimes prove to be too complex.

Sometimes a group has trouble distilling a long list of important factors down to just two critical uncertainties. Group members who fear that they've oversimplified the issues by selecting only two driving forces will be relieved to learn that they will get back all the complexity they want during the next step of the exercise.

Embellishing the Scenario Plots

There is no one right way to design scenarios. Different organizational cultures, different facilitation styles, and different industries may dictate the use of one or another of the approaches for settling on the basic logics of a few scenarios. The inductive approach works well in the oil industry, for example, because going into the exercise everyone knows that at the end of the day there is only one key variable that drives the difference between two or three scenarios: the price of a barrel of oil at some future date. In other industries where there are several, or many, key variables, the deductive approach will help to cut through the complexity.

While it is the most important/uncertain forces that shape the logics that distinguish and drive these scenarios, the other significant environmental factors identified in the brainstorming phase should also be used to compose the scenario plots. These might include such things as political changes or events resulting in more or less restrictive trade policies or regulations; differential or volatile economic growth; indicators of increasing environmental degradation; the emergence of new technologies, products, or processes; or changing consumer values. Each of the key factors and trends should be given some attention in at least one scenario; some (including the predetermined elements) are likely to show up in all the plots. Demographic trends, for example, are likely to be implicit in all the plots, although they may have different implications depending upon how political, social, and economic factors affect such things as education, employment, immigration, and consumption.

Tools for Amplifying Scenarios

Several tools are available for elaborating on the initial premise of the scenarios. Examples are systems thinking for deepening the scenario plots; narrative development for lengthening the basic premises into stories with beginnings, middles, and ends; and characters for populating the scenarios with significant or illustrative individuals who personalize the plots.

Systems and Patterns Systems Thinking. Studying the way the parts of a system interact can be a powerful tool for exploring the logic of a scenario. Most of the time, we focus on individual events—for example, a sudden and dramatic decline in stock prices, a war between two countries, the election of a new president or prime minister. But sometimes we need to explore the underlying patterns of events so we can understand the appropriate plot for a scenario. Studying the way the parts of a system interact can illuminate the logic of a scenario.

To help the scenario team to think more systematically, we often use an iceberg metaphor borrowed from Professor Peter Senge, author of *The Fifth Discipline*. At the tip of this systems iceberg model (see Exhibit 4.3) are the events, such as the election of certain politicians or the rise and fall of companies. When we delve into the middle of the iceberg, we can find the patterns that these events suggest, such as increasing priority given to social issues, or industry consolidation. Beneath these patterns, at the lowest point in the iceberg, we find the important structural changes that define meaningful scenario logics. Samples of these are fundamental shifts in values or industry restructuring.

Here's how this iceberg metaphor of events, patterns, and structural changes helps clarify the evolution of the information technology arena. First, the scenario team might focus on the behavior of an industry leader at the events level. Samples include the creation of the MSNBC network (a joint venture of Microsoft and NBC), Microsoft's announcement that

Exhibit 4.3
The Systems Iceberg Model

The Systems Iceberg Model

Systems

• Visible manifestations

• Trends and combinations

• Causal relationships

Events

Patterns

Structure

Scenarios

• The Story

• Sequences and form

• Driving forces
• The scenario logic

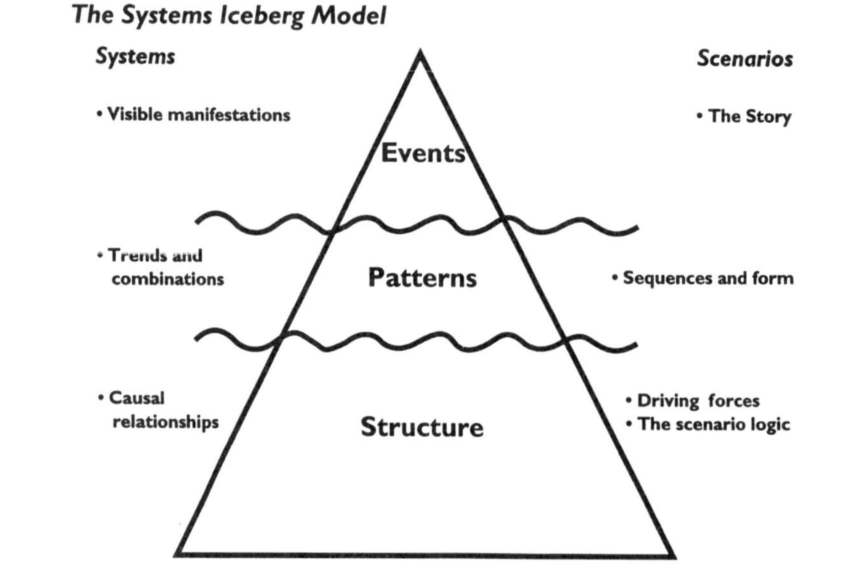

it is helping Apple Computer to build Internet software, and the integration of Internet-style tools into Microsoft Office. Such events signal a move on the part of Microsoft to strengthen its competitive position. Taken together, these moves by Microsoft form a pattern. The structural implications are profound: The events and pattern are evidence of a shift from a desktop-oriented environment to one where most work is done on the Internet.

If the scenario team is having a difficult time understanding the interactions between different forces, it is often useful to have them map out the events, patterns, and structure separately and then create a systems diagram of how different forces interact. There's a three-step process for doing this efficiently by grouping and regrouping notes with the names of the forces on the wall of the meeting room:

- Describe and then cluster (and recluster) events.
- Recognize and link patterns.
- Identify the underlying structural issues.

Building Narratives

When the basic logics of the different worlds have been determined, it is time for the group to weave those pieces together to form a narrative with a beginning, a middle, and an end. How could the world get from the present to the reality proposed by the new scenario? What events might be necessary to make the end point of the scenario possible? One of the most frequent mistakes made by fledgling scenario teams is falling prey to the temptation of settling for a single state description of, for instance, the year 2000. A static description sacrifices the opportunity to see how the "moving parts" in an industry can interact, and then interact again, sometimes producing counterintuitive consequences well on down the road. Narratives are also important to capture issues of timing and path dependency. We may all agree that 20 years from now the twisted-pair telephone line and the cable TV will be largely replaced by optical fiber. But billions of dollars will be won and lost depending on whether the Regional Bell Operating Companies or the cable companies are the gatekeepers. Shorter-term issues of regulation, technology, economic competition, and industry consolidation will have a lot to do with which path we take toward the final rationalization of broadband communications.

Headlining.   A productive exercise at this stage of the workshop is to ask the scenario team to write newspaper headlines describing key events or trends that take place during the course of the scenario; for example, "Philip Morris Divests Cigarette Business," "Dow Jones Falls to 4000," "Moore's Law Disproved" "Eighth Hurricane in 20 Days Ravages Florida Coast." The headlines are a quick way of defining successive stages of a narrative. Well-chosen headlines could mark a surprising beginning for a scenario, perhaps a turbulent middle period, and a compelling resolution, for example. Imagine that you are looking out to the year 2010. What would the headlines for your scenario read in 2000? In 2005? In 2010?

Characters.   Are there known individuals or institutions that espouse specific changes; for example, the successful promotion of conservatism by Ronald Reagan and Margaret Thatcher? Would a scenario that calls for a radical change in values benefit from the invention of a charismatic leader gaining a following? In most scenarios the "characters" are driving forces and institutions, nations, or companies as opposed to individuals. But sometimes a known or an invented character can embody the logic of the scenario.

Beware of building the entire plot around an individual's personality or power, however. A case in point: Scenarios developed for the future of Mexico identified the political issues being fought out in the impending election as a major uncertainty. One of the scenarios was built around a victory by Colosio, the dominant PRI party's presidential candidate; in another scenario Colosio lost. We put the scenarios in the mail on Friday; Saturday morning the headlines proclaimed Colosio's assassination.

On the other hand, an individual (real or imaginary) can personify the intersection of key structural or driving forces. A plot about China, for example, could begin with the struggle for succession following the death of Deng, not because the individual who assumes power is important, but because this can illuminate the political, economic, and cultural struggles that China may face. Creating characters who personify life in the scenarios is also a way to convey the magnitude and direction of change.

Typical Plots

Each scenario plot or logic should be different, yet relevant to the focal question. Nonetheless, there are a few plot lines that seem to arise over and over. These plots are derived from observing the twists and turns of our economic and political systems, the rise and fall of technologies, and pendulum swings in social perceptions.

To be effective, scenario plots must make people rethink their assumptions about the future. For example, many people assume that Asia's continued economic growth is inevitable with little, if any, downside. In fact, this is a dangerous assumption that could be derailed by a whole host of political and environmental factors. On the other hand, plots that are too frightening or implausible tend to be easily discounted and thus weaken the value of the scenario process overall: a study on the future of paper for a forest products company that suggests that technological advances will result in the disappearance of paper and paper products such as books, for example; or a doom-and-gloom scenario that portrays a complete economic, political, and social breakdown that no company can survive.

Do not assume from reading the following set of common scenario plots that scenarios can be prepared according to a formula, nor that these are the only plots that work or matter. Instead, use these examples in your group's discussion of how driving forces may interact to create plausible plots.

Winners and Losers.   This is a familiar plot, not only in scenarios but in life. It is based on the concept of a zero sum game: If one company, country, or institution wins, then others will lose. Some examples of winners and losers:

- An ascendant Asia Pacific bloc versus Europe in decline.
- Government regulation of the Internet versus free expression and entrepreneurial opportunities.
- Pepsi versus Coke.

In these plots, conflict is often inevitable. But sometimes, after an initial flare-up of contention, the conflict quickly burns down to an uneasy detente or balance of power (covert or overt). Sometimes the potential conflict escalates to outright war, military or economic.

The so-called cola war in the soft drink market is an example of a contemporary U.S. corporate battle. In this hypercompetitive global battleground, every move Coca-Cola makes is met by Pepsi-Cola, and every initiative by Pepsi is quickly countered by Coke. Another example of hypercompetitive rivalry is the battle for market share between long-distance telephone carriers. Any effective advertisement by MCI immediately stimulates a response by AT&T, and vice versa. The result is an advertising war in which collective annual spending has topped $1 billion.

Crisis and Response.   In the early 1980s, Royal Dutch/Shell's scenario team constructed several crisis scenarios for the future of Soviet Union. The defining question: What would be the logical consequences of a crisis—a new Stalinism or, alternatively, a loosening of the system's autocratic control? One scenario was called "Clamp Down" and another "The Greening of Russia." The plot of both these scenarios was crisis/response, and each posed a logical, but totally different future. This is a typical adventure story plot. First, one or more challenges arise, and then adaptation occurs (or fails to occur). If the adaptation is effective, it may create new winners and losers, and may ultimately change the rules of the game. A good example of a crisis and response plot is the scenario that attempts to answer the question, How much development is sustainable? First comes the scenario's crisis: Initial signs of environmental degradation lead reputable scientists to conclude that an environmental disaster is fast approaching. A few leading governments and companies change the way they do business. Disasters begin to occur in countries that could not, or chose not to adapt, and there is a public outcry. The playing field—the organizational operating environment—is suddenly dramatically altered. The innovative firms that learned to make difficult changes in their business practices to avoid environmental degradation are now positioned to become market leaders.

Good News/Bad News.   It's important to incorporate elements of both desirable and undesirable futures. For example, a scenario prepared for a global telecommunications company provided the firm with a valuable look at a world shaped by conflict, violence, and corruption—a scenario in which its high ethical standards would become a distinct disadvantage. When considering possible futures for Mexico in late 1994, the scenario team failed to anticipate the devaluation of the peso, in part because there was an unwillingness to look down the dark cellar stairs at bad news.

Evolutionary Change.   The logic of this plot—that over time, growth or decline occurs in all systems—is based on studies of biology. Systems like businesses or governments tend to plow ahead, at least during the growth period, without giving much thought to their inevitable decline. And even if change is anticipated, its nature and magnitude are seldom comprehended and therefore rarely managed appropriately. A classic example from the 1980s is when IBM turned a great opportunity into a catastrophe by missing the significance of the software operating system for the personal computer.

A variation on this plot is coevolution. Change in one system interacts with and causes change in other systems. Technology often spurs coevolutionary change—new innovations appear and either flourish or fail. They may give rise to other innovations, while at the same time interacting with the political and economic systems. Other typical plot lines include:

- *Revolution.* Abrupt discontinuities, either natural or human-made. Examples: an earthquake, a breakthrough invention.
- *Tectonic Change.* Structural alterations that produce dramatic flare-ups, like a volcano, which cause major (but certainly foreseeable) discontinuities. Examples: a breakup of China, the end of apartheid in South Africa.
- *Cycles.* Economics and politics often move in cycles; their timing is important and unpredictable. Examples: health care reform, real estate booms, gentrification.
- *Infinite Possibility.* The seductive idea that continued growth is possible, often enabling sights to be set higher than before. Examples are: the computer industry in the 1980s, global connectivity via the Internet today.
- *The Lone Ranger.* This plot pits an organization or a main character against the established practices of politics, trade, or technology. Often the protagonist group sees itself as battling a perceived evil, a corrupt system or an antediluvian competitor. This plot frequently matches up a start-up firm and a market leader—a David and Goliath scenario. Some examples: Apple Computer versus IBM, MCI versus AT&T, Ted Turner versus the TV networks.
- *Generations.* This plot revolves around the emergence of new cultures—groups with different values and expectations. Examples: the baby boomers, Generation X, or the overseas Chinese network.
- *Perpetual Transition.* This plot is a variation on the evolutionary and infinite possibility themes. It expects change to be continuous and predicts that adaptation will be anything but uniform. It posits that there will be no New World Order or rules of the game; the Internet—enabled by new products that continually push the

boundaries of speed and connectivity—will become a vast, ever-evolving marketplace with no regulation, control, or limits.

When constructing scenario plots, remember that expecting change is only half the chore. Scenario developers must also anticipate a response to the change. Most forecasters make the mistake of assuming that a powerful, highly successful organization can control its destiny to a large extent. For example, Japanese car makers assumed they could continually sell more and more cars in America by making their products better and better. But every system has the capacity for response and self-correction. Continued fast economic growth leads to resistance. The threat of war results in demands for peace. High oil prices promote exploration, new discoveries, more oil, and an eventual lowering of the price, as happened in the mid-eighties.

Wild Cards

Scenarios are about conditions that you can plan for, but wild cards are events that you plan against. Wild cards are surprises that have the power to completely change your hand—and the outcome of the entire game. Wild cards might be:

- Wholly discontinuous events like natural disasters or assassinations.
- Discontinuities that might be anticipated but that have significant unintended consequences. A good example is the formation of ERISA, a governmental agency that was designed to ensure pensions for the elderly, but as a side effect created institutional investing.
- Catalytic developments so different in degree or scale that they have unique effects on society. Mosaic/Netscape, for example, transformed the World Wide Web into a global meeting and marketplace.

In scenario exercises built around a matrix of four logically contrasted scenarios, we will sometimes include a fifth wild card scenario that takes into account a dramatic yet relevant surprise that doesn't fit neatly on the matrix. After constructing four logically related scenarios for Oregon's Department of Public Health, for example, we added a fifth wild card: What if Mt. Hood blows? Other examples: cold fusion works; a breakthrough in nanotechnology (tiny machines) accelerates its commercialization by a decade or more. Wild cards scenarios can encourage an organization to stretch its collective mind and "think outside the box."

GUIDELINES FOR A SUCCESSFUL SCENARIO WORKSHOP

Having had time and experience enough to make many mistakes, we offer some tips to keep others from stepping into various familiar pot-holes:

Stay Focused.   Your scenarios should be developed within the context of the focal question: a specific decision to be made or a critical issue or uncertainty of great importance facing the organization. Keep your sights on addressing the raison d'etre for the exercise.

Keep It Simple.   Although clever and creative plots that illuminate the interaction of key forces can help to make scenarios memorable, don't get the idea that this is primarily a creative writing project. Simple plots and a short list of characters help managers to understand, use, and communicate the scenarios.

Keep It Interactive.   Scenario plots should be the unique product of your organization's interactive team-based effort. If they are off-the-shelf stories, reflect the prejudices of only the most powerful people in your organization, or do not take into account the insights of all levels of your organization's management, they will likely fail to be relevant, and they will certainly fail to capture the imagination of your organization's future leaders.

Plan to Plan and Allow Enough Prep Time.   Before the first scenario workshop, you will need about a month to select the scenario team, conduct a series of interviews, round up relevant literature, and book a site for the workshop.

Day One

The initial scenario workshop should be at least two days long. It takes time to think of everything that could affect the focal issue. It takes time to pry people loose from the present. A typical scenario workshop will begin with about an hour devoted to articulating the focal issue, about three to four hours to listing key factors and environmental forces, and two or three hours prioritizing forces and settling on an official future or a scenario matrix.

Take Time to "Sleep on It."   After a day of brainstorming, we suggest leaving the evening relatively unstructured to give participants in the workshop a chance to socialize and informally compare impressions. We find that after the participants sleep on their ideas, debates, and conversations of the first day, they often awaken with fresh insights that contribute to generating the scenario logics.

Day Two

Begin the second day with second thoughts about the skeletal scenario logics, then have the group spend one to two hours fleshing out one scenario in a plenary session—tracing a narrative line from a beginning through a middle to an end, before breaking up into smaller groups to flesh out the other scenarios. By the end of the second day, the group should be able to see several different scenarios in sufficient detail so that it's possible to draw out preliminary implications of each scenario—and, if you're lucky, some strategic implications of the set of scenarios taken as a whole. But this work of asking, So what? often takes more time and reflection than a single workshop can provide.

Follow-Up Work

After developing the scenario logics and outlines of their plots, allow for at least four to six weeks of interim research and reflection while writing the final scenarios and exploring their implications. As soon as possible, circulate draft scenario logics or plots to other managers whose opinions you value. To speed up the process of drafting narrative scenarios based on the first workshop, we often recruit an experienced note taker to record the workshop so that the ideas of the participants can be captured and quickly organized. There is brainstorming software that can also facilitate this work.

A key purpose of this interim phase is to research more extensively—both qualitatively (through interviews) and quantitatively—the important forces, trends, and uncertainties. Ask the team members what the factors are that they really don't know but need to know: geographic economic growth trends, industry structure, the financial performance and strength of new or potential competitors, consumer trends, emerging technologies, regulations in different countries. For a recent project in the aerospace industry, for example, substantial research was conducted on the restructuring and convergence of several industries—and what the industry structure might look like under each scenario. The better your scenario team understands the nature, magnitude, and possible interactions of these key forces, the more likely it is that your scenarios will be plausible. On the other hand, if you fail to do good research and your underlying assumptions don't hold water, then your scenarios are likely to be quickly discounted. In practice, some scenarios are abandoned after more research, and others may be substantially redirected based on new research findings.

Hold a Second Workshop

After the interim research has been conducted and preliminary scenario narratives drafted and circulated, reassemble the original scenario team for at least a day, perhaps two. At this second workshop, there are three main objectives:

1. Correct, revise, amend the draft scenarios.
2. Explore the implications of each scenario individually.
3. Answer the question, So what? based on all of the scenarios taken collectively.

EIGHT TIPS FOR SCENARIO TEAM LEADERS

1. *Avoid probabilities or "most likely" plots.* Remember that the some of the most surprising scenario plots may be the ones your organization learns the most from. Though all must be plausible, don't just select those that appear to be the most likely to unfold.
2. *Do not assign probabilities to the scenarios.* Do not categorize scenarios as either the most or least likely. Keep your mind open to all possibilities. Don't fixate on just one scenario that you want to achieve. Scenarios are meant to illuminate different futures, complete with negative and positive dimensions. Choosing one scenario

as a goal may blind you to other developments and possibilities. A classic case occurred in the 1970s when oil companies focused exclusively on high oil prices—in their best interest—while remaining in denial about the possibility of an oil price bust.

3. *Avoid drafting a lot of scenarios that are merely slight variations on a theme.* A number of years ago, a project for the U.S. Environmental Protection Agency used scenarios to look at alternative futures for pesticide policy. The team developed 10 scenarios, but their distinctions were blurred, and neither meaningful nor useful. After editing the set of 10, the team selected three dissimilar scenarios. "How many scenarios should be created?" is an often-asked question. Four scenarios are usually all you need. Groups have great difficulty discussing or even remembering more than four. But beware the "middle of the road" approach trap—that is, selecting three scenarios that offer "large, medium, and small" versions of the future. Too often, managers will be tempted to identify one of the three—usually the middle version—as the most likely scenario. Such simplistic scenarios don't challenge the preconceptions of the decision makers; neither do they provoke managers to imagine innovative strategic options and their implications. When presented with large, medium, and small scenarios, managers have a tendency to treat the most likely scenario as a prediction, thus failing to explore the other scenarios fully. Thus, the whole multiple scenario exercise will be wasted.

   In truth, some people have difficulty exploring scenarios that differ greatly from the probable future. They always want to find the "right" answer, usually expressed as a number that can be derived mathematically. When one or more participants in a scenario exercise feel that they know the "right scenario" and aren't willing or able to entertain others, the process becomes very frustrating. It is important to continually emphasize that there are no right or wrong, good or bad scenarios. The truly valuable product of a scenario exercise is the experience of exploring a set of distinct and plausible futures that could unfold.

4. *Choose memorable names.* Apply a generous amount of creativity to inventing good names for your scenarios. Evocative scenario names quickly convey the idea that your scenarios are about crucial changes in the business environment that will affect your entire organization. Some day in the future, when your managers feel the heat of a

crisis, they should be able to recall the appropriate scenario by name. "We're now getting singed from sudden volatility in currencies. Wasn't that a key force in our Interest Rate Hell scenario? What were the other warning signs that that scenario might be unfolding now?" Cultural icons—popular songs, movies, TV shows—are often memorable. One set of scenarios was named for recordings by the Beatles: "A Hard Day's Night," "Help," "Magical Mystery Tour," and "Imagine."

5. *Make the decision makers own the scenarios.* One of the most powerful contributions to a good scenario process is the direct and ongoing involvement of key decision makers. These are the people who will be responsible for using and communicating the scenarios throughout the organization. If at all possible, these are the people who should actually write the scenarios.

   We have had success getting organization leaders to draft scenarios using various different authoring tactics.

   • *Assign the job to one author.* This works if the organization has an important member who both enjoys writing and is a collaborative thinker (a person who is willing to solicit and incorporate comments from the rest of the team).

   • *Assign a pair of authors—one who writes well and another who is a veteran team leader—to work together to draft the scenarios.* Assign a different author for each draft narrative with "technical assistance" available from an experienced editor/scenario writer. This may result in uneven efforts, but it is a way to engage the most senior executives. However, avoid making a facilitator from outside the organization responsible for drafting the scenarios, especially if he or she is a consultant.

   No matter which participant drafts the scenarios, the author must thoughtfully and fairly solicit and welcome comments and suggestions from the rest of the team.

6. *Budget sufficient resources for communicating the scenarios and their operational implications.* Scenario planning will fail if its product is merely a report that is read once by only a few executives, and then allowed to gather dust on the shelf. Instead, print them in the company newsletter. Ideally, the scenarios will capture the imagination of operating managers who will use them to consider the long-term affects of current decisions. Credible scenarios can become drivers of an organization's ongoing strategic conversation and learning.

7. *Communicate effectively and imaginatively.* We tell our scenario stories from the perspective of a person living in the scenarios. While written scenarios should eventually be produced, consider other ways to introduce them to the organization and get them adopted. To help people "live" in the scenarios, you can use various techniques, including dramatization, role-playing, and multimedia presentations. For one organization's annual board of directors' retreat, members listened to audiotapes of the scenarios before arriving. During the retreat, they watched videotaped "newscasts" of the scenarios set in the year 2010, and then engaged in a role-playing exercise that involved interacting as very different characters in the future worlds.

8. *Have fun.* A bit of show-biz can enhance the communication of scenarios. If you're not having fun, you're not doing it right. Be creative and have a good time. Remember, scenarios are a tool for unexpected learning, and learning about the unexpected.

CHAPTER 5

MENTAL MAPS OF THE FUTURE: AN INTUITIVE LOGICS APPROACH TO SCENARIOS

IAN WILSON

This scenario development methodology offers a straightforward six-step process in Section 1, and shows how to apply it in a case study in Section 2. Because it stresses decision focus and logic, this approach is ideal for many different applications, and fits well with other forecasting and planning techniques. In Chapter 21 the author provides a fuller explanation of how scenarios can be used to develop effective strategy.

DEFINING THE APPROACH

Perhaps the most critical purpose of scenario planning is to challenge, test, and, if necessary, change decision-makers' assumptions about their present and future business environment. Through this process, scenario planning can remake executives' "mental maps" of the world, according to Pierre Wack, a manager who pioneered the use of scenarios at Royal Dutch/Shell. So the first premise of any scenario methodology should be to engage a company's leadership fully in the scenario development process. Their knowledge, insights, and awareness of areas of uncertainty are vital for construction of the final product. Only if executives wholeheartedly take ownership of the scenario-planning process and its product will they truly understand the scenarios and incorporate them into their decision making.

To obtain this crucial executive participation and commitment, Royal Dutch/Shell and SRI International developed an "intuitive logics" approach to scenario planning in the 1970s. The model is intuitive in the sense that it builds on the hunches, "gut feelings," assessments of uncertainty, and possible outcomes of the most knowledgeable people—the management team. But the model is also logical, formal, and disciplined in its use of information, analysis and a structured approach to the task.

Scenarios developed by this approach are frameworks for structuring management's perceptions about alternative future environments in which their decisions might be played out. To make this definition work in practice, management's perceptions about critical trends—not a consultant's, not a futurist's, not even the staff's—must be the main building material of the scenarios.

There are obvious objections to this approach. Can any operating managers, let alone overworked senior executives, be relied upon to seriously challenge the basic premises on which their existing model of "the way the world works" is built? Are company executives who are trained to drive operations really likely to confront uncertainty, to acknowledge that they do not know the future? Will they devote the amount of time and effort needed to make scenario planning (and thinking) worthwhile?

All of these objections to giving executives the reins of a scenario project are valid, and must be addressed. Such objections, however, must be weighed against the experience gained from many previous scenario-planning projects. Again and again, we have found that unless decision makers take ownership of the scenarios, they will not act on them. And if executives don't learn to incorporate scenarios into their decision making, the planning process—however brilliant and insightful the scenarios may be—will be a waste of time. We have learned that the surest way to create "ownership" of the final product—the new mental model of the business environment—is to build executives' involvement, step by step, into the process.

To foster executive ownership, this approach must be "decision-focused"; that is, the scenarios should not be generalized views of the future. One of the common misconceptions about scenarios is that they provide only poorly delineated overviews of the world ahead—fuzzy pictures of utopias or calamitous futures intended to dramatize general economic, social, and geopolitical trends and their possible consequences. Deriving implications for corporate or other action from such generalized futures is indeed problematic. In contrast, the scenario process we use starts (and ends) with clarifying the decisions and actions that the organization must take, along with the appropriate timetable, if it is to deal successfully with an uncertain future. It is this decision focus that structures and channels executives' thinking in a purposeful way.

The Six-Step Process

The methodology involves a relatively straightforward six-step process (see Exhibit 5.1). Two important premises of the methodology are:

- The scenarios should be focused on the needs of some decision, strategy, or plan.
- The scenarios should be logically structured and internally consistent.

Decision Focus.   The range of decisions that scenarios can address is quite broad, from an urgent decision (a major investment in a new market, for instance) to broader, longer-range concerns, such as the strategic posture of a diversified company or long-term prospects for a particular business area. Regardless of what the decision may be, addressing it should be both the starting point and the conclusion of the process.

Exhibit 5.1
The Six Steps in the Intuitive Approach

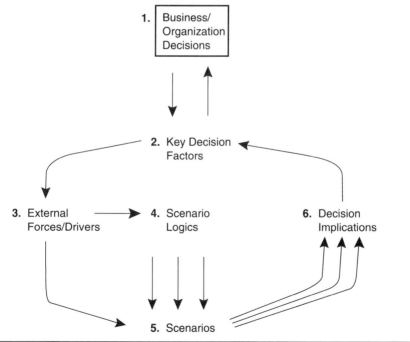

Logic and Consistency.   Logic provides a scenario with its basic thrust or direction. It's a kind of organizing principle or structure for the conditions the scenario describes. The logic of a scenario comes from a theory, assumption, perception, or belief about change.

A scenario process that stresses decision focus and logic is adaptable to many different applications, and fits relatively well with other forecasting and planning approaches. The six steps are summarized here and then illustrated in a case study in Section 2 of this chapter.

Step 1: Identify and Analyze the Organizational Issues That Will Provide the Decision Focus

The first step is to get your management team's agreement on which strategic decision (and the issues surrounding it) should provide the focus for the scenarios. This crucial task establishes the scenario process as a means to help executives make better strategic decisions. Also, by specifying which decisions are to be made, it effectively links the scenarios to specific planning needs. By aiming the scenarios toward making one or two specific decisions, you can prevent the process from straying off into overly broad generalizations about the future of society or the global economy.

Usually, the right decisions on which to focus the scenarios are strategic rather than tactical. This is because scenarios deal more with longer-term trends and uncertainties (often with a 5- to 10-year time horizon) rather than shorter-term developments. Typical examples of such longer-term decisions are:

- Capital allocation decisions in which the main concern may be the long-range viability and payoff of various business areas or projects.
- Diversification or divestment decisions, or new areas of opportunity or risk.
- Major capital investments required for new facilities or to expand or renovate existing ones.
- Long-term market strategies, technology acquisition, and development strategies; or strategic considerations for other business functions.

Virtually any decision or area of strategic concern in which external factors are complex, changing, and uncertain is a suitable target for the scenario process. However, the narrower the scope of the decision or strategy, the easier the scenario construction—and interpretation—will be. Developing scenarios for broad strategic concerns—the long-range positioning of a diversified business portfolio, for example—is more difficult.

A word of caution is needed at this stage. While clarifying the strategic focus is critical for a successful project, it is important to note that this is not the time for strategizing. That should be postponed until the final step of the process. Decision makers, particularly senior executives, have a natural impatience with analysis and a tendency to want to "cut to the chase." This otherwise praiseworthy tendency toward action must, for the moment, be held in check so that the context for action—the scenarios—can first be established.

Step 2: Specify the Key Decision Factors

Having thought through the one or more strategic decisions we want to make, we next need to examine the key decision factors. In other words, answer, What are the crucial particulars we would like to know about the future in order to make our decision? Of course, we cannot actually know the whole future with certainty. Nonetheless, it would still be helpful to have some educated estimate of the direction and pace of change for key components of the future.

Decision factors for an anticipated major expansion of manufacturing facilities, for example, might include:

- Market size, growth, and volatility.
- Competing products or substitutes resulting from new technology.
- Long-range economic conditions and price trends.
- Anticipated government regulation.
- Capital availability and cost.
- Technology availability and capacity.

In contrast, for a charitable organization such as the United Way that is planning its future programs, the relevant factors are more likely to be social values and priorities, consumer spending and saving patterns, government welfare programs, corporate giving, and alternative not-for-profit solutions to social problems.

The important thing to note about these decision factors is that they all relate to external, largely uncontrollable conditions. This is not to suggest that the more controllable internal factors such as a company's strengths and weaknesses, culture and organization are unimportant and irrelevant to the decision. Of course, they are relevant. But because companies have substantial control over such factors, decisions about them belong more appropriately in the strategizing phase of the planning cycle rather than in the scenario-development phase. Scenarios are designed to provide insights into the sort of market and competitive environment and the social and political climate that you may have to deal with someday. Only after the scenarios are developed and you can see how the consequences of your decisions might play out in the future should you make a commitment to action.

Step 3: Identify and Analyze the Key Environmental Forces

The third step is to identify the external forces that will determine the future course and value of your key decision factors. Although no one particular framework exists for making certain that you cover all the relevant forces (the SEPT formula is a start; see Exhibit 5.2). It is helpful to structure your thinking around two areas:

- *Microenvironmental Forces.* These are the important trends in the specific market and industry selected for study. Examples include: customer needs, restructuring of competition, new technology, and industry-specific regulations.
- *Macroenvironmental Drivers.* These are broad (sometimes global) social, economic, political, and technological forces. Examples are: demographic trends, economic growth and development, trading patterns, geopolitical shifts.

The aim here is to start building a good "conceptual model" of the relevant environment, one that is as complete as possible, including all the critical trends and forces. It should map out the key cause-and-effect relationships among these forces.

The next factor in this step is to get a clear picture of future prospects for these environmental forces:

- What the major trends and uncertainties are.
- How the forces are interrelated.

Exhibit 5.2
A Framework for Identifying Environmental Forces

Many different frameworks can be useful for identifying relevant environmental forces. A relatively simple one is the SEPT formula, in which environmental forces are organized in terms of Social, Economic, Political, and Technological trends. The SEPT scheme can be elaborated by considering forces (a) at both the micro and macro levels, and (b) in terms of local, national, and international consequence. A more elaborate framework is outlined here:

Category	Examples
Demographic patterns	Age, family, household, ethnic structures, and trends Regional and national migration Labor force structure and trends
Social and lifestyle factors	Consumer values, needs, and wants Psychographic profiles Education levels Social issues and priorities Special-interest groups
Economic conditions	Macroeconomic trends (GNP, trade, inflation) Microeconomic trends (wages, consumer spending) Regional and national variations Economic structure
Natural resources	Energy prices and availability Raw materials Land use
Physical environment	Air/water/land pollution trends Environmental quality issues (global warming)
Political and regulatory forces	Geopolitical trends and blocs Political policy shifts (privatization, deregulation) Governmental expenditures, deficits Specific regulations and government policies
Technological forces	Basic research trends Emerging technologies Technological infrastructure
International relations	Levels of tension, conflict Trade and protectionism International monetary system, exchange rates
Market forces	Specific customer wants, needs, spending Shopping and distribution patterns
Competition	Changes in industry structure (mergers, acquisitions) Sources of new/substitute competition Sources of competitive advantage

- Which are most important in determining the key decision factors.
- Which best represent underlying, or driving, forces for significant change in the future.

In practice, a complex analysis is not required. The basic thrust of the scenario development here should move quickly to focus on the fewest, most important forces. At a minimum, however, your discussion of these environmental forces should cover:

- Their apparent direction today—that is, current trends and the reasons for them.
- Their future prospects—that is, how much, in what ways, and how fast these trends might change in the future. Your assessment of these prospects should clearly differentiate between trends and developments that you believe to be relatively predictable and those about which you have some feeling of uncertainty.
- Their relevance to the decision focus—that is, the direction and magnitude of their impact on the future course of the key decision factors.

At this stage, you need to start sorting these forces, recognizing that they are not all equally important or equally uncertain. For instance, while the typical scenario process will likely identify a total of 50 or so such forces, the number of key drivers of the business will certainly be significantly fewer. Moreover, while uncertainty is a prevailing condition of the business environment, not everything is uncertain. Indeed, some key demographic trends may be considered virtually predetermined elements of the future. For example, the consumers of the next decade are already born, so their number is already known, but not their purchasing power and taste. In your planning and decision making, you need to be very specific about what is important, and what is truly uncertain, and why.

To be systematic in this sorting-out process, you can use an impact/ uncertainty matrix (see Exhibit 5.3). With a simple high-medium-low scoring system, you can position each one of these forces on the matrix. Rate each of these forces in terms of:

- The level of its impact on the key decision factors (obviously, all the forces are presumed to have some impact, but some are more important than others).

Exhibit 5.3
Illustrative Impact/Uncertainty Matrix

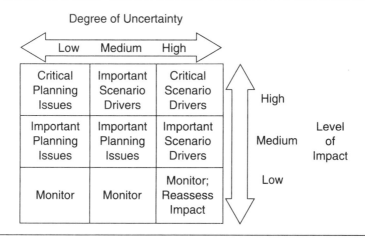

- The degree of uncertainty you feel about the direction, pace, or fact of its future course.

As a result of this sorting, you can focus your attention and the search for scenario logics in the next step on:

- High-impact/low-uncertainty forces (those in the top left-hand cell). These are the relative certainties in your future for which your current planning *must* prepare.
- High-impact/high-uncertainty forces (those in the upper right quadrant). These are the potential shapers of different futures (scenarios) for which your longer-term planning *should* prepare.

Step 4: Establish the Scenario Logics

This step is the heart of this scenario development process. In it, you establish a logical rationale and structure for the scenarios you select to examine in depth. It is also that stage in the process where intuition, insight, and creativity play the greatest role.

Theoretically at least, it would be possible to develop scenarios around all the high-impact/high-uncertainty forces identified in the previous step. Practically, however, it would result in an unwieldy process and an impossibly large number of scenarios. Even if the sorting process in Step 3 reduced the number of critical forces to some 15 or 20, taking all the permutations and combinations of the alternative outcomes of these forces would produce an almost astronomically high number of scenarios, far more than top management could concentrate on or any planning system could utilize.

As a practical matter, even those executives who are prepared to accept scenarios as an alternative to forecasting will balk at having to deal with more than three, or at most four, scenarios in their strategic thinking and decision making. Thus, the central challenge in this step is to develop a structure that will produce a manageable number of scenarios—and in a logical manner.

Defining Logics.   *Scenario logics* are a response to this challenge. This term requires careful definition if you are to understand, and act on, its premise. The operational (rather than a dictionary) definition of the term is the most helpful. You can, for instance, think of scenario logics as being the organizing principles around which the scenarios are structured. They focus on the critical external uncertainties for the business, and present alternative theories of the way the world might work. Each addresses an important area of uncertainty. For example, you could surmise that economic growth will be driven by expanding trade or hobbled by increasing protectionism. Or you could speculate that competition in your markets will be marked by growing consolidation, or restructured by the entry of new players. These alternative future states are logical in the sense that a persuasive and rational case can be made for each of the outcomes.

Step 5: Select and Elaborate the Scenarios

In determining how many scenarios to elaborate, remember a basic dictum: Develop the minimum number of scenarios needed to contain the "area of uncertainty," usually just three or four.

But what happens if you end up with a structure consisting of, say, three axes of uncertainty, giving rise to eight ($2 \times 2 \times 2$) derivative scenarios? Some selection among these scenarios is clearly needed so they don't overwhelm the decision makers who must use them. Once again, you need a combination of intuition and rationality to guide your selection. It is helpful to use five criteria:

1. *Plausibility.* The selected scenarios must be plausible; that is, they must fall within the limits of what might conceivably happen.
2. *Differentiation.* They should be structurally different. In other words, they should not be so close to one another that they become simply variations of a base case.
3. *Consistency.* They must be internally consistent. The combination of logics in a scenario must not have any built-in inconsistency that would undermine the credibility of the scenario.
4. *Decision-Making Utility.* Each scenario, and all the scenarios as a set, should contribute specific insights into the future that will bear on the decision focus you have selected.
5. *Challenge.* The scenarios should challenge the organization's conventional wisdom about the future.

Using these criteria, it is usually possible to quickly select the few scenarios that are most worthy of development. Some of the possibilities may be eliminated because their combination of logics are thought to be implausible or inconsistent. Others can be dropped from consideration because they would not offer any significantly different insights to the decision making or because they do not "push the envelope" far enough.

Once the scenarios have been selected, they have to be elaborated.

There are many ways to elaborate the description of scenarios, but the three most important features are:

- *A Highly Descriptive Title.* The title should be short enough to be memorable, yet convey the essence of what is happening in the scenario. Choose evocative titles that capture the uniqueness of each particular possible future. Avoid nondescriptive titles such as Best Case, Worst Case; High Oil Price, Low Oil Price. Such terms say nothing about why it might be the "best case"—from whose point of view—or why the price of oil is high or low. They tend to promote snap judgments about the scenario, and work against motivating decision makers to examine the scenario conditions and their consequences seriously and thoroughly.
- *Compelling Story Lines.* Remember that scenarios are not descriptions of end points (such as, How big will your market be in 2005?). They should be narratives of how events might unfold between now and a future date, given the dynamics (logics) the team has assigned to that

particular scenario. In simple terms, a scenario should tell a story. That story should be dramatic, compelling, logical, and plausible.

• *A Table of Comparative Descriptions.*   This provides planners and decision makers with a sort of "line item" description that details what might happen to each key trend or factor in each scenario. In theory, this table might include every one of the macro- and microenvironmental forces that were identified in Step 3. But, practically, it is usually advisable to prune this list to the more important forces. It may be difficult to use this table to get an overview of what is happening in each scenario; that is the role of the story line. But the table does provide the comprehensive back-up material—the "flesh on the skeleton"—that will give the scenarios their nuances and texture.

Charts, graphs, and other visual material will help to bring the scenarios to life. The guiding principle in determining the extent of this elaboration is: Provide as much—and no more—as is needed to help executives make the decision. Too much detail, and the scenario could lose its focus on decision making.

Step 6: Interpret the Scenarios for Their Decision Implications

Step 1 was to obtain the management team's agreement on which strategic decision (and the issues surrounding it) should provide the focus for the scenarios. In Step 6, we analyze the scenarios in detail and ask the fundamental questions: What are the strategic implications of the scenarios for the particular decision we selected at the outset of this process? What options do the scenarios suggest to us? Step 6 enables decision makers to turn scenarios into strategy.

That said, the development of an effective, robust strategy requires far more than scenarios. Other elements are a strategic vision, goals and objectives, competitive analysis, and assessment of core competencies, to name a few. But this final step in the six-step scenario process can develop some initial and valuable strategic insights. The needs of each organization for strategic insights will differ somewhat, but some productive approaches are:

Opportunities/Threats Assessment.   First, and most obvious, examine the scenarios in detail to determine the opportunities and threats that each poses for your organization. Then ask two questions:

- Which opportunities and threats are common to all (or nearly all) the scenarios? These are the ones, presumably, on which your strategic thinking should be particularly focused.
- How well prepared are you (or can you be) to seize those opportunities and dodge (or minimize) the threats? These answers provide an initial assessment of the core competencies needed to succeed in the scenarios, and of the gaps in the current organization.

Bringing together the answers to these two questions will suggest some strategy options (though not an integrated strategy) that deserve more disciplined analysis.

Testing Laboratory. A second possible approach is to use the scenarios as a "testing laboratory" for assessing both the resilience and vulnerability of your organization's current strategy. For example, the executive team can assess how well (or badly) the current strategy succeeds in each scenario. For a start, initiate the opportunities/threats assessment, and then use it to address this second set of questions:

- Are you satisfied with the resilience of your current strategy and its flexibility to deal with different possible conditions? Which opportunities does the strategy address; which does it miss? Which threats and risks has the strategy foreseen; which has it overlooked?
- How could you improve your strategy's resilience or hedge your bets?
- Are there contingency plans you should put in place to help the organization move in a different direction, should that be necessary?

Using the Scenarios to Strategize. The third approach is the most sophisticated—and the most difficult. It develops strategy within the framework of the scenarios. This is a highly intuitive process, and there's no checklist that managers can follow by rote. However, if you elect to pursue this approach, you should address the following questions:

- What are the key elements of strategy—for example, geographic scope, market focus, source of competitive advantage, technology, pricing, or distribution?
- What would be the best option for each element in each strategy? For instance, what would be the best marketing strategy for Scenario A? What technologies would you need in Scenario B?

- After reviewing the options for each element, which option seems the most resilient/robust across the range of scenarios?
- Can you integrate these resilient options into an overall, coherent business strategy?

This approach makes optimal use of the scenarios in strategy development, provides management with the widest range of choices, and encourages managers to make a careful evaluation of these options in the context of greatly different assumptions about the future.

EXAMINING A CASE STUDY: SCENARIO PLANNING AT STATOIL

The best way to understand how this intuitive approach works is to follow it, step by step, through an actual case study. I have chosen the case of Statoil, the Norwegian state-owned oil and gas company, because the project was well focused and the process was straightforward. In addition, the discussion can be candid because a great deal of information about the project is already in the public domain.

When we started this project in 1987, Statoil was already experimenting with the use of scenarios to develop overall corporate strategy. This was a year of volatile oil prices, and the near collapse of international financial markets occurred on "Black Monday" (October 19, 1987). It was a year in which it was all too easy to be, as one team member put it at the time, "whipsawed by events."

The management mind-set at Statoil, as in most integrated oil and gas companies, was in a state of seeming contradiction. Their thinking was a curious mix of uncertainty about the timing and strength of "oil shocks," but near certainty about the underlying strength of a seller's market and about the continuing preeminence of oil in Norway's economy. Scenarios were seen as a way to cushion the severity of oil shocks by instilling what-if thinking and contingency planning into the group's strategic management.

This was the setting for a trial run to explore the use of scenarios in developing a long-term research and development strategy for Statoil's Exploration and Production (E&P) Division. Scenarios were far from being the whole of this project, but they were the key to helping R&D managers deal with the inevitable uncertainties they faced in thinking through such a strategy. For example, it's always difficult to predict the consequences that social, political, economic, and technological forces will have for the oil business and its technological needs. Oil and gas prices, the strength of the Norwegian economy, and the availability of technical skills are other examples. But significant questions also require answers:

- How important will the oil industry be in the nation's future?
- What role will technology play in such a future?
- What kind of technologies will the division have to master in the E&P environment of the future?

Step 1: Defining the Decision Focus

In delineating the scope of the project, we determined that there were four defining issues to consider. The project should:

- Deal explicitly and effectively with the full range of uncertainty in the long-term future.
- Take account of future corporate, competitive, and technological conditions.
- Be compatible with existing planning and management culture.
- Be capable of developing a range of plausible technology strategy options.

With these issues in mind, we framed the decision-focus question as follows:

Which technologies should the Exploration and Production Division pursue most strongly in order to best serve long-term business needs?

We determined that the scenarios would have to focus on the future industry and technological environment of the E&P Division, including the structure of both the oil and gas market and Statoil's competition. Given the global nature of the oil and gas industry, the scenarios would be global in nature, but take in account key aspects of Norway's social, political, and economic situation. Technology was also singled out for specific analysis in view of the project's focus on R&D strategy. We set the time horizon for the scenarios as the next 20 years (1987–2010) to accommodate the long lead time and long-term payoff of technology. Ultimately, of course, the R&D strategy would have to address both the short-term and long-term needs of the division.

In a parallel analysis performed at the same time, we conducted an assessment of the division's current technology portfolio in terms of its linkage to the attainment of current Statoil/Division goals (see Exhibit 5.4). This assessment had no bearing on the scenario development work itself, but played a major role later on (Step 6) when we examined the strategic implications of the scenarios.

Step 2: Identifying the Key Decision Factors

In order to determine the optimum long-term technology portfolio for the decision, we reasoned that we would benefit from having answers to five simple questions:

- What will be the division's operating and R&D needs?
- What will Statoil's competitors do? How successful will they be?
- What will be the sources and availability of technology, R&D funding, and human resources? How should the division tap them?

Exhibit 5.4
Linking the Technology Portfolio to Business Goals

Current Technology Portfolio	Linkage to Current Business Goals			
	Goal A	Goal B	Goal C	Goal D
Technology #1	○	●	●	○
Technology #2	○	●	○	○
Technology #3	●	●	○	○
Technology #4	○	○	●	○
Technology #5	●	●	○	○

Symbols: ● = Primary Link   ● = Weak Link
○ = Secondary Link   ○ = Little or No Link

- How will Statoil's charter and government regulations and policies influence the division's R&D strategy?
- What will be the scope of the research network? How should the division utilize it?

This listing then led us to identify seven key decision factors that the scenarios would have to address and project trends for (see Exhibit 5.5):

- E&P operator needs, including future levels of exploration and production; the geographic distribution and geologic characteristics of E&P activities; the mix between oil and gas.
- Competition from other oil companies, including their major strategic thrusts; the extent of their emphasis on strategic alliances and joint ventures; their R&D strategies and successes (e.g., number of breakthroughs).
- Availability of R&D funding—internally and from the Norwegian government and R&D partners.
- Availability of technology—in other companies, universities, and research organizations.
- Availability of needed professional skills (in the Norwegian labor market).
- Statoil's relations with the Norwegian government, including Statoil's charter with respect to its economic development role; its resource production role; safety and environmental regulations.
- Relations with research organizations, both in Norway and internationally.

Step 3: Identifying and Assessing the Key External Forces

Given the scope and complexity of the global, national, industry, and market environment involved in this project, it is not surprising that the scenario team identified more than 60 forces that had some bearing, directly or indirectly, on these seven key decision factors.

Even after being screened by an impact/uncertainty analysis, more than half of these forces remained in the upper right quadrant of the matrix (high-impact/high-uncertainty; see Exhibit 5.6), the area on which the search for scenario logics would concentrate. While this assessment might seem to represent an unusually high degree of uncertainty about the

Exhibit 5.5
Statoil's Key Decision Factors

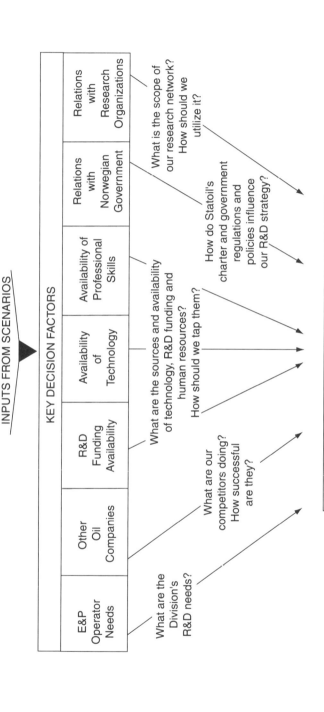

Exhibit 5.6
Statoil's Critical Uncertainties

DEGREE OF UNCERTAINTY			
Low	*Medium*	*High*	LEVEL OF IMPACT
• International economic competitiveness (5) • COMECON energy strategy (9) • Environmental policies (15) • Oil supply—U.S. (37) • Gas supply for W. Europe—North Sea (42) • Gas supply for W. Europe—U.S.S.R. (43) • Norwegian international competitiveness (58) • Norwegian education (60) • Norwegian attitudes/policies on protection (61)	• GNP growth—OECD (1) • Economic restructuring (4) • Taxation policies (13) • Energy technology (18) • Relevant sciences (19) • Demographics—LDCs (21) • Oil demand—Transportation (24) • Gas demand—E. Europe (26) • Oil supply—North Sea (35) • E&P costs (47) • O&G industry—Interests in Norway (49) • Norwegian tax policy (52) • Norwegian industrial policy (53) • O&G technology (62, 63)	• GNP growth—LDCs (2) • International inflation/exchange rates (6) • Geopolitical relations (8) • OPEC energy strategy (10) • U.S. energy strategy (11) • Rate of technological change (17) • National will (22) • Islamic fundamentalism (23) • Oil prices (29) • Gas prices (30) • Oil supply—OPEC (34) • Oil supply—Barents Sea (36) • Gas supply for interregional demand (46) • Restructuring—O&G industry (48) • Norwegian economic restructuring (55)	*High*
• Technology policies (14) • Demographics—OECD/COMECON (20) • Norwegian international relations (50)	• GNP growth—COMECON (3) • Trade policies (12) • Oil demand—Other end users (25) • Interregional gas demand (28) • Competing fuels—Demand (31) • Competing fuels—Price (32) • Oil supply—Canada (38) • Oil supply—U.S.S.R. (40) • Gas supply for other interregional demand (45) • Norwegian entry into E.C. (50) • Norwegian R&D spending (57) • Norwegian interindustry competition (56)	• International debt (7) • Gas demand—Other regions (27) • Oil supply—Asia, Africa, Latin America (39) • Gas supply for W. Europe—Middle East (44) • Norwegian GNP growth (54) • Norwegian national will (59)	*Medium*
• Competing fuels—Supply (33) • Gas supply—Other regions (41)	• Privatization policies (16)		*Low*

future, it was perhaps not surprising, given the nature of the global oil and gas business.

Step 4: Establishing the Scenario Logics

Our search for a simplified logical structure for the scenarios led us into a prolonged discussion of the 35 forces grouped in the upper right quadrant of Exhibit 5.6. We looked for groupings, cause-and-effect relationships, and other linkages among these forces. In the end, we concluded that, for the R&D decision confronting the division, the truly critical uncertainties clustered around three axes of uncertainty (see Exhibit 5.7):

- *The Structure of the Energy Market (Supply and Demand).* Will there be a return to a seller's market, or will the current buyer's market continue?
- *The Norwegian Economy.* Will the economy continue to be heavily energy-dependent, or will it successfully restructure into a more diversified form?

Exhibit 5.7
Statoil's Scenario Structure

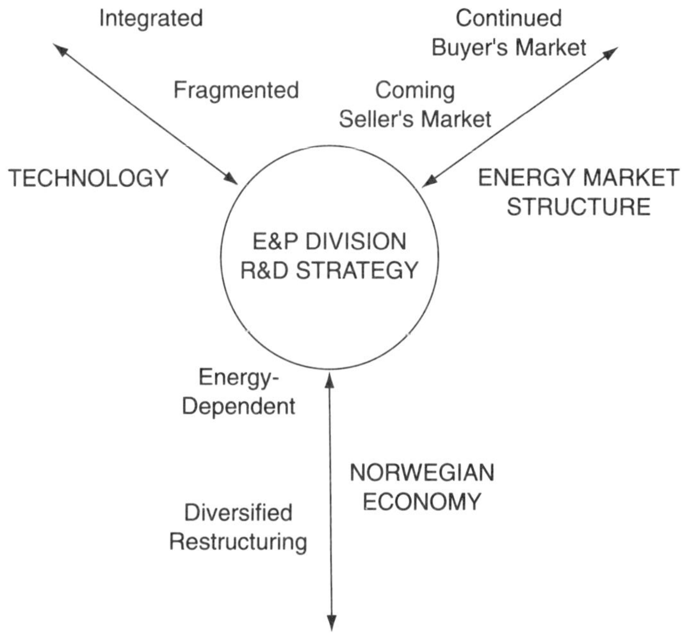

- *Technology.* Will technology evolve, in the general economy and in energy industries, in a fragmented and somewhat incremental manner, or will a more integrated and accelerated evolution take place?

The alternate logics for each axis did, we felt, present radically different, but rational, views of the way the world might work. They effectively defined the most important areas of uncertainty.

Step 5: Selecting and Elaborating the Scenarios

From among the eight possible scenarios, we selected four for study, because we felt that was the most the decision-making system could assimilate. These four scenarios met the requisite criteria and effectively covered the critical area of planning uncertainty (plausibility, differentiation, consistency, decision-making utility challenges).

Scenario A: The Nation's Future Is Dominated by the Oil and Gas Economy

Key Drivers. A seller's market in energy, an energy-dependent Norwegian economy, and fragmented/incremental technology development.

Traditional patterns of industrial and technological development result in a continuing high level of energy dependence. As a consequence, oil prices rebound, and OPEC regains dominance about 1995. The nation debates restructuring its economy, but the actions proposed and taken are not sufficient to divert the strong push toward further development of national oil and gas resources.

Scenario B: Oil and Gas Benefits Lead to a Restructured National Economy

Key Drivers. A seller's market in energy, diversified restructuring of the Norwegian economy, and integrated/accelerated technology development.

A more rapid diffusion of new technology (materials, computers, communications) and the gradual reduction of budget and trade deficits result in higher levels of growth worldwide and closer political and economic relationships among nations. The OECD countries continue to maintain a high level of energy dependence, thus ensuring the return of a seller's market. Norway uses technology and national oil and gas revenues for energy resource development and the diversification of the economy.

Scenario C: The Country Struggles in a Depressed World

Key Drivers.   A buyer's market in energy, an energy-dependent Norwegian economy, and fragmented/incremental technology development.

Structural problems in both developed and developing countries reach a crisis and, lacking resolution, result in a prolonged worldwide recession. Commodity and energy prices plunge, and the politics of protectionism and national self-sufficiency help to generate a siege mentality in many countries. Under these pressures, Norway seeks to leverage its energy resource advantage into a strategy for national economic survival.

Scenario D: The Country Is Driven from Oil Dependence by Global Restructuring

Key Drivers.   A buyer's market in energy, diversified restructuring of the Norwegian economy, and integrated/accelerated technology development.

This scenario represents the furthest evolution of a globalized economy and the "information society." High-tech breakthroughs in such areas as information technology, biotechnology, and materials radically change the structure, mix, and location of global economic activity. The dependence of the economy on raw material and energy declines dramatically, and information-based value increases correspondingly. In this high-growth but highly competitive world, Norway has no choice but to restructure its economy.

A tabular comparison of the scenarios, covering approximately half of the more than 60 forces included in the conceptual model of the division's environment, provided a detailed look inside each of the scenarios, enabling decision makers to make point-by-point comparison of the differing conditions that the E&P Division might encounter. Exhibit 5.8 presents a sampling from this table.

Step 6: Interpreting the Scenarios

One problem with scenario planning has been that managers generally find it easier to imagine how the world might change than to confront the need to change themselves. In this project, we recognized this problem, and sought to deal with it by addressing the need for managers' personal growth in this sixth step. To start the process of preparing for the future, the project team met for an intensive week-long workshop. During the first four days, the team discussed the implications of the scenarios, selecting a different scenario each day for consideration. Addressing a different scenario each day, the team was able to immerse itself into the details of one scenario at a time and thus complete its evaluation before moving on to a different outlook on the future. Then, on day five, we reviewed the results of the first four days of discussion to identify the commonalties and differences of the four scenarios.

To focus our thinking, we needed to refer to the key decision factors that had formed the original decision focus for the scenarios. These gave rise to a series of questions (see Exhibit 5.5) that formed a natural linkage between the scenarios and the development of R&D strategy, and so provided a useful guide for structuring our thinking.

At this stage, the exercise proceeded in five discrete steps:

1. *Review each scenario description.* This was the process of increasing our intellectual and, just as important, our emotional involvement in the conditions of a given scenario. This step was not simply a review of the material we had earlier developed. It required an attempt to "step into" the scenario so that we could believe that it was the future, and that we were part of it.

2. *Assess implications of the scenario.* With the description of the scenario clearly in mind, the team then discussed the effect of the scenario on the key decision factors. To further the discussion, we developed a more extensive list of questions to answer. For example, under E&P Operator Needs, we asked, Which geographic areas of exploration will be most emphasized? Will certain geologic field types have more or less emphasis?

3. *Identify the best strategy, opportunities, and threats.* The focus here was on answering three questions:
   - What seems the best strategy for dealing with this scenario?
   - What are the major opportunities and threats inherent in the scenario?
   - What should Statoil do—and not do?

   To stress the what-if nature of our thinking at this point, we used as a lead-in the following phrase: "If we could forecast the future

Exhibit 5.8
Excerpts from Statoil's Tabular Comparison of Scenarios

Descriptors	A. Norway's Future Dominated by the Oil and Gas Economy	B. Oil and Gas Benefits Lead to Restructured Norwegian Economy	C. Norway Struggles in a Depressed World	D. Norway Driven Out of Oil Dependence by Global Restructuring
Global Economic Development	• Persistent Economic Structural Problems • OECD growth: about 2% • Inflation Higher; Volatile Exchange Rates	• Moderate Growth, Some Progress toward Restructuring • OECD Growth: 2.5% • Cyclical Swings in Inflation, Exchange Rates	• Severe Economic Structural Problems, Protectionism • OECD Growth: 1.5% • Volatile Inflation (Some Deflation) and Exchange Rates	• Strong Growth, Following Restructuring Adjustments • OECD Growth: 3–3.5% • Relatively Stable Inflation and Exchange Rates
Geopolitical Relations	• Increasing Protectionism • Slowdown/Reversal of Privatization Policies • U.S.—W. Europe Tensions Exploited by U.S.S.R.	• Growing International Trade and Cooperation • Privatization Gains in OECD • Relaxation of East-West Tensions; Increased Trade	• Volatile, Tension-Filled World; Protectionism, Nationalism Growth • Emphasis on Govt. Controls • East-West Relations and Trade Deteriorate	• Stable Political Relations Lead to Economic Agreements • Market-Oriented Policies Flourish • COMECON Drawn More into Global Mainstream

Energy Market Structure	• Oil Demand Growth: 1%
	• Gas Demand Growth: 2%
	• OPEC Regains Dominance
	• N. Sea, Barents Sea Pushed
	• COMECON Gas Available
	• Oil = $30–35/bbl;
	  Gas = $3–5/MBtu
		• Oil Demand Growth: 1%
		• Gas Demand Growth: 2%
		• OPEC Power Increases
		• N. Sea, Barents Sea Pushed
		• COMECON Gas Expands
		• Oil = $25–30/bbl;
		  Gas = $3–4/MBtu
			• Oil Demand Growth: 0%
			• Gas Demand Growth: 1%
			• OPEC Struggles to Survive
			• Barents Sea Devel. Delayed
			• COMECON Gas Reduced
			• Oil = $15–20/bbl;
			  Gas = $2–3/MBtu
				• Oil Demand Growth: 1%
				• Gas Demand Growth: 3%
				• OPEC Loose Power and Cohesion
				• N. Sea, Barents Sea Slowed
				• COMECON Gas Reduced/More Former OPEC
				• Oil = $10–15/bbl;
				  Gas = $1–3/MBtu

Oil and Gas Industry Structure	• Only Modest Restructuring —Strong Upstream Operations post-1990	• Moderate Restructuring —More Strategic Alliances —Greater Push Downstream	• Substantial Restructuring —Mergers/Consolidations Multiply —State-Owned Companies Favored by National Policies	• Substantial Restructuring —Strategies Shift from Oil to Gas —Privatization of Some State-Owned Operations
Norwegian Situation	• National Will: Unsure, Drifting • Economic Restructuring: —Few Initiatives Successful —Petroleum Sector Dominant • GNP Growth: about 2.5%	• Moderately Dynamic National Will • Economic Restructuring: —Balance between Petroleum and Nonpetroleum Sectors • GNP Growth: about 2.5%	• Malaise: Discouraged, Divided • Economic Restructuring: —All Sectors Struggling —Govt. Supports Energy Sector • GNP Growth: 1–1.5%	• Strongly Dynamic National WIN • Economic Restructuring: —Most Initiatives Successful —Gas Replaces Oil in Importance • GNP Growth: about 2.5–3%
Technological Change	• Incremental Development: Disciplines Remain Fragmented • Norwegian R&D Spending: 1.5% of GNP with Oil and Gas as No. 1 Priority • Oil and Gas Technology: Focus on E&P Improvement and New Reserves	• Accelerated Progress: Integration of Disciplines • Norwegian R&D Grows to 2% of GNP, with New Priorities • Oil and Gas Technology: Focus on New Reserves Access	• Stalled Development: Restrictive, Protectionist Policies • Norwegian R&D Spending Declines, but Oil and Gas Is Constant • Oil and Gas Technology: Focus on Productivity/Cost-Control	• Rapid Progress: Integration, Global Diffusion of Technologies • Norwegian R&D Grows to 2–2.5% Focuses on High-Tech Restructuring • Oil and Gas Technology: Focus on Gas Conversion, AI/Imaging

with certainty and know that this scenario would develop as it has been described, then Statoil should . . . (name a specific action)."

4. *Evaluate the scenario's impact on the division's goals.* Earlier, we had assessed the linkage between R&D programs and the division's goals (see Exhibit 5.5). That is, we determined which programs contributed how much to the accomplishment of which goals. Here we wanted to assess what changes might be made in company and division goals in light of the external conditions represented by the scenario. Important question were, Which goals might be emphasized and which might be dropped or changed? What new goals might be adopted?

5. *Develop a portfolio of priority R&D programs.* Having a sense of what the major opportunities and threats might be, and how the company might change its business goals, we could use the linkages between R&D programs and business goals to reorder the R&D priorities, and so develop a research portfolio best attuned to the demands of that scenario.

This was not the end of the project. Further steps moved the process from these scenario-specific R&D portfolios toward selection of an R&D strategy sufficiently resilient to be viable in a variety of possible futures.

BENEFITS, LIMITATIONS, AND GUIDELINES

As with any approach to scenarios, the intuitive logics approach has its benefits and its limitations. Among its principal benefits are:

• The methodology is completely "transparent." In other words, the step-by-step reasoning is laid out for critical examination, with no intervening "black box" or computer modeling. This makes for easier communication, understanding, and discussion of the scenarios. Managers can pinpoint exactly where, and why, they agree or disagree with the reasoning.

• Direct participation of the decision makers in the process puts the contribution of staff and outside experts in proper perspective; places responsibility where it should be; and ensures that the decision makers will truly understand, own, and so more likely act on, the implications of the scenarios.

- This approach encourages—indeed, depends upon—free and open discussion of differences of opinion about the dynamics of the business environment, uncertainties and wild cards. In this way, it encourages both individual and organizational learning.
- Because it relies wholly on mental (rather than computer) modeling, this approach has a good chance—perhaps the best chance of any approach—of success in challenging, and perhaps influencing, executives' mental maps of the future.
- Because it is not tied to computer algorithms (which are reflections of the past), it is more likely to engender the sort of lateral thinking that is needed to anticipate future surprises and major "inflection points." It was lateral thinking, for instance, that enabled Pierre Wack to envisage the possibility of an oil world turned upside down by a display of OPEC strength, while conventional industry thinking continued to project the past power of oil-consuming nations into the indefinite future.

The methodology does, however, have its limitations. Among them:

- It is not suited to some organizational cultures. Don't expect it to take root, for instance, in a culture that is rigid, numbers-oriented, unwilling to discuss uncertainties or to tolerate differences of opinion.
- Even where it is accepted, it can cause "culture shock" as the organization moves from traditional forecasting and planning toward scenario-based planning. It is limited, therefore, by the willingness of the organization to undergo this wider culture change.
- It is a somewhat costly—in terms of executive time—and demanding methodology. It requires a broad base of strategic intelligence (often beyond the usual boundaries of corporate information-gathering), and requires its participants to invest considerable effort, thought, and creativity.
- In the end, it is still not the complete answer to futures thinking. Scanning and monitoring are needed to round out the toolkit of external environmental analysis. And it can still miss some surprises.

CONCLUSION

If one follows the guidelines for successful introduction of the intuitive logics methodology, it is possible to reap the benefits and minimize the limitations of this approach to scenario development. It is an approach that is well designed to promote organizational learning; to increase acceptance and understanding of uncertainty; and to elicit and legitimize the inevitable differences of opinion about the future that exist in any organization. It is also a powerful and often underestimated change-agent; and its introduction into a corporate (or any other) system needs to be treated as carefully, and prepared for as thoroughly, as any radical change in organizational culture.

CHAPTER 6

SCENARIO PLANNING: MAPPING THE PATHS TO THE DESIRED FUTURE

DAVID H. MASON

The Future Mapping methodology creates several models of uncertainty that enable participants to experiment with and learn how to gain a greater degree of control over a particular future they desire for their organization. The models are built by first collecting reliable evidence—the events—and then supplying a credible hypothesis—the end state. Next, the participants in the workshop complete the model by creating a logical understanding of uncertainty by studying how the evidence leads to a particular hypothesis. The understanding of uncertainty that they develop by making the models prepares them to manage the opportunities and risks that each future holds for their organization.

Scenario planning begins to succeed the moment management realizes that current strategies, and their related investment decisions need to be thoroughly "flight-tested" in a variety of possible futures. However, the Future Mapping® planning process described in this chapter has a more ambitious goal—to use scenarios to develop entirely new strategic concepts, ones that prepare an organization to take on future challenges with justifiable confidence. Scenarios also provide a low risk "test" environment for introducing an organization to the potential of various alternative strategies. Scenario planning gives leaders an opportunity to reassess the staying power of the strategies upon which the organization is built. Are they all-weather strategies or will they serve the organization well only under certain conditions?

If they survive long enough, most organizations usually have one or two opportunities to re-create their future. They can choose to be in some businesses rather than others, to pioneer certain technologies, to operate in some nations but not others, and to hire certain people. Leaders can use scenario planning to engage groups in a search for direction and to establish a logical framework for decisions that determine direction: Who are we, what do we do, who do we do it for, and why? The process can also set goals the organization can aspire to: Is what we do today what we want to do tomorrow? What are our options?

A PROCESS FOR EFFICIENTLY BUILDING SCENARIOS

Future Mapping is a technique for scenario building that has been adopted by a number of major firms. Participants build scenarios from a "kit" of components that are customized through extensive research by experts in the operating environment of the organization.

In this process, a scenario is defined as a logical list of sequential events that leads to a notable point in time called an end state. The kit is made up of sets of 3 to 5 end states and 100 to 200 events, for use in a workshop where an organization's managers are grouped into teams. End states are one-page, integrated descriptions of the outcome of a scenario, such as, "The Internet becomes the dominant technical infrastructure for computing." Events, such as, "The commercialization of a $300 terminal to access the Internet," are important, easily identifiable milestones that mark the path from the present to an end state. This particular event would be a milestone leading to this particular end state.

At the workshop, each team is assigned to study one end state and asked to identify the logical sequence of events that leads to their end state over time. They primarily choose from the set of events that have been prepared for them, but at appropriate points in the workshop they add other events that they believe help determine the occurrence of an end state. The team's work is focused on thinking through the logical course of events between today and the advent of the end state they have been assigned. One of the most useful products of the workshop is the list of events each team generates. The list is valuable to the organization because:

• It describes an implementation path that management could take to achieve a given end state.
• It describes a way to monitor whether the future is unfolding in a manner that favors a particular end state.

- It provides a basis for comparing the events leading to one end state with events leading to another.
- Events found to be relevant to all end states need to be identified as particularly important points of strategic leverage.

What Makes This Workshop Format Effective?

Workshops for an organization's managers that use a set of events and end states prepared in advance by knowledgeable experts avoid the problems associated with starting a meeting about the future with a blank sheet of paper. The kit gives workshop attendees a jump-start so that they can concentrate quickly on the logic and consequences of the scenarios. By using the kit, the participants don't waste time restating familiar positions; the time needed to get the main ideas on the table is greatly reduced and the time spent working with the ideas is greatly increased.

The key skill of the kit builders is to write the end states and events so that they fully capture and expand on the ideas, problems, and decisions that interest and challenge the group. The workshops are intended to put the organization on the road from where it is today to where it wants to be in the future. The discussions should focus on what do we want and how can we make this happen?

THE GREAT INFRASTRUCTURE DEBATE

A good example of the Future Mapping process in action is the Great Infrastructure Debate® series of workshops, begun in March 1994 and concluded in June 1996. The workshops were aimed at understanding the strategy options for participating in the development of the information highway. The need for scenario planning arises from the complexity of the issues and the interdependent nature of the technical, market, and regulatory issues involved. The workshops brought together high-level representatives of diverse organizations, such as: computing, communications, telephone, cable television, information service, content provider retailing, advertising, banking, financial services, government, and large industrials.

Issues addressed in these conferences include:

- Which business models will be profitable and sustainable for industry players ranging from carriers to information service providers?

- How will the tremendous capital costs associated with building advanced networks be financed?
- What kind of industry participants will win and which are "at risk?"
- Will home and office computing and communications converge or diverge? Will one market "subsidize" the development of the other?
- Will government be a catalyst or regulatory roadblock?
- What will be the role of advertising?

The following description is from the fourth conference on the topic, held in October 1995. The results from each of the prior three conferences were used to refine the kit of materials for subsequent sessions. Earlier workshops in the series had included, for example, more emphasis on government involvement and less emphasis on the concept of extended communities in cyberspace.

THE FUTURE MAPPING PROCESS

The Future Mapping process used in the workshops consists of four primary exercises through which participants explore the future of the infohighway. The four exercises are each described in the following sections using example results from the October 1995 Great Infrastructure Debate.

The Conventional Wisdom Exercise

In this first part of the Great Infrastructure Debate, participants are divided into five teams and asked to vote on the likelihood that each of 166 prepared events will occur. These events reflect ideas described by attendees in interviews prior to the workshop and from 10 years of Northeast Consulting Resources, Inc.'s (NCRI) research in this field. After reviewing the prepared events, the teams are invited to write any missing events they feel are important to add.

The teams sort each event into one of three categories:

- Highly likely (> 80% probability).
- Highly unlikely (< 20% probability).
- Uncertain (20% >-< 80% probability).

In general, if there is significant disagreement within a team or among teams, an event is categorized as uncertain.

The following are some examples selected from the 166 events of the Great Infrastructure Debate (these are just event titles, not full descriptions):

1998   Equal Access Amended

1998   Independent Retail Server Services Proliferate

1999   60 Percent of U.S. Homes Have PCs; Double the Penetration of 1994

1999   Electronic Broker/Distributors Proliferate

2000   70 Percent of Homes Have Three or More Full-Service Network Alternatives

2000   Dollar Volume of Net-Based Transactions Reaches 10 Percent of Total Credit Card Volume

2000   Wholesale Carriers Outsource Retail Collections

2001   More Business-to-Consumer Than Business-to-Business Transactions on the Net

2001   Pricing Plans Continue Subscriber Churn

The workshop facilitators derive the themes of the Conventional Wisdom exercise by clustering the individual events into related topics and time lines. The following themes, for example, were developed from 59 highly likely events and one highly unlikely event in the October 1995 workshop:

- Information commerce will be an early driver of economically significant internet traffic. There will be many early entrants into the information commerce arena, including telephone companies, cellular, cable TV, Internet access providers, and alternative access providers.
- Enough networked electronic resources will be in the home by 1997–1998 to give many "communities" an on-line dimension. For example, your children's classrooms, school, and PTA are a real community that can be extended into the on-line world. In fact, some "communities" only exist on-line. As communication among users over wide areas becomes easier, traditional product or service branding might begin to be undermined, and be superseded, by word-of-mouth endorsement spread through electronic communities with common, deeply held values.

- Shopping and advertising are transformed by the Internet, but only after security and privacy obstacles have been overcome. Shopping will be much slower to emerge as a significant force than digital communities. By 2000, security and fraud prevention measures will be in place to make on-line commerce commonplace. Privacy concerns will lead consumers to protest use of data from on-line activity to create truly personalized micromarketing "segments of one." This customized marketing could enable marketers to profile important customers as individuals rather than grouping them in mass-market segments. Retailers could then offer individual customers the exact product that they want at the exact moment they want it. By 2000, the benefits of personalized offerings will begin to outweigh the costs and consumers' concerns over invasion of privacy.

- Changes in the communications infrastructure will create new challenges and opportunities. Corporate information technology is already recognizing that e-mail, groupware, and telecommuting have become critical applications; if they fail, the business slows to a crawl or stops. Use of the World Wide Web will change the way information is collected and used. Virtual workgroups will continue to expand until they allow fundamental reengineering of the entire industry value chains. This will take longer, but the benefits will be enormous.

- The infrastructure carrying information to and from the home will continue to be broadband in (broadcast TV and cable) *and* narrowband out (phone *and* fax and modem traffic over the phone lines). Wireless broadband—connecting to satellites carrying voice, video, and data—will become a significant option for consumers. By 2000 or sooner, there will be fierce, direct competition between providers, telephone service, CATV, and wireless broadband. For businesses, the Net will continue to blur the boundaries between local area networks (LANs) and wide area networks (WANs).

- For both consumer and business applications, CD-ROM may become a complementary technology that increases the demand for networked services; for example, a CD-ROM catalogue that can take the customer through an ordering process off-line then allow the customer to dial in and send the order over a modem. In addition, bundled service offerings including cable TV, local phone, long-distance phone, e-mail, Internet access, all from one service provider, will become common. Carriers will try to add higher value services to basic offerings.

Scenario Defense Exercise

In the second part of the workshop, teams of participants each advocate and defend a different vision for the future of the infohighway in five years time, delivering a presentation that justifies their position. Participants refine their understanding of how the infohighway will evolve by working in teams that advocate a particular end state. The one-page end state descriptions they are assigned are deliberately brief, leave out lots of detail, and only describe the state of the infohighway at the end of the period.

The major tasks for participants are to fill out the details of the end state, and most important, lay out the event path that would be necessary if this end state were to develop. The creation of the event path is, in effect, a simulated hindsight exercise in which participants learn to understand the logical path that led to the end state.

A. *Simplicity.* The market is dominated by six to eight major service players with tightly integrated public networks for voice, data, wireless, Internet access, and other services. These players provide and control the network interfaces linking content providers—such as HBO, NBC, Paramount, MTV, Viacom—to end customers. Each player, or combinations of players (Bell Atlantic and NYNEX might merge, or GTE join with a cable TV company), maintains direct selling to the end customer and a strong consumer brand identity. Pricing pressure is fierce.

B. *Fragmentation.* Fast deregulation, coupled with rapid technological change initiates a wave of intense competition among service providers. Low-cost structures and targeted microsegmentation are the key to winning. There is great diversity of services created by shifting alliances. The consumer relationship begins to be controlled by an entirely new type of value-added telecom retailers who offer one-stop shopping and one bill for satellite, cable, voice, Internet, Internet content, and connection equipment, even if they come from different providers.

C. *Network Affinity.* Participation in electronic communities and interest groups surges. Most content on the Internet is communication between group members—e-mail, chat spaces, games groups, bulletin boards, schedules, and the like. The creation of cybercommunities—currency traders, derivatives experts, investment clubs, professional organizations, car collectors, environmentalists, to name a few—makes affinity marketing on the Internet a new, cheap, and highly effective way to define and reach micromarket segments.

D. *Content-Driven.* Content providers such as Paramount, Disney, Dow Jones, the *New York Times* are in the driver's seat and steering evolution of the information superhighway. Packaging, bundling services, and providing integration creates value. Content, not carrier, drives user buying decisions. Entertainment services are a major source of revenue.

E. *Doing Business Electronically.* Electronic commerce is the killer application on the infohighway. The Net is now seen by companies as a major market and a new channel. Doing business electronically greatly reduces overhead costs, and companies can rely on network security, metering technology, and efficient payment systems.

The Common and Critical Event Exercise

The facilitators in the third part of the workshop identify the subset of events that turn out to be common to all five of the scenarios. They are usually treated differently in each scenario; for example, an event that is positive for two scenarios might be negative for three others. Therefore, at a minimum, they represent decision points—choosing to act one way supports one direction, acting a different way ultimately supports a different outcome. Look for common events with significant strategic leverage to significantly influence how an industry develops.

During the creation of the scenarios, we ask teams to select events that are relevant to the emergence of their end state (in either a positive or negative way). In the case of the October 1995 Great Infrastructure Debate, our comparison of the event selections the teams produced found 14 events common to at least three out of five scenarios. These events describe a set of issues that stakeholders in the information superhighway should be addressing today. The full listing of the events shared by a number of the scenarios is given in Exhibit 6.1.

In an actual planning effort (but not in the public workshop being described), the teams can be asked to analyze these events in more detail by answering the following questions about each event:

- Describe a desirable outcome for the event.
- How could we influence the outcome of the event?
- Which tactics could be employed to support the desired outcome?

Exhibit 6.1
Events Shared by Scenarios A, B, C, D, and E

A	B	C	D	E	HL	HU	Year	Title
		1	1	1	Y		1996	Common Desktop Applications Become Front Ends to Internet
		1	1	1	Y		1996	Detailed Measures of On-Line Ad Use Offered
1		1	1				1996	Encryption for Secure Communications Is Widespread
1		1	1	1			1996	High-Speed Internet Access through Cable for $50 Per Month
1	1		1				1996	NMF Defines End-to-End Service-Level Standards
		1	1	−1			1998	Equal Access Amended
−1	1	1	1			Y	1998	Independent Retail Server Services Proliferate
1		1	1			Y	1999	60% of U.S. Homes Have PCs; Double the Penetration of 1994
		1	1	1		Y	1999	Electronic Broker/Distributors Proliferate
1	1	1	1			Y	2000	70% of Homes Have Three or More Full-Service Network Alternatives
		1	1	1			2000	Dollar Volume of Net-Based Transactions Reaches 10% of Total Credit Card Volume
−1		1	1				2000	Wholesale Carriers Outscore Retail Collections
1		1	1	−1			2001	More Business-to-Consumer than Business-to-Business Transactions on the Net
1		−1		−1			2001	Pricing Plans Continue Subscriber Churn

HL = Highly Likely
HU = Highly Unlikely

(Note: A 1 denotes a positive "must happen" event for the end state, and a −1 denotes a negative "must not happen" event for the end state.)

- Which resources are required to support these tactics?
- Do we have these resources? If not, how could we obtain them?
- How would we know if our efforts succeeded or failed?
- How would we know the work involved was completed?
- Which organization, or who, should be responsible for this effort?

These kinds of questions lay the simplest, most efficient implementation foundation for scenario-based plans. There is no special magic to implementation other than the willingness of the organization to engage in the work. Some clients are very attracted to the simplicity and discipline of this approach; others view the direction setting of the end states as sufficient.

A Composite Scenario Exercise

In the fourth and final exercise, the teams consider how the five scenarios—(A)Simplicity, (B)Fragmentation, (C)Network affinity, (D)Content-driven, (E)Doing business electronically—could be combined into an evolutionary sequence. Many participants see the emergence of electronic communities as a critical step for creating on-line markets.

Scenario planning often generates significant changes in how participants view their business environment. In this workshop, attendees were asked to rank the five end states with respect to two criteria (see Exhibit 6.2):

- *Attainability.* Assuming you were responsible for implementing the company strategy, rank the end states from easiest to most difficult.
- *Desirability.* Assuming you have no responsibility for implementation, rank the end states from most desirable to least desirable.

In the case where the most desirable outcome is the easiest, there's a straightforward path to decision making. The more common case is that the most desirable end state is also the least attainable. In this situation, decision making is more complicated.

Take note of the following changes the data in Exhibit 6.2 suggests (keeping in mind that these changes occurred in a single two-day workshop):

- By the end of the meeting, attendees had completely changed their view of end state C's attainability (5, hardest, changed to 2). They also found increased attractiveness in the scenario (5, least desirable, to 3). What had been an undesirable, extremely difficult-to-attain scenario had become much easier to attain and significantly more attractive.
- End state A clearly fell out of favor, falling from first in attainability beforehand to the middle of the pack. A world dominated by a half-dozen large, integrated communications companies came out as the least desirable outcome by a wide margin.

Exhibit 6.2

Ranking the end states according to attainability/desirability before and after the workshops shows how the rankings changed from the beginning to the end of the Great Infrastructure Debate.

TEAM	Attainability Before	Attainability After	Desirability Before	Desirability After
A	1	3	4	5
B	3	1	2	2
C	5	2	5	3
D	4	4	3	4
E	2	5	1	1

- Team B persuaded the conference that both economics and regulation made more fragmentation of the communications infrastructure the most likely outcome.
- By contrast, Team E convinced the conference that there was a lot of work to be done before new computing and communications technologies would allow complete reengineering and virtualization of business value chains. However, end state E's promised benefits made it easily the most attractive scenario.
- Views of end state D, which focused on information content businesses, did not change much, but the overall low marks for attainability appeared to be at odds with the group's conventional wisdom belief that information commerce would be an early driver of the Net.

This scenario planning creates a shorthand language in which a group can have clear conversations about very complex changes in their industry. They can see how different arguments influence their peers, and subsequently change their hearts and minds about where they should take their company and where they should lead their industry. Using scenarios to establish a framework for such conversations improves the odds that a large organization will make needed changes.

ADVICE ON APPLYING SCENARIO TECHNIQUES TO DIFFERENT KINDS OF PLANNING PROBLEMS

The different origins of scenario techniques say something about the different styles and uses of scenarios. Future Mapping, for example, originated from client work at A. D. Little, Inc. in the mid-1970s, first for IBM, and later for Citibank. The needs of the clients were rooted in information technology, a fast-moving field where change and speculative investments are a way of life. By contrast, approaches like the Royal Dutch/Shell techniques are rooted in the oil industry which, like other heavy industry, requires a deep understanding of risks related to very large-scale brick-and-mortar investments in an industry that is subject to global political risks. The point is that practitioners of scenario planning need to carefully consider what kind of problem they are trying to tackle before picking one method or another.

How Companies Use Scenarios

It is important for a practitioner to have agreement on the purpose of scenario planning and the definition of a successful outcome. Choosing the correct scope for the effort involves getting answers to the following questions:

- *Exactly which topics is the firm trying to understand?* If the work is too narrowly focused, important topics may be missed. If the work is too broadly focused, it may not be seen as relevant to the task at hand. Global scenarios are not going to be useful to a hospital in Boise, but they are likely to be crucial for global oil companies.
- *Is the scenario effort supposed to be a learning and teaching experience or a strategic decision-making process?* Exposing team members to new ideas and frameworks for thinking is an appropriate outcome for a learning experience. But strategic planning efforts often require managers to reach one or more key decisions. Learning might be required to chose a new strategy, but it is a means of getting to a decision, not an end in itself.
- *Who is the target audience?* The target audience might be the leadership team of a large organization, the managers of a part of the organization, or the planners from all across the organization. Each of these groups will have different amounts of time to devote to the task, different goals, and different personal expectations.
- *What types of information should the scenarios contain?* Are they global or regional? Are there significant regulatory issues? What are the different classes of technology involved? Are the relevant markets

highly segmented or more like commodities? What is the potential impact of networking and electronic commerce on the industry?

• *What sort of existing planning system are scenarios meant to supplement?* Is there a financial plan? A budget? Is there a plan based on traditional competitive strategy techniques? Does the firm have a strong understanding of its markets and competition?

Getting answers to these questions should lead to an understanding of how the organization can use scenarios infuse new thinking into their current planning system.

CONCLUSION: THE EXPLORATION OF THE DESIRED FUTURE

Many corporations' attempts to plan for their future have been remarkably unsuccessful. The libraries of plans that never get read, never get implemented, and never achieve their goals are evidence of the failure of planning based on forecasting to engage the hearts and minds of stakeholders to create the future. In contrast, the scenario-planning process described in this chapter seeks to engage stakeholders in a creative journey—the exploration of how their organization could grow and evolve if they pulled and pushed it toward the particular future they desire.

CHAPTER 7

TESTING YOUR STRATEGIES IN SCENARIOS

CHARLES M. PERROTTET

Most organizations have a success formula, a core strategy that enhances or maintains their competitive position. But will the formula work in various possible future business environments? Scenarios can be used to test the current formula and derive contingent strategies. In the concluding section of the chapter, a number of specialized uses of scenarios are also briefly described.

Though future sight is usually murky in most industries at most times, conventional strategic-planning techniques implicitly assume that the future is governed by some sort of "success equation" that is knowable. For example, for many years, American Express believed that the formula for continuing profits was simply to use top-quality marketing of a premium product to put more and more cards in the wallets and purses of customers. As another example, in the 1980s, many companies thought the formula for ever greater profits was ever greater sales. Sales growth was pursued with single-minded focus. When the times are right, such equations seem to be as unchangeable as the law of gravity.

Even when the good times begin to go bad, most executives don't consider a variety of alternative futures. Instead, challenges to assumptions in the plan typically result in the organization modifying just one or two of the "variables" in its time-honored equation. As a result, many companies have floundered in the past 20 years when they weren't prepared for disruptions in the fundamental cause-and-effect relationships of their business.

One problem is that conventional strategy techniques are so rigid that they don't permit the exercise of intuition or useful speculation. They don't pose the penetrating question, In what alternative future business environments could our organization's old model for success be irrelevant? They don't ask, What alternative futures might come to be and how might they evolve?

If the conventional approaches to strategy are too limiting, how can scenarios help? Rather than being predictive, scenarios treat the future as a boundary issue. That is, they systematically identify the range of uncertainty in the broad factors that will define the business environment in which an organization will have to operate. They embrace uncertainty, and in some cases, elevate it to the status of a competitive weapon. They do this by helping managers to rehearse a variety of futures, so that when new conditions that are included in one of them comes to pass they will be able to react more nimbly than their unprepared competitors. Alternative scenarios provide a tool to probe a number of plausible futures and to test for combinations of factors that could be important. If prepared well, a group of scenarios will, as a set, cover the full range of issues that could threaten or open opportunities for a firm. Conversely, offering management too many scenarios to consider could damage the utility or even the credibility of a scenario effort. So one of the arts of scenario-based planning is to create the smallest number of scenarios that embrace the full range of opportunities and threats facing an organization.

A single scenario can challenge decision makers to think about particular issues or to think about them in unique combinations. For example, a single scenario, by providing a view of the future that lies outside the compass of conventional strategy analysis tools, often causes managers to consider issues that are not associated with the firm's current strategy. By using the more sophisticated scenario-learning methodology presented in this chapter, requiring a carefully written set of four or five scenarios, managers can create a range of virtual business environments in which to test their current and potential strategies. The result, in short, is that managers can have greater confidence in their choices and actions.

In summary, if the goal of strategy is to create competitive advantage; the role of scenarios is to increase the relevance of a strategy. The scenarios should include the full range of threats and opportunities that may be encountered as events combine to change the future in unsuspected ways.

The probability of success of any strategy is greatly enhanced when:

- Top management can identify those elements of strategy that are not subject to changes in its basic "success equation," and then has the confidence to execute them. As a case in point, the huge IBM division that produced and sold mainframe computers tried most strategies that could be suggested. Its management was not sure, however, which ideas to stick with as the industry went through seismic shifts. After completing a scenario-based strategy exercise, they developed the confidence to continue implementation of a small set of strategies despite the day-to-day vagaries of their marketplace.

- There is a clear identification of areas of uncertainty, such as shifting regulations, a changing customer environment, or potential structural shifts in the industry.
- Plans are rehearsed to respond to identified threats or opportunities that require special treatment. For a defense contractor, an example would be the impact of the demise of the Soviet Union on the mission of the U.S. armed services.

Scenarios, because they are structured specifically to probe areas of uncertainty, provide an excellent testing ground for strategies. The entire scenario process is built around identifying and managing areas of uncertainty. But rather than trivializing the analysis of uncertainty by asking assorted what-if questions, scenarios force the strategist to consider interactions among the full range of uncertain forces. Scenarios can be used to test strategies in a broad range of possible situations, so those that prove to be robust—that is, successful in widely different circumstances—can be quickly implemented with greater confidence. Moreover, managers are not easily surprised by dramatic turnarounds in their markets because they have "lived" in a number of such situations during the scenario exercises and, in many cases, rehearsed specific responses to contingencies that arise.

Scenario-based planning now refers to a range of related techniques that are most often used to develop long-term strategies; but they can also scan and monitor external change, prioritize large-scale research activities, game competitive responses, and create or extend a learning organization. Their content runs the gamut from highly qualitative (with some scenario-specific quantification) to highly quantitative (with some scenario-specific qualitative justifications). Focus varies from primarily end-state descriptions to extensive future histories.

We will first review the use of scenarios to develop long-term strategy. This is the most common use of scenarios and is usually where a company first tries to use them. There are, however, other uses of scenarios, all of which relate directly or indirectly to the development and use of scenarios. A brief description of several of these follows the broader discussion of scenario-based strategy development.

SCENARIOS TO DEVELOP LONG-TERM STRATEGY

When the objective is to develop strategy, at either the corporate or business-unit level, the team should use a scenario process (see Exhibit 7.1) designed to produce highly customized, macro-level backdrops for strategic visioning and planning.

Identify Business Issues.   The process shown in Exhibit 7.1 starts with a comprehensive analysis of issues that are important to the existing business today. This analysis must carefully probe the forces shaping the industry and broader competitive arena to expose conventional wisdom. When Thomas J. Watson, the founder and first president of IBM stated, "There is a world market for about five computers," there were few dissents—except perhaps in the science fiction literature. Even 30 years later, most participants in the computer industry still assumed that computer processing had to be centralized, an expensive blind spot as it turned out. In fact, most firms have their blind spots. Research and interviews, both inside and outside your firm, can expose many of them and illuminate important business issues.

Sometimes views expressed in the interviews at this stage of the process contrast sharply with opinions floated later when executives and

Exhibit 7.1
Scenarios to Develop Long-Term Strategy

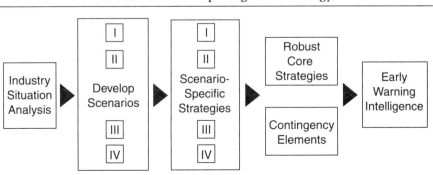

supporting personnel develop responses to the scenarios. Executives at one firm found outside factors such as exchange rate volatility, consumer activism, investment community pressures, and policies of international development agencies relatively unimportant during the interview phase of a scenario-based strategy project. Surprisingly, the majority of strategies that were later developed were designed to manage uncertainties in those very factors.

Develop Scenarios

Developing individual scenarios must proceed through the following four stages:

1. Develop a complete list of drivers that will be treated in the scenarios.
2. Analyze the interrelationships among the drivers.
3. Find dimensions that embrace the areas of greatest uncertainty so that the scenarios can be spread over the broadest plausible range.
4. Write the scenarios.

A group of managers can quickly develop 100 or more individual drivers of success for their company. The intent is to generate a listing of individual drivers without specific reference to their interrelationships or relative importance in explaining any particular change. These individual drivers emerge as managers and others identify the forces they believe are important in the current environment or that might change it in the future.

Consider Anheuser-Busch's beer business. It undoubtedly has a wide variety of drivers—the tastes and health concerns of consumers, consumer activism as represented by such groups as Mothers Against Drunk Driving (MADD), and the price of aluminum and glass, to name but three. The beer business is also driven by a variety of regulations at local and state levels, by trade restrictions, and by a number of technologies. Assembling such a list is not as difficult as it might first appear. With well-organized facilitation, an experienced group of managers can usually generate such a list of 100 to 200 in several hours.

The scenario team must then explore the interrelationships among the individual drivers and identify groups that cluster around common themes. This is hard work, and usually requires much iteration before a small number of themes can be found that includes all of the most important drivers. It is also helpful if people representing several disciplines, such as economics, political science, and some relevant field of technology, are represented on the team.

Armed with the conventional wisdom and facts that could challenge it, the team holds a series of workshops. These are used to define the broad characteristics of the future business environments that could occur, and then to select the four or five that will include among them the broadest set of challenges.

Two Examples of Dimensions.   The Steering Committee on Future Health Scenarios in The Netherlands published a set of scenarios in 1995 that were created to analyze the future of health care policy in Europe. The committee used "the degree of coordination" and "attitudes toward technology" as dimensions.[1] The degree of coordination was a policy variable describing the government's role in health care. Attitudes toward technology referred to the willingness of people to try solutions based on new technologies.

In another case, in 1993, when Fleet Financial Group created a new strategy using scenarios, "freedom to act," "economic buoyancy," and "growth in customer sophistication" were adopted as dimensions that would define the future business environment within which Fleet would have to operate. Deregulation of the financial services industry had stalled in the wake of savings and loan failures. Banks, however, were fighting for more freedom to act. The buoyancy of the economy affected both the level and the nature of demand for banking services. Finally, the sophistication of their customers affected the willingness of consumers to try new delivery vehicles (such as electronic banking at home), as well as the complexity of products they will use. Various combinations of these dimensions resulted in very different market environments for bankers.

Ironically, elements that are absolutely critical to a firm's future often make poor scenario dimensions. It's a bit like saying, "If the sky fell tomorrow, how would our business operate?" A good rule of thumb is to select dimensions that can produce a positive or negative impact and that cannot be affected by the firm. This usually means that the dimensions should be a step removed from the specific organization. So for the U.S. Air Force, "reduction or increase in the U.S. defense budget" would make a poor choice for a dimension. The Air Force would want to understand the conditions that caused the change in funding so they could better understand how that change would affect its strategic options. For IBM, "breakthroughs in critical technologies" may not be the best dimension. IBM has a chance to affect the probability that the breakthrough will occur. They will learn much more from analyzing how to enhance the probability of a needed breakthrough given a different condition with which they must cope.

Equal parts of analysis and imagination are required to define the dimensions. Usually, we will find a number of themes that meet our requirements, but that seem to operate independently of other factors. These will not make good dimensions because we need themes with subtle relationships with each other to produce the kind of complex interactions that occur in the real world. Eventually, a small group of dimensions, usually three to five, emerge that, taken together, can explain variations in the majority of drivers. Using these themes as dimensions, we can now define the scenario space. This scenario space can be shown graphically. The Netherlands health care scenarios were defined by only two driving forces, as shown in Exhibit 7.2.

As discussed earlier, a group of scenarios needs to be chosen that encompass the greatest divergence among the drivers and dimensions, and in which a full range of opportunities and threats can be explored. The first step is to characterize each of the worlds that would be defined by

Exhibit 7.2
The Netherlands Health Care Scenario Space

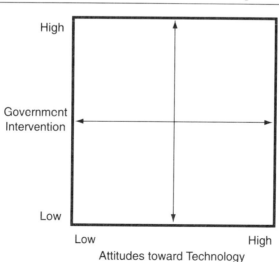

combinations of the dimensions. For example, using the Fleet Financial Group dimensions, consider a world characterized by a high degree of freedom to act, a buoyant economy, and rapid growth in customer sophistication. This must be a fast-paced world and, we thought, a world driven by markets.

We examined eight different worlds and developed a notion of what each might be like. The next step was to choose the worlds that would be most helpful for planning. A series of questions such as the following helped:

- Which world is a "dream" world?
- Which world is the "nightmare" world?
- Which world is the most surprising?
- Which world is most like today?

At The Futures Group, we typically develop our scenarios at selected extremes of the dimensions. Thus, for us, two dimensions define a square with four corners (possible end states); 3 dimensions define a cube with 8 possible end states; four dimensions define 16 possible end states; and so on. Usually it is not necessary to fully develop all the possibilities defined by the scenario space. Our rule of thumb is to select the smallest number that, as a set, includes the full range of opportunities and threats that will be faced. In the Fleet Financial scenario project, with three dimensions, eight end states were possible. We chose five scenarios to develop. Their names are shown within the scenario space that was used to define them in Exhibit 7.3.

Next, the work of writing the scenarios commences. It begins with the characteristics matrix, which catalogues the condition of each of the drivers in the end state of each of the scenarios. Suppose the U.S. economy is a driver in a set of scenarios. It could be strong with low inflation and interest rates in one scenario; strong with rising inflation and interest rates in another; hobbled by stagflation in a third; and collapsing with concomitant low inflation and falling interest rates in a fourth.

The characteristics matrix defines each aspect of the scenarios separately. It is rich in detail, but does not yet convey the fabric of a real world. It is like the outline an author might put together before starting to write. This "writer's guide" must be carefully tested for internal consistency and redone until it passes. The scenario team must determine the condition of each of the drivers by asking themselves

Exhibit 7.3
Fleet Financial Scenario Space

Driving Forces			Scenarios
Freedom to Act	Economic Buoyancy	Customer Sophistication	
High	High	High Growth	*Free Market Triumphs*
High	High	Low Growth	
High	Low	High Growth	*Cutthroat*
High	Low	Low Growth	*Cost-Driven*
Low	High	High Growth	*USA, Inc.*
Low	High	Low Growth	
Low	Low	High Growth	
Low	Low	Low Growth	*Sustained Malaise*

what each would be like given the dimensions that have been assumed. Then they must assure that each is consistent with all the other drivers within a scenario. Further adjustments need to be made as the scenario is written. During this process, a future history describing the path from today to the end state is fleshed out.

We can see the transition from outline to scenario in the Cutthroat scenario developed for Fleet Financial (see Exhibit 7.4). As delineated by the characteristics matrix, GNP growth is moderate, volatile, and unpredictable. In the scenario, this translates to a rapid succession of business/economic crises and an end state with "maverick" businesspeople operating in a volatile environment. The dry description of consumers' attitude toward wealth determination and savings is similarly translated into authentic human responses: A world of brutal price and nonprice competition and street-smart consumers, who have grown cynical, jump for the best deal. Fads and get-rich-quick schemes proliferate to the extent that they seem to pervade all parts of society. This scenario raises many issues that are quite challenging for the banking industry.

Imaginatively drawn but highly relevant end states can effectively call into question management's sacred cows. For example, scenarios completed for the Air Force in 1983–1984, helped it prepare successfully for missions in a future less threatening in terms of nuclear confrontation but just as dangerous because of new emerging political and technological threats. Though the withering of long-powerful antagonists and the rise

Exhibit 7.4
Worlds of Fleet Financial Shows a Few Excerpts from
Some of the Worlds Developed in 1992–1993 for That Firm

	USA, Inc.	Cutthroat	Cost-Driven
GNP growth	Early steady moderate growth; high at end of the period	Moderate, volatile, unpredictable	Low; uneven among sectors
Confidence in the future	Very high and with a national purpose; Apollo image of a national goal	Low, with highly defensive attitude	Moderate but uninspired
Infrastructure building	High in private-sector spending/incentives; government guarantees new initiatives	Low by government; may be high by private; poorly coordinated	Low early; moderate later in the period; mostly patch and repair
Tax policy and structure	Focus on investment incentives; simpler; progressive	Drastically simplified	Tinkering; generally supportive of cost-sensitive environment
Attitude toward wealth, debt, and savings	Savings is in; long-term, socially responsible; household incomes rise	Get rich quick for middle class; wealthy are in a wealth preservation mode; stagnant, erratic household incomes	Debt avoided; "rainy day" savings orientation; household incomes fall

of potent new ones seemed unlikely in 1984, just such a future suddenly came to pass with the fall of the Berlin Wall and the atrophy of Russian military power.

It is also important to build into scenarios the kind of instability that in the real world threatens to disrupt current trends and relationships. For example, Japanese cars enjoyed a cost advantage over their American competition for many years, but eventually the many successes of the Japanese economy were bound to impact the dollar/yen exchange rate. By late 1995, with a dollar worth only a little over 80 yen, Japanese cars had to overcome a cost disadvantage in many areas. For a short time, American car makers enjoyed a "boomlet." Now, with a year of strong appreciation of the dollar against the yen in 1996 and 1997, and imports selling well again, U.S. car manufacturers are worried that they will lose substantial share to Japanese car makers.

Good scenarios should also include some counterintuitive situations to help explore the unthinkable. For example, a company heavily dependent on continued development of the Internet might want to consider a scenario that includes extensive regulations at the state level. In this type of world, the states would be effective gatekeepers. Note that this would be only one element of a scenario, so strategies would have to be developed to deal with this regulatory nightmare in the context of many other developments.

Stress-Testing the Firm's Current Strategy.   All too often, a firm's current strategy remains isolated from the thinking and insights involved in developing a set of scenarios. As a consequence, considerable scenario learning is missed. We often inaugurate a new set of scenarios by "stress-testing" existing strategies. To do this, we ask how would the existing strategy "play" in the circumstances and conditions of each scenario world. Often, such stress-testing identifies potential weaknesses of the current strategy, suggesting that the company would not win against certain types of rivals in the conditions inherent in one or more scenarios.

Scenario-Specific Strategies

At the end of this stage, there will be as many sets of strategies as there are scenarios. There will inevitably be areas of overlap across the sets, but there will also be areas of striking difference.

Strategy teams, one for each scenario, are assembled to develop strategies that are specific to the circumstances and conditions in each scenario world. It may be useful to have an outsider facilitate these groups. Outsiders typically are not beholden to any individuals within the organization and have not been subjected to the conventional wisdom as defined and shaped by the organization. It is essential, however, that a policy-level executive lead each team to assure ownership of the strategies. The team can include managers from the various functions, such as planning, marketing, and finance, that would usually contribute to strategy. Also, it is helpful if the team members have some participation in the selection and preparation of the scenarios.

Each of these groups develops a set of strategies that would optimize results if their world actually occurred. We call this process Adopt-a-World.® It is arduous, but filled with discovery, as unfamiliar business environments provide fresh perspectives on daily business challenges. The use of separate teams to work in each scenario tends to maximize the creativity that is put into each set of strategies.

By assigning separate teams to each scenario, their focus is kept to creating a strategy to maximize the benefit to their organization, given that scenario. If, however, the same team works in several scenarios, there is often a secondary focus on which scenario is more likely or which is more pessimistic. Often, a team creating strategies for two scenarios will develop defensive strategies for the more pessimistic, while a team working only in that world will have a greater tendency to find hidden opportunities.

Even scenarios that seem familiar can offer surprises. For example, sensitized by the experience of "living in" an alternative scenario, one manager suddenly caught a glimpse of his real current world from a different perspective and exclaimed, "We're doing everything wrong!" In another workshop, when a manager tried to operate his company's current strategy in the scenario he was assigned to live in, he said in frustration, "We're totally unprepared for this world!"

Robust Core Strategies

The central challenge is to identify core strategies—robust ones, suitable for a wide variety of possible futures—that contribute to competitive advantage. But beware of vague strategies such as "do good and fight evil," which although appropriate in a wide variety of circumstances, are not specific enough to guide most resource allocation issues. One organization determined that a core strategy of adding a (previously unidentified) service element to a line of manufactured products conferred competitive advantage in most imaginable futures.

All the strategies are tested in each world to ascertain which will work in the full variety of business environments. Strategies from each scenario world are inserted into the rest of the worlds to see if they are appropriate in other situations; or if, though required to respond to peculiarities of one world, they would be inappropriate or even damaging in other situations. For example, the strategy of U.S. steelmakers to drive costs down through ever greater economies was fine when their customers' buying decisions hinged primarily on price, but when customization and quality became more important than price, the giant mills were ill-equipped to compete with the minimills that sprang up.

Contingent Strategies

Of course, more than the core strategy is required to run the business, a lesson that can sometimes become painfully clear when the business environment changes suddenly. Scenarios help companies think the unthinkable, and prepare contingency plans to respond. In the 1970s, many banks focused their full attention on their core strategy—making back-office operations efficient, a means of gaining advantage over rival banks and other financial institutions. But when banks in New England relaxed their lending criteria to ride the real estate boom in the Northeast, they were devastated when that boom turned into a bust.

There are generally two types of contingent strategies:

- *Strategy Additions.* Strategy additions are appended to the set of active strategies. These are designed to respond to some specific aspect of the environment that requires an approach that is appropriate only to that particular set of circumstances. These strategies are not robust and may actually hurt the firm in some environments. For example, a pharmaceutical firm might prepare to shift its information strategy in the event that health care providers consolidate into a few massive HMOs, but it would have a very different information strategy if that key customer group remained fragmented.
- *Strategy Deletions.* Strategy deletions are removed from the set of active strategies. Sometimes, as in the case of IBM's support of the "glass house" of centralized computing, shifts in technology and customer needs can invalidate a long-standing strategy. IBM's steadfast belief that its mainframe computers were protected from technological threat blindsided it to the onslaught of emerging technologies and the rapid growth of network computers. Scenarios, by focusing on the world outside the company's walls, help identify the conditions that could force abandonment of a current strategy.

The core strategy by itself is typically only about half of what is needed to succeed: Contingent strategies will also be necessary to deal with specific challenges. For example, political or regulatory changes, such as the gradual relaxation of laws governing companies in the financial services industry, can necessitate extensive overhauls of firms' strategies to reach their customers, form relationships, and create competitive barriers to protect their relationships. A financial services company that used scenarios to develop a new strategy found that low cost and consolidation of several segments within a defined geography was a robust strategy. Changes in regulatory constraints, however, would change the peripheral industries and geographic regions enough to force the financial services company to move into some new segments of the market. It developed a contingent strategy to enter the new markets and identified the conditions under which they would start that process.

Early Warning Triggers

Once a contingent strategy has been developed, it is important to know when to use it. If the company has a business intelligence capability, early warning triggers should be a focus of some of their external environment scanning and monitoring programs. The financial services firm in this example will obviously need to track the regulatory environment for changes that will ease the entry of nontraditional competitors from adjacent industry segments. These early warning triggers must be tied to the appropriate contingent strategy. The primary research investment of one large firm did not make it into the core strategy because its vulnerability was exposed by two scenarios: It would not win under the conditions of these scenarios. That did not mean that the research was a poor investment, but it did mean that an early watch program was necessary to assure a quick response to conditions that would imperil the investments. That company is pursuing what is essentially a contingency strategy with huge investments, but is tracking consumer acceptance of the new technologies very carefully.

SPECIFIC USES OF SCENARIOS

Corporate Scenarios

At the corporate level, scenarios are used to identify the corporate strategies viable against the range of future opportunities and threats. Scenario-based planning at this level is not a one-time exercise but the foundation of a planning process that is self-renewing and contributes to a learning organization. It can provide a platform for focused strategy work at the divisional level. These projects are resource-intensive and time-consuming, since extensive research, workshop interaction, creativity, and scenario-contingent business model development are required.

Corporate-level scenarios have always had the potential for extensive and creative use throughout the organization, but until recently, targeted applications below the level of corporate strategy have not received sufficient attention. The case for doing so is compelling. If product planners, marketing strategists, and human resource managers, to name a few, all utilized the same set of scenario-derived assumptions and insights, far better coordination and many more stimulating contributions would emerge. No longer would everyone craft his or her own (often mutually exclusive) assumptions about future operating conditions. A musical metaphor helps explain why this is true. The corporate platform scenarios are the rich and complex orchestration. Functional units and divisions can utilize the sheet music as-is, or develop harmonized "variations on the theme." In this way rigid, top-down planning is avoided, but coordination is facilitated and maximum innovation is encouraged. The business unit's deliverables are similar to those at the corporate level, but there will be more extensive work on contingency strategies, and the strategies will be carried to a more detailed level.

Scenarios for Scanning and Monitoring External Change and Trends

A company looking for diversification opportunities may sometimes use scenarios as a tool to identify interesting emerging opportunities. These days, companies participating in the computer and communications industries are all focused on how to take advantage of networking opportunities. This is an obvious arena that will spawn many new products and services. But what if the communications structure proves to be inadequate or unreliable, or is regulated in an inconsistent way (for example with state or city regulations creating effective "toll booths" at the entrance to local jurisdictions)? Scenarios about this environment may suggest completely different opportunities. If a product or service can be identified that would also work in the world of highly reliable, low-cost, unregulated bandwidth, wouldn't it be worth considering?

Scenarios to Prioritize Large-Scale Research Activities

Research directors must try to see into a murky future with rapidly changing technologies, uncertain regulations, voracious competitors, and seemingly fickle consumers. Yet companies have to place "bets" on areas that are most likely to be fruitful in the time it will take to get a new technology to market. This can range from months in some fashion industries to decades in industries like defense or pharmaceuticals. In practice, research investments (as opposed to strategies) are subordinated to the overall strategy of the business unit that funds the research. Only when expenditures are disproportionately large, such as the 10 to 15 percent of revenue that pharmaceutical companies spend on research, would we recommend using scenarios to analyze these investments activities.

Most product research is driven by technology. It is ironic then that technology should almost never be a dimension; as scenario developers and users, we are interested in learning about the forces that drive technology change. Since the dimensions are, after all, fixed (most typically as high or low), they are not left to be analyzed or manipulated by managers who are using scenarios. Technology is too important to treat as a fixed assumption when our focus is on understanding what research should be supported and why. Pharmaceutical firms, computer makers, or weapons manufacturers all need to think about which technologies to pursue in a variety of different future environments. In most ways, scenarios focused on research and technology are similar to scenarios developed for strategy. They tend to have a slightly longer time horizon and to include a little more about the host industry, but are otherwise similar. (For a more detailed discussion of this topic, see Chapter 13.)

Scenarios for Competitive Gaming

Competitive gaming is a process in which managers try to determine what a specific competitor will do when confronted with a new environment. This requires detailed information about the competitor's capabilities, as well as a detailed description of the new environment. In the extreme form, this becomes "war gaming" in which separate teams take the role of their own company and that of the competitor. Then a scenario is described and a referee doles out information about what developments occur, including actions of the other side that would necessarily be visible in a real situation.

Some companies, though satisfied with their strategies, are vulnerable to competitive actions that could redefine the market. In this case, key questions they need to ask include:

- What could our competitors do that would disrupt our current plans?
- Which new competitors could change the game with an entry from a peripheral position (such as supplier, partner, or customer)?
- Which new technologies could nontraditional competitors apply in our industry that would change the way things are done?

Issues to be tested revolve around the infrastructure of the industry: What does the value chain look like and where is the greatest leverage? The scenarios in this instance can be written to give more detail about the industry. They must not, however, give specific information about the competitors that are to be examined. We want to be able to imagine how a competitor might respond to our own actions in different situations. The scenarios can be much simpler to craft because they don't require as much background about how the end state develops, and they are, therefore, more tightly focused on issues that are well known to the user.

Industry-Focused Scenarios

Let's examine a U.S. cigarette industry case. The U.S. cigarette market is highly concentrated, with only a few producers in the United States. There are enormous external forces exerting influence on the industry, but the direction of the influence is clearly evident. For example, increasing societal pressure from nonsmokers is steadily curtailing the freedom of smokers in preference to the protection of non-smokers. Specific legislative changes such as further restrictions on cigarette advertising could have a huge negative impact on the cost of acquiring new customers. The major strategic issues in the United States seem to revolve around these clearly delineated influences and do not seem to be affected particularly strongly by other, more general political, economic, or social issues from outside the tobacco industry.

As a consequence, a set of scenarios narrowly focused on the specific infrastructure of the cigarette industry might be a preferable backdrop for strategic planning in this instance. Macro issues, particularly regulation, can and should be included, but they are very clear and tend to operate independently of most other outside issues. The distribution chain and technologies that might be applied by nontraditional competitors that do not have an existing product at risk could provide an appropriate focus for competitive gaming.

CONCLUSION

There are many approaches to developing scenarios, and no single approach is ideal in all situations because they are adopted with varying objectives in mind. This chapter has outlined one approach that has been used by many different types of organizations. It can be adapted for quite distinct uses ranging from broad strategy setting to scenarios for competitive gaming. Whatever their purpose, scenarios invariably help a group of managers test the likelihood that their organization's current business model or success formula will succeed in the alternative futures that may confront them.

A well-designed scenario process has great value the first time it is used but, like a good wine, it improves with age. The tool promotes mental agility by opening minds to multiple possibilities. As one executive said, "If you use scenarios, you'll never read the newspaper the same way again."

CHAPTER 8

DYNAMIC SCENARIOS: SYSTEMS THINKING MEETS SCENARIO PLANNING

EDWARD WARD and AUDREY E. SCHRIEFER

The real world is an ever evolving system, not a static set of conditions that provide enduring landmarks on the landscape of the future. This chapter studies the competitive arena and the broader social and political environment facing business organizations in terms of its complexity and dynamism. Scenarios are one tool for this study. Another is the new discipline of systems thinking. Profound and rapid learning can occur when scenario planning and systems thinking are employed together.

Scenarios depict various imaginary worlds, environments in which an organization's strategy will play out against its rivals. In the real world of competition, however, Newton's Third Law applies: Every competitive action will set off a reaction. And every reaction changes the environment. The real world is an ever evolving system, not a static set of conditions that can be charted on a matrix. In practice, the competitive arena and the broader social and political environment facing business organizations should be studied in terms of their complexity and dynamism.

Complexity refers to the multiplicity of variables that must be considered and the variety of relationships that can exist among them. Dynamism accounts for the types and rates of change that can occur. This chapter shows how scenario learning is increased by an approach that regards the environments in which organizations operate as systems of dynamic complexity. We call the methodology for preparing and using this type of futures analysis *dynamic scenarios*.

In this chapter, using an example from the automobile industry, we explain in detail the steps involved in developing these dynamic scenarios and show how they can be instrumental in the development and evaluation of strategic alternatives.

SYSTEMS THINKING: THE ENGINE OF DYNAMIC SCENARIOS

The concept of dynamic scenarios advocated in this chapter stems from the application of a large body of systems research to the development and use of scenarios. One fundamental principle, reflected in the work of leading systems theorists such as Russell Ackoff, Jay Forrester, C. West Churchman, and Peter Senge, is that complexity and dynamism can best be understood in the context of a "system." Such a system, as succinctly delineated by Ackoff, "is a set of two or more interrelated elements of any kind: for example, concepts (as in the number system), objects (as in a telephone system, or in the human body), or people (as in a social system) . . . a whole that can be divided into parts."

A characteristic of any system is that the behavior of each element has an effect on the behavior of the system as a whole. For example, the actions of an individual doctor can affect many elements in the work system within a hospital. The actions of an individual manager can affect many of the subunits within the operational system of a corporation. The actions of customers can affect many of the other elements in the system that constitutes an industry: suppliers of raw materials and components, various manufacturers or solution providers, distribution channels, retailers, the industry association, lobbying groups, and legislative bodies, among others. In short, any system is more than the sum of its parts.

Another fundamental principle of systems thinking is that one must view the world simultaneously from three levels: events, patterns of behaviors, and structure.

A Simple Business System

We can best explain this three-level view by putting events, patterns of behaviors, and structure in the context of a simple but common business system: the logistics and sales system that connects a manufacturing firm to its many customers. In this system, we'll focus on observing the effect of delivery delays on product sales.

- *Events.* An example of an event is each sale to each customer. These events are recorded in a report, showing the number of products sold in the prior month.
- *Patterns of Behavior.* The report includes a chart, which plots prior monthly sales over a rolling 12-month historical horizon. This graphs the pattern of behavior of the monthly sales rate. The pattern demonstrates a healthy sales increase up until six months earlier, when the sales rate flattened out and then turned down slightly.
- *Structure.* Another chart illustrates the average delivery time to the firm's customers. The pattern of behavior of delivery time over the past 12 months shows that, until eight months ago, delivery times were equal to the industry average, but then began to increase steadily. Taken together, the patterns of behavior of these two variables, monthly sales and average delivery time, suggest that an increasing average delivery time causes a decrease in sales. This relationship is a manifestation of the cause-effect-cause structure of the industry system in which this firm competes.

The implications of this simple logistics-sales illustration can be inferred: Any organization can affect greater change in its environment when it understands a system at the structural level, as opposed to the event or pattern level. For example, the organization analyzing the logistics and sales system, armed with its new understanding of the delivery-sales structure, can make a number of decisions that will shorten the average delivery time, and as a consequence, increase sales.

On the other hand, if the organization tried to fix its delivery and sales problems without understanding the structure of the system, its efforts to affect individual events, such as sales to individual customers, might result only in making some of the underlying problems even worse. For example, new sales might add to the average delivery time if the firm did not invest in additional logistics capacity such as new delivery trucks.

It is important to note that in this example the structure is not readily apparent. Instead, it had to be discovered through analysis and then compared to the mental models and experience of the organization's managers. By identifying the structure of a system, the analysts create a theory of how things really work. That is, they model how, in a particular situation, the organization's logistics and sales interact and influence each other. Creating such theories of "how things work" or how a system operates draws upon and reshapes the "mental models" of managers and other experienced members of the firm.

The goal of applying systems theory to scenarios therefore is to provide decision makers with a methodology that enables them to identify and better understand the complex relationships that are at the heart of any system and the dynamic nature of how these relationships change. The seven specific steps that characterize the application of the dynamic scenario methodology are illustrated in the automobile industry example that follows.

DYNAMIC SCENARIOS: AN APPLICATION IN THE AUTOMOBILE INDUSTRY

The automobile industry in the past 10 years, like most global industries, has undergone a period of tremendous change with increased competition, expanding markets, higher-quality standards, and changes in technology. The industry can expect further discontinuous change, possibly at an accelerated pace. For example, environmental concerns may cause a shift to alternative means of transport, force major technology shifts to cleaner vehicles, or even increase pressure to telecommute instead of driving to work.

As an illustration of the dynamic scenario methodology, we will consider a major U.S. auto manufacturer's decision to enter an emerging market in Asia. The manufacturer needed to understand the range of possibilities, and to map out strategies that were robust and adaptable under a variety of circumstances. In this case study, we will illustrate how the process was used to improve the quality and timing of decision making. This composite example is based on several engagement experiences using the dynamic scenarios methodology.

Step 1: Generate Scenario Event Ideas

The case begins when a cross-functional team within the firm is assigned to develop a successful entry and growth strategy for the target emerging market.

Intelligence Gathering.   As might be expected, this *Fortune 50* multinational company had already collected data on the competitive environment and customer demographics for the passenger and truck vehicle industry in this market. This proved to be a valuable and essential resource for the scenario team, and provided information that could be expressed in time series charts for important variables. In addition, the team probed for qualitative information by a number of the stakeholders, including suppliers, investors, customers, and employees.

Senior Management's Expectations. The information in the "mental database" of the leaders of the firm was especially valuable for developing and articulating the key strategic issues. The team conducted individual interviews with each of the senior managers of the firm responsible for making and implementing this decision. In these meetings, it became very apparent that a misguided foray into a new market could mean severe, long-lasting penalties for the firm. Concerned over the high stakes involved, the scenario team decided that the best insurance against such a blunder was to prepare a comprehensive set of scenarios for the evolution of this emerging auto market. Because this company had been very successful using the "systems thinking" approach to complex issues when making other important decisions, the team—with senior management support—selected the dynamic scenarios methodology for this project.

Focus Sessions. After organizing information about the actual and potential auto industry in this market, and about the firm's position and interests there, the strategy team recruited knowledgeable individuals from various levels in all the primary functions within the firm to participate in a series of focus sessions. Each session included a few "maverick thinkers," people whose opinions about the future did not usually conform with those of their colleagues.

Briefings. The focus groups were informed that the sessions would be their opportunity to participate in the creation of a number of comprehensive, plausible, but distinctly different, scenarios describing the future of their industry in this target region. They knew that these scenarios were to be used to test several alternative strategies. Because they would have to implement the strategy that was ultimately selected, the participating mangers understood why it was in their best interest to take part in the half-day meetings.

Clues to the Future. The focus question for each session was: When we consider the vehicle industry in this market over the next 15 years, what are the most important or interesting events, factors, be-haviors, conditions, or outcomes we might observe during that period? All participants had an opportunity to think individually about this question for a few minutes and to list their answers. Then they were in-vited to briefly share their insights, ideas, or issues with each other. The facilitators used a "nominal group technique" that is somewhat different from traditional brainstorming. Each member of the group was asked, in turn, to contribute one of his or her ideas, but without duplicating an idea already expressed. For example, one said: "As soon as demand for cars begins to develop, the government will double the tax it puts on gas." Each person spent a minute or two explaining why his or her conception of future events was important, and how and when it might occur. The facilitators documented each idea and its story in a short "headline" and posted it on the wall of the meeting room where all participants could see it. For example, the complex idea linking demand for autos and government need for revenues was cap-tured in the headline: "Government Likely to Double Gas Tax." In a typical session, between 60 and 100 *event ideas* were generated and posted sequentially on the wall.

Step 2: Discover Scenario Dimensions

After the participants in the focus sessions had a chance to express their ideas about plausible future events, the facilitators helped them arrange the ideas into groupings of events that seemed to "belong together," such as target customers, price, market size, and infrastructure requirements. Each of these "event clusters" was labeled with a memorable word or phrase that captured its meaning for the group. That cluster label is also called a *scenario dimension*.

Each focus group generated about 75 event ideas that fit into 7 to 10 separate scenario dimensions. This first event-clustering exercise is very important because each scenario dimension is a clue to discovering an im-portant determinant of the future that the scenario should address. In this case of the emerging vehicle market, for example, the event clustering work by the focus groups suggested a number of important dimensions of future conditions, including: new products, production capacity, techno-logical breakthroughs, dealer development, pricing, macroeconomics, gov-ernment regulations, environmental factors, competitor strategies, energy policies, and many more.

As a result of several focus sessions, the strategy team had collected several hundred potential scenario event ideas grouped into scores of scenario dimensions. There were, as would be expected, many duplicates. After the team eliminated the duplicate events and scenario dimensions, a complete set of clustered events was documented with flowcharting software. All members of the team and the focus groups were given a copy so they would have a record of this phase of their work.

Step 3: Develop Divergent Scenario Themes

At this point, the strategy team set out to develop several distinctively different perspectives or *scenario themes* based on what had been learned thus far in the research, the interviews, and in the focus groups, on how the future of the vehicle industry in this emerging market could plausibly unfold.

The work of developing scenario themes involves selecting significant events, from the scenario dimensions developed in Step 2 and reorganizing them into several scenario themes. Events can be considered significant, if they have an impact in several scenario dimensions, like volume of imports, cost of fuel, or number of dealers, for example.

The scenario theme clusters are new groupings of events that could logically fit together. For example, the event "large truck demand grows rapidly in 1997" would not fit with the scenario idea: "pullback in road and highway construction." Instead, the team members looked for events within the scenario dimensions, that, when woven together, would create the elements of a provocative, but logically consistent story.

The facilitators encouraged the strategy team to organize emergent scenario themes that suggested significantly different futures such as rapid growth/prosperity versus slow growth/stagnation. This was possible because often two or more events within a scenario dimension could not reasonably exist in the same future! The team looked for events that suggested very divergent futures.

The team began to develop interesting sets of possibilities. This process continued until all the events were contained in five different scenario themes. On careful inspection, it was decided that two of these themes were not sufficiently different to lead to new insights and they were folded into the other three. The team members then reviewed the scenario themes and assigned a preliminary name to each that symbolized its core meaning or message.

In this vehicle industry case, the preliminary scenario themes that emerged were:

Scenario theme A: Overarching Environmental Concerns

Scenario theme B: Power and Status Needs Predominate

Scenario theme C: Bifurcation in the Developing Economy

As the group worked to assemble related ideas into scenario themes, the facilitators made notes when the team members commented on relationships among the events as they repositioned them. The facilitators sketched these relationships in simple diagrams. This became the start of the process to understand the dynamics at work in the system under consideration—that is, the forces driving economic growth and the impact of a major new competitor into this market.

Step 4: Discern Patterns of Behavior

The strategy team looked into each of the scenario themes they had created to identify 10 or so events that seemed to be the most important to the underlying story of that theme. For example, the theme Power and Status Needs Predominate required a dramatic increase in "attractiveness of vehicle ownership" and "nonfarm employment." These events were important to the team because of their potential impact on the success of the auto maker's entry into this market. The team needed to understand and describe the key variables associated with these events.

The team looked for three types of variables:

- *Hard variables.* These included expected car sales, the number of employees to be hired, or the number of people in a market who can afford to become customers or who have a use for the product. These are the variables that can be counted, and they include financial and operating unit measures. For example: In 1994, the estimated gross domestic product per capita in this market was $3,600. Competitors' sales only increased from 8,000 vehicles in 1995 to 8,500 vehicles in 1995.
- *Performance measure variables.* These include sales growth rates, ratios of performance to costs, market share, or other financial and operational evaluations.

- *Soft variables.* These are preferences, expectations, confidence levels, and other variables that are difficult to measure quantitatively but are of critical importance to the success of a strategy. Examples include: In 1995, 24 percent of potential buyers in this market had an expectation of vehicle ownership within five years. A survey report put confidence in a pro-import policy at a score of 4.3 out of 10.

In the auto case, the next step was to track how these three types of variables changed over time in this market and in similar developing markets. The purpose was to understand the way these variables were likely to change in the future based on their past performance.

Exhibit 8.1
A Buyer Saturation Problem

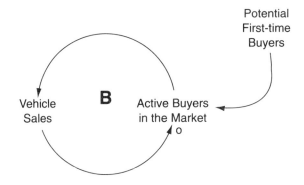

The annual sales rate in the emerging market will not grow because there are just not enough active buyers in the market. Until there are more people who are capable of coming into the market, it does not make sense for us to make investments there.

Key to symbols in the causal loop diagrams:

"R" denotes a "reinforcing" feedback loop.

"B" denotes a "balancing" feedback loop.

"o" at an arrowhead signifies that the associated "effect" variable changes in an "opposite" direction from the "cause" variable at the source of the arrow. When an "o" is not present, the linked cause-and-effect variables move in the same direction. *An odd number of "o's" in a feedback loop determines it to be a balancing loop. An even number of "o's" (or none) indicates a reinforcing feedback loop.*

"=" or "||" crossing a link means there is a significant delay between the cause and its effect.

Step 5: Diagram Scenario Structures

After the team had identified the set of key variables associated with each scenario theme, they noticed that the scenario themes shared many of the same variables, such as pace of economic growth, oil price, and vehicle purchase price. The team then analyzed how these variables could be linked in relationships, which they sketched in simple causal loop diagrams. The diagrams made by the facilitators—those described in Step 3 that were based on the relationships between events—were especially helpful here.

Many causal loop diagrams were created, often sharing one or more of the scenario variables. Examples are presented in Exhibits 8.1 through 8.6. These causal loop diagrams, each describing only a small piece of the story, could then be joined to create one diagram of the entire system.

Exhibit 8.2
Making It Attractive to Own a Vehicle

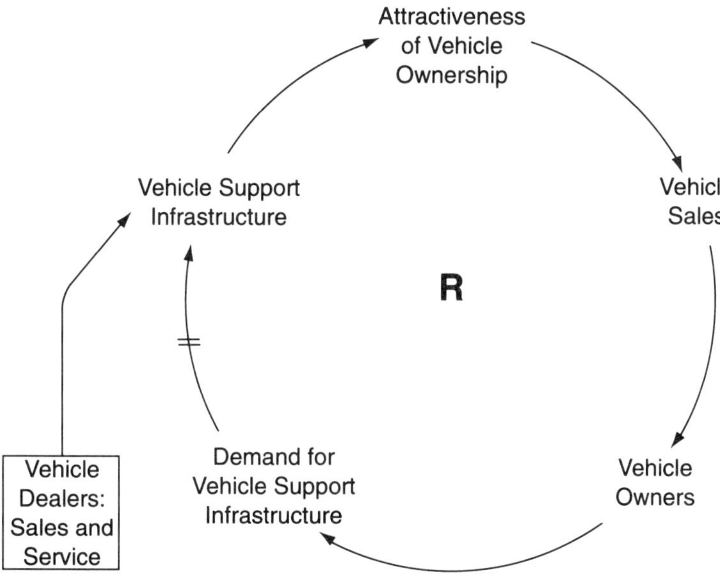

The sales rate has not grown because, for most people, it is not sensible for them to own a vehicle. Prices are extremely high relative to their incomes. There are too few dealers, and they are too far away to provide the service and support an owner would need. Beyond that, the quality and scale of the road network is not well suited for many of the models we now sell. The vehicle owners in the country today do not, by themselves, have the influence necessary to demand greater investment in vehicle support infrastructure.

Exhibit 8.3
Economic Growth Stimulated by Vehicles, Roads, and Highways

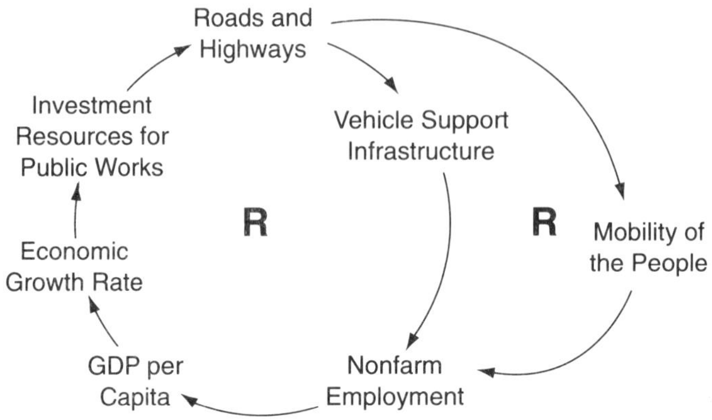

We have seen some authentic indications of economic growth. Nonfarm employment has increased, and the GDP per person has increased steadily over the past five years. This accelerating economic grow rate, combined with the willingness of the government to work with Western investors, has allowed the IMF to arrange investments in the country's infrastructure. The more of that investment that goes into roads and highways, the more opportunity and resources will be there to provide the mobility for people to leave rural agriculture for construction and manufacturing jobs.

This diagram of the complex system is a *dynamic scenario generator* (DSG). In this example, the emerging DSG is illustrated in Exhibit 8.7, which combines all of the variables introduced in Exhibits 8.1 through 8.6.

At this point in the process, the development team had a preliminary dynamic scenario generator representing their theory of how many of the principle variables in the system interact with one another.

Step 6: Write the Scenario Scripts

The dynamic scenario generator (DSG) is a low-tech, high-leverage tool to model the dynamics within complex systems. With this diagram as a plot outline and the scenario themes to provide content, the team was able to write scripts for plausible but distinctly different scenarios by assuming a substantial and significant change to one of the key variables, or *critical uncertainties*. For example, the team could assume that the worldwide price of oil plummets, and then trace this effect

Exhibit 8.4
Imbed Dealerships and Distributors in the Power Structure

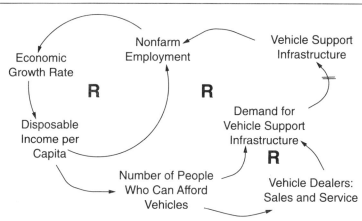

It seems to take a while for the economic growth rate to produce an average disposable income per person that is sufficient to generate the justification for launching dealerships. Yet when that happens, these local businesspeople, with ties to the government work hard to build the demand for better vehicle support infrastructure. And this is a very good thing for the economy. There is little doubt that a healthy vehicle industry, tied to growth in road building, has been a powerful force for economic growth in many developed and developing nations.

throughout the DSG. Because a dramatic change in this variable caused many other variables to shift direction, a set of logically consistent responses began to occur, like falling dominoes. The stories that emerged by tracing the logical response to this dramatic change throughout the DSG were logical and plausible scenarios.

Tracing the three scenario themes through the DSG, their stories began to take shape and change direction in previously unanticipated ways. The themes developed into the following scenarios:

Scenario A: The Green Unmachine is a future where environmental concerns drive the demand for small, lightweight, fuel-efficient vehicles, renewable fuel sources, advanced forms of mass transit and alternatives to commuting.

Scenario B: Re-creating the American Dream says that customers in the emerging market want the power, style, and prestige associated with their newly acquired affluence and competitive spirit.

Exhibit 8.5
The Role of Dealers in the Market Is Critical

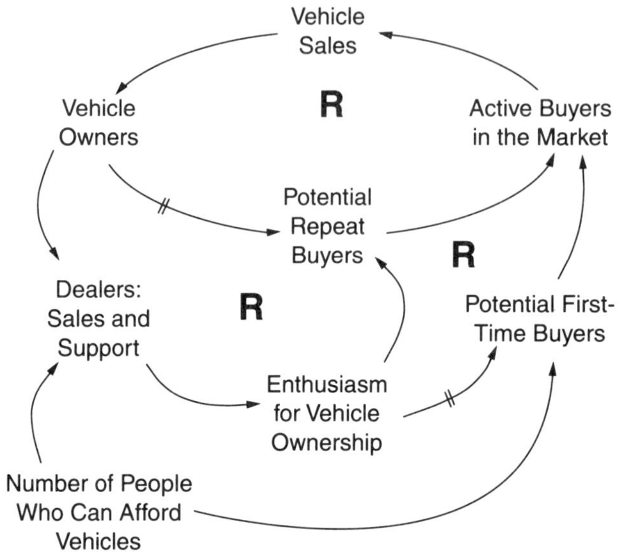

The role of dealers in the development of the market is critical. At the earliest signal that there is a healthy increase in the number who can afford vehicles, even used ones, then we need to get influential dealers onboard. Through them, we will stimulate enthusiasm for owning a car, especially our brand. We will attract owners of competitive brands, who will come over to us. The important thing is dealer presence. That is what is necessary to build vehicle sales.

Scenario C: Road to Nowhere assumes that only a small fraction of the population has sufficient disposable income to afford a personal automobile, and the infrastructure of dealerships, highways, and service stations continues to be underdeveloped.

Each of these scenarios was written as a two-page narrative story. The DSG that the team created could be used to generate a wide variety of scenarios. The team wisely limited the number to those that were significantly different to provide some strategic insights and to be clear, memorable, and compelling.

Exhibit 8.6
Some Factors Influencing the Cost of Vehicle Ownership

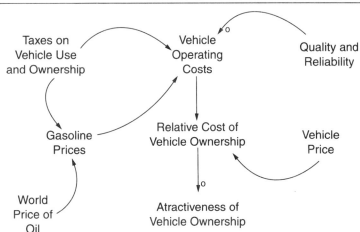

There are several factors that work to reduce the attractiveness of vehicle ownership in the market by making the cost of vehicle ownership very high. A high initial price, especially for new cars is one; and high vehicle operating costs are another. The price of oil, reflected in gasoline prices can adversely increase operating costs, especially when high tax rates are levied on gasoline sales. In all, there is a lot to overcome to make vehicle ownership sufficiently attractive to a lot of people in this market.

Step 7: Assess Strategic Choices

Using some of the accepted strategic management tools for developing alternative investment and operating choices, sets of compatible options were organized and labeled as distinctive strategies:

Strategy 1. Invest heavily in marketing and infrastructure with standard products.

Strategy 2. Acquire or develop major new technology to tailor products to this market.

Strategy 3. Enter with minimal investment to test the market.

The next step was to test the quality of each of these strategies by considering how well it would work in each of the scenarios. The dynamic scenarios matrix (see Exhibit 8.8) is a way of assessing the interaction of

Exhibit 8.7
A Dynamic Scenario Generator for the Vehicle Industry

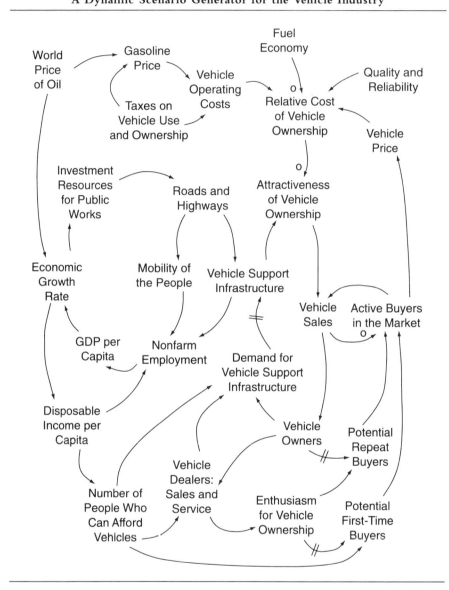

Exhibit 8.8
Dynamic Scenario Matrix

Scenarios Strategies	Scenario A: The Green Unmachine	Scenario B: Re-Creating the American Dream	Scenario C: Road to Nowhere
Strategy 1: Heavy spending on entry with standard products	**Poor:** New products are favored over standard products.	**Good:** Low cost producer wins!	**Disaster:** Over-capacity destroys the company.
Strategy 2: Acquire or develop major new platform technology	**Good:** New tech wins, if the right one. Difficult to do internally.	**Poor:** High-tech development costs make offering non-competitive.	**Poor:** New tech generates limited new markets for firm.
Strategy 3: Enter with minimal investment to test the market	**Poor:** Misses the opportunity to share in industry growth.	**Fair:** Capacity may be attractive to industry consolidators.	**Good:** Avoids over-capacity penalties. 4p2

a strategy with a set of scenarios. The rows of the matrix relate to strategies, and the columns relate to the scenarios. At the intersection of a row and a column, the consequence of each strategy within each scenario can be evaluated.

The result of this evaluation was an assessment of the overall robustness of each strategy. Based on this analysis, the team could look for:

1. *No-risk strategies that work across all of the scenarios.* These can, therefore, be implemented with confidence. In this example, none of the strategies met this criterion.
2. *High-risk strategies that work in one or more scenarios.* These should be further assessed for their risk/reward ratio and implemented only if it is determined that the potential paybacks for the firm are sufficient to justify putting substantial resources behind making it happen.
3. *No-go strategies that don't work in any of the scenarios.* These can be eliminated without a second thought. Surprisingly, they are often the same strategies that the firm would have implemented if they had not gone through this process.

Because most of the strategies fell into the second category, the team had more work to do. They sought to understand more fully the impact of key variables and their driving forces, to hone the potential strategies, to refine the scenarios, and to assess risk and rewards. This leads us into the next step.

Do It All Again: The Iterative Process

A number of important new variables emerged from the discussion and evaluation of the dynamic scenario matrix. One example was Acceptability of Western Ideals. These variables and their historic patterns of behavior depicting their past performance indicated how they might be expected to perform in the future. In this example, research showed that much of the local culture was already interested in Western music and language.

Next the team added these variables to the dynamic scenario generator linking them in cause-effect relationships. As the DSG was being enhanced, the team traced alternative paths that led to different scenarios in order to test the logic and validity of the diagram.

Once these structural relationships had been satisfactorily described, the team had the basis for a great number of plausible scenarios. New scenarios were created simply by selecting an important, high-leverage variable and making a dramatic change in its direction to see how relationships in the system would change. These new scenarios led to a more sophisticated discussion of strategic options. The dynamic scenario matrix was then revised to reflect what was learned.

CONCLUSION: DYNAMIC SCENARIOS SUPPORT ORGANIZATIONAL LEARNING

"Perhaps the single greatest liability of management teams is that they confront complex dynamic realities with a language designed for simple static problems," warns Peter Senge, author of *The Fifth Discipline*. He proposes that the basic purpose of a learning organization is to continually expand and create its future. We concur, and believe that both profound and rapid learning occur when scenario planning and systems thinking are employed. The dynamic scenarios methodology combines the two approaches.

CHAPTER 9

SIMULATION MODELS: A TOOL FOR RIGOROUS SCENARIO ANALYSIS

MARK PAICH and ROY HINTON

This chapter shows how simulation can make the scenario-planning process more effective. It presents case studies of simulations used by a variety of corporations and not-for-profit organizations. It has five sections:

1. *Scenarios, Mental Models, and Mental Simulations outlines the relationship between scenario analysis and simulation. This section describes tested procedures for developing and using simulations in scenario analysis.*
2. *Scenarios, Computer Models, and Computer Simulations explains differences and similarities between computer models and mental models, and explores the benefits of computer models in the scenario analysis process.*
3. *Integrating Simulation and Scenarios shows a detailed application of as-simulation in one large consumer goods company.*
4. *Additional Examples of Simulation in Scenario Analysis provides overviews of several additional applications.*
5. *Guidelines for Implementing Simulations in Scenario Analysis offers practical suggestions for integrating simulation with scenario planning.*

SCENARIOS, MENTAL MODELS, AND MENTAL SIMULATIONS

All managers are model builders by necessity. Few of us have the ability to commit to memory the complete description of a complex system. Instead, we create conceptual maps of the cause-effect relationships that we perceive to be operating in a particular situation. For example, sales managers will often explain that sales are a function of price and product features, when actually there may be many more factors affecting sales—such as service, marketing, availability, receivables policies, sales efforts, and salespersons' skills. Other functions are not exempt from a tendency to explain outcomes simplistically. Managers tend to look for one or two explanations from results and focus our efforts on changing those inputs. Managers routinely transform complex business situations into simple models. For example, in analyzing the impact of corporate downsizing, managers often focus on the direct impact of lower cost, and usually pay much less attention to the important indirect effects that downsizing can have on morale, productivity, and customer service. Consequently, there is considerable evidence that many downsizings have not produced lasting improvements in profitability.

However, mental models of the same business often differ significantly from one person in the organization to another. For example, if you ask a firm's sales manager what causes profits, you are likely to hear a different explanation—based on his or her mental model—than you would get from one of its operations managers or financial managers.

All good managers are instinctive scenario builders. Research at the University of Lund, Sweden, has provided insight into how people use scenarios to respond to uncertainty about the future. According to the researchers, effective people constantly formulate multiple action plans that can be applied to alternative future conditions. The brain also creates a "memory of the future" by remembering these action plans. Managers run mental simulations when they use their mental models to test the latest changes in the interrelationships and the important variables in their scenarios. Often, the output of the scenario builder's mental model is a series of narratives that describe the important aspects of the future environment.

Experienced managers can create scenarios reflecting their deep insight into the important relationships among important business variables. For example, in the mobile communications business, Motorola managers routinely juggle technology development, market dynamics, and long-term profitability issues. Their mental modeling allows Motorola to balance massive long-term investment requirements with the short-term need for profitability and cash flow.

In other cases, an organization's accepted mental model turned out to be a poor interpretation of reality because it was based on too little relevant experience, or the experience was systematically misinterpreted. Several experiments dealing with dynamic decision making have shown that people form poor mental models of complex systems that include multiple feedback loops, time delays, and nonlinear relationships. In these experiments, the performance of experienced managers was measured over multiple trials of a simulation. The simulations involved the formulation of strategy in a rapidly growing market as well as such operational tasks as inventory management. The experiments demonstrated that feedback relationships and time delays worsen performance significantly. Surprisingly, experience with the task does not prevent a bad situation from getting worse. In complex systems, experience is often overvalued and misinterpreted. Too often, managers misperceive the true structure of the business environment. A classic example is to link profits to unit sales. In fact, a targeted sales approach with a limited product line would significantly increase profitability.

SCENARIOS, COMPUTER MODELS, AND COMPUTER SIMULATIONS

Computer models have a lot in common with mental models. Both are based on the relationships among the important variables in a particular situation. The key difference is that in a computer model, the relationships are represented as a set of equations that can be simulated on a computer. These equations include economic, competitive, marketing, finance, and operating models for quantifying a wide range of relationships that exist in business operations. Computer simulations allow managers to derive the implications of the relationships by playing out complex interactions over time. The numerical output of a computer simulation can be displayed in either tables or graphs. For example, the output of business simulations commonly includes variables such as revenue, cost, profit, and market share, all calculated over a number of business cycles.

Many companies have used computer simulations to add significant value to the process of scenario analysis. Certainly, scenario analysis can be executed without the use of computer modeling, but it offers three unique advantages:

- Provides fuller explication of model relationships.
- Reveals implications of assumptions.
- Produces quantitative estimates.

Explication of Model Relationships.   The process of building a computer model—translating verbal statements of relationships into mathe-
matical relationships—forces managers to be precise about how their
mental models work. When creating scenarios, managers begin to articulate their assumptions about the relationships among key variables. For
example, at the consumer goods company discussed in the introduction,
the consultants began by trying to understand the relationships that drive
cost. Often, managers' knowledge of the relationships demonstrates significant insight, but the relationships are imprecisely stated and ambiguous. The process of building a computer model puts these relationships
"out on the table" where they can be scrutinized and clarified throughout the process of discussion and debate. This advantage of computer
modeling is increased when the computer models are built and simulated
by a team that is responsible for acting on the scenarios.

Implications of Assumptions.   Mental models are insufficient for analyzing the dynamic interactions between multiple variables. People lack
the cognitive capacity to keep track of more than a few variables at once.
If they have to track more, they soon complain about information over-
load. We tend to focus on a few numbers or items in most reports and base
our actions on them. Complaints about the need for increased focus, prioritization, and explicit goals and objective also reflect our requirements
for simplification. In contrast, computer simulations can generate the correct dynamics from very large sets of assumptions. For example, in the
case of the consumer goods company, there were numerous interactions
among the company, the market, the production facilities, and the competition. Without the computer, it would have been impossible to quickly
show how these interdependencies combined to determine revenue,
profit, and cost. The computer model processed these interactions without difficulty.

Used creatively in combination, mental models and computer models
provide a management team with a unique iterative learning experience. When employed alternatively by management teams, the crucial intuitive insights of the mental model can be supported by the information
processing power and speed of the computer model. By testing the computer model in a wide variety of business environments, management's
mental model will likely evolve and begin to generate deeper insights.
Once these new understandings are incorporated into a computer model
and tested, the results often lead to improvements in the mental model

and a much higher level of management effectiveness in an uncertain, rapidly changing environment.

Quantitative Estimates.   Computer models provide relative quantitative estimates of the effectiveness of strategies under various environmental conditions. Simulation models generate estimates for important business variables such as revenue, cost, profitability, and return on investment. These estimates provide valuable information about the relative effectiveness of policies and strategies in different environmental scenarios. For example, in the consumer goods case, the simulations revealed that raising the price on some products would reduce unit sales but would also significantly reduce the load on the factory and drastically lower cost. In addition, the model suggested that some of the sales that were lost to the competition would eventually return at significantly higher prices. These quantitative estimates demonstrated that this particular pricing strategy would be a big winner.

A Manufacturing Example

The ultimate objective of scenario analysis is to help managers choose good strategies in the face of significant uncertainty about the environment. Relative quantitative estimates of strategy effectiveness can be an important tool for determining which uncertainties are relevant. For example, a large equipment manufacturer was considering two basic strategic options for entering a large foreign market. The first option was to build a small production facility initially and to gradually expand as the market developed. The second option was to preempt the market by building several large production facilities in advance of market demand. Two of the major uncertainties were the rate of market growth and the degree of competitive entry into the market.

The analysis of a simulation model revealed that, in fact, the uncertainties about growth and competitor investment were not important. The simulations demonstrated that one of the strategies was most profitable under a wide variety of assumptions about market growth and competitor reactions. Of course, the absolute level of profitability depended on these assumptions, but one strategy dominated regardless of whether market growth was fast or slow or the competition was passive or aggressive. These uncertainties became unimportant because they had no impact on the choice of strategy.

INTEGRATING SIMULATION AND SCENARIOS: THE CASE OF A CONSUMER GOODS MANUFACTURER FACING UNPRECEDENTED CHALLENGES TO PERFORMANCE

A major consumer goods manufacturing company faced unprecedented challenges to performance. Although a recent restructuring to make the company more market-driven had increased sales, profits were down. This created a great deal of frustration in a company culture driven by sales in units. In a candid interview, the CEO described the sales areas and plants as being "out of control. The actions we take just don't resolve the problems we have, and we can't get a handle on how to make the changes we need." There was more bad news: higher turnover of personnel, more accidents, and frequent equipment breakdowns. Not surprisingly, the levels of satisfaction of distributors and customers were down.

Management's remedial efforts produced isolated good results, but didn't achieve the comprehensive changes required to improve bottom-line performance. For example, although well-designed new financial and inventory control systems was introduced at headquarters, their companywide installation was delayed.

Taking a longer range perspective, it was obvious that the business environment for the company's products and services had changed significantly in the past few years. A quick list of the consumer goods company's business problems included: excess capacity within the industry, shrinking labor supplies in major markets, changes in distribution channels, and competition from low-cost generic products of comparable quality.

Possible Solutions

The good news was that several viable turnaround strategies—reducing the product line, changing product mix, standardizing production procedures, and eliminating unprofitable business—had been developed by corporate management. However, field management teams still operated under traditions dictated by the old business model: "Simply drive sales revenues and all other good results will follow." The new challenge was: How to get the new approaches out to the field and have them successfully implemented in the least amount of time.

Top management asked consultants to develop a learning experience that would introduce managers throughout the organization to changing competitive and operating scenarios. Two of the goals were to elicit their suggestions for improving performance and to enlist their involvement in implementing new strategies.

The four steps involved in integrating computer simulation with scenario analysis are:

1. Determine the purpose of the simulation.
2. Specify the model structure.
3. Test the model with a small team of decision makers.
4. Use the computer-modeled scenarios to help groups of managers learn.

The next section describes how these steps were followed for the computer simulation project conducted for the consumer goods manufacturer.

Step 1: Determine the Purpose of the Simulation

The first step in building a computer simulation is to define a clear purpose. An effective computer model must focus on a particular issue or problem. To provide the necessary focus, write a concise statement of what a group expects to learn from the process of building and simulating the model. In arriving at an explicit purpose for the simulation, your organization's leaders should address these questions:

- What concerns do you have about current and future performance?
- How do you assess performance? What primary indicators of performance are used in your company?
- What are the performance measures you want the simulation to generate? Are there performance measures that you do not currently use that might be of value?
- What are the causes of each of the performance measures? What drives performance for each one?

Performance measures and drivers are the core variables in a simulation model. Although many of the answers regarding performance drivers are speculations, they help to reveal managers' underlying assumptions about business performance, in addition to clarifying a purpose for the simulation. In the case of the consumer goods manufacturing company, these questions were answered during individual interviews with six field sales managers, the corporate managers in charge of manufacturing, sales, quality, finance, the president and CEO. Field managers were extremely frustrated by the ineffectiveness of the current approach, which prescribed increasing unit sales as the panacea for all problems.

The individual interviews were followed by three group interviews with corporate executives. The first group interview was conducted with the corporate sales and human resources departments, the second with the manufacturing group, and the third with a mix of managers from all functions. This approach to interviewing provided an initial focus on individual concerns and concerns within key functions. The group interviews helped prioritize concerns share by several functions and suggested the most critical relationships to be included in the models. In this case, the executive team was most concerned about the continued decline in profits, increases in workforce turnover, high production costs, and accidents that caused lost time.

The many different performance measures currently used in the company were also identified through these interviews. The most significant measures applied by each of the functional areas and by key executives in the company were incorporated into the simulation models. These included a wide range of financial ratios, manufacturing costs, other production measures, quality indicators, human resource measures, and market share and sales data. Broad categories of performance drivers included pricing and discounting, product mix,and customer mix. This information provided a starting place for building initial simulation models that included exploration of interactions among marketing, sales, production, and competitive response.

Step 2: Specify Model Structure

Once the core variables are identified, relationships among these variables must be specified. For example, what is the relationship between product mix and production costs? How do various marketing and sales tactics affect product quality and on-time deliveries? What determines turnover of personnel in the plants? There is an infinite number of possible scenarios.

In this case, the core variables required the collection of data about the key relationships that determine cost and service levels at the production facilities, and about the relationships that drive unit sales and pricing, including competitive response. Interviews with managers from many locations and functional groups helped the team members determine the primary drivers of performance and the possible interactions among those drivers. Eventually, we settled on a few high-leverage decisions that could be made by management teams in the field to improve performance. These included pricing decisions, product mix, customer mix, workforce training, and limited capital investments.

This information allowed us to proceed to the next step of developing the model structure—specifying the relationships among variables included in the simulation model. For example, at the consumer goods company, the model included relationships that determined the output of a production facility, market demand, market share allocation, and interactions among operations, marketing, and sales. First, the relationships in the mental models were tested for logical consistency and against the available data. These relationships were then isolated through additional interviews with managers and calibrated against available production, sales, financial, and marketing data. The process followed was: Meetings with groups of six to eight corporate and line managers developed simple causal loop models. The procedures for these meetings were:

1. List key performance measures and causal factors (drivers) of those measures (collected during previous interviews).
2. Ask managers to discuss relationships among the performance measures and the drivers. The goal is to reveal their mental models of cause-effect relationships and then draw causal loop diagrams that reflect their assessments.
3. Ask managers to discuss the relationships among the performance measures and drivers included in the model. These questions include: Which of these causes are most important? Which would you like your field managers to change first or most? How do the primary causes (drivers) of performance interact with one another? Which of the drivers are high-leverage? In other words, which ones have the greatest impact for the lowest cost?
4. Collect data pertaining to performance measures and causal variables.
5. Build simulation models that reflect the structure of the causal loop models, but dramatically increase the explanatory power of the models.

Exhibit 9.1 shows one of the early causal loop models developed with the management team of the consumer goods manufacturing client. This diagram was developed in a three-hour meeting with senior managers from operations, sales, marketing, quality, and human resources. Two consultants facilitated the meeting following the procedures just outlined. There was a great deal of debate about what to include in the model and the nature of the relationships. The process of developing the model revealed differences in opinion among the managers and helped them begin to build a shared understanding of the business. There was substantial difference of opinion about the impact of a reduced product mix on overall sales, competitive response to price changes, and the effect of extended overtime on turnover.

The consultants began the process by listing three outcomes on one chart—costs, profits, and unit sales. Managers were then asked to identify the drivers of each those so they could be written on the chart under each of the outcomes affected. We began the lengthy process of building the simulation by starting with a few explicit relationships, such as number of sales routes driving unit sales and number of stock-keeping units (SKUs) driving unit sales. Variables and relationships were then added to the model until there was general agreement that it captured

Exhibit 9.1
Drivers of Cost, Profits, and Unit Sales

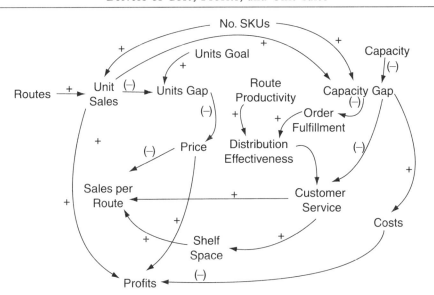

the essence of the business. This diagram suggested a wide range of interdependent relationships among factors affecting profits. Subsequent models were then developed to focus on more specific aspects of the business including market demand, production facilities, distribution, and human resources. The causal loop model shown in Exhibit 9.1 served as the basis for about 5 percent of the comprehensive computer model.

Following development of initial models, the consultants collected more data and made more comprehensive computer-based models of the business. These included financial models, models of the production process, and sales and route structure models. This client had extensive centralized data, and hence was able to provide much of the information required to build the necessary equations. If necessary data didn't exist, a group of managers would meet to share their assessments about the nature of relationships. For example, not enough data existed to estimate the impact of price increases on competitive response. To formulate this relationship in the model, sales and marketing managers met to discuss the most likely competitive responses and the conditions driving those responses. These were then quantified so that consultants could proceed to the next step.

Step 3: Model Testing

After a comprehensive model of the business has been built, the first questions are: Does it work? Does it meet the basic test of producing predictable results under selected conditions? The initial objective of the testing phase is to build confidence that the model is a useful representation of the underlying reality. In this step, the model is simulated using a wide range of inputs such as variations in price, dramatic changes in product line, and shifts in focus from very few to many customer segments. These types of testing help model builders determine whether the model generates plausible results under a wide range of conditions.

One of the variables tested in this model was the effect of capacity utilization on a variety of outcomes, including unit costs, equipment breakdowns, product quality, lost inventory, and staff turnover. Operations were set at capacity utilization levels ranging from 40 percent to 100 percent, and managers were asked to predict results. Then they were shown the results generated by the computer. As a result of the meetings and the extensive data collected in the process of developing the models, very few changes had to be made.

In general, model testing follows five steps:

1. Use management decisions from the past 5 or 10 years to determine whether the model can replicate actual historical results. At the consumer goods company, for example, the model of the production facility was simulated with demand data for the past 10 years. In response, the model generated output for production and cost. The model's version was then compared to historical patterns to assess its accuracy. If a model's results are close to the historical pattern, then we move to the next step. If not, it may be necessary to add additional variables to the model or change relationships among existing model variables.

2. Select extreme inputs, one at a time, and test the model under those conditions to assess the resiliency of the model. In the consumer goods example, the market sector of the model was simulated under the condition that competitors cut their price in half. Nobody believed that this actually would happen, but it was important for the model to generate plausible, explainable results in response to an extreme competitive shock.

3. Enter several extreme inputs simultaneously to stress-test the model. For the consumer goods manufacturer, these extreme conditions included dramatically increasing capacity, adding or reducing routes, and increasing or decreasing the number of stock-keeping units (SKUs or product types). Although these scenarios are unlikely to occur, the model should not produce outcomes that make no sense. The other advantage of this step is that the managers involved are exposed to a wider range of scenarios than they would typically consider, suggesting possibilities that they had not considered and helping them to learn more about the nature of their business.

4. Have a team of experienced managers in the company test the model by inputting a variety of elements and assessing the results. After these initial tests, a team of managers from the consumer goods manufacturing company was asked to play the simulation. During this testing period, managers were asked to describe any differences between the results produced by the simulation models and what they expected to see (their mental models). When differences were identified between the simulation and managers' mental models, the facilitator led a discussion to account for those differences. Sometimes, managers suggested that changes be made to the computer models;

at other times, they began to change their mental models of how the business works. Following this step, the models were revised and integrated into a workshop for teaching managers throughout the organization. The model-testing step is extremely important to the overall success of a simulation project. Too often, time and budget pressures cause this step to receive less than adequate attention. Inadequate testing can cause much time to be wasted tracking down errors that should have been caught earlier in the process.

5. Make revisions as required to the model structure and equations. This is the final step in simulation model development. Once it was completed, other executives throughout the consumer goods company were invited to manage the simulated company, exploring a wide range of scenarios and the effectiveness of decisions within those scenarios.

Step 4: Using Scenarios to Help Groups of Managers Learn

Once a reasonable model has been constructed, the process of analyzing scenarios and testing alternative strategies with a larger audience can begin. *Exercising scenarios* is our name for the process of designing and delivering a learning experience to a targeted group of managers throughout an organization. The simulation is a core activity of the learning experience, and allows managers to assess the impact of various strategies under different scenarios. A primary outcome of the experience is implementation of new actions in the workplace. This process has four steps:

1. Ask senior management to specify their target goals as defined by the performance measures built into the simulation. Clarify exactly how they will know they have succeeded at the end.
2. Identify possible barriers to achieving performance targets.
3. Identify capabilities required for managers to meet performance targets.
4. Develop and deliver a workshop that teaches new capabilities to managers, allows them to practice those capabilities during simulation play, and increases their understanding of cause-effect relationships in different market and competitive scenarios.

The program designed for the consumer goods company, a two-and-one-half day seminar, focused on distinctions pertaining to systems thinking, marketing, managerial accounting, and integration of market and opera-tions strategies. Approximately 200 managers throughout the company took part in this program. Each workshop had about 25 participants.

Meetings were organized so that the managers responsible for different geographic regions could experiment with alternative pricing and mar-keting strategies under various competitive scenarios. Competitor policies were varied to determine whether any of the consumer goods company's possible strategies were superior no matter what the competitor did. If there is a strategy that generates intended results regardless of competitor responses, then that strategy makes most sense for implementation. In this case, the strategies of reducing the product mix and focusing on a smaller number of customer segments produced intended results regardless of com-petitive responses.

During initial simulation play, line managers would typically make choices (price, discounts, product mix, and customer mix) based on their existing mental models, resulting in poor overall performance. During a debriefing on the results, managers would begin to explore possible causes of poor performance. Ideas about system dynamics, market structure, com-petitive response, and managerial accounting were then introduced over the course of the next two days, and managers were asked to take these ideas into consideration as they played the simulation. Different compet-itive scenarios were incorporated into the simulation models, and a wide range of strategies could be tested under these scenarios. In most cases, re-sults improved and managers had more valid explanations for the results being produced. The simulation provided a more rigorous test of the var-ious strategies under different competitive conditions. It also allowed man-agers the opportunity to practice applying new behaviors in a realistic business context. A final benefit was that it increased their confidence in introducing new strategies into their own work situations.

Real-World Results.   In addition to showing that reducing product mix and targeting fewer segments were promising tactics, the simula-tions also revealed a pricing strategy that generated superior perfor-mance for a wide variety of competitive conditions. The strategy involved raising the price on some products in order to discourage un-profitable business. The model predicted that the strategy would produce much larger increases in revenue, much smaller reductions in unit sales, and greater reductions in costs than most of the managers originally anticipated. To date, several of the geographic regions have implemented the strategy suggested by the model and have experienced very significant increases in profitability.

AN EXAMPLE OF SIMULATION IN SCENARIO ANALYSIS

An Arabian Oil Company's Price and Production Strategy

The objective of a scenario project for a major Arabian national oil company was to help management develop production and distribution strategies in the face of significant uncertainty about the world oil market. In this situation, there were two fundamental unknowns:

- Long-term demand for oil.
- Competitor response to price changes.

There is no simple picture of the evolution of the world oil demand. It is driven by factors such as economic growth, tax policy, and the prices of substitute fuels. For the purpose of this project, it wasn't feasible to build a comprehensive model of world oil demand. Instead, the consultants prepared this simple model: A baseline level of demand was influenced by world oil price according to published estimates of the elasticity of demand. Then they used baseline demand as a scenario variable in order to learn more about pricing and production strategies if worldwide demand increased or decreased.

The second major uncertainty concerned how other oil producing companies would respond to price changes initiated by the Arabian oil company. Although the competitive response was uncertain, it was possible to make some reasonable judgments about how the other producers might respond under various circumstances. We were able to create alternative decision rules that represented the competitive behavior of other major producers. The rules specified how other producers would react to different market conditions. For example, one rule specified the conditions under which Saudi Arabia would retaliate by drastically increasing production in response to a price cut by the client.

The consultants combined the alternative competitive responses to the client's potential increased production with different assumptions about baseline demand to create a set of scenarios. Teams of managers from the client company used interactive versions of the computer models to set production levels and price for their own company under various levels of worldwide demand and various competitive responses. Measures of revenue, cost, and profitability were generated for each scenario. Each session with the computer model was followed by an extensive debriefing and discussion of the results. Managers speculated about the likelihood of such results being produced within a given scenario, and discussed how pricing and production strategies would generate the best results for their organization in both the long run and the short run.

Previous competitive responses were useful in creating decision rules for the competition. These rules enabled us to build scenarios for different levels of baseline demand and types of competitive response. If we had not modeled the competitive decision rules and had instead treated competitor price and production as a scenario variable, we would have failed to discern the interaction between the firm's decisions and the competitor's responses. In this case, a scenario model that ignored such competitive interactions would have been flawed. Saudi Arabia, in particular, had the capacity and resources to dramatically increase production and cut price, actions that would have severe consequences for the client company. The management team of this company played a wide range of simulations under different competitive response scenarios and was able to determine with greater confidence the production levels that would generate the greatest profitability without triggering major competitive retaliation.

GUIDELINES FOR IMPLEMENTING SIMULATIONS IN SCENARIO ANALYSIS

Simulation modeling should be viewed as an integral part of the scenario-building process. It is particularly useful under the following environmental and organizational conditions.

Some useful guidelines:

1. *Graphic techniques for building simulation models are very effective in involving managers in the process of building simulations.* Graphics-based simulation languages, such as ITHINK, allow a model to be built from simple graphical building blocks. The structure of a model can be created in real time with a group of decision makers.

2. *Keep the model structure simple and focused on a specific learning goal of the organization.* There is a tendency to try to build "the ultimate model"

of the system. Trying to build an all-encompassing model often results in an extremely large model that is inflexible and may not be finished until the project is over. The best way to keep a model focused is to have a clear purpose. Always keep in mind that managers need to take action relevant to the issue which the model is supposed to address. In some cases, several simple models are better than one big model for analyzing different issues in a scenario analysis.

3. *Internal expert or consultant assistance can be very helpful in creating the model equations.* Many modeling packages have graphical interfaces that make it easy to create model structure. Unfortunately, it is still relatively difficult to develop and test the algebraic relationships that enable simulation.

4. *Allot enough time to analyze the simulations.* Often, because of pressure to make deadlines, most of the time in a modeling project is spent on building the model, and as a result there is too little time remaining for analysis. However, the true payoff comes when managers fully understand how the model behaves and when they absorb the important insights gained from their simulations. Many times, it has taken several weeks of carefully analyzing model behavior before the meaning of a simulation becomes clear and a significant "aha!" insight emerges.

5. *Allow decision makers to experiment with models and to create their own scenarios.* We have found that a great deal of learning can take place when managers are allowed to run their own simulations. But for this learning process to occur, the managers must have a clear understanding of the model's behavior. Well-structured introductory and debriefing sessions combined with appropriate choice of diagnostic graphs and tables make it possible for managers to accurately assess model behavior.

CONCLUSION

As conversations for exploring alternatives in our environment, scenarios open up a wide range of possibilities that we may not otherwise explore. Eventually, however, exploring possibilities is not enough. We must reach resolution about those possibilities and commit to courses of action that contribute to effective performance. Simulations of scenarios help us choose those courses of action that are most likely to support us in achieving our goals and fulfilling our commitments to customers, our workforce, and owners. Simulation models can reveal background assumptions and force rigorous inquiry into the nature of relationships among variables within our operating environment. We must prioritize variables in order to select those that we believe are the most fundamental drivers of future outcomes, and then specify a wide range of relationships among them. These activities will help us move away from excessive focus on a few understandable hypotheses about cause and effect within the business and allow us to consider a larger scope of interdependencies and possibilities for explaining results.

While discussing model development, managers also reveal their individual perspectives of the business to one another. Sharing and utilizing that range of perspectives can help them develop more detailed and valid explanations of results. Shared perspectives usually include broader scope of variables with more detailed understanding of their interdependencies than individual perspectives.

No model or group of models will reveal the "truth" about the future. They can, however reveal useful distinctions about our operating environment and certain limitations in our capacity to understand that environment. Having done so, we can make more informed choices.

CHAPTER 10

SCENARIOS FOR GLOBAL INVESTMENT STRATEGY FOR THE NEW CENTURY

PETER SCHWARTZ and JAMES A. OGILVY

Most large international companies are facing an era of fundamental uncertainty about the future of markets, the evolution of technology, major changes in the world trade map, and the course of the economies of leading trading nations. And these uncertainties will not be resolved easily, either by the passage of time or by better analytic methods. Global scenarios offer leaders a guide to a number of distinctive future environments that each have different implications for long-term investments, operating decisions, and options analysis.

$\mathbf{A}$mong the most important of the political, economic, social, and technological forces that have created and shaped global uncertainties are:

- The turbulent geopolitics of the post–Cold War era rocked by players (from giants like China and India to dismaying organized crime syndicates in the former Soviet Union) and new modes and sources of conflict (ethnic wars in central Europe and central Africa; and ecological issues).
- Shifting geo-economic relationships in an emerging era of trade blocs as Europe pursues economic integration within its union; North America and parts of Latin America integrate within the North American Free Trade Agreement (NAFTA); and Asia moves toward new levels of integration within several regional trade pacts such as the Asia Pacific Economic Cooperation (APEC).

- Rapid change in fundamental technologies, systems, standards, regulatory structures and markets, particularly for companies in high-technology industries.
- New forms of global strategy and organization based on a broad and complex array of alliances.
- The changing meaning of brands in an era of global communications and rapid change.

The resulting discontinuities force business decision makers to ask very difficult questions as they attempt to assess the risk arising from their various options. Where should we put our investments geographically? Asia is "hot" today, but will it remain a strong growth area, or will it go through a boom and bust cycle as Latin America did starting in the late 1970s? On what terms will we gain access to some markets? Will protectionism lock us out of key markets? Will gaining market access sometimes challenge our ethical standards? What should be the targets and nature of our technology investments? Who should our partners be in this new era of global alliances? Will brand strength remain a valuable asset, and how much will we have to invest to sustain that value?

Scenarios are a valuable tool for exploring such complex questions and for helping companies to evaluate the strategic investment options that emerge. Scenarios provide managers with logical stories about a number of alternative futures—in effect, a valuable set of learning experiences.

CASE: A TECHNOLOGY COMPANY EXPLORES ITS FUTURE

A *Fortune 500* firm, a global leader in technology, has faced fundamental uncertainties in its businesses before. The company's leadership has confidence in its ability to manage uncertainties, particularly given its strong market position and reputation. In addition, the company has set ambitious goals for growth—13 to 15 percent annually. This implies a doubling of sales every five years, with a tenfold increase over 20 years.

These goals herald enormous challenges, especially to develop the management and leadership needed for such growth. For example, the chairman of the company recognized that a key skill new managers would need was the capacity to anticipate and commit to the future with confidence. He believed that scenario planning was the best approach to building that capability. At his request, at the end of 1992 and the first half of 1993, the senior management of the company examined their long-term global investment plans through scenarios. After this approach proved successful, the company added scenarios to the official strategic thinking and planning process throughout the organization. In all, more than 60 scenario planning projects have since been launched, with most having a dual purpose:

- To address real strategic issues.
- To educate the management in the use of this strategic-thinking tool.

Global investment strategy was chosen as the first target for scenario planning for several reasons. Not only is technological innovation increasingly global, but technology delivery involves many players pursuing competitive strategies and new alliances in new markets all over the world. Indeed, both the evolution of the industry and access to new markets were central issues for this project. Until recently, this company's industry was dominated by public and private monopolies. In this time of rapid change, privatization and competition are sweeping the globe, but how quickly? The competing forms of capitalism—American, European, and Asian— have shaped the new terms of access.

The company's objective in the first scenario project was to anticipate other possible earthshaking developments, since such macroenvironmental issues would have a major impact on the long-term success of its strategies.

Because these strategies would play out over many years, the date selected for the scenarios was 2010. In this context, the company needed to assess a number of risks, including investing in infrastructure (such as factories and their own telecom infrastructure), and marketing capacities. It also needed to explore its potential market positioning and to get some guidance on a long-term technology strategy.

The Scenario Process

Following an initial set of interviews with a few senior managers to frame the issues of concern, a two-day scenario development workshop took place at a hotel not too far from the company's home offices. The nearly 20 participants in this workshop included the chief executive and most of his senior officers and three senior consultants. In our experience, in order to improve busy executives' focus on long-range concerns, it pays to isolate them from the day-to-day worries of their offices and homes.

On the first evening, the CEO opened the meeting by saying that he was there to learn, and that he expected other executives to be there as learners too. The meeting continued with a brief presentation on the scenario method, a presentation of a set of global scenarios to provide a framework for the focused scenario effort, and a group discussion of the key issues facing the company.

The first full day of the workshop was largely devoted to a discussion of the driving forces shaping the future of global investment strategy. The participants identified those drivers judged to be most significant and most uncertain. Toward the end of the day, the group attempted to develop a structure for the scenarios. The second day was spent revising and expanding the scenario framework and beginning to develop the possible implications of the scenarios. The final discussion of the first afternoon focused on further articulating the scenarios' implications and identifying the project's next steps.

It was decided that the project needed to undertake a research phase. A number of novel issues had arisen during the workshop that required in-depth analysis. For example, in economic terms, how significant were such forces as organized crime, corruption, and terrorism? Could they significantly alter the trajectory of the world economy and the success of the company's strategies?

As the analytic foundations of the scenarios were researched and studied, a quantification effort began. The greatest intellectual challenge proved to be quantifying the scenario studying the impact of organized crime and the underground economy, two factors that are normally left out of computer economic models.

The detailed scenarios were then presented to the top management group for a full discussion of their implications. Two main issues were: management's own assessment of the implications, and the substance of the message that would be communicated to the rest of the organization. Following this meeting, the internal company team presented the scenarios and their implications to the appropriate business units. A number of these business units did use these scenarios as background for their own scenario-planning efforts.

Driving Forces

During the first scenario workshop, six key forces were seen as the most critical and uncertain as the managers confronted major strategic issues. Gaining some insight into how these forces might play out and how they might affect the company's options would be especially helpful in decision making. These forces are presented in order of relative importance, as ranked by the scenario team:

1. U.S. Trade and Political Relations with Other Countries

This company buys components all over the world and relies on worldwide access to manufacturing facilities. Much of its greatest growth is occurring in such emerging markets as China and Southeast Asia. Parts of its businesses require the active cooperation and participation of government and private organizations in many countries.

The company must also anticipate the likelihood of a continued aggressive U.S. posture in global trade politics. Access to markets for all U.S. companies is now affected by U.S. automobile policy, with regard to Japan; U.S. human rights policy, with regard to China; and U.S. conflicts with various Middle Eastern countries such as Iran and Iraq. On top of those challenges, new trade blocs—such as the European Union and NAFTA are evolving. It is obvious that the company's strategic options will be profoundly influenced by the outcome of events.

2. Customer and Partner Relations

As this company's industry has evolved, the key issues are not who does the manufacturing, but which standards and systems will win favor with the most manufacturers. How might the structure of the industry evolve further? Will the current patterns continue? As a maker of components and systems, the company saw this as a key issue. Moreover, nearly every international venture now involves multiple strategic relations among providers of technology, systems builders and operators, big customers, and often governments. Who will determine standards: the marketplace, industry associations, or governments? How will the nature of these relationships be determined? Will the key factors be mainly economic and technical merit, or will politics dominate? These uncertainties will certainly affect how the company plays the game of shaping these key relationships.

3. Technological Discontinuities

In any high-tech industry nowadays, technological tumult is the norm. The personal computer, the massively parallel computer, mobile communications, and the Internet are all discontinuities whose successes have sometimes surprised experienced industry observers. The ups and downs experienced by other technologies—robotics, artificial intelligence, the pocket-sized computer, and high-definition TV have been equally unpredictable.

Fundamental advances in chip technology, new modes of information distribution such as fiber optics and personal communicators, and new arenas such as multimedia, virtual reality, and electronic commerce are together creating unprecedented opportunity and risk. Huge sums are being invested based on the fear of being locked out of emerging industries. But one can be fairly sure that many of the new initiatives will fail or at least be commercialized much later than anticipated. In a recent year, three different modes of digital entertainment storage were launched in the hope of establishing a new standard. It's unlikely that all can find an adequate market, and it's even possible that none will succeed. To quantify such losses, remember that Japan's investment in the analog standard high-density television (HDTV) system exceeded $9 billion, a total loss since it was obsolete even as it was being launched. Because the world has already moved to a digital system, Japanese companies will see no return on investment, not even in terms of significant learning.

Our case study company must continue to make decisions about R&D and product development. It must commit to investments of billions of dollars, and often must do so years ahead of the market. There is a real possibility that the industry will evolve away from the technology it has selected for investment.

4. Business Synergy

Given the scale of the needed investments, a critical question is the degree of synergy among the company's various businesses. For instance, can it use components it develops for one industry segment in another? Will its systems businesses in the United States be like those in Asia or Europe? Will the standards for communications be similar in the United States, Asia, and Europe? If all of these businesses evolve in very different directions, either by industry or geographically, the implied investment levels are much greater than if they evolve in similar directions.

Shaping these uncertainties are the competitive strategies of many different actors, both public and private. Some have an interest in realizing and facilitating synergies while others stand in the way. Today's dominant players—such as Microsoft—have an interest in preventing new players from gaining strategic leverage by capitalizing on synergies.

5. Total Available Market

Clearly, the scale of the investment must be related to the potential size of the market and the market share that can be achieved. Total market growth is, in part, a function of the rate of economic growth of the world's regional economies and the take-off rate of certain technology-based industries, such as electronic commerce and satellite telecommunications. The faster the economy grows, the more likely it is that the new industries will have capital to fund the growth, and customers who can afford to pay the bill. If prices fall rapidly, the market can expand more quickly. But if prices remain high, market growth may be limited. The size of the available market is further related to some of other drivers, such as trade policy and the development of regional blocs. Access to markets can either be more open or more constrained by protectionism.

6. Environment and Health

The firm's business segments in several industries are being affected by concerns about the environment and health. The issues under discussion range from the use and disposal of plastics and other materials in manufacturing and recycling to mounting awareness of the need to monitor health effects in the office to the consequences of close proximity to microwave radiation. Such issues have technological, regulatory, and perceptual dimensions. Technology can eliminate some concerns while creating new ones. Regulators can respond to real issues or to those shaped mainly by political pressures. Customers can respond to real environmental and health threats or to mainly perceptual concerns. Moreover, the media plays a key role in these complex interactions: A story on CNN that inspires alarm and is repeated around the world can have dramatic and nearly instantaneous consequences for business strategy.

The Scenarios

Following extensive discussions among the first workshop participants, the framework used by the consultant, Global Business Network, to develop its own global scenarios was adopted as a starting point for these corporate scenarios.

Most large international firms share economic and political concerns that are reflected in the global scenarios. One scenario dimension considered the degree to which trade regimes would be principally regional (such as the European Union and NAFTA) or global (World Trade Organization). The second dimension charted the sociopolitical domain and addressed whether societies and the world were becoming more fragmented or more integrated. For example, at the same time that social and political integration accelerated under the banner of the new Europe, there was mounting demagoguery in many European countries about non-European immigrants. About this time, the whole world sadly witnessed the dissolution of Yugoslavia into ethnic warfare.

Given the driving forces listed earlier, the scenario team agreed that these two dimensions of uncertainty—regional versus global and integrated versus fragmented—captured some of the concerns of management, but not all. After considerable discussion, another dimension was added, to assess the basis for competition and market access. Would companies entering a new market be rewarded mainly for their technological competence, or would access and success often be dependent on overt and covert relationships with governments, small blocs of the country's power elite, corporate partners, powerful individuals, or even crime syndicates?

The strategic implications of this dimension are obvious. In one case, the company focuses mainly on providing the best technology at the best price. In the other, the company concentrates on developing and sustaining key relationships with partners, government officials, and power brokers. Looking around the world suggested that there was considerable uncertainty as to which approach would become prevalent. For this technology-focused company, a relationship-driven world would pose a major challenge, especially if those relationships were mainly covert.

The Four Scenarios

While a three-dimensional matrix could be used to generate eight scenarios, all are not equally relevant or plausible. In practice, more than four scenarios are rarely useful; during discussions, the distinctions between them tend to blur, and this causes confusion. After consideration, the following four scenarios were chosen because they delineate areas of uncertainty that are of most concern to management.

Two-Bloc Prosperity

In this technology-driven, regionally integrated world, two great trade blocs have emerged, a prosperous Pacific Rim bloc and an expanded but slumping European bloc. Southeast Asia, a model of monolithic capitalism, pulls the United States into its emerging community to help balance China and Japan. APEC becomes the basis for this organizing body. The European Union falters for many reasons: the difficulties of political integration, the inability to create jobs, immigration issues, and the problems faced by new Eastern members like Russia. In this scenario, environmental issues do not inhibit economic development. Deregulation and privatization are key dynamics. Global trade and international organizations such as the WTO continue to develop effectively.

Wobbly Three-Legged Stool

This scenario describes a relationship-driven world that is regionally fragmented into three trade blocs: Europe, Asia, and North America. Europe rebounds and prospers. European-style capitalism, exemplified by Germany, is able to deal with mounting social and environmental problems most effectively. However, the monolithic capitalism of Asia stumbles when confronted with such challenges. Widening income disparities, corruption, ethnic conflicts (everyone against the Chinese and the Japanese), environmental bottlenecks, rising energy needs, and AIDS consume much of the political and economic energy of Asia. Limited access to European and American markets also slows the Asian development.

Techno-Capitalism Reigns

This is the story of a technology-driven, globally integrated, borderless world restructured around information technology. Laissez-faire capitalism led by the United States dominates, giving rise to a completely open global marketplace. Severe environmental problems pose a great technological and economic challenge around the year 2000, leading to a restructured, environmentally conscious, information economy by the end of the decade. The information superhighway and universally accessible information tools facilitate growth and use minimal natural resources. Currency and securities markets are global and electronic with the beginnings of a universal currency. There are more strategic alliances and fewer treaties.

Malefactus

In this scenario, payments under the table are needed to grease the wheels of commerce. It is a relationship-driven, globally fragmented world adrift in economic hard times. The competing forms of capitalism create chaos in the global marketplace with no capacity for cooperation. A vicious circle runs unchecked: Reduced investment leads to slow growth, which results in social conflict, which retards environmental reforms, which fan the flames of environmental conflict, which suppresses investment. Many flash points could ignite in this scenario: immigrants in Europe, conflicts in the former Soviet Union and in the Middle East, war and famine in Africa, conflicts in India, drug wars in Latin America, organized crime, multi-billion-dollar securities frauds, rising crime and terrorism, and mounting international arms sales. This is a dark and difficult world where economic growth takes a back seat to political conflicts and disorder.

Scenario Dynamics

In 1992, when these scenarios were developed, the world seemed nearest to either the Two-Bloc Prosperity or Wobbly Three-Legged Stool scenarios. Thus movements toward either of these scenarios seemed to be the most likely next steps, possibly followed by a movement from one scenario to the other, such as from Two-Bloc Prosperity to Wobbly Three-Legged Stool. On the other hand, if the scenarios were pushed by more extreme developments in the business environment—a real possibility given the history of the last decade—then the world could drift from Two-Bloc Prosperity or Wobbly Three-Legged Stool toward the more positive outcome of Techno-Capitalism Reigns, or instead toward the grimmer conditions of Malefactus. A less likely (but still possible) dynamic would be the long-term devolution of the Techno-Capitalism Reigns scenario into the Malefactus scenario.

Outcomes and Indicators

Once the scenarios had been completed and quantified, the team identified the early indicators of each scenarios to serve as signposts along the way. For example, the growth of trade friction would point away from

Techno-Capitalism Reigns and toward Wobbly Three-Legged Stool or Malefactus. Or, if more of the economy remained in public rather than private hands, this would point toward either Two-Bloc Prosperity or Wobbly Three-Legged Stool. If a large fraction of the economy began moving underground, it would signal a trend toward Malefactus.

The final step in the analytic work entailed an exploration of the implications of each scenario individually, and for the set of scenarios taken as a whole. For each scenario, geographic and technological investment strategies were developed, as well as guidelines for alliances and partnerships. The immediate challenge was to develop strategies that balanced effectively across the Two-Bloc Prosperity and Wobbly Three-Legged Stool scenarios. While it would be difficult to plan for Malefactus, it was nonetheless important to recognize its emergence in a timely way.

CONCLUSIONS AND LESSONS

Participants derived several key lessons from this case:

- *Standard scenarios are useful but need to be customized.* The world view scenarios provided to this organization served as a useful starting point and accelerated the process, but would not have been adequate to address the company's specific strategic issues. Thus, the framework was expanded to incorporate the unique concerns of the company, and the scenarios were modified and augmented to reflect the perspectives of the participants. Although the issues and concerns at stake in this project—such as the dynamics of the global trading system—are shared by many international companies, scenarios must be custom tailored to be useful strategic tools.
- *Quantification of scenarios is difficult but essential.* For the scenarios to be taken seriously in this company, they needed to be reflected in numbers. However, quantification can reduce the scenarios exercise to merely a sensitivity analysis unless there are highly significant qualitative differences between the scenarios. It was especially difficult to model the Malefactus scenario since it describes a future in which much of the economy is hidden.
- *Pay attention to corporate culture.* The culture of this company increased the likelihood of a successful scenario project. The key factor was the participants' capacity for lively, constructive debate. In the workshops

and meetings, they were able to debate intensely, keeping options and possibilities open without creating enduring hostilities. They could leave the conference room as friends and colleagues despite strong disagreements during the scenario discussions. In other corporate cultures, however, a rush to rapid consensus may make disagreement highly risky—either it's poisonous personally or harmful politically. In such organizations, to avoid the risks posed by airing passionate disagreements, the group prematurely closes debate, thus losing the opportunity to address critical issues.

- *Top-level support matters.* In this case, the fact that the chairman and CEO took an interest in the initiative from the very start—and communicated this interest publicly—was enormously helpful. The active participation of the CEO was a strong signal to the organization that the scenario project was important. This also meant that the results actually reflected management's concerns and were therefore more likely to be useful and actionable.

PART III

SCENARIO APPLICATION IN DIVERSE CONTEXTS

CHAPTER 11

INDUSTRY SCENARIOS

LIAM FAHEY

Every industry today is undergoing significant and largely unpredictable change: Industry boundaries are collapsing; new types of entrants are emerging; the dynamics of rivalry are shifting; and entities such as suppliers, distributors and end customers are behaving in new and unexpected ways. It is not surprising therefore that many firms are perplexed by how their industry might unfold. Industry scenarios enable managers to identify plausible future states of an industry and differences between them, to examine how these distinct industry states might evolve, and most important, and to determine what the organization would have to do to win within each industry future.

$\mathbf{P}$ractitioners and theoreticians alike agree that industry analysis is a crucial component of strategy making. For the last 20 years or more, consultants have been coaching managers to analyze their industry by:

- Delineating the scope and boundaries of the industry.
- Identifying current and emerging change in and around the industry.
- Projecting its evolution and future structure.

Effective strategy, well-respected consultants assert, is always predicated upon some understanding of industry evolution. Choosing the right strategy depends upon perceiving how the industry will unfold. Moreover, if the strategy is designed to attain breakthrough marketplace leadership, it can't merely anticipate and adapt to industry change. Instead, the strategy must be designed to drive and direct the process of change, a bold goal.

So you would expect that most organizations would avidly develop scenarios to look at alternative industry evolutionary paths. During the Internet boom, for example, you would assume that firms in many consumer, industrial product, and service industries would be experimenting with scenarios: looking at new ways their customers will purchase products, how products will be sold, and how firms will compete against each other. Or that pharmaceutical firms would develop scenarios that address plausible future directions of biotechnology developments and how they might affect the traditional pharmaceutical industry. But most organizations still don't use industry scenarios despite the successes of a small number of firms. Such a process would seem to be a key step in strategy development and an obvious way of making better strategy choices.

Why don't more organizations see the true potential of learning from industry scenarios? Frankly, it's easy to get lost while trying to integrate industry analysis and scenario development. Some mistakes managers make when they first experiment with scenarios are:

- *They misunderstand the purposes of industry scenarios.* Some organizations view them merely as a means of testing their existing strategies. They do not understand that the big payoff from all the work comes when the scenario process starts generating new strategy alternatives. It is often these alternatives that lead to breakthrough marketplace leadership.

- *They mistakenly limit the scope and domain of industry scenarios.* For example, some organizations fall into the trap of regarding the boundaries of their industry as permanent. As a result, they are not prepared when unexpected competitors emerge, often with products new to the marketplace, and their industry changes radically. Managers should, instead, craft some scenarios that describe a future when innovative rivals are stealing customers in droves and the strategies the organization uses now are no longer viable.

- *They fail to distinguish between wrongly using scenarios as predictions and rightly using them as projections.* Predictions—that is, forecasts of what will happen—are usually wrong. Projections—estimates of future possibilities—help us imagine the future and think out what actions to take if it came about.

- *They wrongly focus on one scenario that they believe has the highest probability of occurring—the most likely future.* Unfortunately, the likely future for most organizations is anything but predictable.

- *They don't understand how scenarios can anticipate and assess likely industry change.* For example, they don't use industry scenarios to identify key indicators that signal which future is unfolding. They are like a boxer who doesn't know until the fight starts which opponent will step into the ring—the slow big one or the fast little one.

Part of the problem is that there aren't many publicly available case histories in which industry scenarios contributed positively to strategy making, so this chapter will illustrate how industry scenarios can be developed and used. It will show that industry scenarios serve four interrelated purposes:

1. To identify plausible future states of an industry and the differences between them.
2. To show how each future state might evolve and to describe the different possible paths.
3. To foster better strategic thinking by helping to identify unanticipated marketplace opportunities and threats, and to illustrate competitive dynamics in different industry contexts.
4. To enable an organization to anticipate what it would have to do—at every level of the business—to win in various industry scenarios.

To those ends, this chapter is divided into two sections:

- How industry scenarios are constructed.
- How they can be assessed and tested.

In short, this chapter demonstrates how managers can learn from industry scenarios and use their new understanding and knowledge to develop and execute strategy. Bear in mind, however, that the methodology presented in this chapter is but one of a number of ways that organizations can develop and use industry scenarios.

For purposes of illustration, this chapter will look at the scenario process at "OPtech," a long-established firm that designs and manufactures hand-held surgical instruments. Though OPtech's current sales were rising steadily, its senior executives had begun to worry that the future of both their company and their industry would be very different from its past. In particular, the executives were concerned with the emergence of new technologies that could give rise to radically new surgical instruments, some of which might make OPtech's current products obsolete.

Constructing Industry Scenarios

Driven by internal and external forces, industries evolve over time. Internal forces include: the actions of competitors; the entrance of rivals offering substitute products or services; innovations by suppliers, channels, and end customers; and of course, changes by your own firm such as the development of new products and services. External forces include political, social, economic, and technological change. While current driving forces usually can be identified, many important elements of the future can escape detection. Subtle but highly significant changes in the environment often go unnoticed when they first occur, and key events that create discontinuity and new circumstances may be impossible to foresee or anticipate. A number of steps, designed to capture these changes and events, must be completed in developing an industry scenario (see Exhibit 11.1). Each of these steps is briefly described.

Delineate Current Industry Context

Managers crafting industry scenarios have a dilemma. If they stray too far away from the current industry context, their scenarios may appear to be fanciful or wishful thinking. Their peers may judge that their attempt at bold thinking is useless for making current or future decisions. Nevertheless, scenario makers need to venture outside the bounds of current expectations for their industry.

The true goal of industry analysis is to be the first organization to figure out a future that is substantially different from current expectations, and then to use that scenario to foster decisions that help the firm to outperform its rivals. In other words, industry scenarios must not only be plausible; they must also be competitively relevant, a quality that requires timeliness. Thus, managers involved in developing and using industry scenarios must creatively challenge current expectations and test current decisions, and do so before anyone else does.

Various widely applied methodologies such as Porter's Five Forces model or industry value chain analysis can be used to describe and analyze the current industry. All the analysis frameworks that describe and analyze an industry will surface a number of important issues or decisions. These include:

- Which products broadly similar to those of your own firm should be included as part of the industry? For example, if the *New York*

Exhibit 11.1
Constructing and Industry Scenario: Steps and Questions

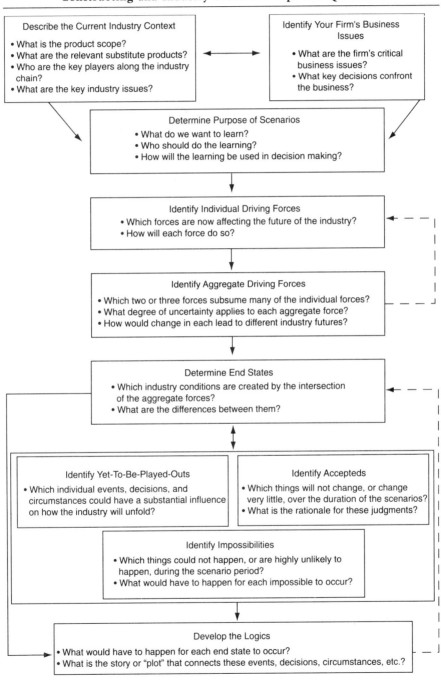

Times is developing a set of Newspaper of the Future industry scenarios, should magazines such as the *Economist, Time, Newsweek,* and the *Financial Times* be included as rival products in the "newspaper" industry?

- Which substitute products are now available, in the pipeline, on the drawing board, or may emerge from the lab soon? Will the new 24-hour cable sports channels attract away readers who previously depended upon newspapers for their news about sports?
- Which new entrants should be considered part of the industry? Only those that are on the verge of entering or those that may enter two or three years from now?
- Which distribution channels should be viewed as part of the industry? For example, a number of firms in many industries are now grappling with whether to include the Internet as one of their distribution channels for reaching consumers with product information.
- Which customer needs should be emphasized?
- Who are the relevant suppliers?

Answers to such questions strongly influence the scope, content, and outcomes of industry scenarios. Three specific items merit particular attention.

Boundaries.   First is the unavoidable issue of industry boundaries. Executives of the case study company, OPtech, suspected that emerging technology and many other environmental changes would destabilize their industry. But they couldn't picture how their industry would evolve. So OPtech executives wanted as broad and as inclusive a definition of the industry as possible. Its industry scenarios included all substitute products, all surgery locations, all distribution channels, and all types of suppliers as part of the industry.

Uncertainty.   Second, identification of current (and prospective) issues or key uncertainties greatly shape the content and domain of scenarios. As the OPtech case is developed, it will become clear that a number of issues identified by managers at the time of the scenario work strongly influenced the specific scenarios that were crafted.

Time Period.   Third, the time frame of the scenarios also greatly influences their content. In the OPtech case, a time line of four to five years was chosen, chiefly because it would take about that long for a number of substitute products to penetrate the marketplace.

Identify Your Firm's Current and Anticipated Business Issues

To be worth the investment of executive attention, industry scenarios ultimately must influence how managers understand the firm's strategy issues and decisions. Otherwise, they degenerate into merely an exercise aimed at understanding the future. Let's look at how two different approaches use the firm's current business context as an input to strategy making. They have distinct implications for how scenarios are developed and used.

Approach 1.   Most consultants who train companies to use scenarios advocate identifying the firm's current and anticipated business issues and the decisions to which they may give rise before scenarios are considered and elaborated. These issues and decisions influence the scope, content, and direction of scenarios. For example, the OPtech surgical instrument firm initially decided to study two central strategy issues:

- Which product line extensions might be possible?
- How to compete against anticipated new "look-alike" entrants? That is, firms that would market largely similar products.

Approach 2.   In some cases, industry scenarios are first developed with little if any consideration of their relevance to the firm's current or future issues and decisions. After they are drafted, the participants consider such implications as:

- What do they imply for the firm's current strategies?
- To which strategy alternatives do they point?
- To which competitive issues the firm must pay attention?

This approach has an important advantage: It frees decision makers and others from their preoccupation with their day-to-day competitive and operating issues. It thus encourages them to take as dispassionate and objective a view as possible of alternative futures in and around their industry and their implications for their organization. This approach allows them to be imaginative, and then to test the fruits of their creativity.

Indeed, the two approaches can be combined. One set of scenario developers can adopt the "guided" approach and another group can employ the "open-ended" approach. They can eventually meet and integrate both sets of projections and implications. In the case of OPtech, the tensions between these two approaches were quite evident. Some managers did not want to waste any time in developing "irrelevant" scenarios; they wanted to quickly identify the most significant business issues and to build scenarios around them. On the other hand, some senior managers were not at all convinced that anyone within the organization knew what the relevant issues were. They wanted to slow down the scenario process and allow every manager the opportunity to grapple with all the uncertainties that pervaded the surgical instrument business. In this way, over time, the firm would reach a consensus about which business issues should receive attention.

As part of the outcome of their initial efforts to consider the state of their own business, the managers at OPtech concluded that they faced a number of strategy issues and decisions:

- How could the firm extend its current product line?
- What should it do to preempt and move ahead of competitors' technology advances designed to improve their products?
- How should it respond to the continued flow of new entrants with products quite similar to its own?
- How should it respond to the threat of substitute products, which most likely would not penetrate the market to any extent for two or three years or possibly more?

Determine Purpose of Scenarios

A common mistake industry scenario developers often make is that they don't clearly establish the purpose of the scenario project before initiating the process. Which business issues should it try to illuminate? In many cases, clearly articulating the firm's current business uncertainties and critical issues enables managers to craft scenarios to investigate crucial, specific questions. For example, at OPtech, the future state of specific technologies was a fundamental business issue, so scenarios could obviously be aimed to explore the evolution and interactions of these technologies.

Whether a guided or open-ended approach is adopted, identifying broad purposes in the early stages of scenario development compels managers to articulate why the scenarios are being developed, what they hope to learn, how that learning is different from what they currently know (or think they know), and most important, how that learning might be put to use. Putting these considerations on the table often forces managers to openly discuss some formerly taboo topics:

- How scenarios might challenge existing assumptions about the industry.
- The wisdom of past decisions.
- The need for new strategies.

OPtech wanted to develop a set of scenarios that would reflect possible industry settings within the following three to five years. In particular, senior managers were concerned that the industry might soon be transformed by new competitors selling innovative products with distinct benefits over all currently available offerings. By anticipating the advent of competitors marketing such "substitute" products, OPtech could rethink its strategy choices: the products it would develop; the customers it would pursue; and how it would endeavor to build and sustain differentiation from its rivals.

As the OPtech managers found out as they engaged in the scenario process, the specific learning goals of industry scenarios can change significantly during the course of the project. A common initial purpose is to test the robustness of the firm's current strategy in a range of distinct competitive environments. As the scenarios are developed, managers might discern that a range of technologies could interact to create a totally new business environment they had not foreseen. The scenarios might then be directed to project and explore a range of technology futures—various competitive environments that would be the consequence of different technology evolutions. The managers might then return to their original concern: How would the current strategy play out in these technologically distinct end states? They might also ask how these scenarios might generate new strategy alternatives—alternatives that most likely they had not previously considered.

Identify Industry Driving Forces

Much of the uncertainty and angst felt by OPtech's managers was in large measure caused by the fact that they did not know which forces would drive and shape their industry over the foreseeable future. The future seemed to be an uncertain blur: Many events and circumstances could happen; each one in turn would affect what could happen next. For example, if one competitor initiated a sales and promotion blitz, others might ignore it, or they might match it. If a new competitor launched a new substitute product, some leading hospitals might immediately switch to the new product causing others to follow suit; or the product might receive very few adoptions.

OPtech's uncertainty is neither surprising nor uncommon. Regrettably, most firms don't take the time nor engage in the analysis needed to identify the forces that are shaping the immediate future of their industry or how it will evolve over time. All too often they rely on the "wisdom" of senior managers or staff who have lived through the ups and downs of the industry for decades. Unfortunately, as an industry changes, the wisdom relevant to an earlier era may produce precisely the wrong recipe to succeed in the new competitive environment. Many firms in the computer, software, electronics, pharmaceutical, energy, automobile, and media industries have painful stories to tell about how they fell victim to the untested knowledge of self-described "experts" who supposedly "knew the industry."

Many factors or forces drive industry evolution. Some originate from inside the industry, others from outside it. A number of different models can help managers identify specific industry driving forces. Many firms employ Professor Michael Porter's Five Forces framework to create an initial list of internal forces. To apply his framework, managers must ask and answer basic questions about change taking place with customers, suppliers, substitute products, new entrants, and competitive dynamics among rivals. As an alternative, managers can search for individual driving forces by analyzing the industry value chain—raw materials, procurement/logistics, manufacturing, distribution, marketing, sales, and service. For example, a firm in a product segment of the chemical industry might ask what changes are occurring in existing components and supplies; the development of new raw materials; the way raw materials, components, and supplies are transported from their source to where manufacturing takes place; how manufacturing is done;

and how the finished product is distributed, marketed, sold, and serviced.

External or macroenvironmental forces—that is, change in the political, regulatory, social, technological and economic milieu—can also influence growth in industry sales, entry of new competitors, emergence of substitute products, and rivalry among competitors. For example, demographic shifts, such as the increasing number of elderly persons, have profoundly affected sales in many industry segments. Technology change has led to the emergence of many substitute products. First, overnight delivery services competed against the fax machine, then against electronic mail, and now against satellite and cable broadcasting of text and video.

As occurred within OPtech, knowledgeable individuals inside and outside the firm should be asked to identify relevant driving forces. "Outsiders" are more likely to nominate important future driving forces because they are unlikely to be burdened with the same biases and preconceptions as the organization's managers. Be sure to ask all participants why and how they expect various forces will shape industry evolution. A partial listing of individual industry and macroenvironmental driving forces affecting the surgical instrument industry is shown in Exhibit 11.2.

Identify Aggregate Driving Forces: Key Change Uncertainties

Even the attenuated list of individual forces shaping an industry's evolution, such as the sample shown in Exhibit 11.2, may seem both daunting and impenetrable. In most industries, the complexity of potential interactions among such forces is beyond the grasp of any one person's mind or any simple analytical tool. Thus, managers must decide which forces are likely to be most critical in shaping industry evolution.

Managers need to distinguish between individual and aggregate forces. The latter are those that are central to shaping the evolution of an industry. They always subsume many individual forces. For example, gross national product, which is an aggregate force that affects many industries, combines many individual economic forces. Demographic shifts, another aggregate force that affects many industries, represents the cumulation of many individual social, cultural, and economic forces.

Managers should plan to spend considerable time discussing and analyzing a listing of individual forces, such as those noted in Exhibit 11.2,

Exhibit 11.2
Individual Driving Forces

Industry Forces	Macroenvironmental Forces
Raw Materials Cost of materials Availability of materials **Suppliers** Development of components Commitment to partnering **Logistics** Cost of logistics Actions of logistics firms Just-in-time delivery **Competitors** Strategy changes New products Strategies they pursue **Substitute Products** Types of products Firms introducing them Strategies they pursue **Distribution Channels** Emergence of new channels Distribution decisions Pricing decisions Partnering decisions **End Customer/Users** No. of surgeons doing this type of surgery No. of procedures Rate of product substitution **Technological** Information technology to connect entities along value chain Technology change in the operating room Technology change leading to change in the historic product	**Political** Change in party affiliation of those in power Change in the influence of key industry groups **Regulatory** Change in regulations regarding product use Approval of substitute products Approval/rejection of industry alliances and partnerships Change in regulations around health care insurance **Social** Attitudes toward physical fitness and general wellness Change in values around health care costs **Economic** Changes in general economic conditions Changes in patterns of income distribution **Technological** Key technological breakthroughs affecting surgery in general R&D developments in related industries such as pharmaceuticals Technology developments allowing more health care delivery outside of hospitals

before deciding upon a small set of aggregate forces. A good analysis technique is to persistently ask questions such as:

- Which forces currently are shaping industry evolution?
- Which new forces may emerge to influence industry evolution?
- Which forces are most likely to affect how the industry will evolve?

These questions guide managers toward identifying a short list of aggregate forces. As the short list begins to emerge, managers need to ask the following two questions:

1. *What degree of change is possible within each aggregate force?* For example, regulatory change is a critical aggregate force affecting some industries because a wide range of regulatory possibilities could occur within a few years. In some instances, possible regulatory change ranges from the imposition of stiff new regulations to the lifting of current regulations. If very limited change is possible, then the aggregate force can't lead to radically different industry futures.
2. *How would changes in each force lead to different industry contexts?* For example, a lifting of regulations might lead to a rush of new entrants, as occurred in the airline industry. Imposition of new regulations might result in customers switching to substitute products. The guardian of the pharmaceutical industry, the Food and Drug Administration, has relaxed its attitude toward advertising directly to consumers, now allowing ads that alert the public that a remedy exists for a common health problem, and suggesting that they should contact their physician to find out whether the medicine is appropriate for them. Even such a small change in how regulations are interpreted can dramatically alter the competitive context of an industry.

The OPtech managers arrived at the conclusion that three aggregate driving forces, or fundamental uncertainties, were key to understanding how their industry might involve. It was not an easy process to arrive at these three forces, nor, on occasion, was it polite. They asked myriad questions about possible aggregate forces and how each might lead to different industry futures. In heated discussion, they challenged each other to show how change might occur in each proposed aggregate force. It seemed that each manager had his or her own pet explanation for what would drive the future of the industry. Each of the three forces they finally selected subsumed many of the individual forces noted in Exhibit 11.2. The three were:

- The entry of new competitors into the current product category.
- The extent of marketing/sales expenditures committed by existing and new competitors.
- The emergence of substitute products.

Significant uncertainty was associated with each of these aggregate driving forces. A few new competitors had already announced their intention of entering the market. But, when they would do so and what their product volume would be were open questions. A few other firms were believed to be interested in entering the market, but they had not announced their intentions. Marketing/sales expenditures, as a percentage of sales revenues, could increase significantly (spurred in part by new entrants) or remain at or even somewhat below recent levels. Current and future competitors clearly had a range of options about their marketing/sales expenditures. Technology developments might allow substitutes to reach the market; in particular, the development of laser technology (for noninvasive surgery) and pharmaceutical products (that offered an alternative to surgery for some patients).

Managers must articulate how and why each aggregate driving force will affect industry evolution. Such rationales provide a preliminary understanding of how these forces could affect industry evolution. For example, in the case of OPtech, the entry of new competitors into the current product category could dramatically reconfigure the competitive dynamics over the next two or three years. As new entrants emerge, hospitals may play off one competitor against another, forcing prices to spiral downward. If substitute products prove effective, surgeons are likely to switch from the firm's long-established hand–held product category, thus severely curtailing its sales growth.

Determine End States

Industry scenarios are intended to offer managers multiple views of what the future of their industry might be at some point in time—what we refer to throughout this book as "end states." In other words, what a selected market situation will be at a specific time in the future. In most instances, two or three aggregate forces or uncertainties are sufficient to generate a number of scenario end states that can be used to identify strategy alternatives, threats to the firm's current strategy, and the dynamics of competition that might confront the firm.

The fundamental guiding question is: How might these aggregate forces interact to create distinctly different industry end states? In the case of OPtech, how might change with regard to the entry of new competitors, the extent of marketing/sales expenditures by existing and new competitors, and substitute products combine to create different industry futures?

The first step in developing end states is to assess how much change might be associated with each aggregate force. Is OPtech likely to confront one or many new entrants? One substitute product that takes off in the market could lead to significant consequences. On the other hand, a potential substitute product might not make it through the regulatory reviews and thus would not reach the market at all.

The second step is to identify the appropriate "scales" for each force. For example, the potential entry of new competitors might be segmented as "many" or "few"; the degree of marketing/sales expenditures might be separated into "high" and "low"; and the emergence of substitute products might be segmented as "yes" and "no." There are no definitive rules for establishing scales; nevertheless, some scales must be agreed upon in order to create contrasting end states, that is, distinct industry futures.

The third step is to use the scaled aggregate forces to generate end states. Even two aggregate forces can provide a set of radically distinct end states. Taking two of the three aggregate forces just noted, the degree of marketing/sales expenditures and the emergence of substitute products, provides a set of four industry end states, as shown in Exhibit 11.3: Live-and-Let-Live, Subdued Product Contest, Dog-Eat-Dog Warfare, and A Switching Battle. The dominant feature of these end states is that they reflect fundamentally different competitive conditions. As we shall see in Part 2 of this chapter, it is in the comparison of the differences between these end states that decision makers truly begin to recognize and understand:

- The diversity of the futures that might confront them.
- The need to develop strategies that are appropriate for the environment that actually transpires.

Exhibit 11.3
Four Distinct Industry End States

Entry of Substitute Products

	No	*Yes*
Low *Marketing/Sales Expenditures*	**Live-and-Let-Live** Rivals are generally comfortable with their products, market positions, and economic returns. There is little effort to upset the balance among them.	**Subdued Product Contest** Rivals compete head-to-head to win customers, but they are willing to share the spoils. Both product types continue to attract customers. Rivals are comfortable with their performance result.
High	**Dog-Eat-Dog Warfare** Rivals compete to defend their own customers. Intense efforts are made to add product features, build relationships, add service, and match prices if necessary. Expectations are built around modest gains at the expense of rivals.	**A Switching Battle** Rivals compete around distinct product functionalities. Rivals see winning as a zero-sum game: They compete for every single customer around different forms of surgery. Special sales programs, incentives to customers, and price deals are the norm.

- How to identify the indicators that would suggest which environment was emerging over time.

Before scenarios can be assessed, however, the conditions characteristic of each end state must be spelled out in reasonable detail. Consider, for example, the Switching Battle end state where OPtech products compete with new substitute laser products. Managers in OPtech asked themselves the following types of questions:

- How would the traditional hand-held products and the new substitute products compete against each other?
- What would be the intensity of the marketing battle between these two groups of rivals?
- What would be the purchase choice criteria of surgeons and hospitals?
- Why would individual traditional product or substitute product competitors win or lose?

Box 11.1
Competitive Conditions in the Switching Battle End State

Surgeons now have a choice in the way they perform this type of surgery. They can use the long-established hand-held instrument or they can choose a form of laser surgery. Both the substitute competitor and the traditional product rivals are aggressively marketing and selling their products to hospitals and to individual surgeons. The two classes of rivals are putting considerable marketing and sales resources into the battle: the laser provider because it is buoyed both by its early success and by its sales projections (assuming its product replaces the hand-held instrument) and the traditional competitors because they recognize that a lucrative market can be lost.

The laser product has been adopted by some leading surgeons and hospitals. Although a number of concerns have been raised about this form of surgery, early reports of its success in medical journals have generated inquiries from many surgeons and hospitals and have further motivated the competitor to push quickly into the marketplace.

In deciding whether to switch to the new laser product, surgeons are considering a number of factors including: ease of doing surgery, number of surgeries that can be performed in a given period, medical complications for the patient, and length and ease of recuperation for the patient.

Individual hospitals are also considering a number of issues including: the amount of initial investment to perform the new type of surgery, the amount of training required for hospital staff, the length of stay in the hospital, and insurance consequences. A small number of surgeons are actively touting and advocating the use of laser surgery. This vocal group of "early adopters" are promoting the superiority of the new form of surgery at a number of medical association meetings and in brochures and related materials going out to individual surgeons and hospitals.

Box 11.1 provides some of the details of the intense competitive battle that would be likely in the Switching Battle end state: a world in which customers choose between rival products and heavy marketing/sales expenditures by the purveyors of both product types. This description affords OPtech managers the opportunity to experience what it would be like to do business should this particular future ever come to pass and to contemplate the kinds of issues that will be discussed in Part 2 of this chapter.

It is in the comparison of end states that managers genuinely begin to understand and empathize with the conditions prevailing in each end state. For example, the Switching Battle end state is a fundamentally different "world" than that which would prevail in a Live-and-Let-Live environment. Live-and-Let-Live is a world in which rivals do not have to contend with substitute products, and each rival is reasonably content with its share of the revenue pie. By comparing and contrasting the two worlds, managers begin to see the distinctions between them, and why (as discussed in Part II) a strategy that could succeed in one might fail miserably in the other.

More complex industry end states can be generated from the intersection of the three aggregate forces noted (see Exhibit 11.4). Each of the eight consequent end states represents a distinct industry context with particular competitive conditions. Generally, it will not be necessary to develop all eight scenarios. Sometimes a scenario may be dropped from consideration because the estimated chances of its occurring are judged to be so low, as was the case with the Continued Local Feud scenario.

Identify the Yet-to-Be-Played-Outs

Industries are also influenced by the way that individual events, decisions, and circumstances play out over time. It is thus important for those

Exhibit 11.4
Industry Scenarios: Potential End States

Anticipated Emergence of Substitute Products	Entry of New Competitors into the Current Product Category	Extent of Marketing/Sales Expenditures	Scenario Name
Yes	Many	High	Unmitigated Turbulence
Yes	Many	Low	Direct Old/New
Yes	Few	High	Direct New/Old
Yes	Few	Low	Frontal Challenge
No	Many	High	Extended Focal Product Battle
No	Few	High	Constrained Focal Product Battle
No	Many	Low	Extended Look-alike Battle
No	Few	Low	Continued Local Feud

constructing industry scenarios to identify those events, decisions, and circumstances that could have a substantial influence on how the industry will unfold. Some of these so-called yet-to-be-played-out events typically turn out to be central to specific scenarios that are eventually developed.

In the case of OPtech, three key yet-to-be-played-outs were identified. First, a trial was being conducted with a new form of laser surgery technology—a potential substitute product. If the trial proved successful, FDA approval could pave the way for the marketing of an innovative rival product so feared by many of OPtech's managers. Second, some leading hospitals were reviewing all aspects of their business, including the types of surgery they would perform. The type of surgery in which OPtech's product was used might be eliminated by some distinguished hospitals. Third, a few competitors had committed significant resources to technology programs intended to create the next generation of the traditional hand-held instrument. If the competitors' R&D investments proved successful, then OPtech would be faced with a superior form of its own product.

The benefit of identifying key future events is that each scenario can be assessed for the way such yet-to-be-played-out events might evolve. Thus, for example, each surgical instrument scenario could be assessed for how it depicts the evolution of laser surgery: the speed of market penetration of the new substitute form of surgery and the rationales or logics buttressing the scenario.

Identify the Accepteds

Many forces shaping an industry have a high degree of uncertainty associated with them, as the surgical instrument case shows. In contrast, some forces, or facets of an industry, may be expected not to change, or to change very little, over the course of the scenario time period. These forces can be referred to as *accepteds;* that is, decision makers accept that they will show little, if any, change over the relevant scenario time period.

Three accepteds emerged in the surgical instrument case:

- Growth in the number of this type of surgeries was not likely to experience a dramatic increase over the average of the prior three years.

- The two or three largest competitors would continue their efforts to be major players in the overall hospital market.
- Cost containment pressures in the hospital market would not abate.

Such accepteds help decision makers understand the context of industry scenarios in a number of ways. The data and logics that support (and maybe refute) each accepted help clarify and make visible the important distinction between those factors that can be treated broadly as constants and those that must be treated as sources of uncertainty, such as the aggregate driving forces. For example, recognizing that the two or three largest competitors in the market would continue to fight to gain market share across a number of product sectors would not greatly affect individual scenarios. However, as illustrated, scenarios would be greatly affected if they were to add significantly to their marketing/sales expenditures or to keep them at current levels.

Accepteds also can be used to test and refine aggregate driving forces. For example, if growth in this type of surgery was not likely to experience a dramatic increase, then an increase in marketing/sales expenditures by current competitors would truly lead to a cut-throat competitive environment. Accepteds also compel decision makers to better articulate and challenge their current assumptions about an industry as well as the assumptions underlying any particular scenario.

Identify the Impossibles

Analysis and reflection sometimes identify things that cannot happen or that are extremely unlikely to happen during the scenario period. We call these *impossibles*. Although great care must be taken in designating something as an impossible, consideration of this category has many of same benefits as noted in how the accepteds are handled. Three key impossibles were determined in the OPtech analysis:

- No substitute form of noninvasive surgery was likely to emerge and be accepted by most surgeons for at least two years.
- No drug would be introduced for at least three years that would cause a decline in demand for the type of surgery that used the firm's products.
- All hospitals could not quit performing this form of surgery, even though some were expected to do so.

When considering specific impossibles and their effect on industry evolution, decision makers should ask: What would have to happen for each impossible to occur? For example, what would the providers of a noninvasive form of surgery such as laser technology have to do in order to attract and win public support and approval from leading surgeons within one year?

Develop the Logics

Logics underlies the "story" or "plot" that connects the present to a specific scenario end state or outcome. Any story or plot, viewed as a "future history," must make sense. A plot then is really articulated connections among the relevant individual forces, such as those shown in Exhibit 11.2. It's a process that involves weighing the accepteds, yet-to-be-played-outs, and impossibles. The challenge confronting decision makers is to elaborate how each of the competitive environments depicted in Exhibits 11.3 and 11.4 might evolve. Simply identifying the dominant characteristics of a specific end state does not reveal how it could or might evolve. In developing any plot, decisions makers must deal with the following questions:

- What are the specific events that would have to happen for each end state to occur?
- What might be the sequence in which these events, decisions, circumstances, could occur?
- In each end state, what specific actions or decisions would specific actors—such as competitors, customers, distributors, and governmental agencies—have to make or not make?

The logics at the heart of a scenario can be articulated and elaborated in a number of different ways. One is to simply lay out in narrative form what would have to happen for a specific end state to occur. In other words, managers delineate the key events, decisions, actions, and circumstances that together lead to the specific scenario outcome. One such simple scenario plot is delineated in Box 11.2.

Unfortunately, the underlying forces and, in particular, the interactions among them, often are not self-evident in descriptions of scenario logics such as delineated in Box 11.2. One way to clearly depict such interactions is to diagram these relationships, as shown in Exhibit 11.5. Such diagrams

Box 11.2
Scenario Plot: The Switching Battle Environment

Emergence of Substitute Products and Intense
Marketing/Sales Activity in Current Products

Year 1

Optech's chief competitor establishes a small trial in a teaching hospital for its new laser technology product. This is the first trial in the marketplace. The results are satisfactory. A second set of trials are announced. One or two leading surgeons make statements suggesting this product is the way this type of surgery will be performed in the future.

In part, due to a slowing in growth of total product sales, rivals in the hand-held instrument begin to increase their marketing and sales efforts. The first "deals" are cut with large hospitals. Another new entrant also causes existing rivals to step up their efforts to defend all major customers.

Year 2

Optech's competitor commits to a small number of trials of the product. As the trials unfold, it seeks and finds new product champions, surgeons who will attest to the product's surgical superiority over the traditional hand-held product. The firm begins to target leading hospitals in selected geographic areas.

Most rivals in the traditional product begin to focus upon differentiation opportunities. Slightly different styles and features emerge. One or two firms begin to bundle the product; that is, include it as part of a package of products sold to an individual hospital at a favorable price.

Year 3

The rival firm commits to small-scale manufacturing. It now has sufficient product supply to begin intensive marketing and sales aimed at reaching some leading hospitals and widely respected surgeons in specific geographic areas. Strong testimonials from a small number of leading surgeons lend extensive credence to the competitor's product claims.

Rivals in the traditional product dramatically upgrade their marketing, sales, and service activities. Special presentations are conducted at the medical conventions. New promotional material aimed at purchasing personnel in hospitals is developed.

Box 11.2 (Continued)

Year 4

Optech's rival now commits to large-scale manufacturing. It aims to reach users (surgeons) in all leading hospitals in all geographic regions. It begins to achieve significant market penetration.

Some key hospitals have switched in part or completely to the new form of surgery. Some leading surgeons have further refined the use of laser surgery for this particular type of procedure. The success of the product has attracted the attention of potential new entrants. At least one or two firms, with extensive experience in laser and related technologies, are known to be developing products.

Rivals in the traditional product stage a last-ditch effort to retain a segment of the market. They introduce their long-planned product advancements and market them aggressively to the segment of surgeons and hospitals that have not yet switched to the laser form of surgery.

---

compel decision makers to consider and account for how the factors affect each other. In this way, causal connections are specified.

Industry logics can range from quite simple to reasonably complex. In some instances, only a few factors may be necessary to develop a plot that results in a particular scenario end state, such as in the narrative shown in Box 11.2.

ASSESSING INDUSTRY SCENARIOS

Using scenarios to clearly see the implications of decisions is a learning challenge for every organization. Managers must be willing to ask and answer tough questions. They must be willing to challenge fundamental, long-held assumptions about the industry and their own organization. A number of steps are central to deriving implications from industry scenarios (see Exhibit 11.5), each of which contributes to the derivation of specific strategy and operational implications for your organization. The steps are briefly described in this section.

Scenario Integration and Consistency

A useful point of departure in assessing any industry scenario is to test its internal consistency. Unfortunately, as scenarios become more com-

Exhibit 11.5
Assessing Industry Scenarios: Key Steps and Questions

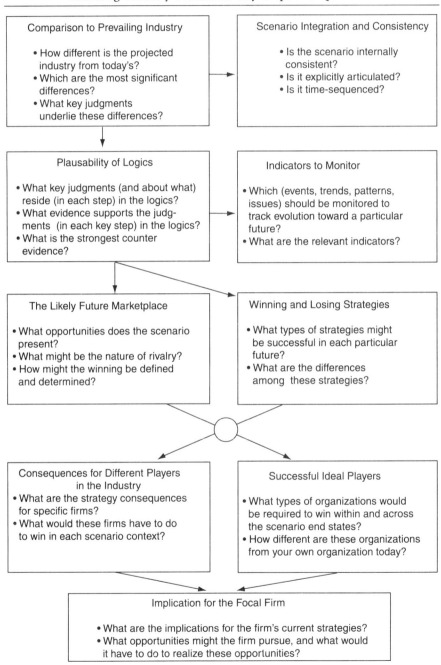

plex and dynamic, and as they take decision makers into unfamiliar competitive contexts, it is not uncommon for the narrative explaining how a specific end state occurred to reveal serious inconsistencies. For instance, the scenario plot might call for certain products to be introduced before it is actually possible to do so. Inconsistencies in a plot reveal problems with the underlying logic. The internal consistency test therefore can force decision makers to clarify and refine a scenario's plot and its underlying logics.

In one surgical instrument scenario in the OPtech case, an inconsistency arose between the projected rate of market penetration of a new laser technology product and the capacity of the competitor to manufacture and market its new product. In other words, the scenario team had projected product sales beyond the likely capacity of the competitor to produce the product. In another scenario, given the assumptions about the overall market size, an inconsistency emerged between the rate of penetration of the new laser product and the rate of decline in sales of OPtech's established surgical product.

Comparison to the Current Industry

Sometimes, decision makers get so involved in constructing and contrasting scenarios that they pay surprisingly little attention to differences between various end states and prevailing industry conditions. This creates a "reality gap" that can be best dealt with by asking, Can we get there from here? And if so, how? Getting answers to such questions will make decision makers reconsider the importance of thinking about what could happen in the future, and reinforces the need for them to articulate and challenge the plausibility of the logics underlying each scenario end state.

For example, even a cursory comparison of the Live-and-Let-Live and Switching Battle end states (see Exhibit 11.3) suggests that these competitive environments have little in common in terms of products available in the marketplace, the choices available to customers, and the dynamics of rivalry among competitors. Thus, even those OPtech managers most committed to the current strategy would have to admit that were they to find themselves in the Switching Battle environment two or three years down the road, blind adherence to the current strategy would only lead to disastrous performance results.

Plausibility of the Logics

A scenario can be logical but implausible. For example, it would be logical for OPtech managers to project that in the event of the successful launch of a new laser technology product, they would be able to develop and introduce a similar product. Because of the differences between the two technologies and OPtech's lack of knowledge of and inexperience with laser technologies, any aspirations or plans on its part to launch a competitive laser technology product would be highly suspect. The logics of each scenario therefore must be tested for its plausibility. Such tests go beyond the concerns of internal consistency discussed previously.

By posing and considering the following types of questions, managers gain a better understanding of a scenario's plot:

- What key judgments reside in each element or step of the logics?
- Who (outside and inside the organization) supports these judgments?
- What rationale or evidence supports each judgment?
- How might these judgments conflict?
- What is the strongest countervailing evidence?
- What is the balance of the evidence or rationales?

Consider again the Switching Battle scenario. With regard to the laser substitute product, OPtech's managers had to make judgments with regard to:

- Technology developments leading to the new product.
- Commitment of one organization (and most likely others) to introducing the product.
- Surgeons preferring the new means of doing this type of surgery.
- Acceptance of this new form of surgical procedure by hospitals.
- The superiority of the new products over the prior hand-held surgical instrument.

With regard to a significant increase in marketing/sales expenditures, critical judgments pertained to:

- The ability of competitors to devote additional resources to marketing and sales.
- The desire of competitors to do so.

- Competitors' expectations about the results of increasing marketing/sales expenditures.

Data supporting judgments about the substitute product had been received directly from some surgeons and from experts in the technology. OPtech's executives concluded from these interviews that the technology was feasible; the substitute product would be developed; and many surgeons would soon prefer it. Some actions and statements by competitors provided evidence that they would increase their marketing/sales expenditures. For example, some had said they would not hesitate to augment their marketing/sales budgets if market conditions warranted doing so.

No apparent significant conflicts were evident in the plots or the judgments underlying them in the early years of the scenario period. But one major potential incongruence emerged in years three and four. If the laser surgical product significantly penetrated the market, under what conditions and assumptions would the hand-held instrument rivals augment their marketing/sales expenditures in the face of quite low likelihood of winning? The scenarios seemed to forecast a case of "throwing good money after bad."

In short, all scenario plots must be challenged. Otherwise, it is too easy to accept an apparently convincing plot. The sternest challenge that can be posed to any plot is to develop strong countervailing logics. For example, a scenario that is built around a logic that postulates a major upturn in market sales can be challenged by demonstrating—by presenting a combination of logic and evidence—that overall market sales will decline. In many instances, the plot of one scenario automatically provides the logic to challenge another scenario's plot. Sometimes such countervailing evidence may be difficult to refute.

In the OPtech example, the evidence supporting the nonemergence of substitute products in the Live-and-Let-Live scenario can be used to challenge the judgments at the core of the Switching Battle scenario—that substitute products would emerge and successfully penetrate the market.

Indicators to Monitor

An observer of the industry who has studied a number of plausible scenarios—and the milepost events that mark the steps toward a given end state—has gained, in effect, a bird's eye view of the future that may actually emerge. Therefore, a critical output of a set of scenarios is the identification of the indicators that should be watched to determine which future, or end state, is emerging. Since the purpose of scenarios is to learn from the future, and preferably to do so before your competitors, indicators that allow a firm to anticipate the evolution of its industry are key outputs of industry scenario exercises.

A set of scenarios can produce a number of indicators that are common to every future in the set and those that are unique to each scenario. Each end state depicted in Exhibit 11.3 shares some common indicators that allow OPtech managers to track competitors' marketing/sales expenditures and the emergence of substitute products. In addition, indicators such as rivals' actual expenditures on advertising, trade/industry shows, promotional materials and salesforce support, announcements of intent to increase such expenditures, and customers' comments about competitors' marketing/sales commitments and plans, can be used to track competitors' current or potential marketing/sales expenditures. These indicators are relevant to each scenario plot or end state. The changes in the indicators you detect and monitor indicate the emergence of one scenario or another. For example, if the marketing/sales indicators noted were to reveal that competitors were adding new advertising programs, creating major new industry/trade show extravaganzas, and adding new salespeople, there would be little doubt but that marketing intensity was on the rise.

When indicators are distinct or unique to a particular end state or plot, they are critical to detecting the emergence of that scenario. For example, in the Switching Battle scenario, one such indictor might be, Are hospitals sharing information about the new laser technology?

When an indicator first appears is also important. For example, the first public support of the new laser product by a prominent surgeon in promotional material or as part of a formal presentation at a medical convention may be a critical indicator of the possible speed with which the laser product may penetrate the community of surgeons.

It is also essential to monitor the rate of change along key indicators. In the Subdued Product Contest and Switching Battle scenarios, for instance, the rate of change in the laser product competitor's manufacturing output or adoption on a trial basis by surgeons in different types of hospitals could significantly indicate the speed with which the laser product is already or is likely to be available in the marketplace, and could potentially penetrate the surgeon market.

Influencing the Likely Future Marketplace

But OPtech's managers can't wait for the future of their industry to happen. For OPtech to continue to be the marketplace leader, its managers must make decisions that can influence that future. And, even more generally, some understanding of the future of the industry always underlies any major decisions they make, such as the commitment of resources to develop new products or to extend their current manufacturing facilities. An extension of manufacturing facilities, for example, presumes that customers will buy the additional output and that competitors will not quickly outmaneuver OPtech by introducing superior products that customers will prefer.

Industry scenarios thus serve the very useful role of providing a context for the development of a number of categories of information and analysis critical to strategy making:

- New product opportunities.
- Emerging and potential competitors.
- New ways to compete against rivals with either new products, the next generation of existing products, or current products.
- Threats to existing or potential strategies.
- Potential marketplace dynamics among rivals.

First and foremost, industry scenarios generate a sense of marketplace opportunities across potential end states: new products that might be possible, new customers that could be reached, new customer needs that might be created. Frequently, these opportunities become apparent only after knowledgeable experts and managers together develop a set of scenarios. The extent of the opportunities may vary greatly across the set of scenarios. For example, the end states represented in Exhibit 11.3 range from little new opportunity in the Live-and-Let-Live context to extensive opportunity in the Switching Battle context. In short, the emergence of substitute products constituted a rich potential opportunity for those organizations with the necessary technological and marketing competencies.

That said, one organization's opportunity may be another organization's threat. An end state that is inviting for one organization may be the death knell for another. In the OPtech case, if laser surgery wins, then OPtech and the other makers of the old hand-held products lose.

The extent of potential opportunity or threat is also affected by the nature of the competitive dynamics at various stages in the industry's projected evolution. Even if substitute products did not emerge in the surgical instrument case, a shift from the Live-and-Let-Live to the Dog-Eat-Dog warfare context would spell doom for those not able or not willing to compete in the more intensively competitive conditions.

Differences across potential end states can also give rise to a need to reassess what constitutes winning and losing. For OPtech, winning could no longer be measured merely in terms of market share against its historic rivals, that is, those with similar products. Winning also meant gaining market share against laser surgery products.

Winning (and Losing) Strategies

OPtech's managers can assess which strategies might win or lose in each scenario's competitive conditions before committing real corporate assets. Consideration of winning and losing strategies has an important side benefit. If the winning strategies vary across the competitive conditions depicted in Exhibit 11.3, it reinforces in the minds of managers not only the need to craft distinct scenarios but to carefully monitor evolution toward them. For example, OPtech managers quickly discovered that a winning strategy in the Switching Battle scenario would most likely require laser technology products, not the case in the Live-and-Let-Live world. OPtech's managers thus became especially sensitive to the need to track and anticipate the development and emergence of the substitute laser products.

There is also the need to carefully assess the judgments involved in labeling strategies as winning or losing. The reasons managers believe a strategy would win or lose must be carefully assessed against the conditions and plot in that scenario. Otherwise, judgments made about strategies may be accepted without being fully tested against a variety of scenarios.

OPtech discovered that quite distinct winning strategies were likely across the scenarios depicted in Exhibit 11.3. In a Dog-Eat-Dog world, winners would have to continually add value for customers. Each change in product functionality, features, service and image would be quickly imitated and matched by rivals. On the other hand, in a Live-and-Let-Live world, market leaders could continue to be successful with their existing strategies. Winning and losing strategies can be used as a foil against which the organization's current and planned strategies can be compared and assessed. For example, OPtech's president could ask and assess whether or how its current strategy to attract and retain customers might succeed if it found itself competing in a Dog-Eat-Dog milieu rather than in its current environment, one that is closer to the Live-and-Let-Live world.

Consequences for Different Players in the Industry

In many organizations, critical learning arises when managers recognize that a set of industry scenarios may have distinct consequences for different industry players: for example, different competitors, different segments of customers, different distribution channels. There may be distinct consequences for different groups of competitors (such as high- and low-market share rivals or domestic and foreign rivals), different distribution channels (such as products moving from one type of channel to another), different suppliers (such as one type of component or supply becoming dominant), or different end customers or users (such as some customers acquiring greater product choice than others). It is essential to note that these differences may arise both within and across scenarios.

The four surgical instrument scenarios in the OPtech case did indeed have sharp differences in consequences for various industry players. For example, surgeons and hospitals would be faced with different surgical options. The rate of increase in competitors' marketing/sales expenditures could give hospitals very different price alternatives. Suppliers of components for hand-held instruments could see their sales increase or decline, depending upon the emergence and success of the laser product.

Successful Ideal Players

Another common source of insight in assessing industry scenarios is to ask: What type of organization would be required to win within and across the competitive contexts depicted in these scenarios? Again, the purpose of this question is to compel managers to step outside the bounds of their own organization and to give them a foil against which both the current and projected states of their own organization can be assessed. In the case of OPtech, if the ideal laser technology organization in the Switching Battle scenario turned out to be an entrepreneurial entity, with a culture driven by an unrelenting desire to build a new business, then OPtech would have to ask whether or how its own culture would impede its efforts to win against this type of competitor. Such comparisons can become a useful means of convincing managers that their organization, even though it is successful today, might need to undergo some radical change in order to win tomorrow.

Implications for OPtech

The ultimate purpose of each of these assessment steps is to generate specific implications for your firm—that is, what it should do. One useful way to integrate and extend the learning and insights generated in these assessment steps is to begin by considering whether your firm's current strategy is "robust"; that is, how well would it succeed in all of the scenarios?

A candid assessment of the lack of robustness of current strategy can cause managers to experience a type of future shock. This is what happened in OPtech when senior managers concluded that the firm's current strategy would not succeed in the face of a successful substitute product. The analysis on this point was convincing and conclusive: Surgeons would quickly adopt the new laser product. Since rivalry with the providers of the substitute product would be a zero-sum game (because the number of surgical procedures was not expected to grow), any gains by the new substitute competitors could come only from losses by the existing product suppliers. Indeed, even more intense shock waves were experienced when OPtech's managers argued that its current strategy most likely would not lead to market share gains, even in the absence of the new substitute product. If a number of existing competitors were to extensively increase their sales and marketing expenditures (the Dog-Eat-Dog scenario), OPtech would be faced with a rivalry intensity that it had never previously encountered.

In the absence of a robust current strategy, the firm must identify potential strategy alternatives. It must ask:

- Which strategy alternatives suggested by the industry scenarios might make sense for the firm?
- Which alternatives might take the organization in new strategic directions—divesting the current product line or acquiring new products, for example?

Once a group of managers has been shell-shocked by the realization that their current strategy is unlikely to succeed in a diverse set of potential competitive conditions, they are more willing to look at strategy alternatives that previously might have been totally beyond the bounds of consideration.

OPtech identified its strategy alternatives for each scenario end state. It recognized that three alternatives in both the Subdued Product Contest and Switching Battle environments would be:

- To develop a laser technology product.
- To acquire an organization with the technology to do so.
- To develop an alliance with either the firm currently developing the laser product or some organization with the capability to do so.

Such alternatives do not just pop up like Eggo waffles from a toaster. They only become evident when managers seriously commit themselves to asking what options they might have if each scenario were to occur. It is in the process of choosing among alternatives that scenario learning should prove most useful and most critical. Managers must challenge themselves by asking a number of questions:

- Which alternatives would be necessary if each scenario or end state were to come to pass?
- Which alternatives would succeed in two or more scenarios?
- When might the firm need to commit to a particular alternative?

The process of choosing among the identified alternatives crystallizes the strategy issues and decisions confronting the organization. For example, consideration of the alternative, acquiring an organization with a laser technology capability, compelled OPtech's managers to assess:

- Whether they had the financial wherewithal to make a substantial acquisition.
- How they might finance it.
- How the debt implications might affect the firm's ability to compete aggressively in the marketplace.

It was at this stage that OPtech's management asked another round of what-if questions:

- What would the company do if the laser product did not materialize?
- What would it do if the laser product emerged slowly or quickly?
- What would it do if competitors proved reluctant to add significantly to their sales and marketing expenditures?

These types of questions forced the decision makers to link their actions to possible futures. For the long run—in this case, three or four years—they concluded that if the laser product emerged and was successful, they would "milk" their current product line; they would not put any further investment behind the product line. Furthermore, they would leverage their manufacturing and technology competencies by developing a new line of surgical instruments. For the short run, they would continue to market and sell the current product line, but cut back extensively on their planned product development and manufacturing technology investments. They would immediately commit resources to exploring ways of developing a new line of surgical instruments.

CONCLUSION

Industry scenarios succeed when they grab managers' attention about a range of possible industry futures and about their strategy implications. Scenarios achieve this by convincing managers to "live" in a competitive world that challenges their current mental models about the fate of their business. When industry scenarios confront managers with industry futures that they have not previously considered, as happened to OPtech's managers in this case study, managers become more tentative about their long-held assumptions about the future; in many instances, they are forced to abandon them. Managers are then willing to entertain and assess new strategy alternatives. The premise and hope underlying industry scenarios is that the firm will be first to perceive these alternatives and understand how to exploit them.

CHAPTER 12

COMPETITOR SCENARIOS: PROJECTING A RIVAL'S MARKETPLACE STRATEGY

LIAM FAHEY

A key purpose of strategy is to outmaneuver and outperform competitors, present and future. But all too often, organizations are caught off guard by their competitors' strategic initiatives. Sometimes, too, they are surprised by a competitor's responses to their own strategic moves. Competitor scenarios offer a unique method of identifying and testing plausible competitor strategy alternatives. They also allow an organization to assess its responses to competitors' moves and to select a strategy that is viable in a variety of competitive conditions. This chapter provides a number of distinct approaches to developing competitor scenarios and shows how your firm can fully understand the implications of issues identified in the scenarios.

$\mathbf{S}$cenarios offer a proven means to generate an understanding of competitors' strategies, capabilities, and likely future actions. The success of any strategic move, such as the introduction of a new product, adding new forms of functionality to a solution, or entering a new geographic market, always depends upon the current initiatives of and potential reactions available to competitors. In short, strategy making that pays no attention to competitors is extremely risky. Consider the introduction of Netscape's innovative Internet software, which for a brief moment seemed to promise stellar market and financial returns. Analysts applauded wildly and the public stampeded to buy stock. But as soon as big competitor Microsoft set its targeting radar on the same product-customer segment, the stock analysts reacted as if they were on the verge of cardiac arrest, and share price plummeted. Microsoft didn't even have a product ready for market; it merely announced it was interested in developing one.

When the future of Netscape's stock looked so good, why weren't analysts drawing up scenarios about what competitors could easily do to capture Netscape's market? Even a move as simple and expected as lowering prices should be undertaken only after anticipating how, when, and why competitors will respond. Each year or so, airlines seem to forget that a massive discounting of prices causes rivals not only to meet their new price structure but entices at least one other airline to drop prices even further. Consequently, they stumble into a price war in which all rivals suffer profitability downturns.

If winning is about outmaneuvering and outperforming rivals so that value is continually enhanced for customers, shareholders, and other stakeholders, then every organization has little choice but to better understand its competitors. Competitor scenarios are intended to satisfy this quest. In particular, they serve three purposes:

- They provide an opportunity to generate knowledge about current and future competitors. For example, they help an organization anticipate the strategic moves available to its competitors, which ones they might be likely to adopt and execute, how they might do so, and what the results might be.
- They offer another avenue by which an organization can explore the nature and type of competitive dynamics that might characterize various product-customer segments at some future time.
- They generate critical input to the development, execution, and monitoring of the organization's strategies and action plans.

Each of these purposes will be illustrated in this chapter.

The competitor scenarios addressed in this chapter emphasize marketplace strategy—marketplace scope, posture and goals, as delineated and discussed in Chapter 2. Other types of competitor scenarios might address, for example, the technologies a competitor might develop and how it might do so; how a competitor might use alliances to achieve some purpose such as completing some type of basic research or gaining access to particular markets; or how a competitor might develop a new low-cost way of manufacturing and delivering its products to customers.

TWO TYPES OF COMPETITOR SCENARIOS

Although competitor scenarios can be developed in multiple ways, this chapter details two distinct, though related, approaches. One type of scenario stems from open-ended or unconstrained what-if questions that suggest possible end states, such as a completely new competitor strategy. These then require the development of a plot or story that would allow the competitor to trace a path to that future end state from its current strategy. On the other hand, scenario developers can also ask what the competitor would do under distinctly different competitive or industry end states. These constrained what-if questions generate scenarios requiring the development of very different plots, which enable scenario developers to project and assess widely disparate sets of competitor actions and their results.

Both types of what-if scenarios are intended to identify and assess potential competitor strategy shifts, their plausibility, consequences for the competitor, and implications for an organization. Both take an outside in view of competitor change by allowing scenario developers to ask what-if questions about the macroenvironment and then assess their implications for the competitors, other rivals, the industry, and their organization. Both are especially appropriate for dealing with discontinuous competitor maneuvers, which are often unexpected by rivals. As a consequence, competitor scenarios often challenge fundamental elements in managers' mental models, or understanding of their competitive environment, and thus present a new perspective on what it takes for their organization to win.

Unconstrained What-If Scenarios

The following what-if questions allow the scenario developers to raise any issue that occurs to them. Some examples are:

- What if the competitor fundamentally altered how it competes to win customers in the marketplace?
- What if the competitor launched a series of new products or quickly introduced a series of product line extensions?
- What if the competitor initiated one or more acquisitions as a means to quickly gain market share and position itself to be the dominant market leader?

- What if the competitor entered into a series of alliances in order to create a stream of products or solutions that was new to the market?
- What if the competitor suddenly decided to dramatically reduce the number of its product lines or business units?

The purpose of these what-if scenarios is threefold:

1. To identify what a competitor would have to do to execute specific types of strategic change.
2. To determine whether or how it could do so.
3. To assess the implications for the competitor itself, the marketplace, and the organization.

These scenarios thus involve consideration of competitor strategy end states that may be radically different from the competitor's current strategy.

Unfortunately, there is no simple methodology to determine which or how many what-if questions should be asked. Although there is essentially no limit to the extent or type of what-if questions that might be submitted, the following guidance may be helpful to ensure that a full range of such questions are posed. The breadth of the questions reflects the intent to generate a set of plausible potential competitor strategies that will lead to useful inputs to strategy making in your organization:

- Which generic strategy types found in any business strategy textbook might the competitor pursue? For example, might it try to be the low-price provider? Might it try to customize its solutions for all customers?
- Given what we know about the industry, what strategy alternatives might make sense for this competitor?
- What strategies of firms in other industries might be applicable to the competitor?
- Which strategy alternatives is your firm considering that might be appropriate for the competitor?

Four steps are involved in constructing a what-if scenario. To illustrate, we will use the example of an electronics competitor, "Pyrolectron." Historically, Pyrolectron had been a product and technology leader in a number of markets. Although its long-established offerings were still the share leader or a close second in most cases, it had not launched a successful major new product in more than a year. Many of Pyrolectron's rivals had begun to wonder what its likely strategic moves might be. The steps are:

1. *Clearly identify the strategy end state.* This requires specifying the content of the strategy; that is, determining the possible products or solutions; which customer needs and segments would be addressed; how the firm would differentiate its offerings from rivals; and what the driving market, financial, and other goals might be. What if Pyrolectron were to develop a network of alliances that would allow it to develop a range of breakthrough products? If the products were successful, Pyrolectron would open an avenue to a new set of customers. The intent of this strategy would be to leapfrog existing rivals and to be the first in the market with a new type of product or customer solution.

2. *Project what the competitor would have to do in order to execute the strategy.* The sequence in which these tasks would be accomplished constitutes the plot or story of the scenario. Among the tasks to be accomplished would be the following:
   - Identify the relevant types of alliance partners. These would include suppliers of key components, new technology sources, one or more institutions such as universities and specialist research organizations, and possibly a current product competitor.
   - Identify specific potential alliance partners.
   - Develop and execute alliance agreements.
   - Coordinate research programs that draw upon the knowledge and capabilities of the alliance partners.
   - Execute the research.
   - Manufacture and test the products.
   - Introduce the products.
   - Market the products to gain market penetration and share.
   Developing a time line, however tentative, around these tasks provides a frame of reference for monitoring the competitor's execution of the projected strategy.

3. *Identify the forces internal and external to the competitor that might drive this scenario plot.* In other words, what might drive the competitor to pursue this strategy? Competitor-specific forces for Pyrolectron would include: the aging of the firm's current product line; a modest deterioration of its market share position; and the intentions of

its chief executive to make the firm into the dominant competitor before he retired. External or competitive forces that might support this strategy direction included: entry of new competitors with products largely similar to the competitor's; a speeding up of new product launches by a small number of rivals; changes in many of the relevant product technologies; and customers seeking more cost-effective solutions.

4. *Elaborate the logics that would connect the driving forces, such as those just noted, to explain why the competitor would pursue and execute this strategy.* This requires that the scenario authors generate a series of cause-effect statements that would lead to a plausible set of arguments to justify the strategy for this particular competitor.

Here's a sample of the supporting logic. If the competitor does not create a networked organization involving a number of key alliances, it will not be able, using only its own resources, to develop and introduce a breakthrough product line. If, on the other hand, the competitor demonstrates the necessary organizational leadership, it could succeed in bringing the key technologies together that are necessary to create a new breakthrough product line. By working closely with a small set of customers, the competitor could shorten some of time required to develop the product line and increase the likelihood of developing solutions for real customer needs.

Clearly, developing supporting logics takes time. But it also gives the scenario authors an opportunity to expose and test their understanding not just of a competitor but of the entire competitive or industry context. For example, if Pyrolectron succeeded in shortening the product development cycle, it could lead to significantly new competitive dynamics. Rivals would have a shorter time period in which to recoup their research and development investments, causing them to be more aggressive in seeking and retaining customers. It is in this way that competitor scenarios contribute to industry learning.

Constrained What-If Questions: Comparative End-State Scenarios

These competitor scenarios are derived by asking what the competitor would do if a specific set of competitive or marketplace end states or conditions were to arise. These what-if questions are "future backward"; that is, they start with some specification of the competitive conditions at some future point in time and then ask, What would the competitor do under those conditions? They are therefore constrained what-if questions.

Scenario Purposes. These scenarios are intended to:

- Identify what the competitor would do under clearly specified marketplace conditions.
- Understand why the competitor might adopt one strategy or course of action as opposed to another.
- Assess decision implications for the organization.

Because these scenarios are derived from distinct industry or competitive end states, they facilitate assessment of what a competitor might do, and why, across different competitive conditions.

Consider the case of a software firm "SoftFollower" that has always been an imitator of the market leader, "SoftLeader." As soon as SoftLeader introduces a new product or the next upgrade of an existing product, SoftFollower generally follows suit. The lag time might be as short as two or three months or as long as one year. Currently, however, SoftFollower is trying to determine how it can wrest away product leadership from SoftLeader in one particular product area. As one input to its own strategy development and assessment, SoftFollower wants to anticipate what SoftLeader, its major competitor in this product area, might do under different competitive conditions. Constructing these scenarios involves a number of steps.

Determine End States. End states are derived by determining aggregate driving forces, or key uncertainties, that affect the product or industry sector being considered. Two key uncertainties were identified by SoftFollower:

- Research developments that could lead to new software products that would be considerably superior to the current product.
- The possible entrance of a significant new competitor that would compete directly against the existing product.

These uncertainties lead to four distinct end states that are briefly described in Exhibit 12.1.

Exhibit 12.1
Competitive Scenario End States

| | New Competitor Enters (Existing Product) | |
	Yes	No
Yes	**Pac-Man End State**	**Displacement Battle End State**
	The new product priced only marginally higher than the current product attracts new customers into the market. In response to the new product and the new entrants in the old product, the overall market begins to grow again. A small segment of old customers immediately switch to the new product. New rivals with only slightly superior old products target old channels and end customers. Old competitors reduce prices and launch new promotion programs to maintain their existing customer base. Many of them move to rapidly upgrade their products to close the gap with the new product.	New product priced considerably higher than the current (old) product attracts few new customers. It gains market share slowly as old competitors move quickly to retaliate, launching extensive marketing, sales, and promotion programs to shore up relations with existing channels and customers. Old competitors begin to market directly against each other. New product is heavily advertised. Channels slowly begin to push new product.
Emergence of Functionally Superior Product	**Local Battle End State**	**Carry-On End State**
No	Rivalry greatly intensifies but is strictly between combatants in the current product. There is little growth in the overall market. Since there is no distinct functionality advantage for any firm, rivalry revolves around image, service, and relationships with the trade. Prices remain relatively similar, although competitive pressures begin to push them lower. Combatants speed up commitments to research to generate the next generation of product.	Rivalry is between current combatants in and around current products. Each rival is relatively comfortable with its market position. It seeks to make small gains in market share through special marketing, promotion, and sales activities. All rivals begin to worry about how they can create the next generation of the product.

Identify Strategy Issues for the Competitor.   In developing a competitor scenario for each end state, SoftFollower must identify a number of issues and questions that SoftLeader would have to identify and analyze. Here are some of the issues and questions that would have to be considered by SoftLeader in each competitive context:

- What is the opportunity set that would be available?
- What threats would be posed to its existing business?
- What threats would be posed to its presumed or projected future strategies?
- How might it go about pursuing these opportunities and/or fending off these threats?

These issues and questions familiarize SoftFollower personnel with strategy challenges that would confront SoftLeader. In addition, they can begin to consider these strategy challenges in the context of their own organization. For example, they might assess whether the opportunities available to SoftLeader would also be available to SoftFollower.

Develop the Scenario Plot Outline: Strategy Choice.   A scenario can be developed for each end state. The story or plot can be built around a number of items: the strategy challenges confronting the competitor such as an opportunity or threat, the options available to it, the actions it might take, and the timing and sequencing of the actions.

Let's take the Pac-Man end state for purposes of illustration. As noted in Exhibit 12.1, in this end state, a new functionally superior product has been introduced by a new entrant to this product sector. As yet it has gained only modest market share. Customers have only begun to test the product. The trade and industry press gave it mixed reviews and faulted it for a lack of "customer-friendliness."

What will SoftLeader do, if confronted by this competitive context? An initial step is to identify what its options might be. These include:

- Fighting the new product with its existing product.
- Moving quickly to upgrade the functionality of its existing product and then going head-to-head with the new competitor.
- Invigorating its own R&D so that it could come to the market within a year or two with a product that would be directly competitive with the new market entrant.

- Using its own R&D to develop a product that would move to the next generation beyond the new entrant's product.
- Withdraw from this product area by milking its existing product for cash flow while slowly withdrawing technical and service support.
- Some combination of the preceding options.

Consideration of which option SoftLeader might choose depends upon what criteria are employed and, to a lesser extent, whose perspective is adopted. For example, it is sometimes useful to use as a criterion the following question: What would the competitor do if it wished to gain or retain a dominant product or market share leadership position? Another criterion is: What would the competitor do if resources were not an obstacle to its choices? This criterion often leads scenario developers to identify strategy options that might otherwise be overlooked. A criterion that sometimes leads to tough questions being asked of our firm is: What would the competitor do if it wanted to make life as miserable as possible for our organization? Consideration of criteria such as these helps to provide some insight into the logics that undergird the scenario story or plot that is ultimately adopted.

If your intent is to develop a scenario that most closely resembles the choices the competitor is likely to make, then your knowledge of the competitor is critical. In particular, a thorough understanding of the following facets of the competitor is essential:

- *Overarching goals*—its intent, vision, and mission, which will greatly influence the choices it makes and the options it rejects.
- *Recent strategy changes,* which will indicate commitment to pursuing specific goals.
- *Resource availability,* which will indicate capacity to pursue goals or changes in strategy.
- *Capabilities and competencies* it possesses or is trying to develop and extend, which will indicate ability to create or pursue specific strategies.
- *Culture*—its core values, beliefs, norms, and behaviors—which will indicate which options it is likely to support or reject, and how it will pursue their execution.

In the case of SoftLeader, the judgment was made that it would go to any extremes to retain its leadership position in this product sector. The option it would most likely choose therefore was: Develop a new product that would rival the new introduction.

Detail the Scenario Plot. Choosing an option does not identify how it will be executed. Indeed, a full understanding of what the option entails can be attained only when what the competitor has to do in order to make the option happen is detailed. Thus, detailing the story or plot involved in what the competitor must do to realize an opportunity or fend off a threat is a fundamental part of the learning experience in scenario development.

SoftLeader would have to accomplish a number of tasks if it were to develop and introduce a new product to go head-to-head with the new market entrant. The main tasks are:

- Determine the scope of the research and development challenge.
- Identify the specific research and development projects.
- Redirect some existing research and development activity to the new product.
- Commit resources to accomplishing these projects.
- Monitor and manage the projects.
- Identify alliance partners or other external sources of relevant knowledge.
- Create one or more alliances.
- Develop a plan to introduce and launch the product.

As we shall see in the discussion of assessment, identification of these tasks provides a means for SoftFollower to gauge the magnitude of the challenge confronting SoftLeader and to assess whether it can execute this strategy option.

Articulate the Logics. To identify the action elements required to execute this strategy option is not to explain why SoftLeader might pursue it. Thus the question must be asked: Which forces internal or external to SoftLeader might drive it in this strategic direction? A number of internal forces seemed relevant. Its senior managers had frequently stated that this product area was central to their aspirations to be a "powerhouse" in the software world for the corporate market. They would thus seem to be strongly committed to winning against any rivals who might enter this product area. Its design, development, and service capabilities were all geared to powering its growth around this product. Both its espoused and actual values clearly addressed doing what it took to win in this product sector. For example, its close working relationships with a variety of customers indicated that it meant it when senior managers talked about the importance of learning from customers and integrating customer experience and knowledge as an input to product development.

Some external forces also seemed to support this strategic direction. SoftLeader's image and reputation would be severely damaged if it conceded leadership of this product area to a new entrant. Also, success in this product area was essential to leveraging its power with the distribution channels and to affecting economies of scale in its marketing, advertising, and sales activities.

The linkage between any competitor scenario and your own organization can be made in a preliminary way by determining the business issues for your organization that stem from the competitor's projected actions and possible results. Doing so has a number of merits. It can quickly draw managers' attention to potential implications. In other words, a competitor scenario shifts from being a nice-to-do exercise to one that may significantly affect the organization's current and/or future decisions. If significant implications are detected, they can in turn sharpen the resolve and incite the motivation of the scenario authors to further refine and test the scenario. In short, the scenario begins to have a purpose and relevance for those involved in its development.

A number of issues were quickly detected for SoftFollower:

- If SoftLeader did in fact succeed in creating the new product, it would essentially guarantee that the product sector would shift away from SoftFollower's current product.
- Even if SoftLeader found it difficult to bring the new product to market, its efforts to do so would become known to some leading customers, who might then be less inclined to purchase SoftFollower's current product or even an improved version of it.
- If the new entrant and SoftLeader were to succeed in establishing the new product, SoftFollower would have little choice, if it wished to remain in this product sector, but to commit to extensive research to develop a similar or superior product.

ASSESSING COMPETITOR SCENARIOS

Scenario learning, as noted in Chapter 1, goes beyond just constructing a set of scenarios. It also includes assessing those scenarios for their action implications for your firm. A number of steps are typically involved (see Exhibit 12.2), and they are briefly outlined in this section.

Scenario Consistency

There is a basic test for any scenario: Is it internally consistent? Unfortunately, initial, and sometimes even refined, scenario plots manifest inconsistencies. Sometimes these are not evident until the scenario plot is carefully scrutinized. This is especially likely to be the case in scenarios in which scenario authors are projecting what a competitor would do under specified competitive conditions that have not yet arisen (the Comparative End State scenarios) or are asking what the competitor would have to do to achieve a particular end state or type of strategy (the unconstrained What-If scenarios).

Among the questions that always need to be asked are the following:

- Are the projected actions in an appropriate sequence?
- What actions, if taken, would preclude other projected actions?
- What inconsistencies might arise among the projected goals?
- Can the projected actions lead to the projected goals?

For example, the electronics competitor, Pyrolectron, cannot introduce new products until all the relevant research has been conducted. However, Pyrolectron's alliance partners cannot begin to do joint research until the alliance contracts have been agreed and signed.

Plausibility of Logics

The logics underlying competitor scenarios need to be carefully challenged and tested for a number of reasons. Scenario authors may unwittingly impose the logics prevalent in their own organization upon assessments of competitors' current and future strategies. Managers who protest that a competitor's actions and intentions "are not rational" often betray the conventional wisdom within their own organization. There is also an inherent danger that scenario authors may overly downplay the potential of

Exhibit 12.2
Assessing a Competitor's Strategy/Scenario: Key Steps and Questions

---

Scenario Consistency

Are the projected actions and events internally consistent?
Which actions and events must happen in what time sequence?

↓

Plausibility of Logics

What evidence supports the logics?
What might happen in the competitive environment
 that would impede executing the strategy?
What is the strongest counterlogics?

↓

Marketplace Dynamics

How might the projected strategy lead to change in the
 broader marketplace?
What would be the consequences for the entry
 and exit of rivals?
How might the dynamics of rivalry be affected?

↓

Competitor Consequences

What results does the projected strategy generate
 for the competitor?
Can the competitor execute the strategy?
How can the competitor leverage the strategy?

↓

Implications for Our Organization

How does the strategy augment our understanding of the competitor,
 the broader marketplace, and our own organization?
How does the projected strategy, its results, and consequences
 serve as input to our strategy development and execution?
How can the projected strategy help us analyze our own organization,
 our assumptions, resources, and capabilities?

competitors to adopt new, innovative, and entrepreneurial initiatives or to deny the potential value of those strategic moves.

Key questions that should be asked are:

- Would the alleged driving forces give rise to the projected strategic direction?
- Could the driving forces counteract each other, that is, pull the competitor in opposite directions?
- What would happen to the projected strategic direction if some of the driving forces dissipated or were countered?
- If the projected results did accrue, what position would the competitor be in?

Each element of the argument or reasoning in any logics must be critically assessed. For example, in case of SoftLeader, consider carefully the argument that the aspirations of senior executives to make it into a "powerhouse" in this product sector would lead to the emotional commitment and managerial resolve necessary to create, develop, and launch the necessary new product. If the competitor has not previously developed and launched a significant new product, the aspiration is less credible. Moreover, if other stated aspirations also have not been acted upon, the assertion loses additional credibility. The scenario authors may come to the judgment that the espoused aspiration is nothing more than "loose words."

An indispensable means to test the plausibility of any scenario logics is to develop the strongest possible counterargument or logics. Thus, the scenario authors might develop a set of arguments to support the contention that SoftLeader does not possess the aspiration, motivation, or capability to develop and launch the new leapfrogging product. Extensive learning about a competitor always takes place in the discussion and debate over competing logics. Scenario authors must listen to and consider countervailing arguments; thus, assertions without evidence or supporting data tend to be exposed.

Marketplace Dynamics

Although it is often receives little attention, a number of competitor scenarios can be interrelated to develop projections about the marketplace in which their strategies will play out. For example, a set of scenarios addressing how several book publishers might begin to use electronic media to market, promote, and distribute books in competition with the book selling chain of Barnes & Noble and Internet based sellers such as Amazon.com. could be used to depict the nature of rivalry between these publishers three years from now. In this way, competitor scenarios can serve as an input to projections of competitive conditions that might be faced by any competitor.

In the SoftLeader case, if its new product did reach the market within 18 months, the competitive dynamics would be significantly altered, for at least two products would be vying for the same customers. Marketing strategies of any new entrants with a rival product including SoftFollower would now have to take into account two rivals rather than one.

Competitor Consequences

To project a competitor strategy is one thing; to have to execute it may be quite another. Even if the competitor can execute the strategy, it may not give rise to marketplace and financial results that it would find acceptable. Thus, each projected competitor strategy must be assessed for the results it generates for the competitor and whether the competitor can actually execute it.

Strategy Results.   Every projected strategy leads to results for the competitor, including market position, financial returns, and technological advancement. The actual results of course depend to some extent upon the strategies of rivals and other factors outside the control of the competitor, such as governmental interventions, technology developments, and changes in customers tastes. Thus, strategy results cannot be separated from the competitive conditions in which they are realized. Nevertheless, it is essential to project what the results might be; otherwise the strategy simply cannot be evaluated.

SoftLeader, for example, in a direct clash with the new entrant, based upon its brand name, marketing and service capabilities, and the new entrant's lack of these assets, might be able to gain 25 to 40 percent of the market within six months. These market share gains might be especially likely if the new entrant's product did not live up to its promises. Assuming that the new product replaces the existing product, such market share would generate significant financial returns. The real market battle, however, would begin only as other rivals, including SoftFollower, entered the market.

Assessment must also weigh whether the competitor would be content with the results. Considerable learning can occur when it becomes apparent that a coherent competitor strategy that appears to be entrepreneurial and innovative would not lead to acceptable results. For example, the costs associated with developing and executing the strategy would not generate acceptable margins or profits. In certain cases, projected market share gains would not satisfy a competitor's espoused goal of marketplace dominance or to be the number one provider in a particular product category.

Given SoftLeader's culture and its often stated aspiration to be the dominant competitor in this product area, SoftLeader almost certainly might be satisfied with a 25 percent market share but it would want to grow that share significantly in the following months.

Execution.   Another critical element in assessing results is to ask whether or how the competitor can leverage the projected strategy and its results. Key questions typically include:

- Can the projected products be a stepping stone to the next generation of products?
- Can the competitor attain further economies of scope or scale?
- Which synergies might be developed with other products?
- Which capabilities associated with the strategy can be further developed?

Leveraging the projected strategy into further successful generations of the product would be central to SoftLeader's desire to be the dominant player in this product area. To do so, it would have to continue augmenting its research and development and building alliances with other sources of relevant knowledge—something it has done in other product areas.

Implications for Your Organization

The assessment steps discussed so far are intended to help identify decision and action implications for your organization. Although implications will clearly vary from one competitor context to another—that is, different competitors with different strategies—they can be assessed usefully with regard to your firm's knowledge, strategy, and organization.

Knowledge.   Successful scenarios enhance decision makers' understanding of the present and the future. Competitor scenarios should specifically augment their understanding of competitors, the broader marketplace, and their own organizations.

Projecting and assessing competitors' strategies enhances our understanding of their future strategy options, why they might choose one option rather than others, how they might execute their strategies, and what the results might be. Competitor scenarios have demonstrated many times how incomplete our knowledge is of which strategy options are available to competitors and why they might choose one rather than another. As a consequence, we are surprised when they make some choice or do not respond in the way we had anticipated. In short, the intent of competitor scenarios is to understand specific competitors so well that we can imagine their choices under a variety of circumstances and anticipate their decisions.

Furthermore, as should be evident from the preceding discussion, competitor scenarios also lead to insights about the emerging and potential marketplace. Knowing that SoftLeader could decide to pursue the new entrant with all its might and power, we can anticipate a radically different picture of the competitive conditions in that product area in 12 or 18 months. Stated differently, projections of competitor strategies force us to articulate and challenge our implicit views of what the marketplace might look like at distinct points in the future.

An often overlooked benefit of this competitor scenario process is that it helps us to get to know our own organization. For example, we can use our evaluation of a competitor's resources, capabilities, and managerial commitment as a benchmark of our own capabilities. In some cases, when compared to one or more competitors, we end up having to alter our judgments about the quality or quantity of specific assets possessed by our own organization, or the extent and potential of specific competencies. For example, SoftFollower's view of its marketing and service skills is diminished when they are contrasted against those of SoftLeader. Such judgments become a "reality check" on how we grade our own organization.

In addition, assessment of our own organization's knowledge can lead directly to decision and action implications. For example, SoftFollower is now confronted with a number of decisions about its marketing and service skills. What should it do to augment and enhance these capabilities? How can they be combined and integrated so that the firm can compete more effectively against SoftLeader? Or should they be directed toward products that would be aimed at competitors other than SoftLeader?

Strategy.   Assessment of knowledge, as discussed, is clearly an important input to determining strategy implications. Competitors' projected strategies, their results and consequences become an input to our firm's strategy development and execution.

Consider the options open to SoftFollower: If it assumes that SoftLeader will pursue the projected strategy, and that this product will replace the current product over the next two years or so, then it must immediately identify which strategy options it has and how they should be evaluated. One radical implication for SoftFollower is that its prior assumption that its strategy built around its existing product would allow it to follow Soft-Leader for the next two or three years would have to be abandoned. In short, SoftFollower would have to approach its strategy development and evaluation process from a fundamentally new point of departure. Its prior assumptions about the marketplace and itself could no longer be an acceptable starting point.

SoftFollower can also consider the implications for its current strategy if the competitive conditions in the Carry-on scenario transpire: A new product breakthrough does not occur and no successful competitor enters with a largely look-alike product (see Exhibit 12.1). Although this scenario represents a fundamentally distinct set of competitive conditions, SoftFollower can also clearly consider all the strategy options identified in the Pac-Man scenario. The strategy challenge confronting SoftFollower in the Carry-on scenario is how to take market share away from the dominant leader and position itself to win in the battle that will inevitably be fought around the next generation of the product in the next two years or so.

Consideration of multiple scenarios with regard to a specific competitor allows decision makers to search for a robust strategy. This is the strategy that would make sense no matter which strategy the competitor pursued. In the case of SoftFollower, product development emerged as the key ingredient in any likely robust strategy. The type of research, how extensive the research, and how rapidly it was pursued hinged upon the competitive conditions that were expected to emerge.

Though a robust strategy may not exist, assessment of distinct competitor scenarios alerts decision makers to the indicators that should be

monitored to anticipate and track which strategy the competitor is actually pursuing.

   Organization.   Strategy and organization implications go hand in
hand. Considerations of strategy change always give rise to questions about
whether or how key organization attributes such as structure, decision-
making processes, resources, capabilities, and culture need to be changed.
   Competitor scenarios must be incorporated into your organization's
decision-making processes. For example, the content of competitor scenarios has direct relevance for almost every stage of an organization's
strategy-making process or strategic planning system. They affect the
assumptions that are developed at the early stages of the planning process, assumptions not only about competitors but also, as noted previously, about the general marketplace conditions and the firm itself. They
affect the opportunities and threats that are identified. They affect the
criteria by which strategy choices get made. As noted in the case of
SoftLeader, a competitor's potential strategy moves can cast your own
organization's moves in a favorable or unfavorable light.
   Also as discussed, one of the great hidden benefits of treating competitor scenarios seriously is that they give decision makers an external refer-
ent to assess their own organization, especially its resources and capabilities.
One output frequently is alternative action plans to augment and invigo-
rate particular resources and capabilities.

ORGANIZING TO PREPARE COMPETITOR SCENARIOS

Constructing and assessing competitor scenarios takes time, resources,
and commitment. It is therefore important that your organization address some central issues and questions in order to enhance its return on
the effort it expends on competitor scenarios.

Who Should Be Involved?

The development of competitor scenarios should not be left to any one
department or unit. Individuals from different departments or functions,
such as research and development, marketing, finance, manufacturing,
sales and service, should be involved in the scenario development and
assessment process. The reason is very simple: They possess different

insights into competitors, have access to different types of data and data sources, and are likely to ask different types of questions about competitors. Moreover, these individuals can take the learning that accrues from being involved in competitor scenarios back to their departments or functional units.

What Drives Competitor Scenario Team Effectiveness?

Forming an ad hoc team is a useful way of getting individuals from a number of business units who otherwise might have little contact with each other to concentrate their energies upon learning about competitors. For best results, the team needs to have:

- *A clear agenda.* For example, to understand potential strategies of recent new entrants.
- *Specific tasks to accomplish.* For example, to develop scenarios for two competitors.
- *Agreed time lines.* For example, preliminary scenarios to be completed by a specific date.
- *A leader.* To shepherd the team through the scenario development and assessment process.

Teams serve the important function of allowing the benefits of scenario learning to be experienced across a number of units and levels in the organization. For example, in the SoftFollower case, forming a team consisting of representatives of various departments—research, development, product engineering, strategic planning, finance, and marketing— helps to ensure that each department has a shared understanding of the likely strategies of SoftLeader and their implications.

Should the Team Have Access to External Experts?

It is always essential that a competitor scenario team, at a minimum, have access to knowledgeable people outside the organization. These include: customers, channels, suppliers, technology experts, management consultants, and others who have interaction with the target competitors. If your organization has little experience in developing scenarios, it is advisable to use an external consultant, if for no other reason than to avoid many of common pitfalls associated with firm's initial scenario efforts.

Should Scenarios Be Linked to Specific Strategy Issues/Decisions?

Often it is appropriate to develop competitor scenarios in response to a particular strategy issue or current or potential decision. For example, SoftFollower developed its set of scenarios with regard to a specific strategy issue: How could it wrest away product leadership from Soft-Leader in one particular product area. Such decisions or issues provide a context for the development of either unconstrained or constrained what-if scenarios.

Are Open-Ended Competitor Scenarios Helpful?

It can be useful to develop competitor scenarios first and then determine which strategy issues or decisions they generate for your organization. The starting point then is not your own organization's issues or decisions but the strategies one or more competitors might pursue. Both types of what-if scenarios can be used for this purpose.

The benefit of this open-ended approach is that it typically induces more open-ended thinking and questioning about competitors, and sometimes leads to surprising strategy and decision implications for your organization. It is especially appropriate if one purpose of the scenarios is to motivate a number of individuals to think more openly and critically about what competitors might do and why, how the broader industry might evolve, and what their own organization might do to influence the actions of competitors and the direction of the industry.

Which Competitors Should Be Targeted?

This is not an easy question to answer with a generalization. It never makes sense to develop scenarios for all competitors. Nor does it make sense to do so for a single representative from classes or groups of competitors such as large and small market share rivals, domestic and foreign, wide and narrow product lines, wide and narrow geographic coverage. There should be a specific reason for developing scenarios pertaining to any competitor. An unavoidable issue for any scenario team to grapple with therefore is which competitors should be subjected to scenario treatment. A number of questions can help guide this discussion:

- Which competitors might be the greatest source of learning about (for example) customers, channels, suppliers, and future dynamics of rivalry for your organization?
- Which competitors are most likely to be negatively affected by your firm's strategies and actions?
- Which competitors are most likely to embark upon major new strategic initiatives?
- Which competitors have demonstrated a tendency to engage in surprising strategic actions?
- Which competitors could do your firm the most damage?

CONCLUSION

The two competitor scenario approaches outlined in this chapter provide scenario authors with distinct but related ways to investigate the strategies that might be available to a competitor. Regardless of how they are developed, competitor scenarios generate an understanding of competitors' plausible strategy options, and provide indications of which options they might choose and why. They can then be used to generate many different types of insights and implications, and help to understand not just which strategy alternatives a competitor might pursue but what it would have to do to execute each alternative. They generate a variety of data such as competitors' likely new products and modes of competing that contribute to developing broader industry scenarios. A major benefit of these competitor scenarios is that they can also identify possible strategies by which your organization can respond to or use to preempt competitors' potential strategic moves.

CHAPTER 13

SCENARIO-BASED PLANNING FOR TECHNOLOGY INVESTMENTS

CHARLES W. THOMAS

Technology decisions are among the most crucial that a company makes. Investing in unique high-technology offerings or service capabilities to gain competitive advantage are strategic decisions best made with top management's full participation and understanding.

Good technology choices are those that have the potential to succeed in a variety of possible future markets. Bad choices gamble a company's competitive position on the arrival of only one possible future. If that "single-point forecast" does not emerge, the stage is set for a slide into noncompetitiveness. Scenario planning can help management make better technology decisions by better understanding the choices—both the opportunities and the risks involved in preparing for a dynamic, turbulent, and uncertain future market.

A team of technical experts that evaluates a technology in terms of its uniqueness, performance growth potential, or against the current competition is likely to miss critical future marketing opportunities and fail to see important potential risks, especially nontraditional ones. Just because developers have detailed knowledge of an emerging technology or have developed a superior product, does not guarantee market success. In contrast, when scenario-based technology planning is skillfully employed, it combines a thorough knowledge of the technology with a wide-ranging assessment of what the future market will demand. Scenarios can help managers evaluate the technology future customers will need.

The second section of this chapter will be devoted to various applications of scenarios to technology decisions, as demonstrated in four case studies. But before looking at applications, we must set some ground rules about scenario planning and how technology scenarios are developed.

Scenarios are decision-making tools, and like all good tools, scenarios must be used correctly, and for the appropriate job.

DEVELOPING SCENARIOS FOR TECHNOLOGY DECISION MAKING

Scenarios are developed first by casting your net widely to identify the many potential issues, trends, and factors in the business environment—past, present, and future—that can have an impact on your business. These issues and trends are called *business drivers,* and whether your objective is to explore the corporate business portfolio strategy or a technology investment strategy, you should not restrict this initial research and brainstorming activity. No matter how narrow your planning objectives, it is crucial to consider all influences at this early stage.

Don't fall into the trap of seeking out "good" drivers and ignoring "bad" ones. In the context of future business environments, you will not know which are important drivers and which can be ignored, so collect all the potential significant influences. These can be systemwide issues, such as global war or the power of the World Trade Organization; and issues closer to home, for instance, worker education programs or your corporate benefits package. Drivers can be issues over which you have influence (regulatory legislation or the level of your technology investment) or those you do not (the U.S. national debt or the liquidity of unfunded pension liabilities in France).

When you have compiled a broad list of significant influences, the next step is to reduce the breadth of your examination and bring some rigor and systematic analysis to categorizing the business drivers. This involves clustering and synthesizing all the drivers (typically as many as 150 to 200) into the macrolevel issues that define the overall decision-planning environment. These macrolevel clusters become the fundamental assumptions of your planning effort, the base assumptions upon which you build the scenarios. These macrolevel assumptions are called *dimensions.* They define the boundaries (dimensions) of the scenario planning space. Where drivers have no rules of inclusion and exclusion, dimensions have very specific rules:

- They are defined at a macrolevel.
- Their future "state" is uncertain.
- They are factors over which your organization has no control.

To understand this process better, try imaging the visual image of a cube in "future space." Somewhere inside that cube is where your company's future lies. The dimensions of the cube define your planning space. The first task is to make sure that the cube encompasses all the issues relevant to your business. Everything you, your colleagues, and external experts think is important to consider must be "inside" that cube—those are the business drivers. When you define the dimensions, you are describing the boundaries of that cube or planning space. By defining the dimensions, you are setting the boundary conditions of the planning environment. Eventually, you will be choosing your planning scenarios from the inside of that cube.

A Defense Contractor Example

The management team of a typical scenario-planning effort will nominate between 125 and 200 business drivers. For example, the drivers nominated by a defense contractor planning team might include; global defense alliances; economic competitiveness; ethnic tensions in Europe; types of weaponry available; Japanese economic policies; state and local business and tax incentives; types of warfare; U.S. economic strength; global free trade; number of graduates in engineering disciplines; terrorism; sources of conflict; the globalization of industry; isolationist foreign policy; location of conflicts; frequency of conflicts; telecommunications developments.

The dimensions selected to define the planning environment emerge from a clustering of the business drivers. For example, clustering some of the drivers just given (types of warfare, location of conflicts, terrorism, sources of conflict, and frequency of conflicts) suggests that one possible dimension is Level of Global Political Instability. Sometimes a driver becomes a dimension (the Strength of the U.S. Economy, for example) but that is rare. More frequently, managers select appropriate dimensions after they go through the process of categorizing, synthesizing, merging, and blending the large set of original business drivers into macrolevel dimensions. The goal is to select those dimensions that will represent future market and business issues in ways that stretch conventional wisdom and encourage innovative thinking, yet still present the business environment in ways that are meaningful to the operating managers.

Selecting the dimensions is difficult work and involves about half science and half art. It also requires good teamwork between the scenario team and line managers. In this defense contractor case, the company managers began with about 175 business drivers nominated from research, internal and external interviews, and a final "brainstorming meeting" intended to explore the interrelationships among the drivers. Such a meeting is often a great help in clustering the drivers into macrolevel dimensions. In this case, the clustering and analysis of drivers produced four dimensions that were used to set the boundary conditions and define the variations in the future business environment in a way meaningful to the company's strategic business interests:

- The level of U.S. global involvement.
- The level of global instability.
- Countervailing military power (to the United States).
- U.S. economic vitality.

The dimensions were then arrayed in a matrix to produce a "scenario space" from which the scenarios were to be selected. The next task was to select the minimum number of scenarios from that planning space that together captured the range of threats and opportunities that must be explored (see Exhibit 13.1). The scenarios were chosen to reflect the need for a defense firm to think about the range of its business opportunities and constraints, and the products and technologies it should develop to accommodate a range of future business settings.

This defense firm project, circa 1988, was primarily an effort to make some critical long-term strategic decisions about technology investment. Yet, despite its importance to the study, technology was not among the defining dimensions of the planning space. Usually, technology makes a poor defining dimension (or assumption) for scenarios intended to be used for technology decisions. That is often a hard predisposition to overcome. Technology-based firms are comfortable with technology concepts, and, after all, they wish to make technology decisions. But using technology terms to define the planning setting—the scenarios—can cause serious problems.

The decisions faced by the defense contractor illustrate this problem. The first dilemma was, How do we define a technology dimension? What macrolevel expression can be used to capture future technology states? Initially, the managers thought of defining some worlds as "high technology" and some as "low technology." Later, and perhaps more realistically, they tried "high technology growth" and "low technology growth." But

Exhibit 13.1
Scenario Space: Future Global Defense Market to 2005–2010[1]

	Name[2]	Level of U.S. Global Involvement[3]		Countervailing Military Power[4]		U.S. Economic Vitality		Level of Global Involvement	
		High	Low	Focused	Diffuse	Vibrant	Weak	High	Low
1	U.S.-Driven Market	•		•		•		•	
2		•		•		•			•
3	Dangerous Property	•		•			•	•	
4		•		•			•		•
5	Regional Markets	•			•	•		•	
6	Peace and Prosperity	•			•	•			•
7	Confused Priorities	•			•		•	•	
8		•			•		•		•
9			•	•		•		•	
10			•	•		•			•
11			•	•			•	•	
12			•	•			•		•
13			•		•	•		•	
14	Isolationist Dream		•		•	•			•
15			•		•		•	•	
16			•		•		•		•

[1]Average weapon system R&D cycles in the defense industries are between 10 and 15 years. This planning horizon was chosen to take the analysis beyond consideration of products currently "in the pipeline."
[2]Named worlds are those chosen for analysis. They are selected to represent the plausible range of opportunities and constraints to be faced.
[3]Included military, economic, and diplomatic involvement.
[4]Is military power in the world "focused" on counteracting the "American preponderance," or is it more generally aimed at various local and regional threats?

as they thought through the implications of those dimensions, they asked themselves, "Why should we expect that all the technologies will develop in similar ways or at a similar pace?" And, "Isn't the potential for differential growth in competing technologies something we might want to test?" Finding a satisfactory technology dimension that does not restrict your planning options turns out to be quite difficult.

A serious planning (and logic) dilemma is produced when the very thing you want to explore—potential technology investments—is fixed as a defining assumption of the planning environment. Finally, the defense contractor's managers concluded that, for them, technology was too important an unknown to make possibly unwarranted assumptions about at the beginning of the planning effort.

Technology is often one of a firm's most promising ways to respond to or to create a future business environment. It should be left to the planners who develop the scenarios to select strong and robust technologies suitable in a range of futures. The scenarios should not constrain their imaginations about technology.

Scenarios provide managers with plausible hypothetical business environments where they can test and explore the viability of a range of technologies. But how can scenarios depict opportunities in technology investments if technology is not part of the definition of the future world they describe? First, the scenarios must provide rich detail about the forces that drive personal and business decisions so that the scenario user can decide which technologies will flourish. For example, the scenarios should provide detail about the business and lifestyle priorities of your customers, and where appropriate, of your customers' customers. Well-drawn scenarios simulate complex, richly detailed, often confusing business environments into which managers can venture armed with their business expertise and ask, "Which products and technologies would work here?"

However, scenarios that are intended to aid in long-term technology investment decisions have some special requirements. The planning horizon must extend well beyond the current R&D cycle to divorce future technology decisions from the biases caused by technologies currently in the pipeline. The scenario environments must contain certain information required for technology decision making.

Although information needs differ from industry to industry, there are some common threads. The terms at which capital resources will be available—the cost of investment capital, the status of interest rates and inflation, government monetary and fiscal policies—must be addressed in each scenario. Trends in regulatory issues—not just those directly affecting the technology but background regulations like those of the Environmental Protection Agency (EPA) or Office of Safety and Health Administration (OSHA)—also must be well documented. If the time horizon is a bit distant, attention should be paid to trends in technical graduate schools and changes in the general social setting for the introduction of new technologies.

The scenario team should not be content merely to enumerate the list of technology decision drivers and include them in the scenarios. The scenarios must provide the logic for thorough analysis of those drivers and their interrelationships. For example, not only must capital availability be examined in all three scenarios:

- Available but very expensive.
- Tightly controlled by government priorities.
- All but nonexistent in the advanced industrial countries but flowing in the emerging markets.

In addition, the interrelationship between capital and other key drivers must be logically explored. This is critical if the scenarios are to be a reasonable reflection of true business issues.

Finally, scenarios should be used to challenge an organization's conventional wisdom. Scenarios offer an opportunity to test the assumptions that a firm simply never thinks to question, such as, "The infrastructure investments needed to enter our industry are so huge that we have an effective barrier to new competitors."

Assume that you have developed a set of scenarios for your specific organizational planning needs. The scenarios capture the range of threats and opportunities for which you must plan, and they thoroughly assess both the business environment and the priorities of your customers. In addition, assume that the scenarios were developed initially for corporate planning and that the firm has already used them to devise a core set of resilient strategies that will work across a range of futures. That is a sound starting point for technology planning, since the technology decisions will be coordinated from the outset with corporate priorities.

Now what? How can technology insights be derived from these scenarios?

Picking the Lineup. The next task is to pick managers who will participate in the technology-planning process. Effective leaders of the corporate-planning process can join this more focused effort. Most scenario-based technology planning efforts will also include members of the science and technology staff, marketers, business developers, manufacturing staff, and, occasionally, representatives of the finance staff. The team will be asked to learn to "live" in the futures that have been created. It will be their job to analyze and evaluate the new products that future customers will demand in each scenario. Then they must match those customer demands—the firm's potential future products—with appropriate technologies.

Two Methods for Adopting a World

There are two distinct approaches to this effort. In both, the planning teams break up into "world teams" and investigate the products demanded by customers in each scenario independently. At The Futures Group, we call this process "Adopt-A-World"[1] because we ask each of the world teams to "adopt" a scenario world and assume for a time that it will be the only one that actually occurs.

Technology Linkages.   In the first approach, all the products from all the scenarios are examined for technology linkages. The goal is to identify the core set of technologies that are required to develop the products that emerged from all the scenarios. This is certainly the most comprehensive approach, but it is also the most resource-intensive. Unfortunately, this approach does not provide technologists with a clear understanding of how their colleagues would decide among various alternatives before making a product selection. The list of products that is collected is usually too much like a "wish list," and worse, this approach avoids answering the question, What will you give up to get your wish?

Technologies Needed for Tomorrow's Products.   The second approach (see Exhibit 13.2), is more commonly used. First, a set of products that don't exist yet but probably will be needed in all the scenarios is identified. Then this set is used to evaluate current technology alternatives. This process helps the technologists prioritize their own work and take into account corporate priorities. The goal is to select a core set of technologies that support likely customer needs in a range of futures, and that correspond to corporate goals. As is the case in all good scenario planning, this should never be a onetime procedure, but a continuing part of the technology evaluation process.

SCENARIO PLANNING IN THREE TYPES OF TECHNOLOGY-RELATED DECISIONS

There are numerous technology-related decisions that will be enhanced by adopting scenario-based planning techniques. The following four case studies were selected to capture a range of applications for this technique. In the first case, the scenario user, "Consolidated Finance," was not a technology firm at all, but was making business decisions and investments

Exhibit 13.2
Technology Needed for Future Products

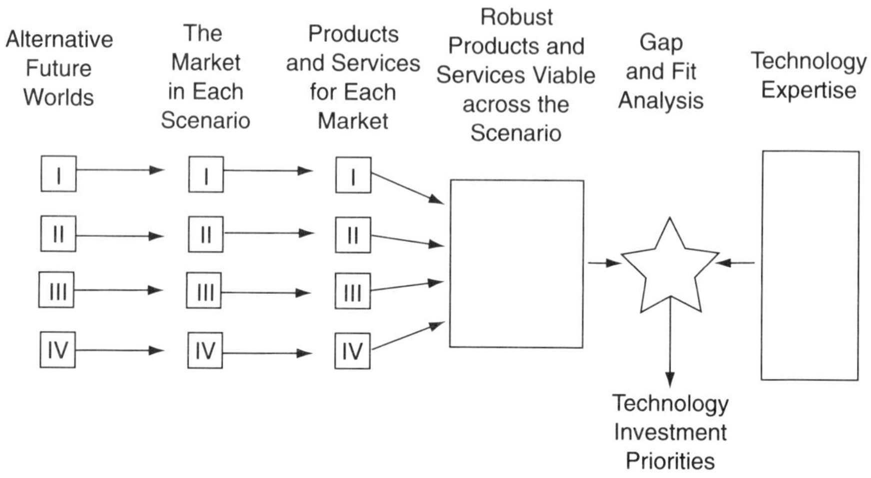

Alternative Future Worlds	The Market in Each Scenario	Products and Services for Each Market	Robust Products and Services Viable across the Scenario	Gap and Fit Analysis	Technology Expertise

Technology
Investment
Priorities

based on which future technologies would succeed. The second case study looks at a more typical application of scenarios to technology decisions. In this case the firm, "The Knowledge Bank," used scenario-based planning to choose which technologies would form the foundation of new business processes (primarily "product" production and distribution). The third and fourth cases examine the technology decisions that firms—"Industrial Visions" and "White Hat Aerospace"—had to make to meet future customer product needs at a time when their markets were in considerable turmoil and unusually unpredictable.

Case Study: Consolidated Finance Invests in Technology Markets

This first case study may seem a bit out of place in this chapter because the company employing scenarios in this case was not a technology firm and had only rudimentary technology knowledge in-house. It is included for two reasons: First, technology is an ever more central feature of the global economy, and many different kinds of investment strategies require a technique for selecting among various technology investment opportunities. Second, this case study suggests that a scenario analysis can provide any organization with an "investment due diligence" tool that it can use to attract investment capital.

"Consolidated Finance" is a financial services firm with a strong regional base, a full range of services, and a national presence in a few niche markets in which it competes very successfully. Consolidated's introduction to scenario-based planning began with top management. The CEO had, over the past decade, driven the firm's growth with shrewd mergers and acquisitions. His strategy was to establish an unassailable position in:

- A select group of markets that corresponded to long-established core competencies in regionally based products and services.
- High-volume transaction processing for a few select national customers.

By nearly every measure, the strategy was unfolding quite successfully and had several years of life remaining.

However, the CEO was concerned that the firm's management was becoming a bit complacent. Though the strategy was clearly understood by all the key executives, a noteworthy communications achievement, its execution had become a matter of "mere" operations and tactics. Additionally, he anticipated that the vision and goals of the original strategy—which was based on regional growth—was soon going to become a hindrance to expansive and innovative thinking. Consequently, Consolidated needed a new vision, new goals, and new strategies. Scenario-based planning was selected as the foundation process for developing new corporate strategic goals and strategies. The planning focus was, itself, quite expansive: To explore any and all potential financial services needs of society (with emphasis on Consolidated's current core competencies) across North America. The planning horizon was 10 years.

The planning process was moving along so successfully that about the time that the executives were involved in the Adopt-A-World exercises (before strategies had been developed), they decided to apply the scenarios to another, more immediate "bottom line" problem. Over the past five years, Consolidated had taken a rather large investment position in several areas of the transportation sector. The nature of the investments made Consolidated's position rather vulnerable to technology choices being made in dozens of original equipment manufacturers (OEMs) and integration firms across the country over which they had no influence. Further, the long-term viability of transportation invest-ments was going to be affected by technologies outside of the transport sec-tor—primarily in information processing and telecommunications. How safe were their investments? Should they reduce their commitment to some long-standing clients in this area?

After the addition of some transportation-relevant data into the scenar-ios, the executives of the transportation investment group engaged in an Adopt-A-World exercise of their own. This was a much more focused ac-tivity than the initial CEO-led effort. The goal of this project was to un-derstand the consumer priorities in each scenario world and how they would affect choices made about personal transportation alternatives and the logistics business that supplied consumer and retail delivery services. Consolidated recruited outside experts to help with the analysis of the technology implications of the range of future transportation needs.

The Adopt-A-World exercises revealed both critical transportation needs in North America over the next 10 years and some alternatives to conventional transportation. New concepts for vehicles and services that met those needs were identified, and the group ascertained which cur-rent and emerging technologies supported them. Finally, the current investment portfolio was compared to the list of technologies that sup-ported transportation needs in a variety of scenarios. Consolidated man-agers had a pleasant surprise: Not only was their current technology investment strategy sound, but, if they brought in-house some specific technology and business expertise, they could safely increase their in-vestments. On the other hand, it was also clear that those technology in-vestments were vulnerable to sudden obsolescence as the decade passed, so a technology-tracking system was installed in the transportation group and a hedging strategy was developed. Finally, various telecommunica-tion alternatives—such as teleconferencing—were evaluated as potential nontraditional competitors to transportation. As a result, the group rec-ommended several technology investments to Consolidated's telecom-munications investment group.

Case Study: Improving Business Process Technology

"The Knowledge Bank" (TKB) is an information services firm that had few real or potential competitors in its business area until the 1980s. TKB's competitive advantage had rested on its expertise at converting raw government data into well-indexed information, and at efficiently publishing, distributing, and aggressively marketing the information. The firm's employment of scenario planning began with a technology-scanning project commissioned by a new president and a recently hired technology director. The business had not altered much since the 1920s, but all of a sudden a confluence of new technologies appeared to threaten the comfortably lethargic pace of change they had become used to over the decades.

The technology scan confirmed the company's fears and doubts. Developments in information-processing hardware, publishing and analytical software, and telecommunications signaled an approaching revolution for their industry. Particularly disturbing to TKB executives was the possibility that the barriers to entry in their niche business that once seemed so high might soon disappear.

Instead of predicting a new technology trend, the scanning effort had actually produced greater uncertainty throughout the company. The results of many of the technology scans seemed to point in different, often contradictory, directions. The research had produced only "possibilities" that "seemed" to portend threatening change. TKB executives had no method for testing or selecting from among the technology trends; they had no sense of coherent future direction. Which trends would dominate? Which would demand a large investment but never become a major market?

The Knowledge Bank decided to implement scenario-based planning to support its immediate decision making and as an ongoing analysis process to test the relevance of emerging technologies. With scenarios developed, an Adopt-A-World approach (using the scenarios separately to derive alternative strategies, then synthesizing the results into a core robust strategy) led TKB executives to recognize the potential of a significantly different business model.

The scenarios analysis of customer needs indicated that the intelligence-intensive analysis portion of TKB's information product would remain unassailable for at least another 10 years. So, management did little to change this key source of competitive advantage. Instead, they moved their entire internal process of data coding, indexing, and analysis from paper and workshops to computers and e-mail. This was done gradually to avoid undue disruption for employees who faced huge changes in their work, and to avoid a reduction in the quality of the firm's product while the transition took place. TKB executives could afford to move deliberately because both customer interviews and scenario analysis of their customers' industries indicated that their best clients would themselves move slowly into the electronic data revolution. However, making a start at the transition process immediately was considered an important hedge for the potential success of expert system software.

Their new insight about their customers' future reactions led to another strategy. They brought their customers along with them as they explored electronic distribution of the product they would soon produce electronically. They not only codeveloped some of the distribution system with their customers, but set up education and training systems for their other clients. The scenario analysis of the future business environment led them to a sound and robust technology investment strategy. For example, they selected a combination of laser discs for yearly "publications" (although disc technology meant that it would be easy to produce them more often) plus an on-line service that could be inexpensively customized for individual client interests.

Many firms would have been pleased with achieving this much innovation, but key TKB executives understood just how lucky the company had been, and they were left with a sense that they had "just caught it in time." The president was determined that emerging technologies or unexpected shifts in the business environment would not catch them unawares in the future. A tracking system was set up based on the combined use of scanning and scenarios. Technology trend scanning was initiated in conventional fashion, but an extra step was added to the analysis process: Each technology forecast or trend is "stress-tested" through the scenarios. This test asks the question, What is the impact on TKB if this particular technology emerges in this particular scenario? In a sense, the scenarios are used as a future "industry-relevance" filter to test for impact on TKB and to explore the impact of the trends in the set of scenarios.

The insights from this process flow in two directions. The trends examined in the scanning process are often selected based upon scenario analysis. The following are two samples of how this worked in practice:

- "Trend X turned out to have a huge impact on the regulatory environment in our industry in three of the scenarios. Get an outlook function for trend X set up in the scanning system."
- "Two of the scenarios implied an unmet customer need for self-diagnostic safety systems. Be sure to scan for emerging technologies that would enable them."

In other words, the scenarios are not just passive analytical tools for testing the relevance of emerging trends or technologies. They are also a source of insight into trends not yet on the horizon that should be included in the scanning process.

The system set up by TKB is simple and elegant. It has the virtue of being an ongoing process that keeps everyone thinking about technology in the context of scenario insights; it nicely reinforces the linkage between company strategy and technology investments. An additional advantage is that TKB executives will know quickly when the scenarios need revision.

TECHNOLOGIES FOR FUTURE PRODUCTS

Identifying future customer needs and selecting appropriate technologies for inclusion in new or modified products is perhaps the most powerful application of scenarios for technology planning. This process facilitates the identification of robust future customer needs—that is, those that will persist in a variety of future circumstances—thereby helping mangers select the technologies most likely to be applicable in a wide range of future business environments. In our experience, companies that have adopted scenario technology planning have found that by developing strategic planning priorities derived from scenarios and prioritizing technology investments, they greatly increase their control over their own destiny. Scenario planning not only links technology decisions to future customer demand but forges strong ties between corporate strategy and the technology investments. Thus, technology choices are made within a strategic context that includes the new corporate vision, the market segments identified as most viable, long-range financial plans, and competitor assessment.

Case Study: Industrial Visions Tests the
Viability of Its Recently Developed Products

"Industrial Visions" (IS) produces diagnostics equipment for manufacturing processes. Its product line was moderately successful in a very competitive market. The company recently completed an expensive R&D program intended to allow it to make it a quantum leap in performance over the competition. But, because of the surprising success of the research, Industrial Visions faced a propitious dilemma. Researchers had made two totally unexpected and quite dramatic breakthroughs, one in well-understood and commonly used analog sensor technology and the other in digital-scanning techniques.

To make matters more complicated, it seemed that either of these technologies could be successfully married to two newly developed image storage techniques, stable, high-resolution microfilm and digital electronic storage. All the combinations of new technology received enthusiastic support when explored with current clients. And, of course, all combinations had their internal supporters. Indeed, some serious factionalism within the firm was developing among the "preferred" approaches. However, there was only enough development money available for one combination.

Technology benchmarking measures that compared the new technology with all potential competitors in forecasted performance growth were not decisive, and customer focus groups gave no useful selection criteria. To resolve this quandary, the vice president for R&D decided to see if a scenario examination of future market conditions would provide some insight. He was skeptical, but the CEO had suggested such an approach. In fact, the CEO was considering using scenarios for strategic planning, and thought this technology decision might make a good test of the technique.

Some unique characteristics of the market concerning the motivations of their customers' customers, plus the need to explore global opportunities and threats made the study complicated enough to require seven scenarios. Although an unusually high number, it was not an unworkable one because the managers wanted to stress-test their new technology combinations, not invent new product ideas.

Industrial Visions top management was in for a number of surprises. First, they did get several unexpected new product ideas from exploring the future priorities of their customers' customers. Second, they got a much keener appreciation for the potential market strengths of one of their competitors. This was a rival that they had previously wrongly tended to dismiss as "second string." Third, they ended up spending a bit more money than originally intended because they picked two technology combinations.

The scenario analysis of the manufacturing diagnostics market for their equipment in the developing countries indicated a far larger, faster growing and more robust market than trend-based market analyses had forecast. However, this was a market with unique conditions. Less educated employees, difficult climate conditions, and poorly performing power-generating equipment in this "emerging markets" sector pointed to the need for more rugged, easier-to-use, and easier-to-repair digital equipment. But this equipment would be more expensive. On the other hand, Adopt-A-World scenario analysis of the advanced industrial markets in the United States, Western Europe, and Japan indicated a strong tendency to prefer the best sensor resolution possible at the lowest price—a combination of preferences that implied the market would choose film-based sensors. Conversely, several of the scenarios indicated that future environmental regulations could restrict the film-based approach because it required several hard-to-dispose-of industrial chemicals. For the advanced industrial markets, the high-resolution analog system was married to the digital storage approach; but digital technology was a long-term hedge in the event that restrictive environmental regulations were enacted.

Industrial Visions' final decision was: digital storage for both markets; analog sensors in the advanced industrial markets; digital sensors in the developing countries; and a new strategic alliance with that competitor that had seemed second string. Since implementing that decision, Industrial Vision has gained some market share in the advanced industrial markets—it grows modestly, while all competitors but one stagnate—and it now dominates its market in the developing countries.

Case Study: Corporate Scenarios Employed to Prioritize Technology Investments

"White Hat Aerospace" is a defense company with expertise in air-launched missiles, communications, and several other defense technology areas. A year ago, it had completed a corporatewide scenario-based strategic-planning project. The first application of scenarios had been to analyze the overall business portfolio of the company, during which the scenario team studied future markets but not in great detail. The planning effort had resolved many market priorities and corporate organizational issues. Three businesses were in the process of being sold off and a foreign infrared sensor firm was being acquired.

A new Adopt-A-World exercise was begun with a focused look at future combat missions and future customer needs 15 years out. About 25 new product ideas that seemed viable across the scenarios emerged from the process. Seven of the new products were missiles—three air-to-air and four air-to-ground. White Hat managers had to decide which missiles to invest in, given reduced defense spending and limited corporate resources.

Exhibit 13.3
Using Scenarios to Indentify Core Technologies

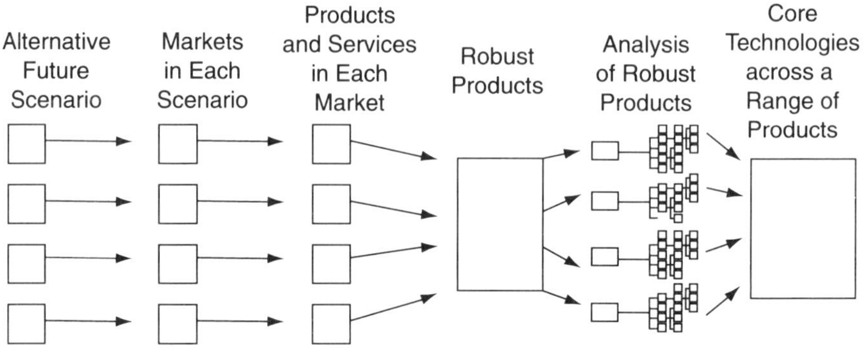

But if you have seven potential products—in this case, missiles—how do you select the right one to produce? The first step is the one taken by White Hat, and it follows the scenario philosophy of managing uncertainty. Technology road maps were developed for all seven missiles. A sensitivity test was run to find the core technologies across all the missiles. That core set of technologies, those that would be needed regardless of the missile chosen, became the priority technology investments (see Exhibit 13.3).

White Hat would first need to choose the missiles to be developed in four years; and some years later it would have to impose a technology freeze—a point at which key component technologies must be "set in stone" so production requiring long lead time could begin. This freeze would have to be imposed by the company in six or seven years. The time preceding the freeze was used to hone the scenario analysis, involve clients in that analysis, and run classic mission studies on the missiles. Eventually, four missiles were chosen for development, and one of these projects was subsequently canceled. Additionally, several current production missiles from several competing manufactures have now been required to incorporate White Hat's new technologies into ongoing missile upgrade and modification programs.

CONCLUSIONS

Scenario-based planning for technology decisions can be a powerful tool to manage the uncertainties that surround important technology investments. The scenarios provide managers with a window on potential future market needs, a tool for systematic and innovative consideration of new customer needs, and a method for evaluating the long-term viability of current product ideas or technology developments. The scenarios help you to set market-driven priorities on your technology investment plans so they are more than just a lengthy wish list.

However, the greatest leverage will come from incorporating technology scenario planning into your regular ongoing planning process. Scenario planning offers managers a powerful new way of thinking about their business future with its myriad unpredictable opportunities and threats. Managers who have "rehearsed" various technologies futures will be better prepared to address discontinuous change than their competitors. They will react faster and with a greater sense of confidence. That is a meaningful competitive advantage.

CHAPTER 14

CUSTOMER-DRIVEN
SCENARIO PLANNING

JOHN KANIA

The customer-driven scenario planning methodology reveals new opportunities created by changes in the customer landscape. It explores these critical issues:

- *How will the evolution of customer needs shape the future of an industry? How might existing customer segments or distribution channels change over time?*
- *What different types of providers will customers switch to in order to satisfy their needs?*
- *How should the company evolve in response to potential changes in the needs of customers and the options available to them?*

"**I** don't pay anyone," Sam Walton once told a gathering of several thousand Wal-Mart employees. "The customers pay us all. I just handle the money." Walton's folk wisdom underscores a basic but often overlooked imperative of modern business: It is only by understanding customers and providing what they value most that a business can remain profitable and viable in the long term.

Back in the days when he was the operator of one dry goods store in Bentonville, Arkansas, Walton perceived that the shopping requirements of rural Americans were woefully underserved. He also foresaw that stagnating real incomes would make a broad range of consumers increasingly price-sensitive. To capitalize on these trends, he built a highly sophisticated, technologically advanced business model that enabled Wal-Mart to grow with such vitality that in a few decades it became the largest retail chain in the world. Walton's prescient reading of his customers and his ability to respond and adapt his business to their changing needs have been identified as the most important factors behind Wal-Mart's creation of $50 billion of market value in the past decade.[1]

Was Wal-Mart's success merely the lucky result of changing demographics and the migration of affluent families to exurbia? In the years that Wal-Mart was beginning its meteoric, customer-driven rise, the retailing giant Sears was losing touch with its customer base and beginning to stagnate.

From 1985–1994, $140 billion of new market value was created by publicly held retail companies such as Wal-Mart, Circuit City, The Home Depot and Toys 'R Us. During this time period, Sears created less than 1 percent of the total $140 billion increase. While Sears' failure to respond to shifts in its environment was caused by many factors, two major management perception failures can be blamed for much of the trouble. First, many managers were still operating with an outdated model of the customer and the competitive environment. Second, many of those who did recognize the structural shifts in the industry were unable to make everyone in the chain of command—their direct reports and their superiors—recognize the urgency of the situation.

While Sears debated, the lion's share of the market opportunity was won by its upstart competitor. Sear's Merchandising Group created $1 billion in market value from 1985–1994. In stark comparison, The Home Depot became a national rival and generated $18 billion in value during this same period.

CUSTOMER-DRIVEN SCENARIO PLANNING

Every organization eventually encounters the need to accommodate major changes in its markets. The late Sam Walton's success record is inspirational, but what if you and your organization lack Walton's extraordinary foresight? Or what if some individuals in your organization have useful perspectives on the evolution of customer needs—as many Sears managers did—but can't act on those insights because of opposition from their peers or superiors? Does your organization have a process for creating a reliable consensus about what customers will want in the future?

Customer-driven scenario planning was developed to help overcome the types of barriers to effective change that many organizations must confront today. But it is more than a problem-solving system. Customer-driven scenario planning enables managers to capitalize on new opportunities created by changes in the customer landscape. It explores these critical issues:

- How will the evolution of customer needs shape the future of an industry? How might existing customer segments or distribution channels change over time?
- To which different types of providers will customers switch in order to satisfy their needs?
- How should the company evolve in response to potential changes in the needs of customers and the options available to them?

To address these strategic questions, customer-driven scenario planning was designed to collect the most critical facts, to chart changing customer requirements, and to hypothesize on future environments. It develops this new flow of information through a step-by-step process that enables managers to escape the limitations of the conventional wisdom of their industry and engage in a structured discussion about the change imperatives facing their organization.

Would customer-driven scenario planning have enabled Sears to avoid stagnation and extend its record of retail industry innovation? Obviously, we will never know. Experience has proven, however, that customer-driven scenario planning can help managers reshape their mental models of the future, particularly when new technology, new demands from customers, opportunities to reach new populations of customers, or rapid entry by nontraditional competitors threaten to fundamentally alter an industry's landscape.

Most important, customer-driven scenario planning provides managers with the confidence to implement a major strategic shift. The customer-driven scenario-planning process often shows that the key to generating significant revenue, profit, and market value growth is not by simply "sticking to your knitting," as one of the favorite slogans of troubled companies that are trying to reinvent themselves by focusing on their core business recommends. Instead, as industry environments change, the organization must be prepared to fundamentally rethink the value proposition it offers to customers. Abandoning the past is unnerving, but ultimately value is created by those who are willing to confront uncertainty and commit to a new course. Yogi Berra, baseball's renowned player/manager/philosopher once advised, "When you get to the fork in the road, take it." Customer-driven scenario planning enables a company to rationally examine the implications of taking one fork versus the other.

CUSTOMER-DRIVEN SCENARIO PLANNING: WHERE IT COMES FROM AND WHERE IT CAN TAKE YOU

Customer-driven scenario planning draws on and contributes fresh thinking to two management disciplines: knowing your customer (also called customer comprehension) and knowing your marketplace.

Knowing Your Customer.   Since the mid-1980s, managers have placed increasing emphasis on "getting in touch with their customers." In the consumer sector, this imperative has driven the development of sophisticated database marketing and personalized customer communication by companies such as L.L. Bean, Kraft/General Foods, and Toyota. In the business-to-business sector, the quest for a closer relationship with and understanding of the customer has led organizations such as Hewlett-Packard to discard geographically based sales and marketing structures in favor of customer-centric "global account management" programs. These and other customer-based initiatives help organizations maintain a closer relationship with their customers day to day. Customer-driven scenario planning takes a longer view, enabling managers to begin preparing their organizations for the fundamental changes that will reshape their industries.

In the drive to acquaint managers with the strategic implications of their changing marketplace, customer-driven scenario planning probes much deeper than traditional market research. Where the latter typically measures the past and present customer satisfaction, customer-driven scenario planning identifies and explores the fundamental forces that will shape customer priorities and decision making going forward.

Knowing the Evolving Marketplace.   The second managerial discipline on which this approach builds is the scenario-planning method pioneered by Pierre Wack and other managers in the Planning Group of Royal Dutch/Shell.[2] Like Wack's approach, customer-driven scenario planning develops different future "worlds" for the purpose of evaluating different potential strategies. In contrast, customer-driven scenario planning supplements traditional scenario planning with a sharper focus on the changing identity and priorities of customers. It constructs and explores future worlds from the perspective of the customer, generating insights on new threats and opportunities that may be less likely to emerge from traditional scenario planning.

Traditional Scenario Planning Revisited

In his *Harvard Business Review* articles on scenario planning, Wack emphasizes that the key elements of future "worlds" are:

- Predetermined events.
- Critical uncertainties.

Predetermined events are those that are certain or nearly certain to unfold based on what has already taken place. To illustrate the concept, Wack explains how heavy rains in the Himalayas make flooding in the Ganges river the following week a predetermined event.

Critical uncertainties are the contributing factors that will have consequences that can't yet be measured. These are addressed in the form of questions that urgently require answers; but the substance of the answers is not predictable. For the purposes of constructing future worlds, it is important to focus on a relatively small number of critical uncertainties that could most fundamentally alter the environment.

World Building. Traditional scenario planning uses predetermined events as a common platform and then creates possible future worlds around different combinations of critical uncertainties. In this process, it is important that participants develop fundamentally different worlds, not merely different outcomes in the same world.

Two worlds are fundamentally different when their key drivers, the forces that influence all other aspects of the world, contrast dramatically. For example, in the retail industry, the balance that consumers strike between saving and spending disposable income—as measured by consumer confidence indexes—can be a key driver that profoundly affects every other dimension of the landscape. Therefore, a scenario that postulated a boom in demand for consumer credit would describe a fundamentally different future world than one that postulated a sudden increase in the national savings rate. On the other hand, different outcomes in the same future world occur when the same basic set of key drivers yields only slightly different results; for example, a scenario that anticipates a boom in consumer credit. One outcome could be that existing credit cards will benefit most from the growth. In another outcome, the growth could occur in new credit cards. For the scenario-planning process, these are characterized as different outcomes of the same world.

Each world must be internally consistent. If some elements of the world are fundamentally incompatible with other elements, the scenario-planning process will be more confusing than clarifying. In our retail example, we would create an internally inconsistent world if we hypothesized that Americans will significantly increase their savings rates, yet also assume a simultaneous boom in demand for consumer credit. These two trends could underpin fundamentally different worlds, but they couldn't be long-term trends in the same world. To ensure consistency across the different elements of a single world, participants in the scenario-planning process should articulate the predetermined events and critical uncertainties that define the world, then methodically consider their impact on the world's other actors, such as suppliers and competitors.

The Expected Future. One of the worlds that participants construct should be a "surprise-free" world, so named because its key drivers reflect the current expectations of the strategic-planning participants. In this future, change occurs in increments and according to expectations, a rather unlikely prospect nowadays. Nonetheless, preparing a surprise-free scenario furthers the planning process because it serves as a point of reference for participants. Often, in the course of working through the logic of future worlds that take into account discontinuous change, managers realize exactly why their surprise-free world is highly unlikely to materialize.

Customer-driven scenario planning injects customer perspective into the process in three discrete steps: constructing, exploring, and responding to future worlds.

STEP I: CONSTRUCTING FUTURE WORLDS FROM THE CUSTOMER UP

As participants construct future worlds, they sharpen their focus on the customer through an in-depth consideration of the following questions (see Exhibit 14.1):

- How do we best define the current and potential customer base?
- Are there different types of customers?
- How might the identity of key customer decision makers shift?
- How might the priorities of different customer types evolve?

In addition to taking a "customer-think" (as opposed to an "industry-think") perspective, customer-driven scenario planning moves beyond a monolithic conception of the customer base by building customer segmentation implications into each of the future worlds. It's widely understood that customers don't all have the same product and service needs. But

Exhibit 14.1
Customer-Driven Scenario Planning

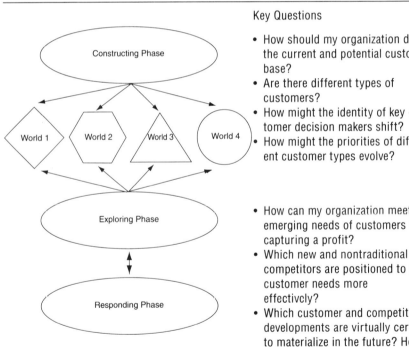

Key Questions

- How should my organization define the current and potential customer base?
- Are there different types of customers?
- How might the identity of key customer decision makers shift?
- How might the priorities of different customer types evolve?

- How can my organization meet the emerging needs of customers while capturing a profit?
- Which new and nontraditional competitors are positioned to serve customer needs more effectively?
- Which customer and competitive developments are virtually certain to materialize in the future? How can my organization begin preparing for them?
- Which "covering bets" should my organization place to position it for developments that might unfold?
- Which trends should my organization monitor closely?

fewer managers understand that different types of customers are likely to change their decision making in different ways and at different rates.

For instance, Nike realized that the shoe-buying priorities of the nation's top high school basketball players evolve faster than (and act as a powerful influence on) the shoe-buying priorities of a much broader cross section of American youth. To capture this leading-edge customer segment, Nike began courting top young players in their midteens by sponsoring city tournaments. Understanding which segments lead, which follow, and how customer priorities may converge or fragment is an essential step in customer-driven scenario planning.

In our experience, the most meaningful lines along which to divide the customer base are not demographic or even psychographic, but behavioral. For instance, in the restaurant industry, very little strategic insight emerges from examining a customer base along demographic lines ("white professional females between 30 and 40"). Instead, if managers think in terms of behavioral purchase occasions, (fast food versus social versus home meal replacement), clear revenue and profit drivers for the business model start to emerge. In any given industry, there are probably four to six major behavioral clusters that must be acknowledged in considering alternatives and changes in the company's business system. Emerging industries may have fewer; mature industries, more.

Channel Evolution

Customer-driven scenario planning also considers the potential for the emergence of new channels for products and services to reach end-use customers. In some industries, the changing importance of channels reflects the changing priorities of end-use customers themselves.

Lotus Development Corporation's successful transition from an applications developer to a communications software provider underscores the importance of channels in executing a major strategic shift. Without a strategic understanding of the end-use customer, Lotus would not have recognized how its R&D focus needed to change from personal productivity tools to groupware applications. But if Lotus hadn't carefully considered how to bring the product to market through alternative channels to the end-use customer, the product wouldn't have enjoyed such resounding commercial success. While customers purchased the popular spreadsheet Lotus 1–2–3 at retail outlets, such as Egghead Software, they purchased Lotus Notes through value-added resellers (VARs). The firms in this alternative channel customized the software to meet the needs of specific organizations. As Lotus developed the Notes product, it began assiduously cultivating relationships with VARs in target vertical markets. No one appreciated the importance of Lotus' shrewd channel management more than IBM, which valued the Lotus Notes franchise at $3.3 billion when it acquired the company in 1995.

Addressing Critical Uncertainties

To build customer segments and channels into future worlds, participants must consider how purchasers will be influenced by the critical uncertainties. For example in the financial services sector, a critical uncertainty might be the rate at which consumers become more sophisticated and knowledgeable about different investment vehicles, such as mutual funds, CDs, and annuities. Combining this critical uncertainty with a behavioral segmentation, managers might develop a world in which only the most diligent savers become knowledgeable and sophisticated. In developing another scenario, participants might hypothesize that the sophistication of all customer segments increases rapidly with the proliferation of investment information through books, the business press, or the Internet.

Clearly, each customer segment will have different sets of priorities. For example, in the first scenario, highly sophisticated consumers would value low-cost access to a wide range of investment vehicles but have no need for advice. Conversely, in the second scenario, less sophisticated customers would be willing to limit their range of investment options and pay higher fees in exchange for knowledgeable counsel and financial-planning services.

STEP II: EXPLORING THE FUTURE WORLDS FROM THE CUSTOMER DOWN

After constructing the different worlds, participants in the customer-driven scenario planning process explore each one in detail. The key questions to consider in the exploring process are:

- How can providers meet the customers' emerging needs while capturing a profit for themselves?
- What new and nontraditional competitors are positioned to serve customer needs more effectively?

Having charted the priorities and characteristics of each customer segment, the scenario-planning process next establishes the capabilities that providers must master in order to meet those priorities. This analysis is not as simple as it may sound. For example, retailers may easily reach the conclusion that cost-conscious consumers would make their shopping decisions based on their search for everyday low prices. But substantial analysis is required to consider and identify all the capabilities a retailer will need to support an everyday low pricing policy three to five years or more in the future. Support skills needed for the next generation of retail competition range from creating state-of-the-art logistics systems that shrink inventory needs to designing employee stock ownership plans that allow management to keep base salary expenses low.

In the process of constructing each scenario, participants consider the effect of changing customer priorities, predetermined events, and critical uncertainties on their existing competitors. In the process of exploring the ramifications of each scenario, participants place themselves in the position of their various customer segments and evaluate a broad range of competitive value propositions.

Detecting Competitive Threats

One common type of competitive threat easily missed by routine competitive benchmarking is the piecemeal market entry by multiple business models, which eventually function together as a system. Taken by themselves, each new player in a market might seem relatively innocuous, but together, the various offerings may provide customers with an advantageous choice.

Managers can use the customer-driven scenario-planning process to recognize such a potential threat. For example, the VCR represented only a marginal competitive threat to network television until one day many consumers could drive a just few blocks to low-cost, large-selection video rental store chains in their neighborhood, such as Blockbuster. Together, VCRs and video rental chains offered the customer a "movies-to-go" home entertainment option that has seriously eroded the competitive advantage of network television.

Competitive threats from innovative combinations of business models are especially difficult for entrenched incumbents to identify because each component may seem harmless in isolation. But by taking the customers' point of view—a constant reassessment of the best value—participants in the scenario-planning process may better anticipate potentially dangerous competitors before they gain critical mass.

The Additional Challenge for Established Companies

The constructing and exploring phases assist management in:

- Charting options for changing customer needs.
- Developing strategies that meet those alternative needs while earning a profit.
- Identifying the organizational capabilities required to execute the strategy.

For the entrepreneur, these last three steps conclude the strategic-planning process. Though much ingenuity and hard work will be required to realize the strategic vision, managers designing businesses "from a blank sheet of paper" are well positioned to begin building.

But top managers in an established company (with substantial existing revenue streams, physical assets, and human resources) face an additional strategic challenge: moving the organization from its current form to the form that will be able to capture profit and value in the future. Without this change in organizational structure, customer-driven scenario planning may prove enlightening, but it won't spur a management team to act.

STEP III: RESPONDING TO FUTURE WORLDS WITH CUSTOMER-THINK

To respond effectively to future worlds, managers in established organizations must ask and answer three sets of questions. The three response modes are:

- *Just do it.* Which changes in the marketplace and competitive environment are common across all future worlds and therefore virtually certain to unfold no matter which future world emerges? Which steps should we begin implementing today to prepare our organization for these eventualities?
- *Place your bets.* Which possible marketplace changes would be most significant if they did come to pass in one of the future worlds? How

can our organization "place a covering bet" that would create a strong position in case these changes do materialize?

• *Monitor closely.* Which trends or developments may not be predictable enough to base immediate investment on, but make sense to monitor closely?

By choosing from these three levels of response—"just do it," "place your bets," and "monitor closely"—a management team can take decisive action on the many insights generated in the construction and exploration phases. The first two options require investments. Deciding exactly what form these investments will take requires consideration of such issues as: the pace of change the marketplace demands, the level of risk the organization is willing to assume, and the trade-offs associated with growth from existing business versus seeking growth from joint ventures or acquisitions. Every industry has its traditional biases about these trade-offs. Too often, conventional industry wisdom is only the formula for yesterday's success. To capture profit and value in the future, it is necessary to ask what today's customers will want tomorrow, who tomorrow's new customers are likely to be, and what they are likely to want.

A Mutual Fund Case

Mutual fund companies have traditionally been very cautious about sharing customer data with any outside organization such as financial planners. But what if a fund company seeking to grow into new markets bundled its products with financial-planning services, and developed the advice capability internally? We can anticipate that sophisticated customers would tend to distrust its recommendations because it had a vested interest in influencing a purchase decision. An assessment of what its potential customers value might suggest that it needs to take an innovative course of action.

Because objectivity is so highly valued by all potential customers for financial-planning services, a mutual fund entering this market might do well to form an alliance with an independent financial planner. Charles Schwab, a distributor of mutual funds with a successful record of experimenting with and implementing nontraditional strategies, has taken this course with considerable success.

IBM's Landmark Acquisition

Another example of a decisive break with traditional thinking was IBM's purchase of Lotus. The transaction represented a strategic leap for IBM, which had never in its history initiated a hostile takeover. By acquiring Lotus, IBM also made a break with the prevailing pattern of mergers and acquisitions in the computing industry. Although acquisition is nothing new, the usual industry pattern is to consolidate a market niche or build economies of scale.

IBM's purchase gave the company instant access to a new technology and a set of skills that are both scarce and highly valued by today's computing customers. It signaled a return to IBM's roots as a customer-driven, externally focused organization.

CASE STUDY: THE FINANCIAL PRINTING INDUSTRY

A leading competitor in the financial printing industry with $500 million in revenues used customer-driven scenario planning to gain a strategic understanding of its customers and the future of its industry. Historically, financial printers have provided a full range of document production services—typesetting, composition, printing, binding, and distribution—to corporations issuing securities on the public capital markets. The Securities Exchange Commission (SEC) requires a document for all such transactions. The document is also used by the issuing corporation to market the securities to institutional buyers. This dual role confers enormous importance on the document and makes the financial printer an important and valued player who can often command fees up to $250,000 for production of an initial public offering (IPO) prospectus.

The printing organization's management team was no stranger to volatile business conditions. The demand for financial printing services rises and falls with the financial markets, sometimes jumping up or down as much as 30 percent in a given quarter.

But in 1993, three disquieting trends further complicated the always nerve-wracking cyclical swings of the industry. First, prices had been steadily softening; sales representatives were coming under unremitting pressure to give customers greater and greater discounts off the established list price. Second, armed with new, sophisticated word processing and desktop publishing technology, customers were learning how to perform some of the composition services previously provided by financial printers. Last, the SEC was in the process of introducing an electronic filing system that would allow corporations to record and register their transactions by modem, without producing a paper document.

While these disconcerting changes in the marketplace were obvious, their underlying causes remained in doubt. Was price erosion due to particularly aggressive sales tactics by competitors or to a profound shift in the balance of power between corporations, their legal and financial advisors, and the financial printers? Were the new technological developments a flash in the pan or the future of the industry? In this uncertain business environment, the president of the organization and her direct reports in manufacturing, finance, sales, and marketing embarked on the customer-driven scenario planning process. One of the first steps was to thoroughly debrief the sales staff.

The Constructing Phase

In the past, the sales representatives carefully guarded their relationships with individual customers. Now, through the scenario process, the group's sales and marketing management, working together, developed new insights about the company's customer base. As a result, the participants began clustering their customers not by demographic characteristics such as geography (West Coast clients versus East Coast clients) or industry classification (computer industry versus packaged goods industry) but rather by their pattern of usage of financial printing services. The key parameter was the frequency with which customers issued securities on the public markets. Focusing on this variable, the team divided the customer base into the following clusters.

Frequent Issuers: The Scientists. Frequent Issuers interacted with he capital markets regularly as a core component of their business. Examples of frequent issuers included government agencies, such as Federal National Mortgage Agency (Fannie Mae); the finance departments of major consumer goods manufacturers that regularly converted their receivables into securities, such as Chrysler Credit Corporation; and utilities with high ongoing capital requirements, such as Long Island Lighting. Repeated trips to the public markets made these players highly sophisticated consumers of financial printing services. Because these customers approached financial printing with expert knowledge, exact procedures, and no tolerance for errors, participants dubbed them "Scientists."

Fortune *1000: The Dabblers.* In contrast, the core activities of the customers in the *Fortune* 1000 cluster lay outside finance, but their size and business scope required regular, though less frequent, interaction with the public markets. As its name suggests, the *Fortune* 1000 segment included many large companies such as Boeing, International Paper, and MCI. These customers used the services of financial printers when issuing secondary debt or equity, producing their annual compliance documents, or consummating a merger or acquisition. Because the *Fortune* 1000s' in-house legal and finance staffs engaged in the financial printing process only occasionally, the participants called them "Dabblers."

IPOs: The Artists. The initial public offering customer segment was made up of hot young companies making the leap to public ownership. The officers of these companies knew virtually nothing about financial printing. Caught up in the heady rush of going public and focused on "the art of the deal," these customers were both highly impressionable and highly emotional about the process, earning them the nickname "Artists."

Law Firms and Investment Bankers: The Cruise Directors. Though not direct consumers of financial printing services, influencers such as law firms and investment banks play an important role in the financial printing purchasing process. As advisors to the true customers (the issuing corporations), the influencers were in a position to recommend or blackball particular providers of financial printing services. These process experts collected a fee for guiding the customers through what was often a complex and bewildering process. So they played the role of "Cruise Directors."

After segmenting its customer base into these four groups, the management team began identifying the predetermined events that would be common to all the future worlds. The first step was to marshall a comprehensive set of facts about customers, competitors, technology, and the economics of the financial printing business. Next, the management team was able to begin searching for patterns of facts that would have important consequences that were at least 90 percent predictable; these are the predetermined events. The two most important ones the team ultimately identified are shown in Exhibit 14.2. The same fact review process that generated the list of predetermined events also identified two critical uncertainties—important unresolved questions about the future of the industry. These critical uncertainties were:

- Which customers will be able to publish financial documents themselves, and to what degree?
- Will customers who are required by the SEC to file their documents electronically begin supplying them directly to end users of financial information?

After reexamining the customer base, establishing predetermined events, and identifying critical uncertainties, the participants were prepared to

Exhibit 14.2
Predetermined Events

Predetermined Event	Supporting Facts
• By performing some composition activities in-house, customers will significantly shrink the revenue stream of financial printers.	• Percentage of draft documents submitted by clients to the printer on disk (versus on paper) increased dramatically from 1990 to 1993.
	• Significant increase in functionality and user-friendliness of desktop publishing and word processing software.
• The SEC's electronic filing initiative will both reduce demand for printed products and educate customers about new media that will compete with print.	• SEC conducting educational seminars and disseminating free explanatory software describing electronic information transfer.
	• Declining run lengths requested from customers that have recently been phased into the SEC's electronic filing initiative.
• End users of financial information (institutional fund managers) will increasingly value and even expect financial data from SEC filings in a manipulable electronic form.	• Time-pressured fund managers with many new issues to evaluate and little time express high interest in efficient analysis tools.
	• Financial information companies (Quotron, Reuters, Bloomberg) are cash-rich and able to invest in new product functionality.

construct several future worlds. They sketched out numerous possibilities, but eventually narrowed their focus to the following four scenarios.

Four Future Financial Printing Worlds

Primarily Printers Scenario.   Based on management's expectations of the future, the scenario Primarily Printers served as the "surprise-free" world. It incorporated the predetermined events but ruled out any dramatic or discontinuous change. In this scenario, advances in personal computing technology empower all customer segments to perform a larger percentage of the composition activity themselves. Nevertheless, all but the frequent issuers continue to rely on printers for most composition, and all manufacturing and distribution services. Disappointed by low levels of service across the industry, these customers refuse to pay the printers' list price. Customers' demands for price concessions, printers' high fixed costs, and slow overall market growth combine to create a downward pricing spiral that permanently erodes the profitability of the financial printing industry.

Composing Customer Scenario.   The defining feature of the Composing Customer scenario is the rapid advance of personal computing technology. Armed with high-powered PCs, laser printers, and new network software, such market segments as the Frequent Issuers, *Fortune* 1000s, and the Law Firms and Investment Bankers can perform most composition activities in-house. As a result, the incumbent financial printers experience severe revenue decline. The decline in profitability is even more pronounced (on a percentage basis), because the lost composition revenue commanded a high margin, relative to other financial printing activities.

Multimedia Madness Scenario.   The central development in the Multimedia Madness world is the explosive growth of the market for high functionality and interactive, electronic financial information. As in the previous scenario, the speedy adoption of computer technology continues to reduce customers' reliance on printers for composition services. But in this future, customers who previously cared only about standard paper-document distribution now expect printers to be able to disseminate their documents in a variety of different media (CD ROM, on-line, diskette, for example). Printers' profitability is directly related to their capability to make information scanable, interactive, and easy to manipulate, then disseminate it in the media format their customers' customers require.

Composition Free-for-All Scenario.   In a Composition Free-for-All World, desktop publishing and word processing functionality advance, but customer segments vary widely in their ability and desire to incorporate it into their business processes. Some continue to require full service; others perform all composition but need downstream printing support; still others unbundle the process and contract with different vendors for the composition and printing and distribution processes. The result is a much more fragmented and heterogeneous cast of financial printing service providers, all competing for a reduced pool of revenue.

The Exploring Phase

After identifying the basic features of these various possible future worlds, the participants entered and explored each one in greater detail. Adopting the economic logic of each world, the team progressed from discussing general market trends to probing specific implications for their business model. Exhibit 14.3 summarizes the insights generated in this exploring phase.

As the exhibit indicates, the exploration significantly enhanced the insights the printing firm's management team gained during the process of constructing the scenarios. For example, when they created the Multimedia Madness world, they realized that financial printers might potentially capture an entirely new revenue stream from a different set of customers for the electronic dissemination of financial documents. However, it was not until they explored the world in more detail that they realized how greatly demand for distribution would be likely to vary by segment. The government agencies that dominate the Frequent Issuer segment essentially place all their securities with a relatively small number of buyers before the documents are even finalized. Consequently, the Frequent Issuers' need for highly sophisticated electronic marketing from an external provider would be limited. In fact, one Frequent Issuer customer had already set up an in-house system that, while relatively unsophisticated, was adequate to meet its needs. On the other hand, IPOs rely heavily on the prospectus as a means to market their securities to fund managers. For them, fast distribution to certain managers might

Exhibit 14.3
Exploring Future Worlds

	Emerging Customer Priorities	Provider Capabilities Assessment	Competitive Landscape
Integrated Printers Rule	• Hassle-free support for sophisticated document production. (Frequent issuers lead in composing in-house.)	• Strong customer service and account management skills • Distributed typesetting/composition	• Traditional financial printers
Composing Customer	• Easy "hand-off" of final document for printing only. (All segments compose in-house.)	• Fast, accurate print capabilities	• Software firms • Low-end commercial printers (anyone with press capacity)
Multimedia Madness	• Multichannel distribution of high-functionality financial information.	• Strong data-manipulation capabilities • Fluency with multiple output media	• Financial information companies (Bloomberg, Reuters)
Composition Free-for-All	• Fragmentation of priorities by customer segment.	• High degree of focus on carefully chosen scope of services • Partnering with key customers	• "Composition-only" niche providers • Integrated printers • Software firms

have significant value. The critical question was whether a law firm or investment bank would develop such a system.

The participants found the exploring phase to be akin to playing a highly structured game of "what if . . . ," the bond traders' pastime described by Michael Lewis in his best-selling book written from a Wall Street insider's perspective, *Liar's Poker* (Norton, 1989). In the game, players select an event at random, such as an earthquake in Japan or a switch in the papal stance on birth control, and logically play out its consequences, ending with the effect on the price and yield of U.S. government bonds. In both "what if . . . " and the process of exploring the worlds in customer-driven scenario planning, the key to success is the ability to detect meaningful patterns among seemingly unconnected events.

The Responding Phase

When the printing company's management team began the customer-driven scenario-planning process, it lacked a strategic perspective on its customers, on their priorities, and on the implications of changing customer needs for the future of the financial printing industry. However, by the time the scenario process reached the responding phase, the participants all agreed on the need to change the business model. Their unanimous agreement is especially significant because each participant began the exercise with a unique set of preconceptions and prejudices, including substantial reluctance to change a business model that had been very successful

Exhibit 14.4
Potential Action Steps

Potential Action Step	Motivating Factor
• Reduce costs.	• Customers' dissatisfaction with service levels and printers' willingness to cut price to preserve baseload volumes together threaten to push prices steadily lower. • Customers place low value on *printing* of the document (versus composition and distribution).
• Broaden product line to offer "Corporate Printing Solutions," including facilities management, forms printing, and customer communications.	• Increasing acceptance of outsourcing of noncore functions among large corporations.
• Improve customer service.	• The better the service at traditional printers, the less likely customers will be to take the composition process in-house.
• Focus on a consultative sales approach (key factor is the cumulative expertise of the printer) versus a purely "relationship sell" (primary factor is how well the key decision maker likes the print sales representative).	• Customers unfamiliar with the new SEC regulations on electronic filing will require a new level of technical advice.
• Exit the print business and become a provider of on-line financial information.	• Growing market for high-functionality, user-friendly financial information.

in the past. At the conclusion of the exercise, they also agreed on specific action steps to start aligning the organization with emerging customer needs.

Each action step required initial financial investment. Before the customer-driven scenario-planning exercise, the management team lacked the conviction to compromise short-term earnings or to propose capital expenditures based on mere theories about future needs to the corporate finance department. But thanks to what it had learned from the customer-driven scenario-planning exercise, the management team was finally able to commit to specific investments.

Each of the actions that the organization ultimately took was motivated by one predetermined event, critical uncertainty, or observation from the scenario-planning exercise (see Exhibit 14.4). While the first two actions were intended to prepare the organization for events that were certain to take place, the third represented a "covering bet" designed to capitalize on one specific potential outcome.

The financial printing management team used customer-driven scenario planning to gain a strategic understanding of how new technology might change the priorities of different customer segments. As noted at the beginning of the chapter, the process can also be used to gain perspective on the changing importance of different channels.

CONCLUSION

For many large and successful businesses considering their future, it is easier to "stay the course" than to venture into new and uncharted waters. However, as the Sears and IBM organizations discovered in the 1980s (and many other companies are discovering today), changes in customer decision making often result in future profit opportunities that differ radically from the opportunities of the past. Executing customer-driven scenario planning cannot remove the risks of taking an organization with existing human and physical assets in a new direction, but it can make managers fully aware of the (often greater) risks of not moving. It can also provide managers with the confidence to keep looking forward and encouraging others in their organizations to do the same.

CHAPTER 15

FUTURING CONSUMER PRODUCTS: AN ILLUSTRATIVE EXAMPLE OF SCENARIO ANALYSIS

STEPHEN M. MILLETT

This approach differs from the more widely used intuitive scenario development process. It employs the same set of issues—developed from expert judgment about the future—to develop all scenarios. It interrelates all issues and their alternative outcomes with each other in computer-based modeling using the cross-impact technique. It provides a format for expert judgment probabilities to produce the "most likely" scenarios. By computerizing the scenarios, it facilitates simulation and the playing of what-if games that are based on a consistent logic.

Battelle Management Consulting uses scenario analysis as a key part of a quantitative methodology called *futuring*. Futuring is the process of recognizing an organization's most likely emerging opportunities and then developing strategies to take advantage of them. It is neither predicting nor forecasting, but it is the identification of trends, their likely outcomes, and the development of effective strategies. Instead of trying to divine the future or estimate a specific data point, futuring teaches managers to recognize how multiple and interacting trend patterns exert forces that can be charted and measured. By modeling the key forces driving the future, managers can anticipate and manage changes. The goal is to create strategies to make desirable outcomes happen.

One product of a futuring exercise is a set of likely scenarios. They allow the futuring team to explore relevant, challenging futures that are based on the synthesis of many disparate issues. The futuring exercise also creates a set of less likely scenarios, each describing a significantly different future with conditions that are logically consistent and explicit. Each scenario provides a rational story that the managers of the organization can learn from and use to understand a given dynamic environment.

Exploring the scenarios gives managers foresight into how actions, investments, and strategies will succeed or fail under a particular set of conditions and logic. It is not a question of learning whether a good or bad future is going to happen, but rather a question of the desirable futures that could be made to happen and how.

A CONSUMER PRODUCT COMPANY USES SCENARIOS TO REVIVE AN AGING LINE

In the early 1990s, an international consumer products company was having difficulty making a strategic business decision concerning a product line that had fallen on hard times. The company's policy was to maintain or reach first or second place in worldwide market share for each of its many product lines, old as well as new. Yet this product line, one that had been a sentimental favorite of the company for decades, had fallen to fifth place in world markets. The product line still made money, but both its margins and its market share were declining. The general market for the product line showed large annual growth rates, but competitors were dominating this growth.

The business problem lent itself well to futuring through scenario analysis. The company senior managers wanted to understand the interplay among many diverse factors, such as how likely the general market was to grow and what they would have to do to reposition their product to increase sales and market share. The concerns of senior management were converted into a topic question for the scenario analysis: What will be the most likely competitive advantages in consumer products—under what worldwide market conditions—by the year 2005?

At the outset of the scenario project, almost every manager in the organization already had formed a favorite opinion about what he or she supposed was the cause of the product line's failure to thrive. In fact, each part of the company had its own pet theories:

- The R&D community believed that the problem was technological; that is, the old design of the product failed to include new capabilities that would provide greater consumer value.

- Manufacturing asserted that production modes were outdated and inefficient.
- Financial managers wanted to economize by purchasing large quantities of a few materials for a limited number of basic products. This would allow the product line to become the lowest-cost producer.
- Marketing blamed the problem on inadequate distribution channels and unfair competitive practices.

The challenge of the scenario analysis was to sort out the facts and determine which factors were the most important to the success or failure of the product. Our assignment was to assess technology capabilities and to provide impartial facilitation for the futuring process.

How Futuring Methodology Works

This approach differs from the more widely used intuitive scenario development process in several important ways:

- It employs the same set of issues—developed from expert judgment about the future—to develop all scenarios. Variations occur in the alternative outcomes for each issue.
- It encourages the participation of many experts, both from inside and outside of the client company. The role of the core team is to facilitate the structure of the scenario, but the ownership of the content remains with all participants.
- It interrelates all issues and their alternative outcomes with each other in computer-based modeling using the cross-impact technique.
- It provides a format for expert judgment probabilities to produce the "most likely" scenarios, not just archetypical scenarios.
- By computerizing the scenarios, it facilitates simulation and the playing of what-if games that are based on a consistent logic.

This scenario method uses cross-impact analysis derived from social science research pioneered by the RAND Corporation. To perform cross-impact analysis, we build formal models for studying the effect of trends. Cross-impact analysis explicitly interrelates all the significant trends and issues identified in response to a topic question being researched by an organization. This interrelationship is measured using a matrix model and assigned numerical values.

Trends and Probabilities

For a topic question such as: "What will be the competitive advantages in a consumer product by 2004?" sample descriptors (trends, issues, factors, and elements) and their probabilities are detailed in Exhibit 15.1.

The selection of descriptors is expert judgment, as in all forms of modeling and forecasting. We typically derive the descriptors from two to five expert focus groups. The probabilities given are expert judgments for outcomes by the target year 2004 based largely on interpretation of trends (a step that is covered in cross-impact analysis).

The Model

The interaction of these descriptors can be studied in the matrix model shown in Exhibit 15.2. Again, the index values of interactions (read columns against rows) is a matter of expert judgment—which is explicit and subject to peer review and revision. We use index values ranging from +3 (strong positive impact) to −3 (strong negative impact) to relate the occurrence of one descriptor outcome to the adjusted probabilities of other descriptor outcomes also occurring. In other words, we ask, "Do diverse trends reinforce each other so as to increase their likelihood of happening, or do trends adversely affect each other?"

For example, in Exhibit 15.2, the occurrence of rapid product innovation (1.A) has no direct impact on any alternative outcomes for manufacturing mode (2), but the occurrence of agile manufacturing (2.A) has a moderately positive impact (+2) on the probability that rapid product

Exhibit 15.1
Sample Descriptors and Probabilities

1. Product Innovation
   A. Rapid (less than 1 year)   0.30
   B. Gradual (1–2 years)   0.50
   C. Slow   0.20

2. Manufacturing Mode
   A. Agile: quick changeover   0.25
   B. Flexible within limitations   0.40
   C. Rigid production lines   0.35

3. Distribution
   A. Multiple, independent distributors 0.50
   B. Strategic relationships   0.30
   C. Self-distribution   0.20

Exhibit 15.2
Interaction of Descriptors

	1.			2.			3.		
	A.	B.	C.	A.	B.	C.	A.	B.	C.
1. Product Innovation									
A. Rapid	0	0	0	2	1	−2	1	0	−1
B. Gradual	0	0	0	1	0	−1	0	0	0
C. Slow	0	0	0	−2	−1	2	−1	0	1
2. Manufacturing Mode									
A. Agile	0	0	0	0	0	0	1	0	−1
B. Flexible	0	0	0	0	0	0	0	0	0
C. Rigid	0	0	0	0	0	0	−1	0	1
3. Distribution									
A. Multiple independent distributors	0	0	0	2	1	0	0	0	0
B. Strategic relationships	0	0	0	1	0	−1	0	0	0
C. Self-distribution	0	0	0	−2	−1	2	0	0	0

innovation will occur. In other words, the move to agile manufacturing increases the likelihood that the trend in product innovation will move to rapid, based on the expectation that more flexible manufacturing provides the means and the motivation to go to rapid product innovation. Conversely, rigid production discourages rapid product innovation and encourages slow product innovation.

How the Computer Model Works

The computer program is designed to translate the probabilities into simple yes or no answers for each descriptor; that is, will it occur or won't it occur? On a 60-element matrix, the software will produce 120 single scenarios. But many scenarios will be identical to others. For example, the calculations might produce 24 single scenarios that are the same (the same set of occurring descriptor outcomes), and another set of 18 single scenarios that are the same (except that they differ in one or more descriptor outcomes from the first set of scenarios), and another set with 10 single scenarios, and other sets with even fewer scenarios that are the same. Since 24 is larger than 10, we infer that the first set of scenarios is more likely to happen than the third set. This isn't a precise calculation based on probability theory, but it does reflect proportionality—that one set of outcomes is higher in frequency of occurrence, and hence more likely than another set of outcomes.

Once a set of four or five distinct scenarios is selected, then we can play what-if games by changing the initial set of outcome probabilities or by adding new descriptors (like a possible corporate action). The numbers may have little meaning in absolute terms but they generate insights with relative meaning. How the scenarios shift in content and frequency gives us a way to simulate potential company strategies to see whether they do or do not produce desired results. Obviously, this method is quite different from the intuitive approach that many scenario consultants offer.

Back to Our Case in Point. In the international consumer products company assignment, once the topic question was approved by senior management, we conducted five expert focus groups to identify the descriptors—important trends, issues, or factors—to be included in the study. The focus groups were composed of knowledgeable company managers and outside experts. The focus groups generated and prioritized over 200 potential descriptors covering all aspects of competitive advantages. From the master lists generated, the core project team consolidated all the expert judgment into 18 descriptors. They included: product content technology, manufacturing processes, marketing, distribution, packaging, regulatory restraints, product variety, and intensity of competition.

Each descriptor was researched, analyzed, and assigned likely alternative outcomes by the year 2005. For example, the descriptor on packaging might include at least three alternative outcomes: value-based packaging, convenience packaging, and price-driven packaging. The probabilities of occurrence of these alternative outcomes were judged by select experts. At this stage, these probabilities are really gross judgments of occurrence—such as 30 percent, 50 percent, and 20 percent (as shown in Exhibit 15.2).

Next, the write-ups and probabilities were widely circulated among experts, including those who participated in the expert focus groups, for further comments and revisions. All points of view were considered and accommodated to the greatest extent possible. In some cases, we had to rewrite the descriptor outcomes based on different expert views or change the probability judgment.

The core team performed the cross-impact analysis and then submitted it for review by many people, in much the same way that the descriptor white papers were reviewed. From the cross-impact analysis we were able to generate scenarios using the algorithm of the BASIC-PC software program, which calculated all the numbers so that probabilities were driven to 1.0 (it occurs) or 0 (it does not occur).

For example, initially the probability for value-based packaging may have been .30 (30 percent), but several other descriptor states impacting it with high positive cross-impact values may increase its probability to 1.0 (100 percent). The conclusion is that value-based packaging will almost certainly occur because of the influence of other trends and issues that are likely to develop. The process allows us to determine which occurring descriptor states go with other occurring descriptor states.

At this stage we made a major discovery about how out of date this company's "insights" were about this product line. Surprisingly little information existed within the company on product trends, market figures, and competitive behavior in this particular market area. We were taken aback by this strange lack of competitive intelligence and product benchmarking for one of the company's oldest product lines. While many individuals had experience and information, there was no central library on this product line. A study of the market done a number of years ago gave us no information on a host of emerging trends.

In comparison, our new research on the 18 descriptors that would be used to develop the scenarios demonstrated the crucial need for fresh, comprehensive information on this product line's consumers, competitors, and market changes. We were intrigued to learn that in this company this "research gap" was limited to this one product line. Comprehensive market information was already available on the company's leading products.

Is it any wonder that this product was struggling? Its dwindling market share could be attributed to a certain amount of resignation and indifference throughout the company to the fate of an aging line. In contrast, we learned from other scenario studies that market leaders typically display great passion about their products—a passion that can be translated into the number one market share position.

The core project team produced many scenarios; just five were selected for intensive discussion. We briefed several audiences about these five scenarios, collected their comments and made further refinements. This step helped people to see the alternative futures, to begin to think of responsive strategies, and to encourage them to feel a sense of project participation.

This study proved an important rule we had also learned from previous projects with other companies: The corporate politics of scenarios is just as important, if not more so, than the intellectual content of them. The changes derived from scenarios have to be fermented slowly in the minds of both corporate leaders and business unit staff. Scenarios can lead to corporate cultural changes—such as a willingness to "visit the future" in the sense of taking part in scenario planning—but only if the process is managed so that knowledgeable line managers are driving the process. The operating managers and corporate decision makers, not the consultants, must own the futuring process. The role of consultants is to provide fair facilitation and expert guidance for scenario creation and development. However, the most important content of the scenarios—the major lessons learned—must belong to the people who are responsible for strategy implementation.

The five scenarios for the aging product line are:

Scenario 1: Strong market growth with strong industry leadership.

Scenario 2: Moderate market growth with many copycat products.

Scenario 3: Market growth, but with small profit margins.

Scenario 4: Market collapse.

Scenario 5: Moderate market growth with strong industry leadership.

Strong Market Growth with Strong Industry Leadership. This scenario showed the potential for further strong market growth when one or more companies provides market leadership by introducing attractive new products that anticipate what consumers want. The strong growth rate of recent years, largely driven by increased consumer demand, could accelerate even further with strong industry leadership. In this scenario, growth and leadership occur in an environment of technological advancements in product engineering as well as production processes. New products would greatly stimulate demand. Competition among a relatively few number of market leaders is fierce in this scenario, and a key source of competitive advantage is the capability to provide diversified, value-added products. For example, the consumer will have many different options from a few basic products that can easily be customized.

The first scenario expects consumers to continue to be difficult to please—ever more sophisticated and more exacting about their requirements. Each consumer will want it his or her own way—precisely the right size, shape, color, texture, and fragrance. Moreover, customers will want their particular wishes, their "customized" purchases, available faster than ever before—right off the shelf if possible.

Innovative companies are seizing upon individualized customer satisfaction as a competitive advantage. For example, Levi Strauss is offering ladies' jeans measured and fitted to an individual buyer's contours. Many buyers consider paying a premium for this service quite reasonable, especially because the jeans are delivered within just a week or two of purchase. In other consumer markets, new stores are already opening that offer moderately priced mass-customized products, such as shoes and swimsuits. After the customers' measurements are taken, a computer-controlled manufacturing process makes the products to precisely fit each customer.

A surprising lesson learned from the first scenario is that despite consumers' preoccupation with quality and choice, product quality won't be a reliable source of differentiation. As all companies improve their product quality, the consumer will find it more difficult to choose among competing products on quality alone. Important new sources of differentiation will be innovation, appearance, and easy availability. In the first scenario, future competitive advantages will be quality with low price or quality with uniqueness. Both product diversity and flexible manufacturing will be extremely important in the next century.

Moderate Market Growth with Many Copycat Products. In the second scenario, market growth will occur, but not to the extent shown in the first scenario. In this scenario, industrial leadership will be lacking, with several companies offering copycat products. The proliferation of more-of-the-same offerings—variation without genuine innovation—will bore consumers and cool demand. An example of this market situation is the proliferation of private label canned foods in supermarkets.

Market Growth, But with Small Profit Margins. The third scenario shows some but not much growth in a highly competitive situation where quality will mean little and price will determine sales. This is truly a commodity market. Product engineering will count for little, but profit margins will require low-cost production tactics. In this situation, the strategic technologies to invest in will be manufacturing processes rather than product content technologies. For a case in point, over many years toothpaste has become a commodity that is easier to differentiate by price than by quality.

Market Collapse.   The fourth scenario portrays a set of circumstances in which the market collapses. Consumer apathy turns to hostility, and the product dies. Competition may still be intense, but largely irrelevant now that share in a dying market counts for little. The corporate strategy here is, obviously, market exit. For example, about a decade ago long-playing records, in the form of vinyl disks, were marketed by "record companies." But these firms were really in the music business and they jumped at the chance to sell tapes and CDs when that technology became widely popular. The companies that actually pressed the vinyl records lost a whole product line to the alternative record formats.

Moderate Market Growth, with Strong Industry Leadership.   The fifth scenario is a variation on the first. It warns that a company might do all the right things but the market growth may be only moderate rather than strong. This is the "smart" scenario without the luck that figures into the first scenario. Such a scenario often occurs when a new product is ahead of its time. That is, the product concept makes sense, but the consumers are slow to actually purchase it. An example is the Internet, which was used by relatively few people for a decade until an explosion in e-mail traffic began about 1994.

WHAT THE SCENARIOS ACCOMPLISHED
The scenarios were a wake up call to company management. The lesson was: If the company wanted strong market growth, then it had to create strong markets. The old product platform was adequate as a launching pad for product variations, but the core product needed to be reinvented. If the company feels that a product is boring, the consumer will feel the same way. Product innovation and creative marketing are continuous challenges.

To remedy the situation, the company began an R&D effort to create fresh offerings from established products and to repackage the current line attractively for new markets. Current trend data verify that the company is on the right track to reach the first, most likely to occur, scenario. Some observations indicate that the changes in the marketplace are taking place sooner than expected. The company changed its portfolio of

R&D investments and has already launched some new products designed for the marketplace that were envisioned in the first scenario.

Even more important, the company has invested encouragement and vigor into the management of this product line and produced new hope for it among all the stakeholders. The message of the scenarios was that a strong effort may not guarantee complete success, but that making no effort nearly assured that the fourth scenario—market collapse—would come true.

CHAPTER 16

THE ROLE OF ECONOMIC SCENARIOS

NARIMAN BEHRAVESH

The future dynamics of the global and national economy play a critical role in the scenario-planning process of both large and small organizations. Over the past three decades, corporate leaders and planners have learned the perils of ignoring the critical macroeconomic uncertainties and possible discontinuities facing their corporations. Throughout the world, companies that erroneously assumed that the economic environment would change slowly, rarely, or in predictable ways were badly mauled by unexpected turns of events.

$\mathbf{S}$trategic plans and scenarios that don't take into account macroeconomic issues risk being suddenly rendered obsolete by a reversal of economic trends. A sample list of major issues that strategic planners should consider as they construct scenarios includes:

- Will inflation rise (or fall) significantly over the scenario horizon?
- When is the next business cycle downturn likely to occur?
- How likely is another oil shock?
- What is the future course of exchange rates?
- Are there likely to be major changes in the tax and regulatory environment?

Such issues need to be incorporated into a scenario learning process (see Exhibit 16.1).

Some of the more spectacular examples of the failure to plan for major changes in the economic environment occurred in the mid-1980s. Many energy companies, financial institutions, and even governments expected

Exhibit 16.1
Scenario Planning

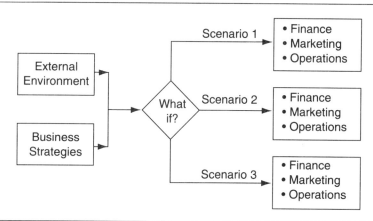

that, even in the worst-case scenario, oil prices would continue to rise. Only a handful considered the possibility that the price of crude oil would fall and stay low. Exhibit 16.2 is a very typical set of oil price projections that were run in the early 1980s. A large number of energy companies, real estate developers, local planners and savings and loan institutions that used the types of projections shown in Exhibit 16.2 were in serious trouble just a few years later.

There is, perhaps, an even more compelling reason why the economic foundations of scenario building have become more important. With the rapid integration of the world economy through trade and financial

Exhibit 16.2
Oil Price Projections

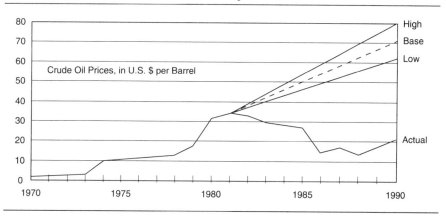

flows, economic drivers have become a central element in the strategy development and execution process. Increasingly, companies have to grapple with questions such as:

- How will the formation of trading blocs—NAFTA, APEC, and EU, for example—affect investment opportunities and decisions about how to do business abroad?
- As national and regional governments expend vast sums to make businesses they support more competitive, what effect will such initiatives have in the global marketplace?
- Which countries or regions offer the most favorable risk/reward trade-offs, and what is the most effective way of doing business in each of these markets? For example, should businesses buy, build, export, start joint ventures, or make licensing agreements?

The best way to consider some of these broader issues is to explicitly incorporate them into the scenario process. Scenarios that explore one or more of these sources of economic uncertainty will prove to be an especially useful tool for planners.

THE BASIC TOOLS OF ECONOMIC SCENARIO BUILDING: ECONOMETRIC MODELS

Exhibit 16.3 is a schematic diagram of the DRI/McGraw-Hill model of the U.S. economy. This relatively large model has over 1,000 variables, which fall into two categories: exogenous and endogenous variables. In the diagram, the exogenous variables are grouped together in the diamond-shaped box, and the endogenous variables in the rectangular-shaped box.

Exogenous variables are determined by events and decisions that occur outside the framework of the model. Such variables rise or fall based on, for example, decisions made by the Federal Reserve to control monetary policy; by legislation to raise or lower tax rates; and by plans to increase or decrease defense spending. Significant international economic influences, such as foreign demand for U.S. goods and the price of imported oil are other major exogenous factors.

Endogenous variables are the influences the model can account for. The model is designed to reflect how a set of major endogenous variables—such

Exhibit 16.3
DRI/McGraw-Hill Model of U.S. Economy

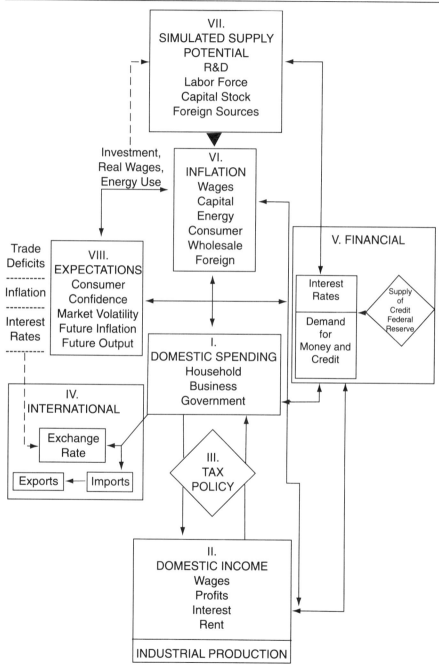

as consumer spending, housing starts, retail sales, capital goods expenditures, import demand, average hourly wages, the Consumer Price Index and corporate profits—can describe the dynamics of a real, interactive economy.

Why Use Econometric Models to Construct Scenarios?

Econometric models offer a number of advantages over more informal ways of creating scenarios. First, they provide an explicit framework that clarifies which assumptions were used to develop a scenario. For example, whether a U.S. business cycle scenario is based on an oil crisis, a hike in interest rates by the Fed, or because of an inventory correction can have vastly different implications for a business. Therefore, articulating exactly how a business cycle might occur is an important part of a scenario exercise.

Second, using an econometric model imposes internal consistency on the scenario process. For example, a model adopts a common set of assumptions for key exogenous variables, such as oil prices or exchange rates. As a result, changes in these variables affect all the relevant endogenous variables in plausible ways.

Third, comprehensive econometric models provide more reliable projections. There are feedback loops in the models that capture most, if not all, the interactions among the endogenous variables. For example, an increase in tax rates will initially increase tax revenues. However, this will reduce take-home pay, which in turn will reduce consumer spending and gross domestic product (GDP). Finally, lower GDP means lower national income and lower tax receipts, offsetting some or all of the initial rise. Economists refer to this as a general equilibrium, rather than a partial equilibrium, response to a change in the economy.

The power of world events to influence the structure of national models waxes and wanes. For example, the opening up of the U.S. economy—as measured by the rise of imports and exports as a share of GDP—makes policies set in Tokyo and Bonn of great importance to U.S. businesses.

THREE TYPES OF ECONOMIC SCENARIOS: TECHNICAL, POLICY, AND STRUCTURAL

Economic scenarios are created by using the model to preview what would happen in the real world when changes occur in specific variables (see Exhibit 16.4). Different assumptions about such exogenous variables

Exhibit 16.4
Constructing Economic Scenarios

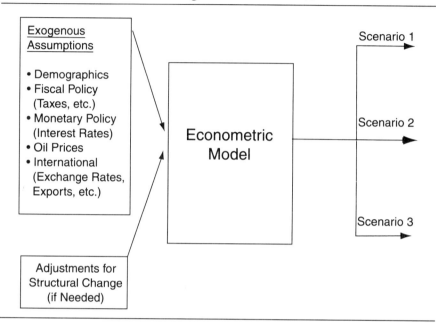

as demographics, taxes, interest rates, exchange rates, and oil prices will produce different scenarios. Depending on the needs of the scenario planner and the scope of uncertainty being considered, scenarios can be constructed by making different assumptions about one exogenous variable, such as oil prices, or many variables. There are three basic types of economic scenarios, technical, policy or shock, and structural, which are defined in the following subsections.

Technical Scenarios. These are developed by making plausible but largely mechanical changes to the exogenous variables of a model to produce pessimistic or optimistic alternatives around a base-case scenario. Alternatively, the exogenous variables can be set to produce either a trend or a cyclical scenario for the U.S. economy. To create cyclical scenarios, the analysts make assumptions about exactly when and how a business cycle downturn in the economy might occur. For instance, they might postulate that a downturn had been provoked by an external shock or contractionary fiscal or monetary policy. (The next section provides several illustrations of technical scenarios.)

Technical scenarios are particularly helpful when companies are planning for their capital expenditures over a medium- to long-term horizon. Typically, companies requiring alternative scenarios—especially a cyclical scenario—are in industries that routinely make large capital expenditures, including the chemical, aircraft, and electric utilities industries. Over a short-term horizon, technical scenarios can also be used for inventory planning and cash-flow management.

Policy or Shock Scenarios.   These are based on actual or anticipated events such as a deficit reduction package, tax reform, an oil crisis, or a currency devaluation.

Unlike technical scenarios, there is usually no attempt at the outset to impose a particular pattern (trend, cycle, etc.) on such scenarios. Rather, econometric models are used to assess exactly what the impact of the policy change or external shock will be. The flat-tax scenario described in the next section is an example of such a scenario.

Policy or shock scenarios are most useful for impact or sensitivity analysis. Many planners are interested in testing the sensitivity of their base-case scenarios to changes in specific variables such as oil prices, exchange rates, or tax rates. Shock scenarios are also useful when considering whether to hedge against oil price hikes and currency fluctuations. Many banks have used these types of scenarios to look at the vulnerability of their portfolios to risks in specific industries or countries, as well as susceptibility to risks that cut across many industries and countries.

Structural Scenarios.   These typically push econometric models to their limits by considering major changes in the economic environment such as:

- The formation of regional trading blocs.
- The introduction and rapid diffusion of new technologies.
- Pressures to move toward environmentally sustainable growth.
- Changes in the economies of scale-of-key industries.

Companies can use economic scenarios, especially structural scenarios, as inputs to risk or decision-tree analysis. In such exercises, planners will assign probabilities to a variety of scenarios in an attempt to assess the mean value and variance of key variables such as return on investment or net operating income. This type of analysis also allows companies to measure the size of the investment risk premiums they must consider, for example, when doing business in a country where the AIDS epidemic is becoming a major drag on growth.

A SET OF TECHNICAL ECONOMIC SCENARIOS FOR THE U.S. ECONOMY TO THE YEAR 2010

The following four scenarios—Trend, Cyclical, Optimistic, and Pessimistic—were created with data from the standard set of alternative economic projections that DRI/McGraw-Hill prepares twice a year (see Exhibit 16.5). The major exogenous assumptions of the DRI/McGraw-Hill U.S. econometric model have been changed to produce four different profiles of the U.S. economy over the next 25 years.

Current Trends: The Surpriseless-Future Scenario.   This projection of current trends provides the baseline scenario. It assumes that the economy suffers no major mishaps between now and 2020, with actual output approximately paralleling potential output. This projection assumes that the economy will follow the middle of all possible paths and will experience no major disruptions. In the trend scenario, demographic forces slow the pace of growth, so its rate averages an unspectacular 2.0 percent per year over the next quarter-century.

Exhibit 16.5
DRI Scenarios

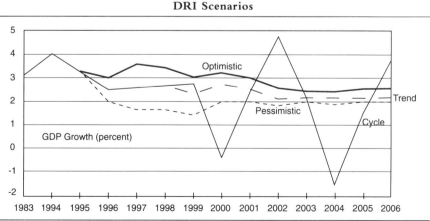

Cyclical: Expecting Ups and Downs Scenario.   The primary alternative scenario assumes that an economic cycle will occur in a few years. This scenario remains completely consistent with the short-term baseline forecast through 1998, but thereafter economic growth proceeds in a series of starts and stops. Periods of rapid growth are followed by externally or policy-induced recessions. The uncertainty this pattern generates causes slower capital accumulation and lower productivity, thus reducing the average rate of growth by about 0.2 percentage points per year relative to the baseline. Experience has proved that it is impossible to predict the exact timing of business cycles much in advance.

Optimistic: Consistently Good News Scenario.   In an optimistic scenario, growth proceeds smoothly but considerably more rapidly than in the baseline version, and inflation remains at current low levels. In this projection, benign changes in population, labor force, and capital-stock growth, as well as exogenous technological factors, occur more rapidly than in the Trend Projection scenario. Potential output thus climbs 0.5 percent per year faster. Inflation averages 0.9 percentage point below the baseline, partly reflecting lower energy prices.

Pessimistic: Slower Growth and Nagging Inflation Scenario.   This pessimistic projection assumes that growth will proceed smoothly but considerably less rapidly than in the baseline version, while inflation accelerates to around 5.5 percent. In this projection, population, labor force, and capital-stock growth, together with exogenous technological changes, occur less rapidly than in the trend. Potential and actual output climb 0.5 percent per year slower. Meanwhile, inflation averages 1.8 percentage points above the baseline, partially reflecting higher energy prices.

Business Implications.   The usefulness of each of these four scenarios to business planners and scenario builders depends a great deal on the nature of their company's business environment. The cyclical scenario is most useful to companies in cyclical markets. These include the capital goods, construction, and chemical industries. Companies in these sectors have learned that it is almost impossible to predict exactly when the next downturn will occur. Nevertheless, they need a plausible business cycle scenario that maps out a downturn sometime in their planning horizon. However, companies in less cyclical sectors (such as many of the service firms) are more likely to find the Trend, Pessimistic, and Optimistic scenarios more useful. These scenarios allow planners to construct alternative strategies around a plausible range of sales and cost outcomes.

ECONOMIC POLICY SCENARIOS: ANALYZING THE IMPACTS OF A FLAT TAX

The following scenario analyzing the effect of a major change in tax policy and tax law in the United States was produced in late 1995 by DRI/McGraw-Hill. It is a good example of a policy scenario, as it changes a limited set of exogenous variables in the DRI/McGraw-Hill econometric model to measure the impact of a specific policy change. The case involves analysis of legislation proposed in Congress to shift the United States from income taxation of corporations and individuals to the equivalent of a value-added tax.

The tax is popularly referred to as a "flat tax" because the net income or spending stream for any business or individual would be subject to one, and only one, tax rate.

The Impact of a Flat Tax on Households and Businesses. Under the proposed flat tax, the tax base for both individuals and businesses would be significantly enlarged but then subject to a lower, common rate. The tax base for business would be gross sales minus wages and purchases from other businesses. Interest payments would not count as purchases from other businesses and thus would not be deductible. The tax base for individuals would be wages and pensions less standard personal exemptions. Consequently, a business in the economy pays a tax on each dollar of every final sale, except for wages paid; the worker reports the wages and pays the tax. Both tax bases of businesses and individuals are subject to an equal flat tax rate that could be near 22–25 percent, depending on assumptions about exemption levels and other special factors. Proponents of the legislation claim that it would produce the same revenues as the current corporate and individual income taxes.

Consequences for the Housing Market. The flat tax would remove all government incentives for owner-occupied single-family homes. Interest and property taxes would not be deductible, thus the after-tax cost of housing would rise substantially unless the market price of homes falls.

Collectively, home owners would lose an estimated $84 billion per year in tax savings. This annual loss can be capitalized with a conservative 5 percent real discount rate to estimate an implied aggregate loss in the value of owning a home equal to $1.7 trillion (the result of dividing $84 billion by .05). This equals approximately 15 percent of the market value of all U.S. homes, a loss that would be surely be reflected in a drop in market prices. Expensive homes would likely fall more than 15 percent, since many occupants of smaller homes do not itemize their deductions. In other words, the $1.7 trillion capitalized value of current savings largely applies to middle- and upper-income groups, and it would be their homes that fall in value.

Other Macroeconomic Effects.   Powerful macroeconomic forces (Exhibits 16.6) would be put in play if current versions of a flat tax were to pass Congress. For example, one version offers businesses a major reduction in the effective cost of business equipment and structures.

The DRI/McGraw-Hill scenario shows that this proposed flat tax would provide a powerful stimulant to business investment. The draft legislation permits immediate expensing, not just phased depreciation, of the cost of plant and equipment. The present value of this tax benefit is far greater than the currently allowed deductibility of debt financing. Therefore, a full analysis indicates that, after the economy gets beyond the probable slump created by a sharp drop in home values and household net worth, investment would pick up and drive market interest rates back toward current levels. The net result might be a real risk of a 30 percent-plus decline in the price of homes owned by the middle class. To be

Exhibit 16.6
The Medium-Run Impacts of a Flat Tax

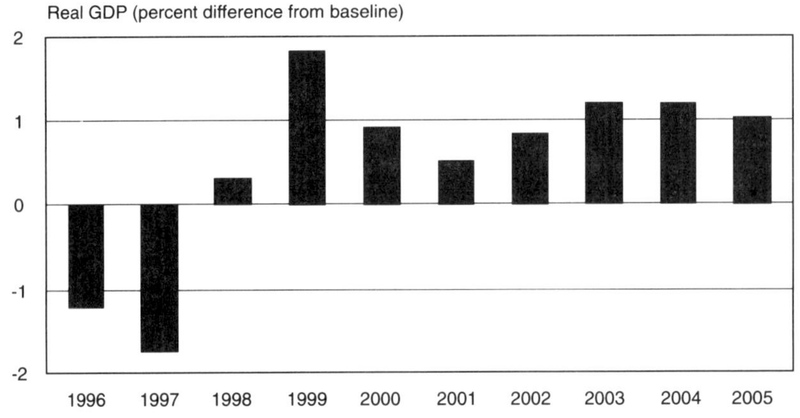

conservative, however, the DRI simulation begins with an assumption of only the initial 15 percent shock calculated from the capitalized value of lost deductions.

DRI concluded that a shift to the flat tax would encourage greater total capital formation and significantly but not dramatically higher long-term growth. In our projection, higher real incomes eventually exert a positive influence on housing, as does the accumulation of pent-up demand. Household net worth, however, damaged by the loss in the value of homes, remains well below baseline levels throughout the 10-year forecast horizon. The American middle class would be asked to pay a high price to achieve tax code simplification and to eliminate the double-taxation of corporate income.

Business Implications. The scenario on the flat tax is of critical importance not only to home owners but also to real estate developers, construction companies, and financial institutions that hold the existing stock of mortgages. All of these sectors would be adversely affected by such a tax change and should factor such a scenario into their plans. Similarly, capital goods industries would receive a boost from such a change and would be shortsighted if they did not factor such an upside scenario into their plans.

CONCLUSION

This chapter described how economic scenarios support the scenario-planning process and offered specific examples of how several different types of economic scenarios are used by planners. Though technical, policy/shock, and structural scenarios have been described as though they were distinct types of scenarios, in reality, planners can and do combine the different types of economic scenarios. Depending on the nature of scenarios being considered and how they are to be used by a company, the three types of economic scenario can be used on a stand-alone basis or in combination with one another. For example, assumptions about different oil prices (shock scenario) can be used to develop optimistic and pessimistic scenarios (technical scenarios). Similarly, a change in the tax law (policy scenario) can have a profound effect on the behavior of households and businesses and, therefore, on the structure of the economy (structural scenario). Whichever method is adopted, the economic dimension offers a useful tool for rigorous scenario analysis.

CHAPTER 17

HOW SCENARIOS ENRICH PUBLIC POLICY DECISIONS

THOMAS W. BONNETT and ROBERT L. OLSON

State and regional governments can use scenario development to improve their planning capacity, to enrich strategic public policy decisions, and to guide their major capital investments. A scenario development project for the New Jersey Long Range Statewide Transportation Plan conducted by the Council of Governors' Policy Advisors (CGPA) and the Institute of Alternative Futures (IAF) provided state leaders with new insights about the opportunities and risks involved in making decisions about public transportation that would have major consequences for the development of the region during the next several decades.

Scenarios can assist public sector leaders to think in a disciplined way about the future when making public policy decisions, especially public investment decisions. Scenario learning helps private and public decision makers consider the range of plausible futures, to articulate a preferred vision of the future, and to use what they learn in the formal decision-making process to foster exceptional leadership. Scenario learning enables decision makers to break free of their conventional obsession with immediate and short-term problems.

CAPITAL BUDGETING AS LONG-TERM INVESTMENT DECISIONS

Perhaps the most difficult public policy decisions are those that relate to strategic choices that have potentially long-term impacts on society. An excellent example is how state governments select projects for their capital budgets, which are substantial public investments in complex systems. How can leaders make thoughtful decisions with such limited information in an uncertain, changing environment?

The Council of Governors' Policy Advisors (CGPA) has taken the lead in promoting the concepts of strategic planning to state governments. An outline of this policy development process (see Box 17.1) indicates how it combines the best of conventional policy analysis and organizational strategic planning. Note the major emphasis placed on thinking about the future, beginning with developing a common vision and scanning the policy environment. These initial steps have helped participants to challenge conventional wisdom about recent trends, articulate their own expectations, and be critical of conventional assumptions about the future.

The process of building scenarios is an important learning opportunity for organizational leaders. Direct involvement in scenario development forces leaders to think critically about plausible futures and appropriate organizational strategies. It forces leaders to understand and articulate some of the implicit assumptions they have about what the future will be like and why they think that. Scenarios developed by consultants, without the active participation of organizational leaders, may be interesting and helpful, but are less likely to lead to breakthroughs in strategy development. Scenarios that focus on an actual decision and its implementation are most likely to affect the thinking of the leadership and be of benefit to the organization.

CASE STUDY: SCENARIO DEVELOPMENT FOR NEW JERSEY TRANSPORTATION PLANNING

In the fall of 1993, CGPA and Institute for Alternative Futures (IAF) began a collaborative effort to develop a Future Worlds component as part of the New Jersey Long Range Statewide Transportation Plan. Developing alternative futures for New Jersey in 2020 provided several long-term perspectives from which to explore organizational strategies and fundamental policy choices.

Background

New Jersey lies between two metropolises: New York City and Philadelphia. The state's economy is linked to these cities, although much less so in recent years as commercial development has spread throughout the

Box 17.1
The CGPA Policy Development Process

1. *Develop a common vision.* Articulate a preferred future. Discuss the elements to be included in a preferred future. Develop consensus on what a preferred future would be.

2. *Scan the policy environment.* Assess key elements of the current environment and their relevance to the issue. Assess how recent trends in these elements could change. Assess elements most amenable to state-level action. Determine which elements are likely to facilitate or impede results.

3. *Assess problems and opportunities.* Define the major problems and opportunities. Determine who is affected by these problems and who could benefit from potential opportunities. Assess how serious the problems are and how significant the opportunities could be. Project recent trends into the future—better or worse outcomes? Determine the underlying causes for major problems. Assign priorities among both problems and opportunities.

4. *Set goals and policy objectives.* Set broad policy goals. Set specific outcome-oriented objectives. Choose indicators to measure accomplishment. Choose criteria for setting priorities. Establish priorities.

5. *Identify effective strategies.* Brainstorm how to achieve results. Research what works. Evaluate what is already in place. Set priorities. Determine when to act.

6. *Select policy and program recommendations.* Test for plausibility and feasibility. Select strategies and programs to achieve specific objectives. Design evaluation and monitoring programs.

7. *Gain support.* Clarify and simplify policy recommendations for the public. Involve key stakeholders—internal and external. Broaden base through local connections. Coordinate communications opportunities. Monitor and adjust for public and media reactions.

8. *Build accountability systems.* Determine the indicators of success. Involve data generators in system design. Organize to gather appropriate data. Develop incentives or mandates for data collection and reporting. Collect and analyze data.

9. *Implement programs and policies.* Clarify expected results. Resolve residual conflicts between existing and new objectives. Target priorities for strategic resource allocation. Provide sufficient guidance and training.

10. *Monitor progress and test results.* Review information from accountability systems. Make decisions based on results. Reexamine the policy environment and the major problems. Adjust objectives and strategies. Adjust implementation timetable. Revise priorities.

state, especially along the corridor between the two cities. The defining characteristic of the state during the postwar period was its rapid, sprawling suburban and commercial growth.

A New Era in Transportation Planning?

As regional planners well know, few public decisions have a greater impact on society than those relating to transportation systems. Building a network of modern highways in the post–World War II era, especially the Interstate Highway System, was arguably the single most important factor in influencing land use and development patterns in the second half of this century. Better highways led to more development and governmental programs to accommodate that growth, which led to more and more demand for travel. Travel needs in many metropolitan areas now exceeds existing highway capacity. However, opposition to building more new highways—by environmentalists and community leaders—has increased in recent years. But other responses to congestion—car pooling, parking fees, and congestion-period pricing—have not yet proven themselves to be popular with the public. Indeed, the driving public wants less congestion, but does not appear to be willing to pay for, or suffer much inconvenience for, whatever might work to achieve it.

There is, nevertheless, a remarkable degree of consensus on one central theme: The efficient and effective flow of goods and people throughout the nation—using all transportation modes—is essential for continued economic and social prosperity. But to add another level of complexity, transportation planners have never faced the kind of challenges that they must confront now. In recent years, they have had to comply with federal Clean Air Act requirements by developing various transportation demand management programs (such as car pooling) to reduce air pollution. They enjoy greater flexibility for federal funding under the Intermodal Surface Transportation Efficiency Act of 1991 (ISTEA), but find themselves in a tugging match with metropolitan planning organizations. Transportation planners must create a new process for engaging the public in making long-term planning decisions. If these challenges are not sufficient to vex even the most seasoned planners, along come the environmental groups who are seeking to use these federal laws as levers to shift resources away from new highway construction and into mass transit, bicycle paths, and other alternatives.

Capital investment decisions for complex transportation systems are among the most difficult choices to be made by state governments. Should public funds be invested to improve freight rail lines or should they be abandoned? If abandoned, should the rights of way be retained? Should additional lanes be added on certain interstate highways? Would adding highway capacity simply increase traffic volume? Should high-occupancy vehicle lanes be tried in certain locations? In which circumstances is light rail a prudent public investment? Will new demand-responsive transit systems such as minibuses meet suburban needs? Will car pooling ever measurably reduce congestion during rush hours? Would congestion period pricing schemes work?

These are not new questions. But the debates about these issues that were once only among a small circle of elite transportation planners, now have been joined by environmental activists, community leaders, appointed members of metropolitan planning organizations, and the general public. Federal regulation (ISTEA) requires state transportation agencies to engage in a public involvement process in formulating their transportation plans, a charge that has thrust these topics into the public arena.

With state transportation officials facing vociferous quarrels about so many uncertainties about the future, who could fault them for being tempted to pursue an abuse-reduction strategy? The core steps include:

1. Combining their agencies' list of short-term capital projects with their business plans to form the ISTEA-mandated transportation plan.
2. Scheduling the requisite public hearings without widespread publicity (hoping the public remains both apathetic and uninformed, and does not attend).
3. Shipping off the edited results to the federal government (while praying that its reviewers check the submission for weight rather than content).

In dramatic contrast, and much to their credit, the top transportation officials in New Jersey developed a study design that included public involvement, scenario development to assess future implications of current policy choices, performance measurement, and other innovative components. At the onset, the study was charged with "setting the course for a 20-year, long-range strategic plan." Throughout the study, its leadership spoke about seeking a widespread understanding of how transportation systems could, should, and would serve social needs.

The Future Worlds component of the Statewide Long Range Transportation Plan was instituted:

- To assure that the plan had a long-range perspective (it was initially called Transportation Choices 2020).
- To provide a methodology for thinking in a disciplined, systemic way about major areas of uncertainty.
- To create a compelling vision for New Jersey and its transportation system.
- To foster creative strategy development.
- To help in evaluating alternative policy actions that might be effective in moving toward that desired future given vast uncertainties.

In the course of our work for the New Jersey Department of Transportation, we identified several key elements that would affect that state's future. They included social elements (such as demographic trends), technology development (for example, smart cars on smart highways), economic growth, environmental conditions and trends, and political factors. These trends formed the basis for scenario planning about New Jersey's alternative futures.

We designed and led a process to create scenarios of alternative futures for New Jersey in the year 2020. This process began with submitting questionnaires to the project's core team and an intensive scenario development session in the spring of 1994. Two sessions on scenario development were conducted later that spring with diverse groups of leaders from business, government, and nonprofit organizations who contributed their expertise in making the scenarios more detailed, compelling, and plausible.

The result of this process were four alternative futures for New Jersey in 2020 that were developed by informed leaders of the state. Each of the four scenarios envisioned a different transportation system, and some of them served the varying needs of the state and its citizens better than others.

The four alternative futures are summarized here. (Exhibit 17.1 provides more detail about each future.)

Muddling Through.   The Status Quo Continues Future for New Jersey in 2020 projects recent trends of incremental improvements in some

Exhibit 17.1

New Jersey Transportation Choices 2020 Scenario Matrix

Element/ Scenario	Muddling Through the Status Quo Continues	Gateway to the World: A Dynamic, High-Tech Future	Bad News: The Worst Plausible Future	Pushing the Envelope: A Sustainable Future
Cultural values and lifestyle choices	Indifference to government; continuing fear of crime and violence; avoidance of racial & ethnic issues; poor sense of community; NIMBYism; love affair with cars and single-family homes continues; fear of change, old ways accommodated; low personal responsibility; expectations are low.	More personal responsibility emerges; demands for efficiency increase sharply, along with greater respect for differences and growing environmental and health concerns.	Hostile to government; fearful; "me first" attitude, polarizations by race and class; loss of community; decline of social, personal responsibility—becomes a quaint concept; many communities become walled to protect against "outsiders"; the "haves" are vulnerable and need 24-hour protection; automobile use is still highly valued, but takes a back seat to personal security.	Major changes occur related to revitalization of community life, personal responsibility, environmental consciousness, energy use, resources, land use; diversity celebrated; movement in inner cities for "community wealth creation"; "love affair with cars" shifts toward "love of convenient mobility"; more desire for urban amenities.
Economy	GNP grows slowly on average, which constricts public spending: jobs mismatch by skill and especially geography.	Modest GNP growth with peaks and valleys; some economic development strategies; better "matching" of education, training with job availability and type.	High unemployment; incomes down, especially white-collar workers; declining public revenues; New Jersey, Northeast corridor becomes "bottleneck" for U.S. growth; education and skills mismatch with available types of jobs; decline of New York City and Philly hurt state.	More peaks than valleys, averaging in to a moderate to high growth rate; rebirth of manufacturing in Northeast based on environmentally advanced technologies; profound restructuring of corporations.

Financing & Investment	With tight government budgets, transportation needs exceed resources; choices are made politically; pressures to build new systems rob funding from older systems; new systems cannot be sustained because funding then has to go to dealing with the deterioration of old systems.	Economic growth encourages private investment; confidence in government provides the will, support, and money for public investment; good management in both sectors restores confidence and optimism; investment in ports, airports, rail, and highways aims to make New Jersey the "Gateway to the World."	Poor economy discourages private investment; taxes low due to the perception of governmental ineptitude, which starves public sector of investment and operating capital; lower funding for transportation at all levels.	A good economy and clear goals allow consistent, long-term capital investment based on the state long-range plan; capital shifted from new capacity to maintenance for highways; greater funding for transit; federal tax shift from taxes on income, investment, savings to taxes on "undesirables"; creative public/private joint ventures.
Demographics	More economically disadvantaged, also more affluent; education falls short of needed skills for some; more elderly, affluent eventually move out of the state; more diverse households.	Expanding middle class; most of the elderly stay in state, but some movement within state toward congregate care facilities that provide some supports; brains drain into the state as young return after college and immigrants with skills find more opportunity.	More poor, smaller middle class; the affluent elderly leave the state while the others remain; talented, skilled young people do not return to the state after college and early work experience; immigration pattern shifts when less skilled people began to settle in the state.	Growing middle class; more educated citizenry; more urban living; more elderly, who choose to stay in state because of modal choices and favorable land-use arrangements; more diverse households; more trips done via walking, biking, transit.

(Continued)

Exhibit 17.1 (*Continued*)

Element/ Scenario	Muddling Through the Status Quo Continues	Gateway to the World: A Dynamic, High-Tech Future	Bad News: The Worst Plausible Future	Pushing the Envelope: A Sustainable Future
Environment & Health	Crisis response; get tough after crisis, then relax; minimum compliance with environmental regulations; air and water quality stabilizes, with improvement in some regions and worsening in others.	Air and water quality get better as many firms invest in technologies that reduce waste and pollution in the production processes; consumers prefer minimal packaging and recycled products; more land is preserved in natural state, and more is purchased for public use.	Hopeless, bordering on tragic. Low public investment to preserve natural resources, reduce pollution, and enforce environmental standards all have devastating impacts on the state ecology. Beaches are frequently closed; whole communities are shut down due to water and sewer system collapse; oxygen canisters are home delivered to the elderly because the air quality has become so hazardous.	Citizens expect and demand solutions that make sense in terms of both environment and development; protection of environment's "carrying capacity" becomes a top priority; focus is on prevention of problems; natural areas, farmlands, and open space are protected.
Role of Government	Government rises to meet crises in shortsighted ways; short-term responsive; local government same as today, but education more equalized; some regionalization forced by economic pressures and regulations (e.g., MPOs); multistate cooperation for special purposes, projects.	Oases of leadership; concentrated effort on key areas, making progress there; "experts" reign; government allowed selective risk taking; some progress in government coordination in transportation area; elected officials increasingly challenged by more informed electorate.	Fragmented; ineffective; poor leadership; parochial; short-sighted; unresponsive; continued home rule; widened gap between "haves" and "have-nots."	Public policy becomes more cohesive and innovative; sustained leadership; government becomes more entrepreneurial, customer-driven and market-oriented; private sector plays large role in implementation; regional planning.

Technology	Implementation of technology lags behind technological development; R&D strategy is fragmented, component-based; information technology available and used, but not maximized; cars and highways are better positioned than transit to take advantage of technological gains; IVHS development is focused on travel management, travel information, and toll/fare collection.	Technological progress is very rapid and its benefits are broadly distributed; universal access to telecom services and applications; advanced IVHS technology is deployed rapidly in all forms and improves utilization of existing capacity; congestion pricing and information systems change travel patterns and needs; efficient cars and zero-emission vehicles improve urban air quality.	Technological progress becomes uneven, partly due to the bifurcation of society and wealth; the affluent have surplus of new and better technologies, while the general public gets few benefits from these innovations. For example, telecommunication systems are very sophisticated, but access is limited; lack of steady or sufficient investment causes sporadically implemented IVHS pilot projects to flounder.	Rapid technological progress includes widespread use of "environmentally advanced" technologies; broadband networks reach homes as well as offices and change travel patterns (e.g., extensive telecommuting, teleshopping, telebanking); IVHS technology applied to transit supports seamless modal transfers, predictability of travel time, and easy access to travel information; "supercar" technology slashes urban air pollution.
Land Use/ Development Patterns	Urban areas struggle; suburbs sprawl; very limited centering; old suburbs decline a little; rateables chase continues to drive development.	Stabilized urban centers (both job availability and population); auto oriented, low-density development continues, but the proportion of mixed-use centers grows slowly; major preservation effort for older suburbs.	Urban decay; low-density suburban sprawl; some suburbs and old towns decline; slower overall development due to economic conditions.	Strong centering; urban revitalization; low exurban growth; sustainable development patterns; old suburbs enhanced, emulated; open space, farmland preserved.

(Continued)

Exhibit 17.1 (Continued)

Element/Scenario	Muddling Through the Status Quo Continues	Gateway to the World: A Dynamic, High-Tech Future	Bad News: The Worst Plausible Future	Pushing the Envelope: A Sustainable Future
Level of Mobility	Mobility improves slightly; high auto use with high congestion; stable transit; modest development of ports, airports, rail.	Improved mobility, high auto use; extensive roadway IVHS deployment limits congestion; improved highway maintenance; modest expansion of transit service; IVHS and port development improve goods movement.	Declining mobility; auto use high with excessive congestion; transit choices low; lost opportunities for improving goods movement because of a failure to develop ports, airports, and heavy rail.	Improved mobility, with expanded choices among modes; auto ownership high but use beginning to decline; major expansion of transit to serve emerging pattern of more clustered, mixed-use development; extensive port, airport, and heavy rail linkages foster movement of goods; walking, biking become realistic options for many.
Pricing	Attempts to implement new pricing schemes prove politically explosive; tinkering results.	Modest steps toward "true cost-ing", coordinated pricing strategy (e.g., "universal" transportation electronic card).	Higher transit fares, tolls; gas taxes up, but not enough to maintain systems (just enough to retire debt service).	True cost pricing becomes a guiding principle; user-side subsidies.
System Integration/Intermodalism	Modest, incremental advances occur toward more integrated transportation planning, fostered by better cooperation between different authorities, agencies, and entities.	Considerable system integration occurs, due to the paramount quest for efficiencies; intermodal connections are established because the public articulates its demands for transportation choices and agencies are willing and able to take a few risks to build linkages among modes.	Very little; agencies defend turf to the best of their ability; modes compete with each other for users and then use those numbers to lobby for scarce public dollars.	Substantial progress occurs in New Jersey and around the country toward an integrated, seamless, intermodal transportation network; transportation-related entities learn to optimize "at the system level."

areas while other problems get worse. Although some aspects of New Jersey's quality of life improved, this was not a terribly promising future. Nevertheless, the participants who built these scenarios considered most of these scenario elements to be most likely descriptions of actual outcomes if present trends were to continue. This also might be called "the official or conventional future" since it includes midrange estimates of most straight-line projections.

Gateway to the World.   In this Dynamic, High-Tech Future improved telecommunication and transportation systems enhance the state's economic development potential.

It also proposes that intermodal transportation system investments in New Jersey, especially those in Newark, Port Elizabeth, and highway I-95, can be a catalyst in boosting the state's status as a global transportation hub and gateway to the world. This scenario emphasizes the strategic importance of: coordinating long-term transportation planning, making capital investment for intermodal linkages, and applying technological innovations to improve transportation systems.

Bad News.   The Worst Plausible Future is dismal for New Jersey in 2020. Virtually every aspect of society suffers from the worsening problems described in this future. The economy suffers, society becomes much more polarized, citizens fear crime and become isolated from each other. The environment gets worse, congestion is horrible, the public funding systems for transportation and other public services are broke and therefore incapable of providing routine maintenance for the transportation system. The participants who developed these scenarios were alarmed by the realization that these terrible outcomes could well develop during the next 25 years. The plausibility of such horrible outcomes focused their thinking about core strategies that might be effective in averting this bad news future.

Pushing the Envelope.   A Sustainable Future describes a very promising outlook for New Jersey in 2020. It is one in which:

- The true costs of natural resources and public goods (such as transportation) are charged.

- Social interaction increases at the community level because employment is decentralized and state land use policy guides compact development.
- Advanced technology and growing affluence provide alternatives to travel by petroleum-burning automobiles. One of the themes of this scenario is the importance of recognizing that land use patterns and transportation systems are linked issues.

Participants in this scenario development process identified five key elements of the preferred future, based on a comparison of the two promising alternative futures: Gateway to the World and Pushing the Envelope:

- Development as a global hub.
- Shift to sustainable development.
- Centering (land use policy articulated in the State Development and redevelopment plan).
- Appropriate true cost pricing.
- Transit expansion.

THE VISION: SCENARIOS FOR THE HEART

The scenario development process helped both transportation planners and members of the general public to widen the range of future possibilities they were willing to consider and to reach a general consensus on major themes of the preferred future. These themes, in turn, were used to develop a vision statement that articulated these aspirations for the future in more detail. A draft statement, "Vision for New Jersey," was revised and improved several times, based on suggestions from participants in the scenario process (see Box 17.2).

The scenarios developed in the project are "futures for the head." They were designed to provide intelligence, stretch the imagination, and identify plausible threats and opportunities. In contrast, the Vision for New Jersey was a "future for the heart." It was designed to move and inspire people, and to align people's efforts around widely shared hopes and aspirations.

Once the Vision for New Jersey was finalized, it became the driver for the more detailed transportation planning that followed. A set of goals and objectives was derived directly from the language of the vision. For

Box 17.2
Vision for New Jersey

In 2020, New Jersey is setting a national example of forging new community and economic development patterns designed to strengthen our economy, protect and restore the environment, and provide a higher quality of life for all segments of the population. Everyone who can and wants to work has a job. Affordable housing is available for all, and we have a wide range of choices of housing types and neighborhoods. Our older cities and suburbs are thriving. A revitalized sense of community in most urban neighborhoods and smaller towns helps prevent crime and reduce personal isolation. The gap between the "haves" and the "have-nots" is narrowing. Discrimination based on race, nationality, gender, and age has declined sharply. The air we breathe and the water we drink no longer threatens our health. Our farms and rural areas have not been overrun by urban sprawl. Natural areas and open space remain to sustain and uplift us.

Within our neighborhoods, we can visit our families, friends, and neighbors, or shop or travel to work without driving automobiles. Our neighborhoods are safe. Attention has been given to the needs of walkers, bicyclists, and the users of other local transport systems. Many of us have access to convenient, high-quality public transit whenever we travel beyond our neighborhoods. Our clean, efficient vehicles have nearly eliminated urban smog. Traffic delays are predictable and avoidable. Every part of our state's transportation system functions reliably because past political commitment to adequate funding has kept the system in a state of good repair and encouraged new investment in innovative technologies.

This is a dramatic change from where many people a generation ago feared our state was heading: toward loss of jobs, loss of community, unlivable cities, isolated individuals, unsustainable environmental impacts, unchecked urban sprawl, increased highway congestion, and little choice in travel modality except driving a petroleum-burning automobile along a crumbling, overcrowded, unsafe highway system.

Many different efforts came together to reverse those negative trends, but three stand out as especially important. First, we aggressively attracted high-technology firms, whose leaders valued the state's commitment to quality education and environmental protection. As a result, the manufacturing base was revitalized by firms that pioneered clean, energy- and resource-efficient technologies. Second, we made significant improvements in our education

(continued)

Box 17.2 (Continued)

system to ensure that all our young people have the skills necessary to fill meaningful jobs in the today's global economy. And third, we fostered "communities of place," the more compact, "centered" community forms advocated in the State Development and Redevelopment Plan of 1992.

Transportation choices have been critical to our state's success. By catching up with the backlog of needed infrastructure repairs, putting a regular cycle of maintenance in place, improving the management of our transportation systems, and adopting innovative measures to reduce transportation demand, we made New Jersey more attractive for business and for all transportation users. Strategic investments to exploit the strengths of our airport and port facilities and to move New Jersey to the forefront in intermodal freight transportation have spurred economic growth. Investments in mass transit, in concert with other public investment decisions, have been used to guide development centered around transit stations and transport hubs.

New Jersey citizens have become surprisingly well informed about transportation decisions and how they affect our way of life. Customers of the transportation system have good, reliable information about options, and access to more realistic choices and quality services. The public is informed about transportation needs, costs, and benefits; agencies and providers work closely to define and meet the needs of affected constituencies. The improved communication between providers and consumers generates the political will necessary to provide stable funding and allow consistent, long-term capital investments to advance agreed-upon goals. Transportation agencies and providers work closely with citizens to define and meet customer needs. Changes in the organizational culture of transportation agencies, and state governments in general, promote innovations in service delivery that are market-driven, competitive, customer-guided, and responsive.

Utopian? No. A stretch? Yes. Achievable? Certainly! If we begin to focus on the choices we need to make now about how we want to live, work, and travel, then we can make a better future possible for the coming generation of New Jerseyans—our children and grandchildren. This requires planning— deciding in advance, to the extent possible—the kind of state we want to live in. This vision of a better New Jersey can be realized if we are willing to take the responsibility to work together to create our preferred future. In making these tough choices, we should keep in mind the admonition of world-renowned pediatrician and author Jonas Salk, "Our greatest responsibility is to be good ancestors."

example, one goal was "Use Transportation to Shape Efficient Development Patterns," and the objectives under this goal were:

- Establish and strengthen "communities of place" (more compact, 'centered', mixed-use forms of development).
- Concentrate development in existing and emerging centers, in concert with other public investment decisions.
- Maintain the rural character of portions of the region.
- Foster transit-supporting development near transit stations and stops.

The goals and objectives derived from the scenario/vision process were checked against another set of goals and objectives drawn from a public participation process using focus groups. A comparison of the two sets found substantial correlation.

In a next step, a wide range of specific actions recommended by transportation agencies and citizen groups were organized into "Strategy Packages" built around nine themes:

1. Bringing Infrastructure to a State of Good Repair.
2. Highway System Management.
3. Transit System Management.
4. Highway Capacity Expansion.
5. Transit Capacity Expansion.
6. Freight System Improvements.
7. Land Use and Community Design.
8. Transportation Demand Management.
9. Market-Based Demand Management Policies.

Participatory exercises were used to generate rough quantitative ratings for each of these Strategy Packages, assessments of how important each Strategy Package is for achieving each of the goals derived from the vision. In another exercise, participants used the four Transportation Choices 2020 scenarios to evaluate the 'robustness' of the Strategy Packages—that is, they assessed whether the Strategy Package made sense across a wide variety of future conditions, or only in a particular situation.

At this point, the scenario planning process reached full circle. At the start, scenarios were used as a tool to imaginatively explore future possibilities and reach general consensus on a vision of the preferred future. Goals and objectives were derived from the vision. Finally, packages of strategies were ranked in terms of their importance for achieving the goals as well as for their workability across the different scenarios.

CONCLUSION

Our mission was to help New Jersey's leadership consider a wide range of strategic transportation choices in the context of high uncertainty about the future. The scenario/vision process described here led to new priorities and innovative outcomes, especially in the area of land use and community design. The scenarios and vision developed for New Jersey have had a significant impact on the strategic planning process of the American Public Transit Association and on the Vision Statement produced by the Task Force on Sustainable Communities of the President's Council on Sustainable Development.

CHAPTER 18

IMAGINING SOUTH AFRICA'S FUTURE: HOW SCENARIOS HELPED DISCOVER COMMON GROUND

ADAM KAHANE

It was uncertain in 1990 when the Mont Fleur scenarios were developed, if there could be a peaceful political transformation in South Africa—whether white minority rule could be replaced by an alliance joined by people of all colors. In fact this occurred, and the Mont Fleur scenarios contributed significantly to the acceptance of a new democratic society for all South Africans lead by President Nelson Mandela. Conflict resurfaced in 1996, after the former Prime Minister, F. W. de Klerk, who shared the Nobel Peace Prize for successful political transition with Mandela, took his Nationalist Party out of the coalition government. Currently, it remains an open question whether de Klerk's white minority party can transform itself into an inclusive and effective opposition.

Though these scenarios served well the needs of the day, new issues and other actors have taken center stage, and new uncertainties lurk on the horizon. For example: In 1997, there are clear fault lines within the governing alliance and fractures may soon appear; the dynamics of what the government calls black economic empowerment and affirmative action are not well understood.

Optimists predict that South Africa might soon be leading the rest of Africa in a resurgence of prosperity. In contrast, pessimists warn that economic forecasts, as measured in traditional terms, are not all that promising.

The Mont Fleur scenario exercise was an innovative public conversation about the future that took place in South Africa from September 1991 though December 1992. Its purpose was to stimulate debate on how to shape the country's next 10 years.[1] The project brought together a diverse group of 22 prominent South Africans from across the political spectrum—politicians, activists, academics, and businesspeople—to develop and share a set of stories about what might happen in the country from 1992 to 2002.[2]

The historical context of the project is important to understanding its impact. It took place during a period in the country's history shortly after Nelson Mandela was released from prison and the African National Congress, the Pan Africanist Congress, the South African Communist Party, and other organizations were legalized, and April 1994, when the first all-race elections were held. During this pivotal time, South Africans set up a number of "forums"—temporary discussion groups that gathered together the broadest possible range of stakeholders (political parties, civic organizations, professional bodies, government departments, trade unions, and business groups, for example) to agree to a new way forward in a particular area of concern. There were forums to discuss education, housing, economic policy, constitutional matters, and many other areas. They ranged from informal, off-the-record workshops to formal, public negotiations. The Mont Fleur project was one that convened unofficially and used a unique methodology: scenario thinking.[3]

This scenario team met for three, 3-day workshops at the Mont Fleur Conference Centre outside of Cape Town. After considering many possible stories, they agreed on four simple scenarios that they believed were plausible and relevant:

- *Ostrich.* A negotiated settlement to the crisis in South Africa is not achieved, and the country's government continues to be non-representative.
- *Lame Duck.* A settlement is achieved but the transition to a new dispensation and approach is slow and indecisive.
- *Icarus.* The transition is rapid but the new government pursues an unsustainable, populist economic policy.
- *Flight of the Flamingoes.* The government's policies are sustainable and the country takes a path of inclusive growth and democracy.

Each of these stories was developed into a brief, logical narrative. A 14-page report was distributed as an insert in one of the important weekly newspapers, and a 30-minute video was produced that combined cartoons with presentations by team members. The team then presented and discussed the scenarios with 100 or so groups, including political parties, companies, academics, trade unions, and civic organizations. At the end of 1992, the work was completed, the project ended, and the team was dissolved.

DEFINING THE PROJECT

Scenario use in the polarized, political, public setting of a South Africa in transition was new. However, the Mont Fleur team's four scenario stories were not in themselves particularly novel. The important innovation of the project was who was delivering the messages—an unusually heterogeneous group of important leaders—and how this group worked together to arrive at these messages.

Mont Fleur cannot be credited with resolving the crisis in South Africa. But it's fair to say that the project, along with other, nonscenario forum processes, contributed to the building of a common vocabulary, language, and understanding. This common understanding, together with other developments, promoted a climate for settling the crisis. The shared language of Mont Fleur, for example, quickly spread beyond the negotiating elite. I heard an exhortation in favor of the Flamingoes scenario in a Sunday church sermon and a concern about the Lame Duck scenario in a rural radio phone in program.

The participants did not agree to a concrete solution to the county's problems. They reached agreement on some aspects of how South Africa worked, on the complex nature of the crisis, and on some of the possible ways things could turn out. More specifically, they agreed that, given the circumstances then prevailing, certain strongly advocated solutions could not work, including armed revolution, continued minority rule (Ostrich), tightly circumscribed majority rule (Lame Duck), and socialism (Icarus). In this way, the broad outline of a credible successful outcome emerged (Flamingoes).

Mont Fleur was not a formal, mandated negotiation. It was an informal, open conversation and dialogue. At the first workshop, several of the participants told me that they did not expect to be able to agree on anything. Over the course of the workshops, they talked until they found some shared understanding and agreement. Some of this shared communication was relevant to the formal negotiations that were being conducted during this period.

Mont Fleur did not deal with the differences among the participants. Traditional negotiation focuses on identifying the positions and interests of the parties, and then finding a way to narrow or reconcile these differences.[4] In contrast, the Mont Fleur process only discussed the domain that all of the participants had in common: the future of South Africa. The team then summarized their shared understanding in the scenario stories. Management author Marvin Weisbord calls this process "finding and enlarging the common ground."[5]

RESULTS FROM THE PROJECT

The Mont Fleur project produced several different sorts of results: substantive messages, informal networks and understandings, and changed ways of thinking.

Substantive Messages.   The articulated public outputs of the project—as conveyed in the report, video, and workshop presentations—were the scenario stories, each of which had a message that was important during this period of the search for a settlement.

The message of the Ostrich scenario was that a nonnegotiated resolution of the crisis—with the result that the country's government continues to be unrepresentative of the voters—would not be sustainable. This was an important realization, especially for elements of the National Party (NP) government and the business community, who believed that some sort of deal with their allies, instead of a negotiation with their opponents, might be sufficient. After hearing about the team's work, NP leader F. W. de Klerk was quoted as saying, "I am not an Ostrich."

Lame Duck's message was that a weak coalition government would not be able to deliver on its promises and would not last long. This message moved the national debate a step forward because the nature, composition, and rules governing the coalition Government of National Unity (GNU) was a central issue in the negotiations leading up to the elections. The right-wing NP was pushing for the centrist GNU to operate subject to various vetoes and other restrictions; and on the left, the African National Congress (ANC) wanted an unfettered "winner takes all" arrangement. Lame Duck explored the boundary in a government of national unity between compromise and incapacitation.

Icarus warned of the danger of a new government heedlessly implementing populist economic policies. This message, coming from a team that included several of the left's most influential economists, was very challenging to the parties of the left, which had been assuming that they would be able to use government money to eradicate poverty quickly. Populist economic policies were one of the business community's biggest worries, and having the Mont Fleur team—and some of the left's key economic thinkers—articulate the Icarus scenario was reassuring. The fiscal conservatism of the Government of National Unity coalition party has been one of the important surprises of the postelection period.

The simple message of Flight of the Flamingoes was that the scenario team believed that a positive outcome was possible. In a country in the midst of turbulence and uncertainty, telling a credible hopeful story had a strong impact. One participant said recently that the main result of the project was that, "We mapped out in very broad terms the outline of a successful outcome, which is now being filled in. We captured the way forward of those committed to finding a way forward."

Informal Networks and Understandings.   The second series of achievements of the Mont Fleur exercise were the informal networks, understandings, and agreements that were reached among the participants—an influential group from across the political spectrum. Such networks and understandings were being achieved in other forums across the country, and taken as a whole, helped set the stage for the subsequent critical, formal agreements.

Changed Ways of Thinking.   Participants noted changes in the language and thinking of the team members as a result of the time spent working together. These language and thinking innovations were transmitted by the Mont Fleur project participants to the people in their political base with whom they discussed the scenarios. This effect is both the most difficult to measure and the most fundamental result of this sort of project. The Mont Fleur team gave vivid, simple names to important concepts that previously did not have well-known names, and therefore could neither be discussed nor addressed. At least one important political party seriously reconsidered its approach to the constitutional negotiations in the light of the scenarios.

Why the Project Produced These Results

How can such a simple, storytelling project produce such significant results? This scenario process has five key characteristics that explain its potential influence:

Logical and Fact-Based.   There is no place in the core of a scenario conversation for positions or values. (Scenario work can be extended to include normative discussions about which future we like or want, but the essence of the scenario development conversation deals with what might happen, not what should happen.) Instead, the discussion is about facts and logic: Can you convince your fellow team members that the story you are telling is plausible? In the first Mont Fleur workshop, a story about the Chinese Red Army helping to liberate South Africa was discarded because it was not credible, not because someone didn't like it or because someone else didn't want it to be told.

Open and Informal.   The scenario-building process can take creative risks because it is "only" about telling stories; it does not require participants to make commitments. This allows people to discuss almost anything, even taboo subjects. Early in the Mont Fleur process, one of the African National Congress (ANC) members proposed a story, which was debated and eventually dropped, called "The Chilean Option: Growth through Repression" (a play on words on the ANC slogan, "Growth through Redistribution"). This was an important discussion, which would not have had a place in a usual left-wing party political debate.

Inclusive.   A story about a country's future has to be able to encompass social, political, economic, cultural, and ecological issues. Furthermore, telling several plausible stories specifically encourages a variety of perspectives to be raised. As a result, participants become aware that since the future is fundamentally unpredictable, there is no one truth. This accords respect to the points of view of all of the participants, and it allows everyone to see more of the world. As American poet Betty Sue Flowers puts it, "In a scenario team, you develop two or three different pairs of glasses to see the world through; you can put them on and off, and by doing that, it gets easier for you to see a fourth and fifth way."

Choice-Eliciting.   One of the premises of scenario thinking is that the future is not predetermined and cannot be predicted. However, the choices we make can influence what happens. In a situation where people feel swept along by overwhelming, seemingly inevitable currents, the idea that choices help determine the future is an empowering world view. During its transition, South Africa was haunted by apocalyptic visions; the scenario stories helped people think through their options.

Constructive.   A scenario conversation turns the attention of a group away from the past and present—where the debate often is stuck—toward the future. It shifts the dialogue away from looking for single solutions to exploring different possibilities (and perhaps exploring how these possibilities can be influenced). It beckons the debate away from the separate interests of the parties (as in traditional negotiations) and toward their common ground and common future.

Former Royal Dutch/Shell Oil Company executive Pierre Wack, one of the first managers to use scenarios in a corporate setting, said that the scenario process involves "the gentle art of reperceiving."[6] These five characteristics of the process—logical, open and informal, inclusive, choice-eliciting, constructive—explain why a scenario project can create shifts in language, thinking, and action.

Conditions Necessary for Success

Timing.   This is the initial critical success factor. Are public leaders ready to talk together about the future? If they are, then two other ingredients become critical: how the process is led and the composition of the team.

Credible Leadership.   The people who convene and lead the project must be broadly respected. They must be seen to be advocates for the process and not for any particular predetermined position or message.[7]

Informal, Imaginative, and Thought-Provoking.   The use of scenarios in these applications must be separate from formal negotiations. The power of scenario work is partly derived from its being an exercise in both reflection and imagination—innovative thinking that is not directly linked to action. Although it is possible to graduate from scenarios (what might happen) to visioning (what we want to happen) to strategizing and action planning (what we will do), these three processes must be carefully insulated from one another.

Inclusive.   The value of this type of project is that it builds the common ground among different perspectives and parties. It is therefore important to make every effort to be inclusive. The Mont Fleur project, for example, would have been even more effective if it had included the

Inkatha Freedom Party, which has been an important dissenter in South African politics.

Team members should be:

- *Respected, influential leaders in their own communities or constituencies.* They do not necessarily have to hold official positions.
- *Open-minded (not political dogmatists) and able to listen to and work with others.* Stakeholders must be able to see their point of view represented by someone on the team. This does not mean, however, that the team members have to be official representatives of groups or positions.

CONCLUSION

The Mont Fleur exercise demonstrated a new way for a society in conflict to approach the future. The informal, indirect scenario approach is different from and complementary to negotiation. Scenarios are a promising tool for public consensus building.

PART IV

MANAGING THE ORGANIZATIONAL CONTEXT FOR SCENARIO LEARNING

CHAPTER 19

ARTICULATING THE BUSINESS IDEA: THE KEY TO RELEVANT SCENARIOS

KEES VAN DER HEIJDEN

Scenarios are like miniature hothouse environments where organizations can experiment with a number of unique growing conditions. However, such scenario experiments will fail to generate significant benefits for your organization if they do not provide a realistic challenge for its core business idea—how your firm provides value to customers in a way that is unique from your rivals. In fact, organizations that have not articulated their business idea will find it difficult to create scenarios that are truly relevant to their future. This chapter suggests one approach to identifying the business idea and testing it in scenarios.

           A set of scenarios provides any organization with an opportunity to test how and why both its current and potential strategies might win across a range of plausible future worlds. As part of this "stress-testing" of strategy, many organizations have discovered that their strategy, either current or proposed, was not as "all weather" as they had assumed. The great benefit of scenarios therefore is that they can be used to discover problems and difficulties with a strategy well before they become painfully evident in the cut and thrust of marketplace competition and to develop ideas for a new strategy.

    But, before an organization can test its strategy against a set of scenarios, it must know what its strategy is. Although every organization has an implicit or emergent strategy, its essential elements often aren't familiar to rank-and-file management. It is thus not surprising to learn that many organizations find it difficult to derive strategy-related benefits from their scenario work. Clearly, if an organization does not know the success formula underlying its own strategy, it becomes well nigh impossible to use scenarios to critique the "content" of the strategy, to challenge its underlying assumptions, or suggest ways in which it might be changed to win against current and potential rivals.

The purpose of this chapter is to briefly outline an analysis and organizational process to determine the basis and essential underpinnings of an organization's strategy, which we shall refer to as its *business idea*. The goal is to show how the business idea can be studied, tested, and improved through the use of scenarios.

THE BUSINESS IDEA OF AN ORGANIZATION

The first task is therefore to understand and articulate the organization's success formula, measured in terms of its twin purposes of survival and growth. Such a business idea drives every successful organization. This idea is specific to each organization, and no two organizations can have exactly the same one. Strategy development can be viewed as assessing this business idea against the outlook for the environment. The scenario planner, aiming to accelerate organizational learning, first needs to articulate the business idea before it can be studied, discussed, modified, and improved (see Exhibit 19.1).

Exhibit 19.1
The Generic Business Idea

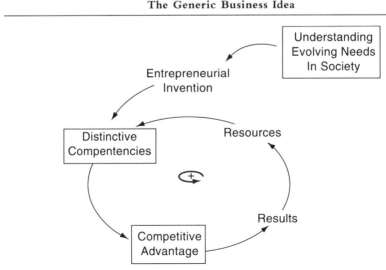

The articulated business idea must be a rational explanation of why the organization has been successful in the past, and how it will be successful in the future. It defines how the business can apply its system of competencies to provide goods and services that the customer values. How much the customer values the services or products and what alternative choices the customer has determines how much economic values the business idea generates.

Let us begin by identifying the four elements that need to be specified in order to develop a complete business idea. These will then be illustrated using a detailed case example.

1. The customer value created.
2. The nature of the competitive advantage exploited.
3. The distinctive competencies which, in their mutually reenforcing interaction, create this competitive advantage, allowing the organization to appropriate some of the value created.

These three elements must then be configured into the fourth element:

4. A positive feedback loop, in which resources generate growth.

KINDER-CARE: AN EXAMPLE OF A BUSINESS IDEA

Kinder-Care, the largest private provider of day care in the United States was started in the 1960s by Perry Mendel who perceived a need for innovative child care. He reasoned that many mothers and fathers experience a feeling of guilt when they provide their preschool children with simple custodial child care. His entrepreneurial idea was to create centers where children would not only be cared for but would also be surrounded by a learning environment similar to preschools, thus creating a positive image in the minds of the parents (see Exhibit 19.2).

The Kinder-Care system can be understood by reference to the four elements making up its business idea:

1. *The customer value created.* The creation of customer value starts with recognition of parents' needs for beneficial custodial care for their young children. By providing an enriching learning environment, Kinder-Care enables parents to feel more comfortable

Exhibit 19.2
The Kinder-Care Business Idea

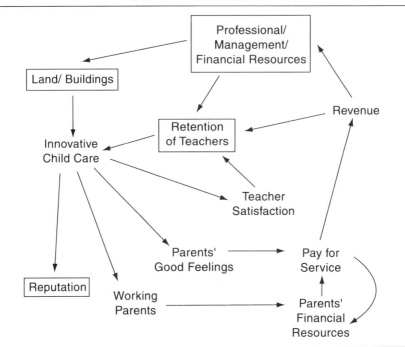

about leaving their children in a day-care program. The entrepreneurial invention, an innovative child-care center that provides a learning environment for preschoolers, creates a new type of value for customers.

2. *The nature of the competitive advantage exploited.* The purpose of the Kinder-Care operation is to offer a new enhanced product or solution to parents of young children. It creates value for customers through its differentiated offering compared to rivals. Kinder-Care does not aim to be a low-price leader.

3. *The distinctive competencies exploited.* Kinder-Care has developed a number of competencies that mutually reinforce each other. Together, they allow the realization of the entrepreneurial idea. They include:
   - Knowledge of required personnel characteristics and attributes.
   - Knowledge of facilities.
   - Management systems and expertise.

- Access to specialized facilities.
- Reputation, resulting in parents' trust.

These competencies reinforce each other as shown in Exhibit 19.2. Note that having hired the appropriate personnel (a scarce resource) does not by itself create a distinctive competency for the firm. Any value resulting from that resource alone would eventually be appropriated by the individuals with the requisite characteristics.

4. *The positive feedback loop, driving growth.* The system of feedback loops as shown in Exhibit 19.2 contains a number of growth drivers. For example, more innovative child care leads to more teacher satisfaction, which leads to more retention of motivated teachers, which leads to more innovative child care. Or, innovative child care allows a parent to feel better about going to frequent or full-time work, increasing willingness and ability to pay for the use of more innovative child care. We see that the main strategic loop is a positive feedback loop. This explains the successful growth of Kinder-Care. Innovative child care induces customers to pay for a service that creates increased management and financial capability. This in turn causes an increase in the amount and quality of innovative child care offered.

It does not seem very difficult to imitate the individual distinctive competencies that together provide the basis of Kinder-Care's business idea. One must ask then why Kinder-Care has been so successful. The answer in large measure resides in the way the company has continually developed its business idea and the relatively slow response of its competitors. By growing fast, well ahead of the ability of the competition to catch up, the company has exploited scale effects to the maximum. It has continually developed and strengthened both its management system and the image and reputation associated with the name Kinder-Care. As it successfully did so, it created barriers to entry for newcomers. The company now needs to consider whether these entry barriers are high enough for sustainable competitive advantage.

EVALUATING THE BUSINESS IDEA: THE LIMITS TO GROWTH TESTS

What business growth can a business idea generate? How can it be sustained? What will limit growth? Can these limiting factors be managed?

One useful framework in which to consider the limits to growth in a business idea is Michael Porter's Five-Forces competitive model:[1]

- Demand limits.
- Supply limits.
- Competition limits.
- Limits imposed by the possibility of new entrants.
- Limits imposed by possible alternatives and substitutes.

Each of these limits can be applied to Kinder-Care or any other business idea. In the Kinder-Care example, growth of the business—that is, parents sending their children to a Kinder-Care type of facility—will ultimately lead to a reduction of demand. The potential market will eventually be saturated—there is not an unending supply of children with parents who want day care. Moreover, parents' ability and willingness to pay will limit the market long before the point of saturation is reached. Kinder-Care is thus an example of a demand-limited business idea.

Some examples of the other four growth limitations include:

- *Supply limits.* The business idea of a mining company may be largely dependent on "legal protection" through a concession agreement. The mine owners are granted permission to do a particular type of mining in a specific place. The company may not be able to extend its ability to do this particular type mining beyond its current location. In this case, the exploitation of the business idea is limited on the supply side, restricted by the reserves or deposits available to it.
- *Competition limits.* A rapidly growing company must expect retaliation from its competitors if its successful exploitation of its business idea threatens them.
- *All distinctive competencies depreciate over time.* Most business ideas can be emulated. Any firm exploiting a successful business idea will reach a point where the market created looks attractive to new entrants. At this point, new competitors are prepared to incur the costs of imitation and to enter the market as alternative suppliers.

- *Substitutes.* The emergence of competitors offering substitute products has undercut the business idea of many successful companies. Just consider what the personal computer did to the typewriter industry.

    Such a new entrant generates a negative feedback loop in the business idea. At first it diminishes the business idea's ability to generate economic value for the enterprise. Eventually, if the company can't defend its markets, it loses the capacity to create surplus value. At that point, growth stops.

SCENARIOS AND THE BUSINESS IDEA

A business idea may be a glorious success in one set of competitive conditions but a conspicuous failure in another. Any business idea therefore must be tested for its capacity to win in alternative futures. Doing so establishes a business idea's "degree of fit." Testing a business idea in this manner can be compared to a wind tunnel where an airplane model is subjected to tests to assess its strengths and weaknesses. The purpose is not just to accept or reject individual designs, but to engage in an iterative process of adjustment and improvement, until a model has been developed that will be successful in a wide range of environments. The wind tunnel metaphor clarifies one of the fundamental rules of scenario planning: Once we have decided on the set of scenarios of the future that are considered relevant to our situation, each scenario is treated as equally likely. In wind tunnel terminology, if the wings fall off under one of the specified test conditions, the model has to be redesigned, independent of any assessment of the likelihood of these conditions occurring.

In the process of testing a business idea in a set of scenarios, strategists often develop a value judgment about the scenarios in the set. It is based largely on the degree of change that a scenario requires in the business idea. If little change is needed, the scenario is considered a "good future," one in which growth is possible by exploiting the competencies associated with the business idea. If the existing success formula does not fare well, the particular scenario is seen as less friendly. The narrower the business definition the more likely that futures are seen as unattractive. Organizations that tend to define themselves too narrowly, for example in terms of a specific product, often incur this difficulty.

Underlying such value judgments of certain futures as "attractive" and "unattractive" is a resistance to change. If change were not typically seen as negative, but rather as the source of new business opportunity, then perceptions of good or bad futures would not arise. In business futures, success is relative, and every viable idea is eventually copied by competitors. It is a race, in which every participant who slows down will be overtaken. The winners are those who quickly develop new business concepts—new business ideas—and exploit them efficiently before the competition arrives on the scene. Companies that see themselves in the business of change will not find any scenarios good or bad, but will distinguish them by the different challenges they offer.

Considering Strategic Fit

The analytical task is to "walk" the business idea through a set of scenarios one by one, to study how it would "play out" if each future were to materialize. At the heart of the analysis are the following two questions:

- Will customers value the offerings generated by the business idea's set of competencies?
- Will the organization be able to appropriate enough of the value generated for its own development? Will its competency system be capable of being defended against competitive emulation?

One outcome of this deliberation may be the judgment that the business idea stands firm as the basis for future business, allowing the discussion to move on to the question of how it can be exploited to best advantage.

Alternatively, a business idea, even one that has proved successful in the past, may not stand up to these questions. The management team may decide that it needs to be developed to create a better fit with the anticipated future business environments.

BUILDING FOR THE FUTURE

The business idea generally needs to evolve with changes in the business environment. Management needs to develop a view on what new distinctive competencies will be called for in the future, and they need to work toward getting these in place. This is best achieved by developing a coherent view of a future business idea that will be robust against the various futures the scenarios indicate (this is sometimes called a *strategic vision*). The challenge is to decide how to develop the business idea for the future.

A unique business idea, one that generates unique customer value, cannot be bought; it needs to be invented and built. In principle, there are two ways in which a business idea can be advanced and developed:

- By entrepreneurial invention.
- By building on the existing distinctive competencies to create new ones.

Both of these imply discovering new customer value potential and/or a new and more efficient way of harvesting existing customer value. The business idea for the future must:

- Respond to future customer values.
- Be a new unique combination of competencies, which can be exploited in a positive feedback loop.
- Be created on the basis of the current business idea, leveraging existing distinctive competencies.

Building for the future means leveraging competencies that are present today. The ability to invent a new combination within these constraints constitutes the entrepreneurial task facing any management team interested in creating long-term profit potential for the company.

CONSIDERING THE BUSINESS IDEA IN THE MANAGEMENT TEAM

Sometimes companies continue exploiting a successful business idea based on a strong set of distinctive competencies built up in the past. The unique business idea is not always well articulated. Although initially the underlying entrepreneurial idea was clearly understood, it often happens in successful organizations that attention moves to the product and the efficiency of its production system. Companies that have been in business for awhile often lose sight of the complex reasons that customers buy their particular products or services. While things are going well, many managers get on with the day-to-day business, relying on the aging business idea to protect them from competitive onslaught. As time goes on, people in the business often come to take customer value for granted, and managers in the company over time may gradually develop divergent interpretations of the business idea. This is dangerous because distinctive competencies depreciate over time.

If the business idea is not clearly and jointly understood—considering the long lead times required to build most distinctive competencies—the company may run into serious difficulties trying to turn things around once profitability has started to decline. There may not be time or resources to adjust the business idea to the current market. To avoid this situation arising, the management team needs to jointly articulate and understand the basis of a company's success. Divergent notions of the business idea in the management team need to be confronted in open debate. The business idea process introduces a thinking framework and language that allows rational consideration of:

- The current business idea.
- The strengths/weaknesses of the current distinctive competencies in their systemic interaction.
- The outlook for the strength of the distinctive competencies against a set of scenarios relating to the everchanging values in society.

Once a business idea has been articulated, strategic priorities need to be determined to maintain its health. Selection of strategic options for the future should be guided by the options' relevance to maintaining and enhancing the business idea.

Workshop: Surfacing a Business Idea in a Management Team

Effective managers carry the elements of a business idea in their head. The process of articulating their collective knowledge for subsequent discussion, adjustment, and agreement in a management team is an iterative one. First, a prototype representation is quickly developed. The managers then react to this model, in the process expressing their understanding of what drives success. Through a number of iterations, the prototype representation is gradually brought into line with the views of the managers. By employing this process, the managers eventually reach a shared view of the business.

The process may need to be facilitated. The facilitator's role is to remind the management team of the concepts involved, to introduce and lead the process, to take the team through the various steps, and to record the views expressed. Choice of the facilitator is important, and should be limited to team members or well-trusted, experienced outsiders.

The process usually takes a series of three management workshops; but if necessary, it can be completed in one full-day session.

Elements of the Business Idea

A cause-and-effect influence diagram is the best way to show the systemic features of the business idea to bring out the positive feedback loop driving growth. If the company is dominated by one or a few major business sectors, customer value, competitive advantage, and distinctive competencies may be easier to define at the business unit level.

It may be useful for the top management team to prepare the ground for their corporate business idea review by arranging one or more sessions with the business sector managers, in order to develop joint understanding of the basics of these businesses in the team. A possible way of approaching this is by means of one or more strategic evaluation sessions, in which top management discusses the strategic aspects of the business in a "for information only" exchange with the business manager.

Initial Data Requirement

The discussion of the business idea in the management team requires a shared database, which ideally should be generated through an interview/feedback round, to be undertaken by the facilitator. Alternatively, the facilitator develops with the client a strengths, weaknesses, opportunities, threats (SWOT) analysis on flip charts. This is done preferably in a separate team session; but if necessary, the management team may start the business idea workshop with a one-hour SWOT analysis.

The Process

Step 1: Deciding on the Company's Competitive Advantage. The SWOT analysis, developed from individual interviews or as a team exercise, is displayed on the walls of the meeting room. The process of drawing up the first prototype diagram starts with addressing the question of competitive advantage. The facilitator should have developed some initial understanding of the key elements that may end up in the business idea diagram, and prepared these as a checklist, to be used during the meeting if required. To get the process going, the facilitator poses the following question: What is the basis of the company's competitive advantage?

A useful way to think about this: How would you explain to potential customers why they should prefer this organization as supplier/business partner over any other competitor? It raises the question, Who are the customers, and what are their cares and worries? The facilitator may introduce this issue by suggesting to the team that they formulate a sales pitch that clearly differentiates the offering in terms that motivate the customer to buy from this organization rather than another one.

The follow-up question focuses on competencies: What does this organization have to do well in order to deliver on this promise? It is surprising how much time many teams need to answer these seemingly obvious questions. The reason is that managers take the basic strengths of the organization for granted, and do not think a lot about the underlying driving forces while they are absorbed with their day-to-day tasks. The purpose of the competitive advantage question is to come to an understanding of the way the organization is or will be successful. Success can be based on doing better things than others or on doing the same things but at a lower cost. The final answer to the competitive advantage question should be one, or a combination, of the following two:

- Product/service differentiation from competitors.
- Cost leadership over competitors.

A company produces a differentiated product if the nature of the market allows a premium on product differentiation, and if its system of distinctive competencies allows it to put a product/service on the market with enough unique features, in design, quality, support, and availability to make the customers want to pay a premium price. A company is a cost leader if it has a system of distinctive competencies that allows it to make a commodity-type product/service available at a cost consistently at the lower end of the industry cost curve.

Step 2: Addressing the Devil's Advocate Question.   Next, the facilitator poses the devil's advocate question: What are the unique factors that allow this company to exploit this competitive advantage, and why are others unable to emulate it? The purpose of discussing this question is to force the managers to rethink their mental model to search for evidence of the underlying system, not stopping at superficial symptoms at the event level. The question to be asked at this point is not, What we are good at? but instead, What do we have that nobody else has, or can easily copy? A company can be a differentiator in the market only if it has competencies that nobody else has or can quickly imitate. Initial ideas on elements of uniqueness are recorded on a flip chart as well, as preparation for the following stages of the process.

Step 3: Developing Cause and Effect.   The facilitator now starts the development of the first prototype business idea diagram. As this is an iterative approach, the most flexible recording medium available should be used. The facilitator begins the development of the influence diagram by recording the agreed competitive advantage. He or she then draws an arrow to an element called "profitability," and from there another arrow points to an element called "investment." An arrow from A to B means: A is a cause of B.

The team has started to discuss the sources of the agreed competitive advantage by addressing the devil's advocate question. The facilitator next invites the group to specify the characteristics of the company that generate the competitive advantage. These are recorded, and arrows are drawn from the sources to the competitive advantage recorded.

The facilitator next asks, "What causes these sources of competitive advantage to exist, and how are they sustained." The "what are the causes of the causes" question is repeated until a connection can be made with the item "investment," which is already on the board. Elements may be sustained by investments, either in capital expenditure or operating expenditure. For example, an R&D capability may be maintained by expenditure; personnel loyalty may require generous rewards; or customer loyalty may be bought by a "low everyday price" policy. In such cases, the facilitator will complete the diagram by drawing an arrow from the "investment" box already entered to the element under consideration. All expenditure made to buy a long-term hard or soft asset is considered an investment.

Step 4: Completion of the Diagram.   At this point the diagram will contain a number of loose ends, elements for which no sources are shown. This may be due to a number of reasons, two of which are:

• The element may be due to investments, sunk or otherwise, made in the past, the fruits of which are enjoyed by the current organization. In relation to these elements, no further entries on the diagram are required, as the explanation resides in the past only.

- In some cases, the organizational success may be related to the leadership by an individual. If the organization is strongly identified with this individual, such as in the case of an owner/manager, then no further explanatory entries are required.

In all other cases, questioning should continue until all elements in the diagram are explained and connected by arrows.

Step 5: Identifying the Distinctive Competencies.   When loose ends have been tied up, the facilitator needs to complete one more task in this team session. This is to identify the distinctive competencies in the diagram. Referring to the devil's advocate question again the facilitator asks the managers to identify the elements in the diagram that are:

- Unique to the company, and by which it distinguishes itself from its competitors.
- Impossible or difficult to emulate by existing or new competitors.

Five categories of distinctive competencies can be distinguished, and the facilitator needs to take the team through this list, making sure that suggestions by the team fit in one of these categories:

1. Activity-specific assets.
2. Legal protection.
3. Reputation and trust.
4. Embedded processes.
5. Networked team knowledge.

Step 6: Cleaning Up.   The first part of the team session is now completed. The flip charts with the SWOT analysis will be displayed again during the next session. The first draft business idea diagram will need to be cleaned up and redrawn in an orderly way.

During the meeting break, the facilitator should, if at all possible, reduce the number of elements in the business idea diagram to its essentials. Very often, a rather complex idea can be reduced by combining elements or by replacing them with other concepts that evaluate the situation from a higher conceptual perspective. For example, the diagram might be simplified without losing anything essential (see Exhibit 19.3).

Exhibit 19.3
Reducing the Business Idea to Its Essentials

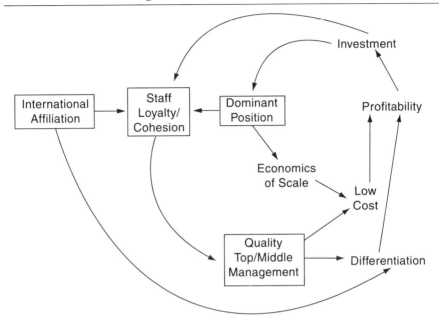

In this example, the essence of the strategic thrust has now been condensed to three elements:

- Investment in people to retain status of most attractive employer and to achieve "best in class" management.
- Maintaining a dominant market position by continuous investment, to retain a cost leadership position and to support status as most attractive employer.
- Using international affiliation as a source of differentiation in the market, and to support status as most attractive employer.

Step 7: Review of the Business Idea. After reconvening, the management team needs to consider the total picture by testing the results obtained so far. The first test is against the strengths and weaknesses developed in the SWOT analysis. This gives rise to the following questions:

- Have all strengths been reflected in the diagram?
- Can the business idea overcome any structural weaknesses identified?

A useful trigger question to open this part of the discussion is: If we, as a management team, swapped places with that of our best competitor, what would we do to eliminate the competitive advantage of the company we now belong to? In the final analysis, it is the distinctiveness that determines the quality of the business idea.

Step 8: Strategic Repercussions.   The vulnerability analysis so far has looked at the business idea against the current situation. Can the result serve as a powerful leading principle for the future as well? In order to consider this, the management team confronts the business idea developed so far with the opportunities and threats identified in the SWOT analysis.

- Does it constitute a strong basis from which to exploit the opportunities?
- What would happen if the threats identified were to become reality?

THE FIT BETWEEN THE BUSINESS IDEA AND THE SCENARIOS

A fully defined business idea first describes the critical success factors in one scenario, the present. The next step is to construct a set of scenarios by identifying the two or three preeminent driving forces of an organization's macroenvironment that are relevant to its business idea, and then by selecting the ones that are most uncertain.

Eventually, after scenarios have been developed and the business idea tested in them, the team should prepare several qualitative strategic objectives. These can take two forms:

- If the existing business idea is seen as a good basis for future business development, objectives will be formulated in terms of existing business areas to be further developed or new business areas to be entered where the business idea can be exploited. The strategy will likely focus on doing more with what the company already has.

- If the existing business idea needs development, objectives will be formulated in terms of building new unique capabilities and competencies, to be created in the company by the leveraging of existing distinctive competencies.

This process is the sort of entrepreneurial thinking that every team can do only for itself. What will be achieved at the end of it is that the team's current success formula will become clarified and tested against scenarios of the future business environment.

Once the business idea has been tested and found viable in a range of possible futures, it becomes the basis of the strategic direction that will be taken. The rest of the strategic management process can then be focused; priorities become clear.

CONCLUSION

Strategy is the art of making choices—investing both for current and future success. To understand these choices clearly, organizations should identify a business idea and test it in substantially different scenarios. This process can help an organization develop a business idea that will serve it well as the future evolves.

CHAPTER 20

THE EFFECTIVE IMPLEMENTATION OF SCENARIO PLANNING: CHANGING THE CORPORATE CULTURE

IAN WILSON

Moving from traditional planning to scenario-based strategic planning requires a transformation of corporate culture. Scenario planning is a new way of thinking through the future possibilities of organizations and of making decisions that benefit them and promote their survival. Instituting scenarios as an integral part of corporate planning requires a substantial commitment to manage the cultural transformation. Many, probably most, of the problems in introducing scenario planning into an organization stem from a failure to recognize the magnitude and duration of the implementation effort that is required to use this technology to change the prevailing management assumptions.

Integrating scenario development into the planning and decision-making culture of the corporation is more of a challenge than most managers anticipate. Indeed, the two greatest hurdles to using this methodology that beginners (and even some old-timers) confront are:

- Finding truly effective ways to use scenarios.
- Changing the corporate culture to make it compatible with scenario thinking.

Changing an organization's culture is clearly a more complex and demanding problem than developing the scenarios or ensuring that they are linked to specific strategic decisions. Royal Dutch/Shell is now probably the premier example in the world of the effective integration of scenarios into planning processes and executive thinking. But the company achieved this enviable state only with great effort and a lengthy training period.

Shell planner Pierre Wack began experimenting with scenarios in the early 1970s when oil prices were driven primarily by the economies of the Western nations. In the halcyon days just before the first oil shock—a sudden scarcity that panicked the public, caused consumer prices and oil futures prices to skyrocket, and ignited inflation—conventional Shell management thinking was that "consumer logic" (to use Wack's term) would always continue to dictate the rules of the game for global oil. In other words, the buying power of the major oil-consuming nations would determine the level of oil production—and its price. Wack's alternative premise, based on an analysis of the production power and revenue needs of the major OPEC producers, clearly showed that a world of "producer logic"—where OPEC could set the price high enough to send a shock throughout the industrialized world—was entirely possible.

Although Wack quickly gained management's attention when the oil embargo and price increases hit in 1973 and 1974, corporate action as a result of the insights gained from the scenario work followed much more slowly. Some five or six years passed before the Committee of Managing Directors felt comfortable using scenarios in its decision making. Getting the operating companies to make a wholehearted commitment to scenario planning took even more time. Even now, the spread of scenario thinking through Shell is uneven and incomplete.

WHAT IS THE "CULTURE PROBLEM?"

Why do companies, even those that are sincere and persistent in their efforts, have such a hard time making scenario planning work? No doubt, there are many explanations for this difficulty, but managers who have the most experience implementing this technology believe that the fundamental problem is largely a cultural and psychological one.

Most corporate cultures are still heavily biased toward quantitative analysis, with its emphasis on precision to as many decimal places as possible. Scenarios, by contrast, are primarily qualitative products (although quantification of key parameters is needed to supply definition to the scenario stories). Scenarios present a range of possibilities rather than one number projected by single-point forecasts. The initial management reaction to scenarios is, often, the suspicion that they are little better than blue-sky visioning with little relevance and insufficient detail for strategic planning.

This prejudice isn't surprising, given the fact that so much corporate decision making is still based on single-point numerical forecasting. This forecasting supports the time-honored managerial premise: Tell me what the future will be, then I can make my decision. Scenarios, by contrast, are a form of multiple-point exploration, and force everyone involved in the process to view the future and decision making in terms of alternatives. But when confronted with multiple scenarios, many managers typically complain, "Giving me four forecasts is no help at all." The fact is that managers may be willing to look at several alternative strategic options, but most don't consider preparing a number of alternative futures a worthwhile exercise. Why not?

The answer is that managerial competence is normally defined in terms of "knowing." Good managers, we often say, know where they are, where they're going, and how they'll get there. Scenarios, by contrast, confront us with the need to admit that we do not, and cannot, know much of the future. To that extent, scenarios seem to force us to acknowledge some degree of "incompetence." Because few corporate cultures allow managers to admit they can't see around the next bend in the road, most managers have a vested interest in not acknowledging what they don't know. Many an organization has placed its trust in the leader who faced the future with the most assurance—and who proceeded to drive off the unseen cliff.

Scenario planning forces management to face the need for drastic corporate culture change in the processes of planning, strategy development, and resource allocation. The most obvious need is to change the system so that managers routinely consider alternatives—futures, strategies, tactics—before making a decision. This process should not merely be desirable, but mandatory and automatic. In most organizations, existing management habits and attitudes are so deeply seated that they will yield only to a prolonged and many-faceted assault. Indeed, to expect to achieve the required degree of culture change to successfully manage the future, a corporation must engage in a concerted and sustained effort in at least the following areas:

- Tailoring scenarios to specific organizational needs.
- Selecting "targets of opportunity" for applying scenario planning.
- Tutoring its leadership and planners on the scenarios-strategy linkage.

- Developing a communications program.
- Emphasizing manager education.
- Fine-tuning and updating scenarios.

To succeed, such a comprehensive program necessarily imposes responsibilities, not only on senior management and the planning staff, but on operating and functional units throughout the organization.

TAILORING SCENARIOS TO ORGANIZATIONAL NEEDS

Scenario planning, like any methodology, can succeed only if it meets the criterion of corporate relevance. Pierre Wack warned in two *Harvard Business Review* articles that scenarios must reflect management's central concerns.[1] Thus, Wack's scenarios were centrally focused on conditions that would affect global oil demand and price—Shell's main strategic concern. This is not to say that scenarios should uncritically accept management's current views of the future. Indeed, a central aim for scenarios should always be to challenge conventional wisdom, as Wack's "producer logic" thesis did. But they must also address management's perceptions of the critical uncertainties and the key issues they face.

This double requirement is perhaps the most potent argument against using "off-the-shelf" scenarios and for involving senior managers in the development of ones specifically designed for the organization. Producing cookie-cutter scenarios for a company is counterproductive. Only by tailoring scenarios to planning needs, emphasizing their "decision focus," and actively involving decision makers in their development is an organization likely to have its executives accept ownership of the final scenarios. Only under these conditions are the executives likely to effectively use the scenarios to make operational decisions.

Executive Involvement

One of the most productive scenario projects I have personally undertaken was at Allied Irish Banks where the chief executive officer insisted that his direct reports should constitute the scenario development team. Because these senior executives actually developed the scenarios themselves, they understood and owned them fully and so were able to incorporate them more easily into their thinking and strategy development.

SBU-Specific Scenarios

Multidivisional companies have a special need for tailored scenarios. Scenarios developed at the corporate level are not likely to be detailed enough to guide strategic business units (SBUs). The fact is, planning needs vary substantially from business unit to business unit. Nevertheless, SBU-specific microscenarios should fit under the umbrella of the corporate macroscenarios so they will be consistent with the major commonalties of the corporate and SBU business environment. These more focused scenarios capture the details of each SBU's markets, competition, technology, and other key environmental variables. In addition, they enhance SBU managers' understanding of the relevance of scenarios to their business, which in turn helps to ensure their commitment to using the scenarios.

SELECTING TARGETS OF OPPORTUNITY

Often managers must find a way to jump-start the scenario process to increase their chances of bringing about the needed culture transformation. A number of years ago, scenario planners thought that the best way to get quick credibility involved "shock treatment." This was achieved by introducing scenarios that painted pictures of awaiting disasters. This approach proved ineffective.

Taking a different tack, Royal Dutch/Shell found that executives need time to develop the skills—and the attitude—to use scenarios instinctively and imaginatively to manage a variety of operations. One way to use scenarios as an agent of dramatic change is to try them out in targeted situations with high payoff.

An important element in the implementation plan is, therefore, selecting the best "targets of opportunity" for the use of scenarios. For example, a company might want to start using scenarios to assess the resilience, risks and payoffs of major investment decisions. Such a target has at least two obvious advantages:

- These key, long-term decisions most readily lend themselves to scenario-based evaluation. Actual examples of such projects include the determination of the pace and timing of opening a new copper mine in Chile, and assessing the long-term payoff and feasibility of a $600 million addition to a firm's paper-manufacturing capacity.
- Because such an investment-approval process involves both SBU managers (the proposers of such projects) and corporate managers or the

board of directors (the approvers), it promotes scenario use at two levels. When a business-unit manager anticipates that corporate executives will use scenarios to evaluate requests for investment funds, both the manager—and the SBU management team in general—are much more likely to use them to help shape a proposal.

Two other appropriate targets for introducing scenarios are planning assumptions and contingency planning. Virtually every strategic plan contains a set of assumptions about future economic, market, competitive, and other trends. Typically, these assumptions are the product of single-point numerical forecasting. These can be better addressed for by scenarios, that assess the strategic significance of trends, uncertainties, and assumptions about the company's future business environment. A scenario can be developed as an alternative to the "baseline" set of assumptions in the current corporate plan. This scenario will provide a test for the robustness of current strategies, and it will likely become obvious from this first experiment that other scenarios are needed.

Similarly, every strategic plan should consider how the business would deal with contingencies—the divergences from planning assumptions that could whallop corporate performance. The scenario process aims specifically to explore contingencies and their consequences. As a first step, corporate executives could use a contingency scenario to reassess all current strategies and investment decisions. Or they could ask business units to detail how their planned actions would change in the event of such a scenario. This is standard operating procedure, for example, at most Shell operating companies. Encouraging this sort of what-if thinking can, over time, build a constituency for fully fledged, scenario-based strategy development.

Whatever target or targets of opportunity managers select, they should recognize the need for changes in the existing strategic-planning system. They should have a clear idea of what innovations are necessary, and establish a schedule for bringing them about. The selected targets should be incorporated into an overall implementation plan and not be a random set of experiments (see Exhibit 20.1).

THE SCENARIOS-STRATEGY LINKAGE

Some managers become so captivated by the process of producing scenarios that they forget that these pictures of the future are not an end

Exhibit 20.1
The Uses of Scenarios in Strategic Management

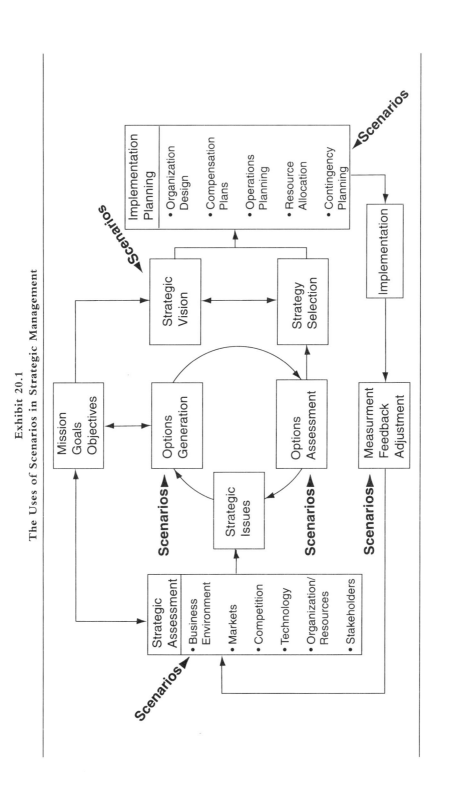

in themselves; they are merely a means of opening executives' minds to new possibilities and new options. Scenarios are a tool to help managers make better strategic decisions. But it is precisely at the point of linkage between scenarios and strategy that decision makers seem to have the greatest difficulty. Too often, top management's response to the completion of the scenarios is an anticlimatic, "Now what?" If there is no immediate and convincing answer to this question, the organization's leadership is all too likely to "file and forget" the work of the scenario team.

In the long run, strategizing within a scenario framework is a skill that requires considerable sophistication and takes time to acquire, as Royal Dutch/Shell's experience so clearly demonstrated. But every manager's immediate need is for a utilitarian primer that explains, step by step, how to move from scenarios to strategy. Some critics will protest that this approach trivializes strategy development, substitutes analytical structure for intuitive insight, and overlooks other vital inputs to the process.[2] There is some validity to their argument. However, in defense of the utilitarian approach, an analogy to learning to play the piano is illuminating. The beginner has to learn the notes, practice scales, and play rhythmically, paced by a metronome. Only after mastering technique can the piano player successfully perform with feeling and insight. So too the beginning scenario player needs to learn some basic techniques that will help to bridge the gap between scenarios and strategy.

Exhibit 20.2 lists some exemplary techniques that a scenario primer might include. Each of these techniques is illustrated with a brief case study drawn from actual experience.

Sensitivity/Risk Assessment

A paper company needed to decide whether to invest $600 million in a new paper-making facility. The plant would have a long life span (some 30 to 35 years) and a relatively narrow range of products, and management had some concern about eventual market erosion because of inroads by electronic communications. The company, therefore, elected to use scenarios to explore the possible variations in market size and growth rate, given the uncertainties about future electronic technology development, consumer values and use of time, prospects for advertising, and general economic conditions.

The scenarios showed, as one might expect, distinctly different levels of demand growth, but similar patterns of eventual decline, with the timing

Exhibit 20.2
Linking Scenarios to Strategy: A Comparison of Selected Approaches

Application	Steps	Evaluation
Sensitivity/ Risk Assessment		
• Best use: Evaluate a specific strategic decision (such as a major plant investment or new business development). • Approach: Use computer modeling (with scenarios providing assumptions) or simple judgmental assessments to evaluate the strategy's resilience or vulnerability to differences in business conditions.	• Identify key conditions in the future market/industry environment (such as size/growth of market, changes in regulatory climate, or technological breakthrough) that would be necessary for a "Go" decision. • Describe and assess the state of these conditions in each scenario. • Compare the scenario conditions with the desired future conditions, and evaluate the likely success/failure and resilience/vulnerability of a "Go" decision in each scenario. • Evaluate the overall resilience or vulnerability of a "Go" decision, assessing the desirability of hedging or modifying the original decision.	• Offers relatively simple straightforward application in a series of descriptive and judgmental steps. • Depends on a very clear and specific "decision focus" that lends itself to a "Go/No Go" decision.
Strategy Evaluation		
• Best use: Use scenarios as "test beds" to evaluate the viability of an existing strategy (usually one that derives from a single-point forecast). • Approach: Play a companywide SBU or competitor's strategy against the scenarios to assess the strategy's effectiveness in a range of business conditions; identify modifications and/or contingency planning that require attention.	• Disaggregate the strategy into its specific thrusts (e.g., "Focus on consumer market segments in . . . ," "Diversify into related service areas") and state objectives and goals. • Assess the relevance, and likely success, of these thrusts in the diverse conditions of the scenarios. • Analyze the results of this impact analysis to identify: —Opportunities that the strategy addresses and those that it misses. —Threats/risks that the strategy has foreseen or overlooked. —Comparative competitive success or failure. • Identify options for changes in strategy and the need for contingency planning.	• Offers natural first use of scenarios in the strategic planning system. • Quickly identifies "bottom-line" issues and provides senior management with immediate evidence of scenarios' utility (particularly when the company links it with competitive analysis.

Exhibit 20.2 *(Continued)*

Application	*Steps*	*Evaluation*
Strategy Development: Using a Planning Focus Scenario • Best use: To accommodate management culture, use as a starting point for strategy development. •Approach: Develop strategy to deal with conditions of one scenario and then test it against other scenarios to assess resilience and the need for modification, "hedging," and contingency planning.	• Review scenarios to identify strategic opportunities and threats for the business. • Determine what the company should do and should not do in any case. • Select a planning focus scenario (usually the most probable one). • Integrate the product of the preceding steps into a coherent strategy for this scenario. • Test this strategy against the remaining scenarios to assess its resilience or vulnerability. • Review the results of this test to determine the need for strategy modification, "hedging," and contingency planning.	• Flies in the face of strict scenario theory (by dealing with probabilities), but can be a useful intermediate step in weaning executives from reliance on single-point forecasts. • In its step-by-step process, addresses many key questions that scenario-based strategy should ask; avoids the pitfall of focusing on only one scenario. • Can close executives minds to "unlikely" (or "unpleasant") scenarios and limit the search for strategy options.
Strategy Development: Without Using a Planning Focus Scenario • Best use: Takes all scenarios at face value, without judging probabilities. • Approach: Develop a "resilient" strategy that can deal with wide variations in business conditions.	• Identify the key elements of a successful strategy (e.g., geographic scope, market focus, basis of competition, technology). • Analyze each scenario to determine the optimal setting for each element (What would be the best market focus for Scenario A? Scenario B?). • Review these scenario-specific settings and determine the most resilient option for each element. • Integrate these options into an overall, coordinated business strategy.	• Most closely approximates the goal of strategizing within the scenarios framework, and makes optimal use of scenarios in strategy development. • Provides management with maximum feasible range of choice, and forces careful evaluation of options against different futures. • Requires effort and patience from involved decision makers.

of key threats remaining a critical uncertainty. Playing out the investment decision in these different environments suggested that only in the most optimistic conditions would the company meet its "hurdle rate" for investments. As a result, the executives decided on a more incremental approach to the investment, significantly scaling back the initial plant size. Interestingly, too, the scenarios also implied a far higher near-term demand for certain key products than conventional industry wisdom anticipated at the time. The company broke with conventional thinking, increased manufacturing capacity for these products, and reaped significant gains during the following decade when its competitors were unprepared to meet the surge of orders.

Strategy Evaluation

A large department store chain introduced scenarios into its strategic planning to explore alternative future patterns of change in the economy, consumer values and lifestyles, consumer buying decisions, and the structure and operations of the retail industry through the year 2000. The company then used these scenarios in three ways:

- To evaluate the likely payoff from its current strategy (that is, the projected return from each of its key strategic thrusts).
- To assess and compare the strategies of key competitors.
- To analyze retail strategy options to identify the most resilient ones for possible inclusion in the company's strategy.

The company expanded its specialty retail outlets in the 1980s as a result of the new market understanding it gained from developing the scenarios. As a consequence, it was able to win appreciable market share (and increased profitability) from the then market leader, Sears Roebuck.

Strategy Development: Using a Planning Focus Scenario

When Shell Canada introduced scenarios into its strategic-planning system in the early 1980s, the company elected to ease into the new process by using one scenario as a "planning focus," that is, as a starting point for strategy development. From this initial point, Shell Canada built up its corporate strategy from the answers to three questions:

- Which strategies should we pursue no matter which scenario materializes?
- Which strategies should we pursue if the planning focus scenario materializes?
- How sensitive are these "base-case" strategies to variations in assumptions under contingent conditions (the other scenarios)?

By adopting this approach, the company tried to bridge the gap between the old and the new strategy-development process while preserving the value of considering, and planning for, the contingencies resulting from widely different business conditions.

One outcome of this initial venture into scenario planning was the company's decision to give up on some of its peripheral ventures (into biotechnology, for example), and to concentrate on its resources and chemicals businesses.

Strategy Development: Without Using a Planning Focus Scenario

The senior management team of Allied Irish Banks (AIB) became both the scenario- and the strategy-development team in its review of the bank's strategic direction. After structuring scenarios around their perceptions of the critical uncertainties facing their business, the CEO and his direct reports first identified the strategic opportunities and threats arising from the scenarios, and used this framework to assess the bank's current competitive position and prospective vulnerability. Their approach to future strategy then led them through the following steps:

1. Single out 11 elements of a well-rounded strategy (product scope, technology, alliances, and the like).
2. Identify the optimal strategic option for each of these 11 elements in each of the four scenarios.
3. Select the most resilient option for each element, and integrate these options into a coherent strategy for the bank.

AIB's strategic-planning officer has credited his company's scenarios with helping to provide a clear and consistent focus for company strategy. Since AIB developed scenarios, he said, "Reliance on strategic adhocracy has diminished."

This approach represents undoubtedly the "purest" and most sophisticated use of scenarios in strategy development. It also has the highest content of "executive insight," for the simple reason that the resulting strategies are the product of their effort, and theirs alone.

DEVELOPING A COMMUNICATIONS PROGRAM

Communications are an essential part of the scenario implementation blueprint. If such a major change in planning culture is to take root, participants must define, clarify, and communicate both its nature and its purpose. And communications must fit the needs of various internal (and some external) audiences.

Thus, "communicability" is a vital characteristic that companies must build into their scenarios. To change the mind-set of executives and planners, the champions of the scenario process must first capture and hold their attention. An excellent way to grab the attention of operating managers is to write imaginative but plausible scenarios about their markets. The term scenario comes, after all, from the world of film and theater: The best scenarios resemble convincing movie scripts or plays about the future. To hold management's attention, these stories about the future need to be both imaginative and logical, opening the corporate mind to new possibilities.

The stories need intriguing titles and captivating story lines. Bland titles such as "Best Case," "Worst Case" or "High Growth," "Low Growth" simply don't stir the imagination. They tell us little about the true character of the business environment and virtually nothing about the forces that drive it. To highlight the fundamental gestalt of its scenarios, Royal Dutch/Shell called one early set "Fragile Compromise" and "Restructured Growth," and more recent ones "Sustainable World" and "Global Mercantilism." Titles that capture the dynamics of the scenario are the most memorable. Each title should convey, in just a few words, a complete picture of complex forces, issues, and business results.

Story lines should give an account of a changeable rather than a static future. These narratives shouldn't merely describe an end point—such as the global chemical market in 2010. They should also offer insights into how such a future will come to pass. Making these possibilities so convincing that they become part of what Pierre Wack called "managers' mental maps of the future" is the ultimate objective of the project.

The most experienced scenario-planning organizations pay a great deal of attention to communications. Unfortunately, newcomers to scenario planning tend to give much less thought to the communications process. Experienced organizations both use the widest range of media available and rely very heavily on audience participation in workshops and seminars. Shell, for example, enhances communications by preparing an elaborate scenario book that describes the scenarios in detail, and presents the overall implications for issues of key importance to the company. In 1992, it also produced an illustrative video of that year's scenarios. But Shell's primary mode of communications is to hold tens of workshops throughout its worldwide organization. These workshops aim to stimulate diverse groups within the company to consider the strategic implications of the scenarios for their businesses.

Most, but not all, scenario planners produce written descriptions of the scenarios and their implications, usually in the long and the executive summary versions. Scenario consultants also provide written briefing reports. But most scenario experts say that, though written materials are useful, they are not nearly as important as presentations and working discussions.

If the scenarios are truly to become part of the corporate culture, communications about them have to occur at two levels:

- Communications from senior managers should clearly convey the seriousness of their commitment to this new way of planning. They can start by explaining how they intend to use the scenarios in their own decision making and by being explicit about how they wish others to use them.
- Members of the planning staff should provide step-by-step guidelines for constructing scenarios and putting them to best use.

EMPHASIZING MANAGER EDUCATION

Learning by doing clearly has merit. However, to achieve a culture shift of the sort that scenario planning entails, on-the-job learning must be reinforced by a formal educational program.

First, institutionalizing scenario planning normally requires a broad review—and some revision—of the existing planning system. At a minimum, both planners and executives need to learn about the requirements of the new system, and guidelines must be available on how to use scenarios.

Some of this education can occur through manuals and other written materials—but not much. Everything we know about adult education suggests that investing in seminars, group interaction, and hands-on exercises pays off.

The core of a manager-education program can be a one- to two-day seminar on the purpose, methodology, and applications of scenario planning. A typical agenda for such a seminar might include:

- The general rationale for using scenarios, and why this company, in particular, is using them.
- Examination of the scenario methodology that is to be used.
- Discussion of scenarios that may have already been developed (normally, a seminar of this sort will follow a preliminary scenario project).
- A presentation by a high-ranking executive (preferably the CEO) to underscore the company's commitment to scenario planning, and to establish the authority for the ground rules for using scenarios.
- Guidelines for the application of scenarios in strategy development.

In such seminars, the most valuable lessons for managers are the need for, and role of, scenario planning; its proposed application in the strategic-planning system; and the changes in culture and decision-making processes that this new approach requires.

Beyond these seminars, the real aim of the education program should be to integrate the implications of scenario thinking into other programs, especially those that touch on management style and organization culture. Scenario planning will not take root in a company whose education programs foster a culture of hierarchical thinking and "going by the numbers." Such an approach is quite at odds with the flexibility and innovative thinking that scenarios require.

FINE-TUNING AND UPDATING SCENARIOS

One good indicator of whether scenario planning has taken root in a company is how faithfully major players update and revise the scenarios. If scenarios are to contribute fully and effectively to a company's strategic thinking, executives must be confident about their continuing relevance and conforming to actual events.

The blueprint for implementation should, therefore, show how to link the scenario process with established corporate monitoring and scanning systems. Monitoring is most useful when it tracks current events leading up to the branching points (or forks in the road) that the scenarios have identified as leading to different futures. Scanning, in contrast, can alert companies to hitherto unanticipated developments—ranging from unexpected research breakthroughs to more subtle social and political shifts—that might form the basis for entirely new scenarios. Both monitoring and scanning are necessary to keep the scenario process alive, relevant, and in the forefront of corporate thinking.

Experience points to three other procedures that help keep the scenario process lively and perceptive:

- First, planners should schedule scenario-development sessions so that their output feeds naturally into the planning cycle. For example, if (as is often the case) the first stage in the planning cycle is examination of future environmental assumptions, scheduled for January, then the preparation or updating of scenarios has to be scheduled for the fall.

- Second, the more people with different viewpoints who participate in the process the better. Restricting participation to members of the planning department is certainly not a good idea. Instead, management should seek the ideas and insights of marketers, technologists, public policy analysts—anyone whose experience covers the driving forces of the scenarios. Such broad-based involvement produces a double benefit: both the scenarios and the participants gain from the process. DuPont and Prudential Insurance have come to the conclusion that the use of scenarios links top executives and operational managers who are tackling external issues, thereby helping to integrate strategic and tactical decisions.

- Third, establishing a provisional schedule for scenario revisions is helpful. Though annual fine-tuning is usually necessary, companies with deep experience in scenario planning have found that they need to engage in more radical rethinking and restructuring of the scenarios every three or four years. The revision schedule depends, of course, on the pace and course of events and on the foresight of the original scenarios.

CONCLUSION

Moving from "traditional" planning to scenario-based strategic planning requires a transformation of corporate culture. Scenario planning is not merely a new planning tool, but a new way of thinking through the future possibilities of organizations and of making decisions that benefit them and promote their survival. Using scenarios on a one-shot basis requires much less investment than instituting them as an integral part of corporate planning. Many, probably most, of the problems in introducing scenario planning into an organization stem from a failure to recognize the magnitude and duration of the implementation effort that is required to use this technology to change the prevailing management assumptions.

This chapter has attempted to provide only a sketch of some of the dimensions of this effort. Like scenarios, this effort has to be tailored to the needs of the organization, but some requirements are constant: senior management commitment, communications, education and guidance, and practice, practice, practice. If we do it right, scenarios can be a strategic-planning tool that will enable management to attain vital insights, learning, and mind-opening that can't be attained any other way.

CHAPTER 21

THE CROSS-SCENARIO PLANNING PROCESS

DOUG RANDALL and ROBERT G. WILSON

This chapter introduces three generic approaches to creating a strategy your organization will choose to test in its scenarios: diving-in (go-for-broke), testing-the-water (experimenting and learning), or all-weather (win/win). Some strategists select a generic approach as a way to better prepare their organization to succeed in almost all scenarios. The main criteria for selecting which of these approaches to pursue is to consider how much influence the actions of your business have on the industry; how much risk your management is willing to assume; and how certain the future operating environment is.

Astute observers of the corporate arena are convinced that building winning strategies is getting more difficult in today's economy. In their agenda-setting book, *Competing for the Future,* Gary Hamel and C. K. Prahalad conclude, "It is not enough for a company to get smaller and better and faster, as important as these tasks may be; a company must be capable of fundamentally reconceiving its industry . . . of getting different."[1] We believe that the bold leap an organization must take in order to "get different" requires a special kind of scenario planning. We recommend a cross-scenario planning methodology that helps companies prepare for the competitive terrain of the future.

This chapter introduces a four-step comprehensive scenario-planning process that explores how to devise a strategy that will serve your organization well in various possible futures. We call this approach, building bridges between scenarios.

BUILDING BRIDGES BETWEEN SCENARIOS

To understand the value of building bridges between scenarios, let's look at how "PublishingCo" conducted a scenario-planning exercise in 1985. Its primary goal was to understand what impact technology would have on its strategy and how it should allocate the limited resources the firm could devote to technology. The company looked at three technology-oriented scenarios for the domestic publishing industry in 1995. The first scenario focused on technology that would bring about increased efficiency in the printing and prepress process; the second looked at technology for alternative distribution channels; and the third focused on outsourcing the management of sophisticated technology.

In the first scenario, prepress and printing technology advances to a point where publishers are able to reduce their printing and production costs by 35 percent. This dramatic savings drives up profits for publishers willing to make long-term investments in state-of-the-art printing technology.

In the second scenario, customers have personal computers and access to computer networks. They shift away from reading everything (from newspapers to books) on printed paper and are moving rapidly toward on-line information as an alternative. As a result, traditional publishers make large-scale investments in network computing services.

In the third scenario, publishing technology has become so sophisticated and complex that many publishers have outsourced technology management. Some smaller, independent full-service integrators have also sprung up to serve publishers. Even printing is being outsourced, which allows publishers to focus less on the rapidly changing technology environment and more on content.

PublishingCo's management selected the cost reduction scenario as the one they thought was most likely to come about. Like many companies in the mid-1980s, they anticipated that computer technology would slash costs in production, prepress, and printing, and didn't want to miss out on being a technology leader. As a result, the business managers invested its limited resources in production, prepress, and printing technology. They gambled the company's future that the basis of competition for the publishing industry in 1995 would be low-cost printing.

What wound up happening in the publishing industry? In reality, all three scenarios came about simultaneously. Advances in printing technology slashed the overall production and printing costs by at least 35 percent for most companies. High-speed networks and lower-cost computing brought the personal computer to more desktops than PC manufacturers ever dreamed of, which led to the introduction of electronic publishing. And outsourcing of expensive, hard-to-manage functions such a information technology became popular among many American businesses.

PublishingCo did not have the resources to invest heavily in preparation for all three futures. Each required significant capital and substantial changes in management business practices. But instead of ignoring the second two scenarios, PublishingCo might have considered how it could prepare for the scenarios without overcommitting its resources. For example, in preparation for the second scenario managers might have thought about forming a partnership with an on-line service, which could act as an electronic distribution channel. Similarly, in preparation for the third scenario, they might have engaged in small-scale outsourcing agreements where they were financially viable.

PublishingCo's mistake—preparing for the future as though only one scenario would come about rather than developing strategies for a range of futures—is one that many companies make when they are first exposed to scenarios. An approach that considers how to "build bridges" between scenarios offers an alternative method of strategic planning.

THE CROSS-SCENARIO PLANNING PROCESS

The cross-scenario planning process consists of four steps. During the first, you'll create several future industry scenarios and explore alternative strategies for your business under each scenario. The second step, which is the emphasis of this chapter, focuses on making decisions about how to use the scenarios as a tool for strategy development. During this step, you will discover how to build links between scenarios. The third step is devoted to the nuts and bolts of your strategy. Here you will allocate resources and outline an action plan. Finally, the fourth step is devoted to monitoring both your strategy and key industry indicators that might influence your strategy.

Step 1: Exploring the Future

The primary purpose of the first step is to broaden management's perspective by spelling out all of the major identifiable changes the industry could face within the planning horizon (generally 5 to 10 years). In the publishing example, the changes would include a shift toward lower-cost printing; the introduction of innovative distribution channels such as on-line services, CD-ROM books and Internet-based publishing; and a move toward outsourcing information technology management. During the second part of Step 1, you will consider the implication of those conditions on your business. For example, PublishingCo decided that if new technology led to low-cost printing, they would want to invest in it. They also might have decided that if electronic publishing became an attractive market, they would acquire a company to help them offer services on-line. By the end of this step you should feel as though you've adequately explored all of the recognizable threats and opportunities facing your business.

Two Tools: End States and Events.   To begin "exploring the future," we suggest developing three to five scenarios, using two critical tools: end states and events. End states are one-page snapshots of the future. Events are specific identifiable actions that might occur sometime during the planning horizon.

End states describe a set of conditions for an industry at a certain time in the future. They capture a range of plausible, high-level descriptions of how the industry might evolve. When written properly, they focus on underlying issues and drivers affecting your business. The brief descriptions of the publishing industry in the previous section are summaries of three different end states.

In contrast to end states, events describe very specific possible future occurrences. Prepped with a list of these key future events, managers will gain new insights from news items in tomorrow's trade papers. Events should be written in a way that makes it easy to identify whether the event occurred. For example, PublishingCo might have considered some of the following events:

1987: Publishing companies spend 35 percent less on prepress and printing than last year.

1989: Expenditure on information services for publishing companies quadruples over the past four years.

1990: Number of users with access to on-line services increases by 500 percent since 1985.

1992: EDS, computer systems giant, launches division devoted to publishing industry.

1995: Eight of the top 10 publishers offer products on-line.

In most cases, a business should draw up a list of between 100 and 150 important events. Event ideas generally come from a series of interviews with "industry experts" and other forms of research.

After developing the end states and events for scenario building, it's time to create the scenarios. You do this by identifying events that are critical (either must or must not occur) to each end state. For example, in the publishing case, the event "1990: Number of users with access to on-line services increases by 500 percent since 1985" must occur in order for the second scenario to come about. The event "1992: EDS launches division devoted to publishing industry," on the other hand, is irrelevant to the scenario. Every event should be analyzed according to its relevance to each of the end states. We consider scenarios to be the well-thought-out combination of end states and relevant events.

In sorting through the events, managers will identify several different categories:

- *Events relevant only to one scenario.* If several of these start occurring, they might serve as an indicator that a certain future is unfolding. Or, if the scenario is truly key to the company's future, the events are critical action items.
- *Events relevant to many scenarios.* These are generally important events that you should act on because they are likely to have an effect on your business no matter which scenario comes about.
- *Events not relevant to any of the scenarios you're working with.* These tend to be issues that some people believe are important to your industry, but in reality are not relevant to any of the futures you've imagined for the company. Thus, they might either point out a blind spot in your end state development or identify issues that are distracting managers from more relevant future concerns.

Step 2: Choosing an Approach

Step 2 is the point in the scenario-planning process where managers tend to have the most trouble, probably because it requires creative conceptual thinking. The primary goal of this phase is to determine which of the three generic approaches to creating a strategy your organization will choose: diving-in (go-for-broke), testing-the-water (experimenting and learning), or all-weather (win/win). Sophisticated planners learn to select an approach as a way to build bridges, or link scenarios. That way your company is better prepared to meet a broad range of future industry conditions. Your choice of approach is critical, as it helps you lay the foundation for your business strategy.

Before you choose a generic strategy, initiate a frank discussion among your company's key decision makers. The goal of the discussion is to determine what kind of impact your company's decisions have on the industry. Who are the other players? How do their decisions influence your customers? How do your decisions influence their customers? What forces affect your business? Regulation? Foreign trade? Suppliers? New entrants? Technology? If PublishingCo's managers were to engage in this discussion today, they would probably find they have little influence over the industry. Increasingly, the publishing industry is becoming influenced by the computing, communications, and networking industries. Rapid technological innovation and the onslaught of desktop publishing has made it easy for nimble newcomers to enter the industry at very low costs. As a result, there are many more players, reducing the power of some traditional publishers.

This discussion about your company's ability to change the industry should conclude with a decision on which generic approach to choose: diving-in, testing-the-water, or all-weather. The main criteria for selecting which of these approaches to pursue is to consider:

1. How much influence your business actions have on the industry.
2. How much risk your management is willing to assume.
3. How certain the future operating environment is.

Let's explore each of the three generic approaches in detail.

Diving-In.   The first approach is diving-in; that is, making a major, probably risky, investment. This is the most aggressive option, and is generally pursued by businesses that have tremendous influence in their industry, are willing to accept a significant level of risk, and are fairly certain of the future operating environment. A company pursuing a diving-in strategy believes it can shape not only its own future, but also the future evolution of the entire industry.

Let's look briefly at "TransparencyCo," a disguised division of a *Fortune* 500 diversified company that is the worldwide leader in transparency film manufacturing. It recently used scenarios to help develop a long-term strategy. With the rapid increase of computer-based presentation systems, TransparencyCo anticipated a future where the market for overhead transparencies would dwindle quite rapidly. Managers explored five alternative future scenarios for their business ranging from trying to block the trend toward computer-based presentation systems (in order to protect their current position in the industry) to proactively accelerating the trend (and consequently growing their business in a new direction).

TransparencyCo's office products distribution network is one of the best in the complex office supply industry. Its relationships with hardware and software vendors around the world as well as its sizeable capital resources make it an attractive partner for most companies. Its incredibly innovative laboratory allows it to develop new products and services and quickly launch new businesses when it wants to gain a key position in the industry. All of this puts TransparencyCo in a unique competitive position. After studying market share, profits, and a variety of other metrics, TransparencyCo concluded that its independent actions have a significant affect on the fundamentals of its industry. This is the first criterion for considering which generic strategy to pursue.

Next, TransparencyCo's managers considered how risk-averse they were. They determined that the threat of losing revenue in the future (as transparency demand fell) was so severe, that they would need to make a bold strategic change. As a result, management was comfortable accepting a high level of risk. After evaluating these criteria and considering the volatility of the industry, TransparencyCo decided to dive in—to pick a scenario and make it happen. They explicitly decided to become an all-encompassing "enabler of electronic meetings." By this they meant they would become industry leaders in providing tools and support to customers that run high-tech meetings.

Today, TransparencyCo offers advanced presentation equipment, support, and consultative services for interactive high-tech meetings. It plans to collaborate with customers and partners so it can introduce new products and services to enhance meeting productivity. At the same time, TransparencyCo continues to track the other four scenarios to be sure its customers and competitors are not moving in a different direction than it is. If certain events start to occur, they will trigger TransparencyCo to consider a different approach to the market. But for now, TransparencyCo's managers are working—full speed—on creating the ideal meeting environment of the future.

To those who are unfamiliar with the process, the diving-in approach might sound as though it contradicts what we've said about not using scenarios as forecasts. But diving-in works because a company must first go through an analytical process for making a commitment. In the example outlined, TransparencyCo chose to pursue a single scenario not because it thought it would occur, but because its managers believed they could make it occur. Only after a careful evaluation of their industry position, risk tolerance, and the industry's certainty, did managers boldly commit to diving in.

Testing-the-Water.   Testing-the-water is another generic strategy. Companies pursuing this approach select a few scenarios that are likely to occur and make strategic investments in each of them. It is, initially at least, a learning experience.

Imagine that PublishingCo decided to adopt a test-the-water approach. Rather than committing the majority of its resources to new printing and prepress technology as it did, managers might have decided to make a few, smaller-scale investments aimed at securing them a strong position regardless of which of the three scenarios came to pass. For example, they could have signed an agreement with Prodigy to publish a journal on-line, outsourced a few key information technology projects, and found an alternative to the hefty investment in printing technology. When a company tests the water, it generally postpones "bet-the-company" investments that would be desirable only in a particular scenario. But it should still make attractive, affordable investments that ensure its future.

EnergyCo Tests the Water.   A leading North American energy company used scenarios to develop its strategy for operating in China. Management was so committed to building a business in China that they shifted most of their global resources toward the company's China strategy. Building business in China was "EnergyCo's" number one priority.

In examining their approach for China, EnergyCo managers determined that many components of their strategy would change depending on what happened to China's political, economic, and social climate.

For example, if China split up along provincial or regional boundaries, having strategically placed, independently managed local operations would be essential. If, on the other hand, the Communist party tightened its belt and curbed the burgeoning capitalism along the eastern coast, a more national approach might win. In this case, operating as a unified entity in a critical industry such as energy might offer good bargaining power with the Communist government. At the same time, a country-wide catastrophe, such as a financial crash or military invasion, might cause China to close its doors to foreign investment, which would require EnergyCo to retrench from China.

Even before they considered their influence on the industry and the amount of risk management could tolerate, EnergyCo managers decided to test the water. They found China's future to be so unpredictable that they wanted to follow a strategy that would help offset risk. By testing the water, EnergyCo was able to make a significant play in China while at the same time, manage the risks of operating in its highly uncertain business climate.

Today, EnergyCo has invested billions of dollars in China. It established a presence in China by opening offices in Beijing, Shanghai, and other important cities well before most of its non-Chinese competitors. Energy Co is careful to consider how its actions would play out in each of the independent scenarios it developed for China's future business climate. After testing the waters, EnergyCo rarely pursues projects that will be beneficial only if one or two scenarios emerge. Instead it strives to find high-leverage actions that will be desirable in several of the alternative scenarios.

All-Weather.   An all-weather strategy is the lowest-risk alternative of the three generic options. Companies pursuing an all-weather approach strive to limit their investments to those projects that will be viable under any of the future scenarios. As a result, it is sometimes described as a "lowest common denominator" approach (because projects are pursued only if they are beneficial to every scenario). In deciding whether to pursue an all-weather strategy, a company asks itself: Can we affect the outcome of our industry, or should we optimize our flexibility and responsiveness? An all-weather strategy is a good choice for those companies that want to minimize risk until managers are ready to make long-term investments in the business. (One warning: A company that pursues an all-weather strategy may have to accept a low rate of return.

By assuming the least risk in its industry, the business may also reduce its profit potential.)

All-Weather at MedCo.   Recently, a small candy company, MedCo decided to use an all-weather approach in building its strategy for entering the medical foods industry. Medical foods producers make over-the-counter food products such as nutrition bars and shakes targeted at distinct patient populations, such as people suffering from renal disease, AIDS, or Parkinson's disease. The candy company, with its ties to the food industry, manufacturing know-how, and excess manufacturing capacity, was well suited to become a player in the emerging medical foods industry.

But MedCo was having trouble developing a long-term strategy because the future of this embryonic industry was so unclear. Nobody knew whether manufacturers would face regulations such as those imposed on pharmaceutical companies (which require very expensive manufacturing plants) or food manufacturers (which require much less expensive manufacturing facilities). Similarly, planners were wondering whether they would be allowed to make health claims the way nutritional supplement makers do (minimal trials costing little money), or if the FDA would require them to prove their claims clinically, as pharmaceutical companies must (lengthy trials often costing millions of dollars for a single product). MedCo's managers were so unsure about how the medical foods industry would evolve, they hesitated to make any long-term investments. At the same time, they didn't want to lose the potential advantage of being an early mover in the industry. After all, there were only a few players in the medical foods industry, and MedCo had already introduced a successful product.

MedCo's management decided to pursue an all-weather strategy—they wanted to hold off on making long-term investments until the future operating environment became more clear. Pursuing an all-weather approach, they focused only on those projects that were likely to pay off regardless of what the future brought. MedCo chose not to upgrade its plant to pharmaceutical manufacturing standards because the costly upgrade would only be desirable if the FDA-imposed regulations on medical food manufacturers required it to meet strict manufacturing standards. If these regulations didn't pass, MedCo could continue to manufacture medical foods in its existing candy manufacturing plant, a lower-cost alternative. Even though they were holding off on expensive investments like the plant upgrade, MedCo managers didn't want to lose the momentum they had gained being one of the first to introduce medical food products. They continued to make short-term investments in their business (minor plant upgrades and inexpensive R&D projects, for example), enabling them to manufacture both existing and new products at competitive prices. In this way, MedCo managed to minimize risk while laying the foundation for a successful medical foods business without making immediate long-term investments.

No matter which approach you pursue (diving-in, testing-the-water, or all-weather), it's critical that you begin with an open and frank discussion of two points: your company's own power to influence the industry, and its willingness to accept risk. Once these have been accurately assessed, you'll know your strategy is based on a solid foundation.

Step 3: Program Your Organization

During Step 1, we used events to identify the range of specific future occurrences that might influence an industry. These were an important tool for creating the scenarios. At Step 2, we developed several scenarios depicting a range of future industry conditions, then determined which of the three generic strategies your business would pursue—diving-in, testing-the-water, or an all-weather approach. Now, we're ready to build your company's strategy, to make explicit decisions about what actions your company should take in the future.

During this step, we'll use a tool called *company-focused events*. The purpose of these events is to identify the range of actions your business might consider taking throughout the planning horizon. Some examples of company-focused events for PublishingCo might be:

- PublishingCo spends $1 billion upgrading printing facilities.
- PublishingCo signs agreement to publish three books on-line.
- PublishingCo launches public relations campaign in key markets.
- PublishingCo outsources network and systems management.
- PublishingCo moves from Boston to New York to be closer to its customers.

Notice that company-focused events are written so that a specific action is within the sphere of influence of a specific business.

Once you've developed a complete set of company-focused events, you're ready to map the events in terms of the scenarios. Using the list of company-focused events, identify which are most viable under each of the alternative scenarios. The goal here is to come up with a "winning" strategy for each of the individual scenarios by identifying company-specific events your business should influence. Each of the scenario-specific strategies you develop should be subject to the same restrictions your company's strategy is. For example, if you have $10 million to spend in the upcoming year, be sure the cost of influencing all of the events on your list (for each individual scenario) is no greater than that sum. Completing this exercise, you'll wind up with a chart that resembles Exhibit 21.1.

After developing a list of critical company-specific events in each scenario, you're ready to consider which of these events your company should pursue. This final list of company-focused events becomes the foundation of your strategy—a listing of action items your company might carry out over the coming years. There are three different approaches to developing this foundation. These correspond with the generic approaches we discussed in the preceding step.

Diving-In.   Companies that are diving in generally have the easiest time with this step. You've already selected a scenario that your company believes it can make happen. Thus, you carry out the company-specific events you've identified as critical for that particular scenario. Don't be too rigid about your approach. Sometimes companies find that funding influencing events that are not critical for the scenario they're pursuing

Exhibit 21.1
Strategies for PublishingCo

Scenario A: Efficiency through Innovation	Scenario B: New Distribution Channels	Scenario C: Outsourcing for Performance
PublishingCo spends $1 billion upgrading printing facilities.	PublishingCo signs agreement to publish three books on-line.	PublishingCo outsources network and systems management.
PublishingCo launches public relations campaign in key markets.	PublishingCo launches public relations campaign in key markets.	PublishingCo moves from Boston to New York to be closer to its customers.
PublishingCo prices drop; profit increases.	PublishingCo forms multimedia division.	PublishingCo launches public relations campaign in key markets.

can be like taking out an insurance policy. If, for example, PublishingCo were diving in to the New Distribution Channels scenario, it might still consider investing in an event like "PublishingCo outsources network and systems management," if it were not too much of a strain on resources. This way, if the Outsourcing for Performance scenario were to actually occur, it might be better prepared (because it is critical for that scenario). After evaluating the list of critical company-focused events for its scenario, PublishingCo might ask itself: What additional actions might complement our strategy for the scenario? What easy-to-influence events might protect us in case another scenario emerges?

Testing-the-Water.   Many companies that are initially testing the water eventually hope to find a way to minimize risk by developing strategies that will work in several different scenarios. These companies should try to identify high-leverage events (ones that will be critical in many of the scenarios). While PublishingCo is in its testing-the-water phase, it would probably hold off on company-focused events such as: "PublishingCo spends $1 billion upgrading printing facilities" or "PublishingCo forms multimedia division," for two reasons. The first is that each of these events will be critical only if a particular scenario comes about (for instance, the first event is only relevant to the Efficiency through Innovation scenario). The second reason these events would not be a high priority is that they probably require a significant commitment of resources.

Alternatively, PublishingCo might consider an event such as: "PublishingCo launches public relations campaign in key markets." The management has already identified this as a critical event in all of the scenarios. It might also consider this event: "PublishingCo signs agreement to publish three books on-line" because it probably requires less commitment of resources, yet it places them in a strong position should the New Distribution Channels scenario comes about.

All-Weather.   Companies pursuing an all-weather approach are generally highly uncertain about the future and may also be highly intolerant of risk taking. Perhaps they're reluctant to make long-term investments because they fear unforeseeable changes in the industry might poison their strategy. Such companies generally select events that will be viable in any foreseeable future. Events such as: "PublishingCo launches public relations campaign in key markets" are particularly low-risk because they're critical to all of the scenarios. All-weather strategies tend to be made up primarily of this type of event. (Warning: Make sure that managers in operations—not just public relations or other staff jobs—are getting the benefit of the learning that comes with an all-weather strategy.)

Success of your strategic plan relies heavily on conducting this phase thoroughly. It's important to develop a good list of company-focused events. By this we mean you must identify the complete set of potential future actions for your business. This often requires a great deal of information gathering and creativity by the people running the planning exercise. You should also remember Peter Schwartz's insight about scenario planning: "At its heart the ultimate goal of scenario planning is to create maneuvering room for management."[2] Don't think of your list of company-focused events as a rigid action plan. Instead, consider it to be a foundation for your company's strategy—which can be adjusted as conditions change.

Step 4: Monitor the Strategy and Key Industry Indicators

Major changes in your industry can completely wreck a strategy. But how do you know that a major change has occurred or is about to occur? How does management know how and when to respond? Monitoring is critical.

Monitoring ensures that your strategy is being followed properly. You need to determine how successful managers are at influencing crucial company-focused events. Monitoring also tracks the currency of the decisions that led you to choose the company-focused events (that is, which generic strategy to pursue). For example, imagine that a company decides to dive in to a scenario because it currently has 80 percent market share and a high level of influence over the industry. Two years later, a new entrant captures 50 percent of the company's market share (and gains tremendous industry influence). As industry conditions change, the diving-in approach is no longer a good choice; and, therefore, the events that had been selected as most critical may no longer be relevant.

Each company will find its own unique monitoring system. What's important in this step is that your company find an approach to monitoring that can be ratified. In other words, can your business carry out the strategy as it's written? Does the strategy continue to be relevant and appropriate given changes in the industry?

CONCLUSION

Scenario planners often think of themselves as facilitators of organization learning. As Arie P. de Geus, former head of planning for Royal Dutch/Shell explains, "The real purpose of effective planning is not to make plans but to change the microcosm, the mental models that these decision makers carry in their heads."[3] While it's true that changing decision makers' mental models is an important part of planning, we've found that today companies are turning to scenarios as an integrated tool for developing strategy. In the face of uncertainty, scenarios offer the best way to develop a winning strategy.

CHAPTER 22

HOW INFORMATION TECHNOLOGY HELPS SCENARIOS ADVANCE FROM CONSENSUS TO DECISIVENESS

PATRICK S. NOONAN and MASON S. TENAGLIA

This chapter explains how to combine the creativity of scenarios with the rigors of modeling and information technology. This combination provides up-to-the-minute information for fact-based analysis and permits a preview of the often hard-to-discern implications of management decisions. The use of vivid, decision-focused scenarios can change planning into a management process capable of discovering radical new consensus and moving decisively to appropriate action. By using scenarios, models, and information technology in concert, managers can rapidly achieve managerial decisiveness—in other words, consensus plus a bias toward action.

CASE STUDY: SQUIBB CORPORATION

The highly respected CEO of an extraordinarily successful multinational pharmaceutical company senses a portentous crossroads in his company's future. He leads a team equipped with a combination of information technology and scenario planning to speedily develop scenarios of the company's alternatives. As a result of applying this combination of methods to address the decision-making process, management is ready in a remarkably short time to take decisive action that will profoundly change the company's destiny. Painfully but quickly the firm managers achieve fact-based consensus about the appropriate strategy to adopt. Here's how it all happened.

For two days in February 1989, the 14 top managers of Squibb Corporation secluded themselves in a conference center meeting room in Princeton, New Jersey, to explore their concerns about the long-term viability of their company as an independent entity. Coming into this meeting, each was keenly aware of the corporation's dilemma: Could

Squibb find a way to sustain its earnings and growth beyond the patent expiration of its antihypertension product, Capoten, that now enjoys blockbuster sales? These seasoned executives had invested decades of their lives helping Squibb surmount other crises, and each had a personal vision of "how they were going to dodge another bullet." However, all the managers harbored serious doubts about the various proposed solutions to the problem.

Through two days of exploring scenarios about the pharmaceutical business, using quantitative models of how Squibb's R&D portfolio might evolve, all the proposed survival strategies were tested, quantified—and dismissed as implausible. Squibb would not survive unless it were big enough to sustain the impact of competition for Capoten by generic equivalent drugs. Furthermore, that jump in company scale could happen only if Squibb acquired a larger pharmaceutical company, or was itself acquired. Three months later, Squibb and Bristol Myers agreed to a merger. On the date of the announcement, the value of Squibb's shares, which were already trading at over 20 times earnings, increased from approximately $8.3 billion to $12 billion.

Thinking about Squibb 2000

The intellectual preparation for the Squibb/Bristol Myers merger decision started early January 1989, when Squibb Corporation President Jan Leschly was already thinking—and worrying—about 1995 and beyond. The company's Pharmaceutical Management Committee (PMC) had recently completed a strategic-planning exercise for the years 1990–1994 and was confident that the continued success of Capoten, its revolutionary treatment for hypertension, would allow the company to grow its earnings per share (EPS) comfortably at greater than 15 percent per year. But what was going to happen just over the horizon, in 1995 and 1996, when Capoten lost it patent protection, first in the European community and then in the United States? In recent years, prescription pharmaceutical products with generic competitors had quickly lost market share and contributed only 25 to 35 percent of their peak years' product sales and contribution to corporate costs. Would Capoten suffer the same fate? And if so, how could the company possibly fund the research and development of the next generation of new products?

Despite the PMC members' deep fears about the future competitive environment for existing products, they also had great hope that the

Squibb R&D portfolio would yield highly successful new products. But all the parameters—markets share, new product launches, the possibility of a research-based "eleventh hour" reprieve that would extend Capoten's patent life—were uncertain, leading to some key questions: What would be the rate of new product approvals for Squibb? Would they get their newest "ACE inhibitors"—hypertension treatments, successors to Capoten—to market before the onslaught of products currently in the pipelines of five competitors? Would Squibb's new agent for reducing blood cholesterol, Pravachol, become the blockbuster that could fill the earnings gap? Could a new formulation of Capoten, or a new dosing regimen, effectively extend its patent life?

Each member of the PMC had his or her own "mental model" of a future pharmaceutical industry and the Squibb portfolio, and each worried that 1995 could bring a sharp decline in earnings, which would in turn cause a sharp drop in Squibb's market value that would jeopardize the company's independence. How could Squibb's management reach consensus about what do and where to invest, given such uncertainty?

CEO Leschly invited PMC members to attend a two-day off-site meeting in February, christened "Squibb 2000," that would focus on creating a common vision for the post-Capoten era.

Preparing for Squibb 2000

During the month they had to prepare for this meeting, Leschly took his team off-site for several days to perform a top management audit of the 1990–1994 strategic plan. Each manager was given a series of Lotus 1–2-3 spreadsheets that modeled the Squibb portfolio and yielded projections of the profit and loss statement (P&L). Testing critical assumptions embedded in these projections, such as prices, market growth, and market share assumptions had been an enlightening experience: His team emerged with a common mental model of the leverage points in Squibb's business for the 1990–1994 planning period. Was it possible to use this basic business model, which they all understood, to test some of his own darkest concerns about the future portfolio and environment?

An internal Squibb team and scenario-planning consultants worked to do just that, developing new baseline models of the business portfolio and extending them to include eight products that potentially could be launched between 1990 and 1999. All products were then analyzed in light of two or three possible external scenarios—largely a function of potential competitor actions and FDA approvals. For example, Capoten scenarios included a base case, an aggressive generic competitor, mandatory generic substitution by an increasingly powerful managed care sector, and FDA approval for once-a-day dosing that afforded the product more protection from generic competition. To ensure that each potential scenario was explored in depth, Leschly had assigned one PMC member to be its advocate.

In the week before the Squibb 2000 meeting, these individual product models were integrated with baseline plans for manufacturing, R&D, corporate services, and several smaller Squibb business units. The resulting consolidated financial model was capable of making EPS estimates using detailed pro formas—companywide financial projections—for the entire decade, 1990 to 2000.

The Squibb 2000 Presentation

At the Squibb 2000 meeting, each major product in the Squibb portfolio was presented in turn, first as its base-case scenario, followed by each of the potential external and internal scenarios. Next, the PMC was asked to vote on a "most plausible" scenario for each product. (Authors' note: As a general rule in scenario planning, probabilities are not assigned to each of the possible outcomes.) Once all products and scenarios had been explored and a set of "most plausible" scenarios had been selected, the financial projections were immediately consolidated to produce 10 years of EPS estimates, a graph of which instantly was projected against the base-case estimates for all products. The first-pass consolidation result was clearly unacceptable: EPS dropped by more than 20 percent in 1995—and again in 1996.

The scenario process, coupled with detailed financial models, had immediately and vividly shattered the managers' old mental models of the business and ruled out their conventional strategies for sustaining growth. Management had to conceive a new strategy—and put the old ones to rest.

The managers' comments during the meeting, captured here in selected quotes, suggest that in order to bury their old mental models, the top management team had to experience an emotional catharsis and evolution of thought:[1]

Denial: "Impossible—let me see the numbers!"

Anger: "How could we have let this happen?"

Bargaining: "Well, certainly our new blockbuster will fill the gap. . . ? "

Depression: "I guess it is time to think about doing something else."

Acceptance: "There is no denying it. We will have to come up with a radically different solution."

This progression from denial to acceptance began the moment the first numbers were projected onto the screen. Immediately, the chief financial officer challenged the math: "There must be something wrong with the calculation." After the vice president of Planning and the senior vice president of Information Resources assured him that the model had been thoroughly debugged and audited, angry conversations erupted between the managers. "They must have forgotten international expansion." "There must be something else in the portfolio." "Why weren't we told about this?"

Bargaining soon began. "What if we could get FDA approval for Pravachol earlier?" (Counterintuitively, models demonstrated that accelerated new-product launch costs would actually worsen short-term performance.) "What about the CHF (congestive heart failure) indication—couldn't that make a difference?" (Analysis showed that this was another red herring. Ironically, although the new indication would have increased sales and profits before the patent expiration, the fall in earnings after patent loss would be even more dramatic.)

All the combinations and permutations the group could offer (including some that were not truly plausible) were explored. None of their proposed solutions would produce the desired 15 percent per year growth in consolidated EPS. In the chart before them, EPS estimates grew sharply, plummeted when Capoten came "off patent," and started growing again in 1997 and 1998. This "lightning bolt" image (see Exhibit 22.1) became central to every single manager's vision of the future, and each wondered: "What can we do to close that gap?" The time required to reach this conclusion: about half of one day. Ultimately, as Squibb entered merger negotiations with Bristol Myers, it was this image that drove the senior managers to support a loss of independence for Squibb.

Exhibit 22.1
The Lightning Bolt in Squibb's Future?

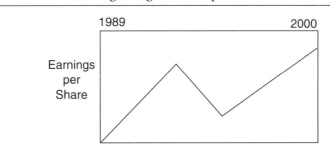

This painful realization of a new truth is the most tempestuous of management events. Minimizing resources wasted on ideas arising from denial, anger, bargaining, and depression, and rapidly "moving on" from acceptance to action could be achieved only through the marriage of scenario techniques and rigorous, interactive and quantitative models of their business.

Later that year, CEO Leschly reflected on the process, stating, "We already knew all that we would ever know about the future of Squibb. We ultimately would have figured out that we couldn't go it alone—but the combination of scenario planning and a comprehensive financial model of Squibb got us to that conclusion maybe a year or two sooner. And certainly before anyone else figured it out!"[2]

HOW INFORMATION TECHNOLOGY ADDS VALUE TO SCENARIO LEARNING

In recent years, the use of vivid, decision-focused scenarios has changed planning into a management process capable of discovering radical new consensus and moving decisively to appropriate action. In a number of leading companies, scenarios promote strategic thinking throughout the organization, reinforced by coherent management processes.

In our view, some additional pressures are now creating a new planning environment: rising business complexity and competitive uncertainty, escalating costs of delay or error, increasingly specialized management, and an explosion of internal and external data. While scenario planning remains the best approach for dealing with these challenges, there is a growing need for it to be augmented with new decision-making models and new group processes.

Specifically, we suggest combining the creativity of scenarios with the rigors of modeling and the high-speed data processing of information technology. Effective scenario-based planning by itself can lead an organization's leaders to consensus on key strategy issues. Models provide concreteness through fact-based analysis, increase credibility through a connection with the operational economics of the business, and permit a preview of the often hard-to-discern implications of management decisions. In our experience, by using scenarios, models, and information technology together executives can achieve managerial decisiveness—in other words, consensus plus a bias toward action.

Information technologies (IT), which recently have expanded in function well beyond modeling and have become more accessible to those with managerial skills, can now be exploited throughout the scenario-planning process to gain more depth, quality, and speed. Indeed, embracing IT-based approaches can have enormous impact not only in scenario planning, but in all types of planning processes.

In this chapter, we discuss how to achieve these benefits—decisiveness included—by integrating models and other information technologies into the scenario-planning process. With so many approaches to scenario planning from which to choose and so rich a landscape of technologies available, a detailed how-to for setting up a single system is inappropriate. Instead, we provide several frameworks, examples, and theories that promote an understanding of how and why IT adds value to scenario planning. Our primary goal is to give broadly useful advice and counsel to managers seeking to transform any of their planning processes using IT.

We begin by describing broadly what IT contributes to the planning process, and how it should be integrated with scenario planning. We then discuss how to look for opportunities to use IT, and some appropriate cautions and potential pitfalls.

RADICAL CHANGES IN PLANNING

What IT Brings to Planning Processes

There is an irony that all providers of services, from corporate market research staff to roofing contractors are acquainted with: Their customers want an offering to be "good, fast, and cheap," but are only permitted to pick any two of the three. Usually, service providers can only offer trade-offs: improving quality by sacrificing time or money, for example.

So it is with planning processes. What top managers need is an effective process leading to high-quality strategic decisions, and not only do they want it done quickly (owing to the competitive demands of the business) but they would like to proceed without breaking their departmental budget.

Fortunately, recent developments in information technologies and infrastructures—in essence, advances in the sophistication of computers, networks, software, and the people and organizations who use them—have improved the economics of planning. Now, for the same (or even fewer) resources, the use of information technology (IT) can add value to the planning process by improving its effectiveness and reducing its cycle times.

IT and Scenario Planning

Employing a range of information technologies in the scenario-planning process facilitates a number of alternative approaches to its usual steps, as illustrated in Exhibit 22.2 and explored further later in this chapter. But doing so accomplishes far more than just speeding up its usual possibilities or improving its quality only by degree—for example, increasing the detail, scope, time horizon, or number of scenarios. As we shall discuss, the collective effects of IT permit quantum improvements in planning by fundamentally changing what is possible.

As the Squibb case shows, rigorous models can vastly improve scenario planning. The identification of alternatives that is central to scenario building first liberates decision makers from the shackles of one-year financial plans. Then, the use of economic models of the business, in combination with a planning infrastructure, enhances this process and prepares managers to act on their plans. To take effective action they need to:

- Identify leverage points with the highest impact and greatest uncertainty; that is, to identify and prioritize the things that need to be managed. For example, cost of goods sold might have a huge impact on earnings but be quite stable, while foreign exchange rates might be wildly unpredictable but not material. Which issues should be keeping managers up at night?

Exhibit 22.2
Illustrative IT Enhancements to Scenario Planning

Scenario Planning Steps

1	2	3	4	5	6	7
Identify defining decisions: What needs to be decided by management team?	Discuss driving forces that create future uncertainties.	Research the selected driving forces.	Rank the driving forces.	Combine driving forces to create plausible scenarios.	Evaluate impact of scenarios on decisions to be made.	Develop and evaluate scenario plans.

Traditional Approach

"Diagnostic" interviews with senior management team	Workshops or individual meetings	Interviews with industry experts, white papers	Workshops or written surveys with ranking requests	Small team and individual work to create scenario descriptions	Scenario-planning meeting	Qualitative assessments of scenarios and implications

IT-Enhanced Alternatives

Structured and unstructured electronic discussions using groupware (e.g., Lotus Notes) Audits of strategic-planning financial models to surface critical assumptions	Electronic discussions using groupware, supported by rigorous planning models	Electronic research (via First!, Hoover, NewsEdge, etc.), circulated via electronic mail	Electronic dialogue using groupware and e-mail Test forces against critical assumptions in strategic-planning model	Interactive evaluation and group scenario-development using groupware	Real-time evaluation of scenarios and their implications using decision support models (based on TM-1, I-Think, spreadsheets, etc.)	Interactive quantification and illustration of plan implications using decision support models

- Explore the firm's numbers in detail to discover the key concepts and external driving forces. Even senior managers with the experience and perspective required to make judgments about scenarios need a frequent refill of objective information.
- Test-operate their personal mental models in order to explore the implications of their own assumptions. A CFO who believes deep-down that company earnings are driven by sales through the wholesale channel can validate this view—or discover its invalidity—if given a chance to experiment in private with a good model.
- Get closure, or at least reduce the array of ideas on the table, through fact-based challenges and elimination of untenable pet theories and hopeful guesses. Many informal predictions that sound plausible when argued in team meetings do not hold up when subjected to quantification and consistency checks.

- See things from a senior management perspective down through divisional and operating unit views. Plans that work at the "big picture" level may, however, run into trouble at the product-market level, or reveal organizational weaknesses. The ability to disaggregate and reaggregate information is constructive.
- Reveal the hardiness—or fragility—of certain plans by gaining an understanding of their sensitivity to slight changes in assumptions. Would you bet your company on a plan that crucially depends on interest rates rising or falling no more than 1 percent?
- Do all this very quickly and with confidence, so that a company's managers understand the evolving business environment sooner—and with deeper understanding—than their competitors, suppliers, customers, and market analysts.

What Scenario Planning Demands of IT

These new planning models and infrastructures do require new information technologies. However, scenario planning is most effective when it involves senior management—traditionally not a natural constituency for IT. Experienced planners, too, are justified in harboring their own skepticism about IT and can readily point to ill-conceived planning processes that tried to incorporate innovative information technologies.

Keep in mind, first of all, that information technology should help promote strategic thinking, not merely create whiz-bang graphics and fountains of numbers. As strategy professor Henry Mintzberg warns, a badly designed planning process can actually hinder managers. When a plan fails, he warns, "most often the real blame has to be laid, neither on the formulation nor on implementation, but on the very separation of the two. It is the disassociation of thinking from acting that lies closer to the root of the problem." Failing to heed this warning dooms any scenario-planning process to the creation of unimplemented goals—wish lists instead of action plans. Therefore, IT must serve a planning process that, at its best, combines thinking and acting, and involves rather than detaches the managers.

This is a lot to ask. If effectiveness in planning thus can require everything from unconstrained brainstorming to disciplined scenario building, modeling, and data gathering, then IT must bring more to the table than mere number crunching. The synthesis of scenario planning, modeling, and IT must promise something other than the seductiveness of detached thought, and it must speak the language of a skeptical senior management constituency. Information technologies of old—insular MIS approaches with their year-long development times and unidirectional, voluminous flows of cold data, or even simple spreadsheets alone—could not begin to accomplish this feat. Fortunately, the IT that exists now can (see Box 22.1).

Box 22.1
Information Technology: Infrastructure and Tools

The term *IT* encompasses products, processes, and competencies. The IT infrastructure includes all hardware, some software, and most "wetware" (individual, group and organizational competencies). It supports a host of diverse functions. IT tools perform more specific, identifiable tasks, and there are a number of classes of tools: analysis, representation, and process.

Analysis tools include model builders (such as what-if modeling, various types of simulation, and optimization tools) and information integrators and refineries (shared databases, plus data retrieval and manipulation tools). Some of these applications permit a rapid "slice and dice" of budget and plan information (by product, division, country, etc.) and the forecasting engine—the model and its algorithms—that translates scenarios into 10-year financial projections. All such tools are increasingly propelled and directed by intelligent agents or implemented as expert systems.

Process tools include the host of functions now often found together in groupware (e-mail, conferencing, collaborative databases, smart document flow, and group decision facilitation) and networking. For scenario planning, for example, a useful tool is a structured discussion database into which various members of a geographically diverse planning team can take initial steps in the collaborative development of scenarios.

Representation tools employ an interactive interface to link human and machine strengths. These tools includes geographic mapping of data, exploratory data analysis using powerful graphics, decision support, multimedia technologies, visual representations of simulations, and more. For example, we might see the mapping of marketing data (market potential versus marketing effort versus sales performance) to permit managers to seek patterns of effectiveness, or a schematic representation that can compactly communicate 10 years of cash flows across 10 countries and 5 product lines.

Reengineering the Planning Process

The scenario-planning process can make use of many of these new, manager-directed information technologies, in many cases without much cost or difficulty, and often using generic solutions. However, rather than thinking of IT as merely a collection of interesting applications for solving discrete challenges in the scenario-planning process, it is often better to be bolder and treat IT as a path—indeed, the only means—to reengineer the entire planning process. The tools and "planning infrastructure" necessary to reengineer planning are now within reach.

So, planning can be reengineered to make use of IT so that:

- Steps are performed in a natural order as needed.
- Roles are integrated.
- Work is performed where it makes the most sense, and by the right people, the senior managers who actually make decisions.
- Processes are flexible and effective under a wide range of conditions.
- Unnecessary checks and controls are eliminated.
- Reconciliation with other plans is quick.

Consider the following brief case examples (and Box 22.2) and their relation to the seven steps of scenario planning outlined in Exhibit 22.2.

Case: Consumer Products Company

The senior management of a consumer products company, whose annual sales were directly tied to the number of new babies each year, went through the process of killing off their old mental model of the business and inventing a new one—a process that progresses from denial, to anger, to bargaining, to depression, and finally to acceptance—in a single day. The facilitating tool was a spreadsheet-like economic model of the market and product revenues through the year 2000. Although the executives intuitively understood that birthrates were declining and that the competition for a shrinking market would be intense, they hoped that immigration, higher usage per infant, and improved market pricing would allow them to grow their earnings. However, graphs of projected sales and earnings all sloped downward, regardless of their attempts to feed optimistic assumptions into the model.

After a couple of hours of "bargaining" to no avail, the senior management team was depressed. After an evening of "accepting" the future, they

Box 22.2
The Lotus Development Corporation Case

In 1992, software company Lotus Development Corporation (makers of the pioneering spreadsheet 1–2–3 and new groupware standard Notes, and now a subsidiary of IBM) used information technologies in its scenario planning. Lotus was facing the classic "two-curve" problem: The old business model based on selling shrink-wrapped software products (individual copy sales) was rapidly going away, but the new business model based on enterprisewide computing and a new product category, "groupware," was not yet profitable. The remaining life expectancy of 1–2–3 was very short, and a scenario-planning process was designed to address the question, Do we or do we not "bet the farm" on Lotus Notes?

Today, many people already know that the answer to the question should be a resounding Yes! However, in the early 1990s, many Lotus senior managers wanted to "ride the old business to the grave": They hoped that international growth plus new products in graphics, word processing and electronic mail would restore their strong position. Others did view Notes as the chance to leapfrog competitor Microsoft's planned groupware product, Exchange. Modeling both of the curves was essential for getting Lotus's senior managers to consensus and action.

Projecting the profit and loss results for even 1–2–3 alone was potentially an infinitely complex problem. Imagine the problem of coherently modeling the units, market share, price, and currency exchange rate over time for seven or eight different platforms—DOS, Windows, Macintosh, UNIX, various mainframes, and even HP130 palmtops—in 10 major geographic markets. Lotus attempted exactly that by creating an aptly nicknamed "Mother of All P&L Models," which, not surprisingly, no one could understand.

However, after reshaping the model, adding in some real-time analytical capability, and putting a graphical interface on the output, the scenario team quickly was able to analyze different competitor and market scenarios for the traditional "shrink-wrap business" (individually boxed software products). One scenario, named Wicked Witch, depicted earnings per share melting down faster than the Witch of the West in the *Wizard of Oz* finale. Most Lotus managers, upon seeing a vivid graphic of this possible reality, resolved to commit to the new business model.

The value of new information technologies in this analysis was their ability to include the amount of detail necessary to honestly evaluate scenarios,

---

Box 22.2 (Continued)

but without burdening the planners in the process. The IT improved on simple spreadsheets in their ability to manage the analytical scale and complexity painlessly, and with more flexibility in representing—depicting and making tables from—the relevant data. The clarity of the answers moved the managers to action.

As one part of the process, Lotus management needed to quantify the payback over the life cycle of the new product. System dynamics—a methodology for modeling and understanding changes over time, especially when the interactions among competitive players are complex and dynamic—was essential here. Modeling the "base case" using I-think software from High Performance Systems, Inc., enabled everyone on the team to understand the critical importance of rapidly building an installed base of workgroup customers. In addition, estimating the time lag between investment and payoff and understanding how results responded to management levers over time was possible only through such dynamic simulations. The base-case model was then easily applied to several competitor scenarios, such as the early or late launch of Microsoft Exchange.

Not only did this second application of technology improve the evaluation of scenarios, but its clarity had the additional value of garnering support for Notes beyond planning, and into the implementation stage.

---

spent the next day focusing on the future and reaching consensus about what had to be done to fundamentally change their business model. The result: a commitment to several new businesses, and a drive to cut fixed costs by 30 percent in the next year.

Once again, IT-enhancement—during Steps 6 and 7, the evaluation of scenarios and plans—led to a major reevaluation of options and priorities. Use of IT throughout the process leading up to the scenario-planning meeting cut the elapsed time for all steps by several months, and the decision time to one day.

Case: Regional Bank

A regional bank was using scenarios to select from three alternative business focuses: international operations, retail banking, or commercial lending. The participative and political nature of the company led to the involvement of about 45 people, three times larger than might be typical for a team of senior planners.

Here, communications technologies greatly reduced the cycle time. Taking the entire group through all seven steps of the process would have been long and arduous, and the initiative might have run out of steam. Instead, a "suite" of Lotus Notes applications was used to drive the discussion and debate. The process lasted only three months, led to consensus, and retained commitment to action at the top of the organization. The result: the acquisition of the company that had been their fiercest rival.

Case: Consumer Products Company

Simulation technologies (system dynamics, Monte Carlo, for example) can capture the uncertainty and complexity of new-product launches in the face of strong competition. One consumer products company was using scenarios to plan the launch of a new product whose success or failure could determine the fate of the company. Typically, the company tested its products in small regional markets. However, a simulation of the economics of different launch scenarios was compelling: The model incorporated the dynamics of competitive response, and it demonstrated that moving timidly would give competitors valuable information and time in which to exploit the situation. As a consequence, the company completely changed its approach and reached a consensus on an aggressive national launch.

FACTORS THAT CONTRIBUTE TO EFFECTIVE PLANNING

The key question is: Which factors consistently lead to effectiveness in planning? An empirically tested, logical checklist applicable to all planning processes, scenario-based and otherwise, was developed by British management professors R.G. Dyson and M.J. Foster. Their research showed a clear relationship: Organizations with a greater presence of 13 critical traits in their planning processes showed measurably greater effectiveness.

Based on our experience, we have modified their original framework and organized their 13 traits into four major themes: framing, scope, analysis, and process. Managers can use this list to find additional opportunities to improve the quality of their outcomes for their own planning processes.

- *Framing.* Effective framing defines the problem correctly to begin with. The biggest barrier to creative thinking is being stuck with the existing problem frame, that is, the status quo view of the world. In scenario planning, managers should be considering many alternative ways of framing their planning issues. Groupware-facilitated discussions and quantitative models aid in clear and precise framing, and they permit the intensive evaluation of alternative frames. Several of our cases illustrated how models changed the managers' understanding of the key issues and led to reframing.
- *Scope.* Defining a scope effectively means including the right amount of issues in the process. Scenario planning should include everything that matters—the entire organization and all its resources, if necessary, plus the invisible world of the uncertain. Managing this process on the back of the envelope can lead to a dangerously narrow scope; the narrowing of scope that must take place during the planning process should be based on the facts that emerge during the process, not on expedience and managerial biases. Only through detailed simulation models can the initial scope be so wide yet still manageable by the planning team.
- *Analysis.* Effective analysis is as rich and complex as required to capture the complex subtlety of the business. Analytical assumptions must be explicit and consistent; quantitative models force explicitness, and their detailed outputs can be analyzed thoroughly for consistency. All aspects of a business must be analyzed, and done so against more than one simple criterion; again, formal models permit this completeness and multifaceted analysis. While the demands for data are great, the intensive use of data should not crowd out creative thinking; today's modeling tools and group-decision facilitation systems permit analysis to take place in "real time" and interactively, which permitted the case companies to pursue new ideas and react to sudden insights.
- *Process.* Finally, effective planning is a dynamic and fluid process, responsive to what is learned along the way. It creates a plan that is itself dynamic, with measurement systems in place that can permit adjustment and course-correction as the plan plays out. An effective process facilitates the implementation of what is being

planned, so barriers are identified, removed, or avoided prospectively; consequently, implementation surprises are kept to a minimum. Most important, an effective planning process is integral and catalytic; it is driven by management but stimulates and involves the entire organization. Integrating IT into a "planning infrastructure" creates an organization capable of quickly learning from and responding to the environment and its changes and surprises. Several of the case companies have used Notes and planning models to make their work on the planning "loop" continuous and evolutionary.

Factors That Lead to Speed in Planning

It is easy to be a champion for quality, but the need for speed is less obvious to many, despite volumes of anecdotes and research lessons on the subject. Scenario planning proponent Arie de Geus contends that the ability to learn faster than the competition is "the only sustainable advantage."

Which organizational characteristics permit faster-paced decisions? Again, the use of scenarios in planning can make a vital contribution, with IT leading to obvious enhancements. First, experience suggests that speed requires a common language and shorthand for scenarios and strategies, plus shared mental models of business levers. In addition, the empirical work by management professors Stefan Wally and J.R. Baum reveals factors consistently associated with fast-paced planning organizations, many of which correspond to IT-enhanced scenario planning:

- Simultaneous consideration of alternatives (scenarios).
- A means of accelerating cognitive processing (graphics).
- Smooth group processes (groupware).
- The ability to act confidently (model-enhanced scenario analysis).
- The use of intuition and learning from experience (combining "soft" and "hard" modes of analysis).
- Flexibility, informality, adaptability, and a tolerance for risk.

CONCLUSION

Increasingly, organizations will be stretched and challenged to become true learning organizations that depend on superior management of intellectual capital to achieve competitive advantage. A scenario-planning process that is truly integrated with information technologies is a prime example of the just-in-time knowledge systems that will be required to stay ahead.

Companies that begin to embrace IT in planning, the most fundamental of strategic processes, will be steps ahead of their competitors in this learning challenge. Further, they will move through the planning loop more rapidly and with greater responsiveness to changes in the external environment. For in the end, it is not only learning faster than the competition that counts, but also having the confidence and capabilities to respond to what is learned.

The use of scenarios has led to major improvements in many an organization's planning processes, but now there are opportunities—and competitive pressures—to do much more. By exploiting the wide variety of powerful, manager-friendly information technologies now available, management teams have the opportunity to explore the future as never before. Whether it involves using specific problem-oriented tools (such as forecasting models) or pervasive planning infrastructures (such as communication and groupware systems), IT enables scenario planning to take place better, faster, and cheaper. And the results are better not only by degree; as shown in the studies, IT actually changes what planning can do by allowing quantum leaps of imagination, surprising insights, unheard-of responsiveness, and 180-degree turnabouts. Organizations that have integrated information technologies into their scenario planning processes have demonstrated this decisiveness.

CHAPTER 23

INTRODUCING SCENARIOS TO THE CORPORATION: ALTERNATRON 2010 AT UNICOM

AUDREY E. SCHRIEFER

It's never easy to convince an organization to imagine operating in future conditions that differ greatly from the present. Here's how one group of managers in one of the world's largest corporations—we'll call it UNICOM—tackled this challenge, starting with the design, development and execution of a one-day "grass roots" event to introduce scenario planning.

Scenario planning offers an organization an opportunity to do some fresh thinking about its future. But the operations managers of many businesses who have recently struggled through reengineering, rightsizing, benchmarking, or other initiatives are likely to be cynical—and reluctant to embrace another new methodology. So what's the most effective way to introduce the thought-provoking concepts, methodology, and goals of scenario planning to both line and senior managers of an organization and to obtain their enthusiastic support?

When introducing scenario planning to an organization for the first time, managers confront a number of immediate challenges:

- How to get senior management's attention?
- How to quickly explain the content, rationales, and uses of scenarios to a cadre of managers, many of whom are likely to possess a bias against "futuristic" thinking?
- How to motivate managers to come together and talk openly about the benefits and limitations of scenarios, and in particular, how they might improve decision making?

Here's how one group of managers in one of the world's largest corporations—"UNICOM"—tackled these challenges through the design, development, and execution of a one-day "grassroots" scenario-planning event—Alternatron 2010. One of the program's major purposes was to establish a network of champions, people who believed that scenario planning could improve strategic decision making and who would educate and influence the senior ranks of UNICOM.

THE NEED FOR SCENARIO LEARNING AT UNICOM

The story starts a number of years ago, when a small team of scientists within UNICOM's research division were preparing a report on how the company had selected its R&D investments in recent years. A frequent complaint voiced by group members was that the corporation's historic mind-set prevented top management from anticipating how their industry would evolve. They concluded that the organization was mired in a mental rut—stuck in its particular ways of thinking about the future, making decisions, and asking and answering questions. This small cadre of scientists concluded that the organization needed fresh perspectives to evaluate key research decisions. Indeed, they hoped that by creating new and different perspectives on the future, the organization would discover high-potential research opportunities that were now being ignored or even suppressed. New views of UNICOM's future markets, they hoped, would generate fresh insight into emerging customer needs, and thus lead to new-product breakthroughs.

The original team members—all scientists—soon decided to enlist a number of UNICOM managers with business backgrounds and strategic management experience. They asked these new team members to help them evaluate strategic-planning tools and techniques designed for decision making in UNICOM's high-technology environment.

After studying the strategy analysis and business-planning methodology used throughout UNICOM, the team concluded that these processes had become stagnant and stale. The current system was no longer able to capture and respond to the firm's fast-changing product markets and technologies. As in so many large corporations today, UNICOM's planning system required the business units to state how they would achieve predetermined corporate goals and related "metrics." The culture did not reward the business unit manager who demonstrated that some goals dictated by corporate planning were unrealistic. As a result, UNICOM's business unit plans universally proclaimed their intention to increase revenue and profits, often with little or no convincing evidence to show how these financial results were to be accomplished.

Several team members suggested that scenario planning—a methodology especially suited for studying markets in flux—would be an appropriate alternative to UNICOM's current formal planning system.

Because of the current and anticipated turbulence in its competitive and technological environment, UNICOM could no longer assume that present trends or past successes were a true indicator of future performance; there were simply too many unknowns. The ad hoc team at the research division could see many potential threats and opportunities that UNICOM's senior managers and their staffs seemingly refused to recognize. The scientists on the team were familiar with many examples of research projects that should have become important new products, but never even made it to the marketplace. And the researchers could also point to a number of worthwhile new products that made it to market but were promoted ineffectively. UNICOM seemed locked in traditional ways of defining markets, taking products to the market, and executing marketing—a serious disability at a time when markets were changing in unexpected ways. Many of the discoveries made at the research center were later successfully exploited by competitors, who derived considerable strategic advantage from being the first to market the new technology.

Somewhat to the surprise of the research team, they soon discovered that several senior managers were familiar with scenario planning, and a few had used it to address specific issues in the past. One manager had used scenario planning when he was working for a competitor and was extremely enthusiastic about its use. He agreed to sponsor the team and have them work on a scenario demonstration project.

PREPARATION FOR THE ONE-DAY EVENT

The secret to winning acceptance of truly bold ideas is extensive preparation. The team recognized that they needed to gain visibility and credibility within the organization for the scenario-planning methodology. The question was, how? They decided on a two-step initiative: to identify innovative thinkers and start networking with each other.

As a first step, members of the team identified a number of UNICOM's strategic thinkers—individuals who had demonstrated their willingness and ability to consider unconventional methods or to challenge long-established business orthodoxies within the corporation. They sought out people in a variety of functions and all levels of the corporate hierarchy. They wanted individuals who were respected by their peers and who were in a position to influence the thinking of major portions of the organization. As a second step, the team decided to bring these people together to introduce them to scenario-planning methodology and to facilitate a strategic dialogue.

The team carefully developed specific goals for a day-long event. Each goal was intended to help "market" scenario planning as a means of making better strategic decisions. The specific goals included:

- To build a network of individuals throughout the corporation who would understand both the value of scenarios and the scenario-planning methodology.
- To position the team as the hub of the network.
- To establish the team as a resource for information on scenario planning.
- To identify specific areas of expertise within the network.
- To identify scenario-planning projects for the team. Selecting these projects would be one of the critical activities of the day.

Developing the Agenda.   To achieve these meeting goals, the agenda identified the topics and issues to be covered, specific tasks to be accomplished in each time period, and the speakers or presenters who would lead each session.

The team wanted those participating in the event to learn about scenarios as well as to actively engage in the work of developing them, so the workshop consisted of both:

- *Presentations on scenario methodology.* These presentations would draw upon the experiences and insights of the participants gained from previous scenario work.
- *Participatory workshop sessions.* These sessions encouraged attendees to experience "how it would be to really operate a business unit in a future quite unlike the present."

Choosing the Participants.   Another key element of success for such events is identifying and attracting the "right" participants. The choice of participants determines not only whether the meeting achieves its immediate goals, but also whether it can have a lasting effect on the organization.

The team first used its own personal contacts to identify influential prospective participants. Corporate databases were scanned for line and staff personnel—in all units, at all levels—who managed strategy development and execution. The list of potential invitees included strategic planners, human resource professionals, business unit managers, marketing personnel, and key researchers. Each person was first contacted by e-mail to gauge their interest and availability. Follow-up phone calls were made to get recommendations for other talented people who should be invited. The solicitation process was similar to that used by employment "headhunters."

The invitation list consisted of 60 people. It was reviewed for balance prior to sending out the formal invitations. One important criteria: Were all functions and business units fairly represented? While the team tried to be inclusive, it also wanted to hint that invitees belonged to a select group. Apparently, the right impression was created. Almost all the 60 people invited were able to attend.

Communicating with the Participants.   The team believed that the long-term the success of the program hinged upon it being perceived and experienced by participants as part of a larger, ongoing activity. To this end they named the long-term project AlternaCOR. The one-day kickoff event was called Alternatron 2010.

Furthermore, the team needed to establish its credentials and expertise before the actual event. First, they created an Alternatron newsletter—promoted as the first of a series—describing the team's experiences with the scenario methodology and their key learnings. It was mailed it out with the formal invitation to the event. Second, they developed a scenario-planning Internet Web site to promote communications with and among the participants. The Alternatron Web site provided useful logistic information and background information about scenario planning as participants began preparing for the one-day retreat. In the months after the event, it enabled participants to continue to learn about scenario planning, to network, to share success stories, to keep abreast of developments, and to share innovative ideas. The Web site and the newsletter would also be used to document and communicate the work of the small groups in the workshops held on the afternoon of Alternatron 2010.

Workshop Design.   The team paid extensive attention to each segment of the event—designing both their process and content, planning their sequence, and setting learning objectives for each one. Facilitators for each Alternatron workshop were selected based on their specific interests and expertise.

The team devoted a number of days to developing the industry scenarios that would be presented in the afternoon workshops. The scenarios were presented as a work-in-progress, and participants were encouraged to contribute to their further development.

Written guidelines were prepared for the facilitators. These covered suggestions for how to ask and respond to questions, a request that facilitators adhere to schedules, and advice on how to deal with specific issues that might surface during the day, for example, questions about possible follow-up activities..

The team was especially attentive to managing the participants' expectations about what could be accomplished in one day. For example, session leaders pointed out that full and complete scenarios could not be completed in one afternoon, but that Alternatron 2010 could make considerable progress, and its work would lay the foundations for the AlternaCOR project.

Preparing the Information Packet.   The information package given to each participant contained industry information, a description of scenario-planning methodology, a reading list, and brief biographies of all 60 attendees.

As part of the advance work, all participants—team members, invitees, and presenters—were asked to submit a biographical paragraph, along with their phone numbers and e-mail addresses. Since one of the twin goals of the event was to link the participants into a network, this information was necessary so that attendees could quickly get to know each other and to be able to reach each other during subsequent months.

"Launching the Brand."   The team wanted to create a distinct "look and feel" to this one-day event. Their objective was to make it so exciting and memorable that participants would be motivated to become informed and committed champions of the use of scenarios when they returned to their business units and departments.

To this end, the team planned the day as if they were "launching a brand." For example, the graphic design of the handouts, name tags, presentation materials, and even the forms used to gather feedback were all coordinated with the Alternatron 2010 name, logo, and colors to create a uniform and professional appearance.

ALTERNATRON 2010: SCENARIO-PLANNING DAY AT UNICOM

The schedule was:

7:30–8:30: Continental Breakfast/Registration. Upon arrival, participants received their name tags and booklets of information, each marked with the distinctive Alternatron logo. The continental breakfast provided the first opportunity for the participants to network. When it was time to convene, lively music gave the participants the signal that it was time to go to work.

8:30–9:00: Introduction to Scope and Purpose of the Day. The team leader opened the meeting by introducing the mission of the team, stating the goals for the day and reviewing the agenda for Alternatron 2010.

9:00–9:45: Methods of Approaching Strategy. A UNICOM senior manager described several strategies companies employ to cope with the future. He demonstrated how each strategy is highly dependent upon the industry structure and the company's position in the industry. The presentation concluded with a brief description of how scenarios could contribute to strategy development and execution.

9:45–10:30: An International Emerging Market in This Industry. A group of leading consultants from another country who specialize in the UNICOM's industry delivered a lively presentation on the topic: How a nation's culture shapes the assumptions of its inhabitants about the future of an industry. The consultants presented a radically different perspective on the dynamics of the industry, the driving forces shaping it in their country, and the various futures that could ensue.

11:00–12:00: Opportunities for UNICOM—Keynote Presentation. A world-renowned scenarios consultant drew a number of parallels between UNICOM's industry and many others in which he had led consulting engagements. He illustrated and diagnosed the uncertainty inherent in the industry: massive technological change, unstable geopolitical and economic environments, declining societal wealth, and multiple forms of social conflict. He used some simple scenarios to demonstrate how this uncertainty could generate both opportunity and crisis for the different competitors in and around the industry.

The team selected this overview session instead of a how-to on scenario planning for a number of reasons. For one, by presenting an articulate, well-known futurist who could share his experiences as scenario-planning consultant for many similar corporations, the team offered a "marquee event," one that would attract senior participants. Second, they wanted to demonstrate how scenarios could have a direct impact upon major strategy and investment decisions currently being considered by UNICOM. They wanted to prove a critical point: Scenarios aren't just imaginary futures; they are tools for studying the implications a variety of possible futures will have on today's important decisions.

1:00–1:30: Introducing the Workshops. To help stimulate the participants to enjoy the afternoon's work—designing scenarios around the industry's future—a video on the future of the industry played on several monitors as the participants returned to the meeting room for the workshops. The video was professionally prepared by an agency that had carefully researched the industry trends.

Each Alternatron 2010 scenario team had its own area of the main meeting room. Participants' badges were color-coded so that each person, upon entering the room, knew where to sit. According to the team's plans, if the four groups were within eyeshot of each other, it would create a sense of both urgency and energy. The ideal working environment was an energetic background hum but not an overpowering noise level.

Graphics and props placed in each area helped the participants define their specific scenario project. A photo montage of poster-sized images designed to elicit "future shock" decorated the wall space of each workshop. Blowups of newspaper headlines, mock-ups of communications devices in use in the year 2010, even a Dow Jones news bulletin helped the participants imagine that they were actually living "in the scenario." Each group's supplies included a white board, a flip chart, Post-it notes, tape, and colored markers.

Once the participants settled into their assigned places, everyone in the room was introduced to the basic outlines of all four scenarios.

Each participant therefore had a brief understanding of all four scenarios: the range of industry futures or possibilities the team felt was needed as a point of departure for the afternoon's deliberations. So that the participants would also understand how these preliminary scenarios had been developed, two team members reviewed the step-by-step process the Alternatron 2010 team had used to craft these distinct, albeit skeletal, industry futures.

1:30–3:30: Small Group Sessions—Rehearsing the Future. Each workshop was structured so that each group spent the first hour "living" in its assigned scenario, which was very different from the present. The facilitator steered the discussion so that it addressed critical elements of the future—that is, those that would profoundly affect UNICOM's strategies. For example, how did each future change the home, work, education and leisure/entertainment? Such discontinuities reveal unexpected opportunities and risks that might confront each division of UNICOM.

Once the small groups fully understood what the daily life of their customers was like in their scenario, they were asked to discuss the question, How do you operate and sustain a successful company in this world? Participants first shared ideas about what the industry would be like:

- The products that were on the market.
- The technologies that were embedded in these products.
- The competitors that were winning and losing.
- The alliances entered into by different industry entities—suppliers, customers, and competitors.
- The needs of different groups of customers.

In sum, empathy with a future industry setting comes not from reading about it, but from envisioning what it would look like, feel like, and sound like from the perspective of UNICOM, its vendors, its rivals, and its customers.

The team hoped that immersion in the scenarios would allow each group to experience making decisions in a world that was yet to be, and most important, a world that often didn't fit participants' expectations of the future shape of the industry. The guiding underlying premise of the workshop can be simply stated: Innovative strategic thinking is more likely to occur when managers and others are given the opportunity to dispense with conventional wisdom, to abandon their old mind-sets, and to discover the future through authentic dialogue.

The team decided to forgo formal "report outs" by each group. Instead, volunteers helped document the discussion, and the results were posted on the Web and distributed in the newsletter.

3:30–4:00: Break. Many participants were overheard sharing ideas from their workshop with colleagues who were in other sessions. The participants were encouraged to fill out their evaluation forms. When they turned in their completed forms, they were given an appropriate memento—a small kaleidoscope decorated with the Alternatron 2010 logo—as a thank-you for attending the meeting.

4:00–5:00: A Practitioner's View of Scenario Planning. The team asked one of the firm's senior managers to recount his experience with scenarios at a previous employer—a competitor of the firm. The manager related how he learned about scenarios first from reading a book about their development and use, and then talking with executives who had put the methodology to work. Eventually, he led a team that generated a surprisingly divergent set of business futures. His message: High-quality scenario work and its outputs can give decision makers new mental models to work from and influence decision making.

FOLLOW-UP ACTIVITIES

Alternatron 2010 team members committed themselves to executing a number of follow-up activities as quickly as possible. Each activity was designed to help build and sustain involvement in the ongoing project—AlternaCOR, the full-development UNICOM scenarios and their use throughout the company.

An electronic thank-you note was sent to every participant the day after the session. The note reminded them to check the Web site and to look for their newsletters. It also invited them to make contributions to both the Web site and the newsletter. In addition, written thank-you notes were sent to the presenters on Alternatron stationary.

The team met soon after the event to debrief on the day. They described and detailed the entire process for future reference, reviewed the feedback from the evaluation forms and other informal means, and planned subsequent steps.

The feedback revealed that the presentations were generally rated very highly, but the small group sessions scored somewhat lower. The rationales for specific numerical evaluations are always difficult to discern. However, the wide range of scenario-planning knowledge and experience among the participants was evident: Some feedback forms revealed that more coverage of the basics of scenario planning was desired, while others wanted to go into more content development in the scenario break-out sessions.

The forms asked whether scenarios applied to their jobs and whether the team could help. Nearly 80 percent responded yes to the second question. The team divided the respondents among themselves for follow-up phone calls to get more details on what types of help they desired and how best it might be provided.

The output of the break-out groups was edited and reviewed with the participants who had agreed to help. The result was posted on the Web site and in the newsletter so that all participants could review the work of all the scenario groups.

The meeting notes were summarized and published in a special edition of the newsletter and on the Web site. A "scenario speakers bureau," a database of internal and external speakers available for unit meetings was set up. The list of network members was also entered into a database for ease of sorting and access.

NEW INITIATIVES BY THE TEAM

Although the team felt that many of the Alternatron 2010 goals had been attained, they were well aware that most of real work necessary to convince UNICOM to adopt scenario planning still lay ahead. They committed themselves to a set of initiatives, each of which was intended to weave scenarios into UNICOM's decision-making process.

First, they began an effort to integrate and extend the work of the individual Alternatron 2010 workshop groups. These initial attempts at writing industry scenarios needed to be augmented, refined, and tested before they could be used by other groups of UNICOM managers to gain more significant insights. As a major step toward accomplishing this task, the AlternaCOR team scheduled a two-day off-site meeting. A number of the workshop participants and UNICOM employees who could add particular expertise and knowledge were invited to participate in the off-site meeting. Prior to the meeting, each

AlternaCOR Project team member was assigned one or more topics to research.

It was obvious to all members of the AlternaCOR Project team that they needed to continue to build the network through ongoing communications and events. A half-day session was scheduled a month in advance. A calendar of events (brainstorming sessions, large plenary sessions, cyberspace events, working teams, training sessions, scenario development sessions) was developed, and a person was assigned to coordinate the execution of these events.

Obviously, for the scenario project to become a dynamic addition to the corporate culture, the AlternaCOR Project team would have to continue as its promoters for some time to come.

CHAPTER 24

WRITING AN ANNUAL REPORT FOR YOUR ORGANIZATION'S FUTURE

WAYNE A. EARLEY

How would your organization respond to the challenge to write its annual report for the year 2010 now, more than a decade in advance? Would such a scenario project inspire the leadership to rethink its current practices and plans? Could the annual report format make a set of scenarios more real and more insistent? Could it create a stimulating environment where your organization explores new opportunities?

Organizations need a way to make the future as attention getting as a bad quarterly report and as urgent as an irate phone call from the CEO. Unfortunately, the stock-in-trade of a number of futurists is macrotrends and warnings of startling new-world alliances—elements of the future that are foreign to most company managers. Macro-futures don't help most of us make everyday decisions. Some futurists are a bit like the soothsayer Mark Twain satirized in his book *A Connecticut Yankee in King Arthur's Court*. This disingenuous crystal ball-gazer purported to be able to describe what kings in far-off countries were doing at that exact instant, yet he disdained to reveal how many fingers the Connecticut Yankee, a commoner, was holding up behind his back.

Scenario-planning projects that begin with a look at long-term macro-economic futures and international risk analysis are as unreal to management teams embroiled in the hurly-burly of markets and competition as news of exotic kings and queens. Worse, glimpses of turbulent post-Cold War tomorrows are not exactly "red alerts" in most companies. To win the attention of an organization's "doers," the people who can make things happen, the future needs to be made as specific as this year's annual report.

So why not create an annual report set in your organization's future? A far-fetched idea? Not really. In fact, a few organizations primarily use their annual reports to advertise their future. For example, Gilead Sciences' 1995 annual report is, by necessity, all about the future. The company had almost no revenues in fiscal 1995. According to the report, "Gilead Sciences is a leader in the discovery and development of a new class of human therapeutics . . . ." The company is spending $40 million a year building a future, and its annual report describes its work and expectations, not its distribution and marketing strategy.

Actually, almost any company would benefit from the exercise of drafting its annual report for 5, 10, 15, or 20 years from now. Such work raises healthy questions:

- Where would we want to be?
- Which trends are driving our future?
- What are the clues to emerging trends?
- Where are the forks in the road ahead?
- What road conditions can be expected?
- What will our destination be like when we get there?

To show how some of these questions can be addressed in the annual report format, we wrote one for "Wonder Building Materials" (WBM), a supplier of materials for residential buildings. Though the company is not real, the events described are based on extensive research on newly emerging industry trends. In fact, our initial trend analysis had 48 pages of citations, a list of sources that is obviously too long and too specialized to be catalogued in this chapter.

For example, one trend incorporated into our scenario was the migration of people to newly created communities in rural parts of the United States. Our goal was to use the annual report format to translate the macrodemographic concept of "migration to rural areas" into niche marketing opportunities. As evidence, a recent *New York Times* article described a new rural development called Stoudtburg Village. In our annual report, we used this authentic project to illustrate how WBM recognized the rural migration trend as a new market segment and concentrated resources on it. We were able to support a concept that we had included in our scenario for the year 2010 with real events that would soon be underway. The following is a quote from our annual report for WBM, which was written as if we were in the year 2010 discussing the company's performance in the year 2009.

> While small communities worked to make themselves more attractive, another phenomenon expanded rapidly, the creation from the ground up of customized communities. Stoudtburg Village in rural Pennsylvania was completed in 2001. The $30-million village is home to 300 residents living in residential units above shops ranging in size from 338 to 850 square feet.
>
> WBM's New Community Construction market share, just 1 percent in 1998, when we virtually created this segment, is now 10 percent. Our lead in the single-family and multifamily home construction materials market continues.

How would your organization respond to a chance to write its annual report for the year 2010 now—nearly 15 years in advance? Would such a project challenge the leadership to rethink its current practices and plans? Could the annual report format make the future more real and more insistent? Could it put market decisions into a context that would reveal new opportunities and risks?

Before you discount such a project as being too challenging or time-consuming, remember that sometime in their career most "fast-track" managers have drafted a part of an annual report or edited a section of one. Preparing a draft of the president's letter for the annual report of the organization for the year 2010 wouldn't be a totally new experience for many top-flight executives. And for future leaders, creating such a report would be a terrific assignment, one that would both broaden their viewpoint and enhance their ability to anticipate change. If an organization developed a set of four scenarios, each one could be assigned to a different team of managers, perhaps inspiring a bit of competition over which team would produce the most eye-opening annual report.

Based on how much discontinuity and transformation a scenario in annual report form anticipated, and depending on how prepared the organization is to accept change, it could be an explosive document, or a learning exercise. A truly subversive document—a provocative view of the future that knocked managerial complacency off its long-time perch—might be just what's needed. Consider these surprising logistic problems of the future addressed in the Wonder Building Materials 2010 annual report as anti-complacency alerts:

Progress in delivery is difficult. Last July 4 (2009), motor carriers were prohibited from all interstate highways from Thursday through Sunday. Seventy percent of interstate highway mileage is now (2010) truck traffic, and our nation's roadways are no longer able to handle the load.

Getting to a destination around the time of holidays at some cities is approaching the conditions at Hyannis, Massachusetts, back in the 1990s, when travelers bound for Nantucket arrived to find 1,500 cars in queue for a ferry service that could handle only 300 vehicles per day. The new privately funded toll roads first built in the 90s that run parallel to existing highways are one solution. But they aren't being built quickly enough.

We at WBM ship long distances as much as possible at times when low traffic loads exist. We have established a new project to investigate creative, innovative delivery solutions. We are evaluating freight carrying dirigibles for delivering large orders of prefabricated housing to rural sites. And as we add new capacity and introduce new technology, we are considering smaller local and regional facilities.

An individual who was concerned that clues from the evolving market were not registering or not being reacted to by his or her organization could write a future annual report and use it to spur the organization into action. By sharing the work with a few key people, the annual report of the future could produce excitement, and open minds to important signals of threats and opportunities.

The annual report is an organization's key document for communicating with internal and external stakeholders. It announces the results of the current year compared with the previous year and presents the organization's mission, vision, and strategy. It tells a new version of this same story every year: "This is where we were, what we tried, what we won, what we lost, what the score is, where we're going, and how we're going to get there."

Writing stories of potential futures in the form of annual reports is also a chance to "get in practice" for making decisions regarding the evolving environment. These paragraphs from WBM's annual report offered the rationale for the firm's investment in "customized" rural developments:

Congress approved moving more federal infrastructure development money to the states in 1999, after nearly four years of contentious debate. Its actions soon resulted in aggressive competition among states and communities as each strove to offer more attractive living conditions and a brighter future for their citizens. Competition for professional sports teams by cities in the 1990s was an indication of state marketing wars to come.

The competition among communities resulted in migration to both rural and urban areas, away from "edge cities." Success in attracting businesses required that a community, big or small, become focused and make itself desirable to specific groups of people. One concept born from this competition among localities was "customized communities." As Harvard professor Michael Porter proposed in the 1990s, "unique advantage, not investments driven by social programs, revitalizes cities."

Of course, such a proposed annual report won't really forecast the future of your business in the year 2010 (or whatever other year that you choose). However, you can, by looking at a number of possible futures, have a more open, flexible approach to the changes—good and not so good—your company will face along the path to the future. And by putting these conceptual pictures in the form of annual reports, you increase their impact on your organization. Nothing is so energizing as the discovery of a new image of key issues. A good picture of the future that challenges existing mind-sets is the best stimulus for innovation.

The following paragraph from Wonder Building Materials 2010 annual report sends a powerful message to the organization. It teaches managers the increased potential of a firm that is the first to develop an important new capability. Even if a particular possible future is "wrong," if it is provocative, it will challenge your associates to develop their own, better, ideas.

> The instant electronic delivery of products like movies and software, and the ability of companies like Hewlett-Packard to, overnight, replace equipment that goes on the blink, has taught customers to expect immediate access to the products and services that they want. Therefore, in 2001, we established a goal of 12-hours-or-less delivery to all customers on any product. At the same time, we set goals to reduce logistics cost per item by 8 percent per year. While we did not achieve that goal, our costs are now only two-thirds what they were in 2000. As a result, we receive frequent requests from other firms to add their products to our system. This allows us to meet customer's complete needs.

The annual report format can support the scenario-planning process in several other ways:

- The CEO can ask division representatives to contribute a section on their unit to an annual report of the future. By challenging individual units to define their contributions to corporate financial goals, the chasms on the path to the future can be spotlighted.
- Plan to prepare several versions of the annual report of the future. The first draft creates a "base case." The second one addresses a future that emerges after the organization has had a chance to study scenarios about its macroenvironment. The third draft sketches the future after the organization has discussed prospects for markets and plans its investment in new technology and infrastructure.
- The ultimate product of a corporate scenario-planning effort—a set of scenarios—can be formatted as a set of annual reports, one for each alternate story.

By distributing an annual report of the future to all employees, management throws open the window of potential opportunity to show both the objectives that can be achieved if the organization works together and the obstacles that must be overcome.

THE PROCESS OF DEVELOPING WBM'S ANNUAL REPORT

Various chapters in this book describe the technique for preparing a set of scenarios. You can write an annual report for each unique future scenario you define. The process we used to prepare the WBM annual report of the future is briefly discussed here, from the point of view of an individual seeking to stimulate his or her organization to undertake a scenario development effort.

Step 1: Which factors are likely to impact your organization in future years? To compile a list of significant influences, first obtain a wide range of credible viewpoints on your industry and business. Include interviews with associates, customers, consultants, academics familiar with the industry, suppliers, and others. Additional sources are industry magazines, futures books, texts related to the problems you feel exist currently, and writings about the industry your business competes in and related industries.

The list of ideas you collect must be broad and varied. Include historic, current, and future views.

Step 2: Aggregate all the change concepts you have identified under a few category headings. Group large numbers of similar ideas under one heading. Don't discard evidence of a potential trend. For example, some concepts that you may be tempted to discard because they can't easily be categorized may eventually be recognized as constituting a totally new category of trend. You will likely have 10 to 20 groups when finished. Some trend concepts will be part of more than one of these categories.

Step 3: Examine the interrelationships among the categories identified in Step 2. Generally, it's the interaction of two or more trends that will evolve into an opportunity or discontinuity for your business or industry. For example, three trends—Congress returning control to local governments, electronic communications, and the problems of "edge cities"—all contributed the concept of "customized communities" in Wonder Building Materials' industry.

Step 4: For each category, what is the range of futures? A useful tool is the "force field analysis" used by quality teams to list the factors driving the change and those retarding the change. For example, if rural population is going to increase after declining for many years, what are the alternate ways this trend will manifest itself that might create turbulence, risk, and opportunity for your industry? Use this range of futures in Step 6.

Step 5: Select a few key variables that will drive your scenarios. To do this, you will first need to prioritize the categories you have identified. Which are likely to have the most important impacts for your business?

Step 6: Write a short description of at least three scenarios using combinations of the key variables and the range of possibilities. It is critical that the variables and their expected future are consistent within a scenario. Construct a paragraph or two that describes a concept of a new future. Ask yourself, how useful would this image of the future be to my organization? You may decide to go through Steps 1–5 a second time. Test your images of possible futures on others in the organization. Is their interest piqued? Are they intrigued enough to ask for further development of the ideas?

Step 7: Search for information that supports the future picture you have chosen. Separate teams can adopt a concept and develop it further. Depending upon the evidence you find that supports or contradicts the concepts in the scenario you are exploring, you may change it. It's also important to make some educated guesses about when key changes will occur. Try to identify important milestones in the change process. These should be highlighted when you write your narrative.

Step 8: Develop the story by drawing on the ideas and supporting materials you (or your team) have collected. Be sure to include such details as when important decisions were made. Ask: Which specific programs generated the results? When did a change occur in the economy, industry, or your business?

This step-by-step authoring process may seem a bit onerous, but it helps build credibility for the final product.

CHAPTER 25

TWENTY COMMON PITFALLS IN SCENARIO PLANNING

PAUL J. H. SCHOEMAKER

Previous chapters have shown you how to create scenarios and discussed the potential benefits of scenario learning. This last chapter takes a hard, practical look at the variety of pitfalls that could undermine an organization's attempts to implement scenario planning. The 20 pitfalls are grouped into two categories:
- *Process. How the scenario exercise is conducted.*
- *Content. What the scenarios should focus on.*

$\mathbf{T}$he distinction between process and content pitfalls is important because it highlights the fact that scenario planning entails a sequence of activities—the process—that can only deliver satisfactory results if the inputs—the content—are of high quality. For the scenario process to work, managers need to master process and content.

My list of pitfalls concerns the initial scenario-building phase during which individuals or teams envisage a limited set of futures that bound the range of possible outcomes. When scenario creation is successful, it helps managers break through the prevailing mind-set and develop valuable insights about the future.

Once this process is completed, an organization can then employ the tools of strategic management—industry and competitor analysis, strategic segmentation, and core competency assessments—to design strategies that will succeed in several of the scenarios.

Process Pitfalls in Scenario Planning

The term process refers to a series of activities that unfold over time and build upon each other to create a particular outcome. The distinct steps usually follow a carefully planned sequence.

Pitfall 1: Failing to Gain Top Management Support Early On

The first step in any scenario process should be to secure the political support and involvement of senior executives, because without them there can be no significant change in strategy at the end of the process. In 1969, the first generation of scenarios at Shell were brilliant, but their insights were not incorporated into the thinking of decision makers.

Since the scenarios were the product of staff managers, Shell's senior executives felt no pride of ownership in them. Those 1969 Shell scenarios actually predicted the 1973 oil embargo by OPEC, but this warning was neither believed nor acted upon by management. The solution: Make decision makers stakeholders in the scenario process.

Pitfall 2: Lack of Diverse Inputs

Outside inputs should be actively sought. Sometimes it pays to put outside experts on the team because even managers who are recognized as technological experts or astute students of specific markets may feel uncomfortable addressing issues beyond the familiar boundaries of their industry.

At the outset, the scenario-learning initiative addresses only the external part of the world, and not proprietary firm strategies or market information. As a result, there should be no problem inviting customers, suppliers, regulators, analysts, academics, or other thought leaders into the process. Since the advent of the Internet, these outside experts can be easily and economically invited into an electronic scenario conference.

Pitfall 3: Poor Balance of Line and Staff People

Too often, the scenario-planning process is driven by staff personnel. Although staffers may initiate the project, they need to make every effort to recruit line managers as project champions. It is the line managers who must shape the scope and focus of the scenarios. So the role of staff should be confined to offering support. Staff managers need to convince line management to invest time in the project by emphasizing that the benefits are improved decision-making capability and competitive foresight.

Pitfall 4: Unrealistic Goals and Expectations

It is important to keep a tight rein on the expectations of those involved in the process. Some line managers expect the scenario-planning process to contribute to the bottom line within a few months. This is unrealistic. The initial purpose of scenario planning is not to produce plans, but to help managers understand what might happen to their current plans in the various possible futures their organization may confront. Sometimes this understanding occurs rapidly. Often, however, a lengthy period is needed to convince managers of a large, successful organization that its future won't resemble its past.

Pitfall 5: Confusion about Roles

It is important at the beginning of the process to clearly define people's roles and the steps the group will need to take. Scenario planning may be a new and mysterious activity to many. Moreover, since this is a mental exercise that calls upon both analytical and creative skills, the process may be unsettling and even threatening to those whose basic world view is being challenged. An excellent first step is to create a core group that keeps the process on track. Have others play supporting roles by studying and summarizing key viewpoints, articles, books, or conference proceedings on issues central to the scenario-building process. Next, the core group should do more thorough research into the key issues, and then ask senior management to select the top 10 trends affecting their business, as well as the top five key uncertainties. Pick the uncertainties the CEO and senior management committee would most like to have clarified by a truly infallible and prescient informant, if such a source actually existed.

Pitfall 6: Failure to Develop a Clear Road Map

The scenario process may start to drift if participants do not have a clear road map, and unless dates, tasks, and the people responsible for them are identified. Set clear milestones and deliverables for the process. For example, you might start by assigning some homework on key social, political, economic, or technological factors that could significantly change your business or industry. After discussing the results of this research, ask participants to evaluate these factors in terms of their (1) relevance, (2) potential impact, (3) degree of understanding, (4) uncertainty, and (5) possible interactions. Do this in teams in workshops, or use e-mail questionnaires when you're dealing with larger groups.

Pitfall 7: Developing Too Many Scenarios

Some companies go overboard and study too many scenarios. This dilutes the attention and energy of senior management. I recommend that at the very most only five scenarios be developed. And, in fact, two to four scenarios are usually sufficient to bracket the range of future outcomes and to provide alternative images to the prevailing view. Don't assume that the initial scenarios must capture and display all possible future states of the world. The team should only make detailed descriptions of a small set of distinctly different ones.

Pitfall 8: Insufficient Time for Learning Scenarios

Most companies have a strong action bias. Their motto is, "Let's get it done and move on." This attitude is fine for day-to-day operations. However, a slow simmering process can be highly beneficial in scenario development. After all, it is designed to be a learning activity. And the learning process matters as much as the outcome.

The aim is not to get it right the first time, but to experiment with the new environments described in the scenarios. Enough time must be allowed for people to move into each scenario and experience what it would be like to live and work in that particular future.

Different teams might tackle different scenarios and compete in making them plausible, the way the prosecution and defense teams are pitted against each other in our legal system. In the end, the dialectic tension created by considering these competing views of the future give rise to better syntheses and judgments about the true implications of each scenario world.

Pitfall 9: Failing to Link into the Planning Process

The scenario process should not be an isolated activity, unconnected to other organizational decision-making processes. Ideally, scenario planning should be tied into the existing planning and budgeting process. However, the transition from using scenarios as thinking frameworks and intellectual lenses to using them for project evaluation requires careful management.

By using such techniques as risk assessment, simulation, and real options analysis, you can combine the big-picture issues raised by the scenarios with such crucial project parameters as demand, costs, customer taste and preferences, competitive responses, and profit. This is where staff managers can play an important role as internal consultants, helping business unit managers employ the scenarios to sharpen their strategies, tactics, competencies, and strategic options.

Pitfall 10: Not Tracking the Scenarios via Signposts

Even when the scenarios and appropriate strategies have been developed, the task is still not complete. Scenarios provide coordinates that help managers better understand the world they're in now, and the futures they might be heading toward. However, scenarios initially look at the world from the perspective of an orbiting satellite, while day-to-day issues have to be managed on the ground. Thus, the scenarios should be made specific and tracked by developing specific signposts or markers.

This can be done by writing imaginary newspaper headlines to characterize the events and driving forces of each scenario. For example, these headlines might postulate provocative mergers, new patents or products, bold competitive moves, lawsuits, customer defections, and regulatory changes. To make the link between the scenarios and the day-to-day world of managers, you will have to reset the resolution of your mental binoculars a few times. Zoom in and out, until the whole panorama is revealed and understood: from Earth orbit to ground zero.

CONTENT PITFALLS IN SCENARIO PLANNING

This next set of pitfalls addresses the common problems scenario builders encounter with the quality of the input.

Pitfall 11: Inappropriate Time Frame and Scope

It's hard for many firms that thrive by managing so well in today's marketplace to take the long view. Too often, scenario developers focus merely on current crises, ignoring unrecognized longer-term opportunities that require investments today. Instead of concentrating narrowly on existing products or markets, it's important to investigate opportunities that lie beyond the current boundary of their business. For example, it is imperative to consider the impact of emerging technologies, potential new competitors, and market developments in other industries and countries.

Pitfall 12: Too Limited a Range of Outcomes

Even though firms may have experienced a tumultuous past—deregulation, globalization, and new technologies that caused havoc in their industries—they may not realize that this turmoil is ongoing, and fail to see that it can be part of their future. Instead, firms should ask, How imaginative and wide-ranging are the key uncertainties and outcomes we're postulating here? This is where historical perspective plays a key role.

Another useful benchmark is making comparisons with other industries that have experienced unexpected discontinuities. Match your industry against others that have progressed further in terms of deregulation, globalization, new technology introductions, or other issues of concern. Since the scenario process is intended to widen the organization's field of view, managers must remain vigilant against inputs that are the product of tunnel vision.

Pitfall 13: Too Much Focus on Trends

Some organizations unintentionally foster tunnel vision by paying too much attention to current trends. This simply projects the past forward. Worse, this encourages the hidebound to pay too little attention to the unpredictable possibilities that are harder to envision. Most managers are more comfortable addressing the issues they know, rather than the ones that are ambiguous, unfamiliar, and unquantifiable. But this is exactly what scenario planning requires: the collective surfacing of our ignorance. As Roy Vagelos put it when he was CEO of Merck and

Company, "Planners and managers should raise more doubts about their plans, strategies, and the future in general."

Pitfall 14: Lack of Diversity of Viewpoints

Even though companies may collect well-quantified data about future trends and key uncertainties, they often fail to synthesize them into truly diverse scenario themes. They make the mistake of seeing the future as if it were a T-shirt that only comes in small, medium, and large.

Some organizations have this problem because they are convinced that the future won't be much different from the present; other organizations have limited imagination. In either case, their scenarios end up being slight variations on one theme, organized around the status quo.

As a test, scenario developers need to ask whether their scenarios reflect the full range of viewpoints within and outside their industry? Do they truly capture the opinions of their industry's innovative thinkers, devil's advocates, and dreamers? For example, if you are a newspaper company, does at least one of your scenarios postulate a world in which mass use of the Internet or broadband two-way TV has forced newspapers to reinvent themselves?

Pitfall 15: Internal Inconsistencies in the Scenarios

Is the logic of the scenarios internally consistent? For example, most economists would not find an economic scenario that postulates full employment and zero inflation to be internally consistent. You can test for internal consistency in at least three ways. Ask yourself for each scenario:

- Are the main future trends mutually consistent with each other?
- Can the outcomes postulated for the various key uncertainties co-exist?
- Are the presumed actions of stakeholders compatible with their interests?

For example, scenario designers shouldn't portray powerful stakeholders, such as government agencies, as sticking to a position they wouldn't like to take. Such unrealities would undermine the credibility of the scenario.

Pitfall 16: Insufficient Focus on Drivers

In their annual reports, firms describe their future in terms that relate directly to their income statement. The focus is usually on margins, market share, costs of raw materials, and other indicators. However, these are merely the symptoms of the deeper forces the scenarios need to focus on. For example, a scenario driven by different assumptions about the interest rate or employment won't provide a full picture of what's going on in the external environment. Economic scenarios should deal with the determinants of these variables, taking into account supply, demand, consumer confidence, and likely governmental actions. The scenarios can be quantified in terms of variables such as interest rates, but should not be based on them initially.

Pitfall 17: Not Breaking Out of the Paradigm

A special challenge in scenario planning is confronting management's key beliefs. A scenario that merely confirms conventional wisdom is of little use. On the other hand, a scenario that totally challenges fundamental beliefs and seemingly has little chance of actually occurring might well be dismissed as "off the wall." A balance must be struck between what the future may really bring and what the organization is ready to contemplate.

It's best to start with an intellectually honest and wide-ranging set of views and then rein in the team—reluctantly and carefully—to accommodate an organization's legitimate political or emotional concerns.

How do you know whether you're breaking out of the old paradigm? Watch people's reactions. Do they exhibit denial, confusion, discomfort, or outright anger? If so, you are challenging their fundamental beliefs in a healthy way.

Pitfall 18: Failing to Tell a Dynamic Story

Many companies write scenarios in terms of end-point descriptions, as though they were snapshot images of what the future may hold 10 years from now. However, instead of a snapshot, a scenario should be thought of as a movie. An effective scenario explains the process of how we get from today to the future world projected in the end-state description. A good scenario presents a persuasive case for unusual outcomes, using a logic that is rooted in today's realities. The scenario needs to explain how we can move from today's reality to tomorrow's possibilities.

Pitfall 19: Failure to Connect with Managerial Concerns

The story you tell must be relevant to the key decision makers. Being brilliantly creative but irrelevant is a waste of time. Scenarios that make a difference must connect with key managerial concerns and yield new insights about strategic opportunities for the business today as well as tomorrow. In telling the story, explicit links should be made to issues confronting managers in terms of the threats or opportunities they face in their markets, or by offering signposts and early warning signals for each scenario. After all, the main objective of the exercise is to change the managerial mind-set about actions and investments. The scenarios work when your organization perceives and acts upon promising business opportunities before your competitors discover them, or avoids making investments that will pay off in only one possible future but would be jeopardized by a number of futures that can be envisioned for your firm.

Pitfall 20: Failure to Stimulate New Strategic Options

The ultimate payoff of scenario planning occurs when the organization embarks on successful new strategic initiatives. But too often, the scenario process fails to create legitimate breakthrough options that the firm can accept.

One problem is that alternatives that are in fact truly breakthroughs may not look attractive when evaluated through a traditional net-present-value lens by people who haven't participated in the assessment of the organization's long-term environment. As a solution, convince leaders to view breakthrough insights about the future as valuable options. Such options, much like financial call options, give the firm the right to play in case one of the scenarios materializes.

FROM LEARNING SCENARIOS TO DECISION SCENARIOS

We can think of scenario planning as creating surrogate crises, which at first engender denial or anger and then lead to bold action. The key is to push people past their comfort zone, and to inspire managers to stop following the pack. This is why scenario planning requires an artful balancing of the known and the unknown.

To be effective, scenarios must challenge the dominant paradigm and yet be intuitively accepted as a spur to needed action. This is the purpose of creating learning scenarios, which are at first presented as tentative hypotheses to be tested and validated through further discussion and research. It is in the act of learning that emotional and intellectual acceptance of the scenario themes occurs. But this process takes time and requires the involvement of the key decision makers.

Once the learning scenarios are revised and accepted, they can then serve as decision scenarios. Strategies can be tested against these decision scenarios to determine which ones will be winners in only one possible future and which will serve the organization well in a number of futures. How current projects would fare in various scenarios can be quantified using Monte Carlo simulation, options analysis, or other tools for strategic risk analysis. The most important use of scenario planning, however, is to devise new insights about the future environment. From this foresight organizations can craft more effective strategies and plans.

NOTES

Chapter 3

1. *Energy: Global Prospects 1985–2000,* Report of the Workshop on Alternative Energy Strategies (WAES), (New York: McGraw-Hill, 1985).

2. Presidential Energy Program, Congressional hearings on proposals in the Energy Independence Act of 1975, February 1975.

3. Robert Chote, "Why the Chancellor Is Always Wrong," *New Scientist* (October 31, 1992): p. 26.

4. John Kay, "Cracks in the Crystal Ball," *London Financial Times* (September 29, 1995).

5. Pierre Wack, "The Gentle Art of Reperceiving," *Harvard Business Review* (September–October 1985 and November–December 1985).

6. David Ingvar, "Memories of the Future: An Essay on the Temporal Organization of Conscious Awareness," *Human Neurobiology* 4 (1985): 127–136. Described by Arie de Geus in "Modelling to Predict or Learn," *European Journal of Operational Research* 59 (1992): 1–5.

7. D. Kolb, *Experiential Learning* (Englewood Cliffs, NJ: Prentice Hall, 1984).

8. Richard Pascale, "Nothing Fails Like Success." *Insight Quarterly* (Summer 1993).

Chapter 7

1. Leufkens, Haaijer-Ruskamp, Bakker, and Dukes. *The Future of Medicines in Health Care,* (Kluwer Academic Publishers, 1995)

Chapter 13

1. Adopt-A-World is a service mark of The Futures Group, Inc. of Glastonbury, Conneticut.

Chapter 14

1. At the end of calendar 1984, Wal-Mart's market value was $8 billion. By 1994, it had increased to $58 billion. All market values referenced in this chapter represent the sum of market value of shareholders' equity and long-term debt, unless otherwise noted.

2. For a fuller explanation of the Royal Dutch/Shell approach to scenario planning, see Pierre Wack, "Scenarios: Uncharted Waters Ahead," *Harvard Business Review,* (September–October 1985) and "Scenarios: Shooting the Rapids" *Harvard Business Review,* (November–December 1985).

Chapter 18

1. Pieter le Roux et al., "The Mont Fleur Scenarios," *The Weekly Mail* and *The Guardian Weekly* (July 1992).

2. Members of the Mont Fleur scenario team came from, among other organizations, the African National Congress (ANC), the Black Sash, the Chamber of Mines, Distillers Company, the National Council of Trade Unions, the Pan Africanist Congress (PAC), Pepkor, Shell South Africa, the South African Communist Party (SACP), the University of South Africa, and the University of the Western Cape. In addition, leaders from the Confederation of South African Trade Unions, the Conservative Party, the Democratic Party, the National Party, and other organizations participated in ancillary workshops.

3. For a description of another forum process, see "Bringing Diverse People to a Common Purpose: Learning in South African Forums" by Louis van der Merwe, in *The Fifth Discipline Fieldbook: Strategies and Tools for Building a Learning Organization,* edited by Peter Senge, Charlotte Roberts, Richard Ross, Bryan Smith, and Art Kleiner (New York: Doubleday, 1994).

4. Roger Fisher and William Ury, *Getting to Yes: Negotiating Agreement without Giving In* (London: Arrow Books, 1987).

5. *Discovering Common Ground: How Search Conferences Bring People Together to Achieve Breakthrough Innovation, Empowerment, Shared Vision, and Collaborative Action,* edited by Marvin Weisbord (San Francisco: Berrett- Koehler, 1992).

6. Pierre Wack, "The Gentle Art of Reperceiving," *Harvard Business Review* (1985).

7. David Chrislip and Carl Larson, *Collaborative Leadership: How Citizens and Leaders Can Make a Difference* (San Francisco: Jossey-Bass, 1994).

Chapter 19

1. Michael E. Porter, *Competitive Strategy: Techniques for Industry and Competitor Analysis* (New York: The Free Press, 1988).

Chapter 20

1. Pierre Wack, "Scenarios: Uncharted Waters Ahead," *Harvard Business Review* (September-October 1985); and "Scenarios: Shooting the Rapids," *Harvard Business Review* (November-December 1985).

2. Scenarios do not replace more detailed analysis of markets, competition, technology and other critical external forces. And they have nothing to say about resource analysis (the

organization's strengths and weaknesses), which must be factored into any decision on strategy.

Chapter 21

1. Gary Hamel and C. K. Prahalad, *Competing for the Future* (Boston: Harvard Business School Press, 1994).

2. Peter Schwartz, *The Art of the Long View* (New York: Doubleday Currency, 1990; revised 1996).

3. Arie P. de Geus, "Planning as Learning," *Harvard Business Review* (March–April, 1988), pp. 70–74.

Chapter 22

1. E. Kubler-Ross, *On Death and Dying* (New York: Macmillan Publishing Co., Inc., 1969).

2. Leschly became chairman and CEO of SmithKline Beecham plc, where he continued to be an active scenario planner. In February 1996, he was selected by the *Wall Street Transcript* as the pharmaceutical industry's CEO of the Year.

About the Authors

Nariman Behravesh is chief international economist and research director for DRI/ McGraw-Hill, an international consulting and research firm headquartered in Lexington, Massachusetts. Dr. Behravesh consults on international trade, finance, governmental regulations, and global market opportunities. His Internet address is: nbehravesh@dri.mcgraw-hill.com.

Thomas W. Bonnett, who co-authored his chapter when he was with the Council of Governor's Policy Advisors, is now a public policy consultant to a number of organizations promoting effective government, including: Alliance for Redesigning Government, the National Governors' Association, the National Conference of State Legislatures, and the National League of Cities. Based in Brooklyn, NY, his e-mail address is: twbparkslo@aol.com.

Wayne A. Earley, a management consultant based in Sylvania, Ohio, was formerly vice president for Strategic Planning at Owens-Corning. His Internet address is: cke4cxqc@aol.com.

Liam Fahey is an adjunct professor of Strategic Management at Babson College, Boston, and visiting professor of Strategic Management at Cranfield School of Management in the United Kingdom. Dr. Fahey has authored or edited six books on management; most recently, *The Portable MBA in Strategy,* with Robert M. Randall, (New York: John Wiley & Sons, Inc., 1994). He has won awards for his teaching, research, and professional activity. He consults for a number of leading North American and European firms. His Internet address is: LFahey95@aol.com.

Roy Hinton is a consultant with The Burgundy Group, located in Evergreen, Colorado. His e-mail address is: rhinton@tesser.com.

Adam Kahane is a founding partner of the Centre for Generative Leadership, L.L.C., located in Hamilton, Massachusetts. He specializes in the design and facilitation of processes that help people work together to anticipate and effect change. He can be reached by e-mail at kahane@cgl-leadership.com.

John Kania is a partner at Corporate Decisions, Inc, a strategy consulting firm located in Boston, Massachusetts. His Internet address is: john_kania@cdiboston.com.

Brian Marsh, a seasoned manager in the Royal Dutch/Shell Group, is now a fellow of the St. Andrews Management Institute (established in Scotland by Shell and St. Andrews University). He lives in South Africa and consults worldwide in scenario planning and strategic management. Internet: bmarsh@iafrica.com.

David H. Mason is president and cofounder of Northeast Consulting Resources, Inc., a strategy and information technology consulting firm in Boston. His Internet address is: mason@ncri.com.

Stephen M. Millett is a Breakthrough Leader of Battelle Consumer Products Group, Columbus, Ohio. His Internet address is: Milletts@Battelle.org.

Patrick Noonan, a founding director of The Planning Technologies Group, is assistant professor of Decision & Information Analysis at Emory University's Roberto C. Goizueta Business School in Atlanta, Georgia. Dr. Noonan consults on strategy, operations, and information technologies issues. His Internet address is: Patrick_Noonan@bus.emory.edu.

James A. Ogilvy is cofounder and vice president of Global Business Network, Emeryville, California, and director of its scenario-planning training activities. Previously, at SRI International, "Jay" Ogilvy developed future scenarios and directed research for the Values and Lifestyles (VALS) Program, a market research consumer segmentation system. A former professor of philosophy at Yale University, his most recent book is *Living without a Goal,* (New York: Doubleday Currency, 1995). His Internet address is: ogilvy@gbn.org.

Robert L. Olson is research director of the Institute for Alternative Futures, Alexandria, Virginia, where he designs and uses methods for environmental scanning, scenario planning, vision development, and strategic decision making. His e-mail address is: bolson@altfutures.com.

Mark Paich is a consultant with The Burgundy Group, located in Evergreen, Colorado. His e-mail address is: mpaich@earthlink.net.

Charles M. Perrottet is vice president of The Futures Group, Glastonbury, Connecticut, a consulting firm that specializes in scenario learning and strategy development. Internet: C.Perrottet@tfg.com.

Doug Randall is a scenario planning consultant based in San Francisco. His articles have appeared in *Long Range Planning, Planning Review,* and *China Business Review.* Internet address: douglas.randall.wg97@wharton.upenn.edu.

Robert M. Randall's publishing company, located in San Francisco, specializes in operating management magazines; editing and writing management articles, books, white papers, and business brochures. He and Liam Fahey co-edited *The Portable MBA in Strategy* (Wiley, 1994). Randall and Fahey are working on another book, *Strategic Management Tools,* also for John Wiley & Sons, Inc., scheduled for publication in 1998. His Internet address is: Randall_Publishing@compuserve.com.

Paul J.H. Schoemaker is chairman and CEO of the consulting firm Decision Startegies International, Inc.; research director of the Huntsman Center for Global Competition and Innovation; and adjunct professor of Marketing at The Wharton School, University of Pennsylvania. In the early 1980s, he was a strategic planner for Royal/Dutch Shell in London. Schoemaker is coauthor of *Decision Traps* (New York: Simon & Schuster, 1989), *Decision Sciences* (Cambridge, MA: Cambridge University Press, 1993), and coeditor of *Wharton on Emerging Technologies* (in progress). Internet: PaulSDSI@aol.com.

Audrey E. Schriefer, president of Schriefer Management, an international consulting firm located in Concord, Massachusetts, facilitates client organizations' strategic conversations using an approach that integrates scenario planning and systems thinking. She is president of the Boston chapter of the Strategic Leadership Forum and has chaired its International Strategic Leadership Conference. She can be reached via Internet at ASchriefer@aics.net..

Peter Schwartz is cofounder and chairman of Global Business Network, in Emoryville, California. GBN is a network of business executives, strategists, scientists, and artists specializing in organizational learning, scenario planning, and strategy development. Schwartz directed the business environment center at SRI International and later headed scenario planning at Royal Dutch/Shell in London. He is the author of *The Art of the Long View,* (New York: Doubleday Currency, 1991) and coauthor (with James A. Ogilvy and Paul Hawken) of *Seven Tomorrows: Toward a Voluntary Future* (New York: Bantam, 1982). The GBN website is http://www.gbn.org.

Mason Tenaglia is founder and managing director of The Planning Technologies Group, Inc., a strategy consulting firm located in Lexington, Massachusetts. He has published a number of articles based on his experience advising corporations in the United States and Europe on strategy development and implementation. His Internet address is: Mason_Tenaglia@Plantech.com.

Charles W. Thomas is a director of Scenario-Based Planning with The Futures Group, a consulting firm based in Glastonbury, Connecticut. He can be reached on the Internet at: C.Thomas@tfg.com.

Kees van der Heijden is the author of *Scenarios: The Art of Strategic Conversation* (New York: John Wiley & Sons, Inc., 1997). He was head of scenario planning for Royal Dutch/Shell and its internal consultancy, and is currently professor of Business Administration at the University of Strathclyde in Glasgow, Scotland. His Internet address is: kees@gbn.com.

Edward E. Ward is a principal of Ward & Company, a consulting firm based in Lexington, Massachusetts, that applies system dynamics, scenario planning, and organizational learning concepts to business and not-for-profit-organizations. He has served as an executive in manufacturing, logistics, and corporate strategic planning for multinational firms in the industrial, capital goods, consumer products, and high-technology industries. His Internet address is: WardandCo@aol.com.

Ian Wilson first experimented with scenarios as a member of General Electric's strategic planning staff in the early 1970s. After leaving GE in1980, he spent the next 13 years as a senior management consultant at SRI International, where he worked with senior managment teams in a wide variety of international companies on scenario-based strategy projects. He is now principal of Wolf Enterprises in San Rafael, California. His Internet address is: Jason415xx@aol.com.

Robert G. Wilson is chairman and cofounder of Northeast Consulting Resources, Inc., based in Boston, a firm specializing in scenario development and futures studies. His Internet address is: Wilson@ncri.com.

INDEX